D1597398

Layers

Personal Narratives of
Struggle, Resilience, and Growth
from Jewish Women

Toby

Shira Lankin Sheps

LAYERS

Personal Narratives of
Struggle, Resilience, and Growth
from Jewish Women

FOREWORD BY

Rachel Hercman, LCSW

The Toby Press

Layers
Personal Narratives
of Struggle, Resilience, and Growth
from Jewish Women

First Edition, 2021

The Toby Press
POB 8531, New Milford, CT 06776-8531, USA
& POB 4044, Jerusalem 9104001, Israel
www.tobypress.com

© Shira Lankin Sheps 2021

The publication of this book was made possible
through the generous support of The Jewish Book Trust.

ISBN 978-1-59264-554-1, *hardcover*

A cip catalogue record for this title is
available from the British Library

Printed and bound in the United States

"...Yet Esther won the admiration of all her saw her"

To celebrate the life of

Batsheva Chaya Stadlan *z"l*

whom everyone loved and was taken from us too soon.
From her loving parents, Dr. Noam Stadlan and Rabbi Marianne Novak
and her dear siblings, Zehavya and Hillel Stadlan.

℗ ℗℗

As I contemplated my 70th birthday, attaining "fullness of years" seemed more like a responsibility than an achievement. So supporting a book of consequence filled an important niche.

The Layers Project has always spoken to my heart because it represents everything that would have been meaningful to my mom, Sarah Baker and my mother-in-law, Pearl Hametz. Their lives were a true testament to courage, strength and wisdom. Working in the marketplace, raising their families, devoted to their communities – education and knowledge were paramount.

The Layers Project gives voice and strength to a new generation of women. May every story be heard and may every woman who needs to be lifted up find what she is looking for.

Denise Hametz

Dedicated in memory of our beloved father:

Stanley "Pop-pop" Edwin Perelman z"l

שלמה בן מרדכי ז"ל

Robert and Holly Lankin

⊱ ⊱ ⊱

We are thrilled to link this wonderful book
with the memories of our beloved parents:

Marion and Herbert Achtentuch z"l

מירים בת יונה וזיסל ז"ל
דוד בן צבי ופסל צירל ז"ל

Shirley and Joseph Lankin z"l

שינדעל בת ישראל לב ז"ל
יוסף בן משה אהרון ז"ל

Micki Lankin z"l

מלכה בת וועלוול ז"ל

Rabbi Dr. Eric and Jeanne Lankin

⊱ ⊱ ⊱

Dedicated in loving memory of our beloved parents:

Ralph and Regina Hessdorf z"l

רפאל בן שמשון הלוי ז"ל
ונחה רבקה בת משה ומנה ז"ל

Herbert and Marion Achtentuch z"l

דוד בן צבי ופסל צירל ז"ל
מרים בת יונה וזיסל ז"ל

Harriet and Michael Hessdorf

We pray that all their neshamot merit an aliya.

For all the women who share their stories.

For those who listen with love.

For my family,
Shmu, Ayelet, and Dovi,
for filling my life with light.

For HaKadosh Barukh Hu,
who made humans "betzelem Elokim," in the image of God.

ॐ ॐ ॐ

Contents

Contents

Foreword

The Layers Project first entered my life after a *Shabbos* meal conversation three years ago. Some guests were discussing an issue they had read about on *The Layers Project* blog that week and how refreshing it was to see a taboo topic getting visibility.

As a social worker and speaker in the Jewish community, I was intrigued by The Layers Project's ability to bring awareness in a way that was translating into meaningful conversation. After all, it's not easy to challenge systemic denial. There are reasons why we don't want to hear or read about things going on right in our backyard. It brings up fear, anger, and confusion, and it pops the bubble of innocence that we desperately chase.

Within minutes of laying eyes on *The Layers Project*, a blog that featured the images and raw intimate stories of Jewish women, I knew there was something different about this endeavor. The way issues were getting focus – it was a totally new forum and space that I'd never seen before. The profiles brought an awareness to issues in a way that was deeply impactful. Wherever I heard people talk about *The Layers Project*, the buzz was always the same: gratitude that stigmatized conversations were finally happening, and relief that others understood.

When the project grew and Shira Lankin Sheps invited me to join *The Layers Project* magazine as clinical director, I joyfully said yes. I knew this was more than a project or a magazine. It was a growing movement that was slowly changing the Jewish community and the way we speak not just about challenge, but about life itself. I certainly wanted to be part of that, and it's been deeply enriching ever since.

The Layers Project magazine has become a healing space through facilitating carefully curated conversations, and our crown jewel is *The Layers Project* magazine profile. Through a storytelling process that is typically six to eight parts, we bring our thousands of readers into the experience of someone else. We virtually gather around into a healing circle and gently listen to a story unfold. Through vivid photographs and delicate narrative, we go on a journey as a group and are together changed.

Some of my most poignant moments at *The Layers Project* magazine have been seeing the responses to our posts. In a world where social media posts can invoke judgment and conflict, almost every comment on our profiles has been validating, supportive, and appreciative. Time and time again, our profiles have yielded a group embrace that has been overwhelmingly loving and kind. The most common sentiment we hear is the notion of people no longer feeling alone. They feel more a part of a group, more understood, and more connected to those around them.

We have learned many lessons about what it takes to cultivate a healing space. The process entails intention, sensitivity, and a heightened awareness of emotional nuance. When those things are in place, safety grows and people feel seen, heard, and for some, truly understood for the first time. And it begins with starting a conversation.

This book is a resource for starting conversations and expanding our perspectives on the complexities of life. In these pages you will read stunning stories of Jewish women in the Land of Israel today. These women are our friends, cousins, neighbors, sisters, grandmothers, mothers, daughters, and aunts. Their stories have real-life endings, imperfect and multilayered. And they are not really endings, because only in fairy tales is the story over and with a neat ending. In real life, the story continues, and we as a community can learn how to be present for each other through it.

If conversation is the melody of this book, the harmony is self-care. Self-care played a significant role in the book production process from start to finish, and as you will see, continues to be a recurring theme between chapters.

Like anything we publish, we spent considerable time ensuring that the women we profiled for this book didn't just have a story to tell but felt ready to tell it and have it published. Opening up the past can be loaded and triggering, and it was essential that all participants felt secure in taking those risks as they entrusted us with their vulnerability. This meant giving people permission to have ownership over their stories – how they were told, which photos were used, and which parts of themselves they ultimately did not want us to share.

For us, going over these stories went beyond an intellectual exercise. Every story was unique and powerful, and its details would reverberate for days after reading it. Seeing chapters of history come alive through stories of the human experience, and looking eye-to-eye at the people who went through it, felt like a tremendous honor but also a heavy responsibility that we took seriously.

As the clinical editor of this book, every story I read became a part of me. There were many times in the production process that I'd find myself going over a story with tears streaming down my cheeks, feeling simultaneously defeated by what the person went through yet uplifted by her capacity to show up for life despite it. There were times that I'd have to take a break away from the work in order to emotionally recharge, and then return to it when I felt ready. I was keenly aware of how the stories impacted me, and I continually considered how they would ultimately impact our readers.

Shira and I regularly took time to pause, reflect, and process together all the feelings brought up for us by these stories. It generated deep and meaningful conversations, and gave us the necessary space to keep moving forward. Having that space inspired us to incorporate sections between chapters to do just that – pause, reflect, and process.

These stories are deep and descriptive. Perhaps a theme will resonate with you in a way that feels uncomfortable, even triggering. Be mindful of your feelings as you read, paying attention to your breathing, your body, and what comes up for you. Each of us will react differently to a story, so keep an awareness of where these narratives land for you. We often find that talking to someone you trust can be a great way to process the experience of reading meaningful or challenging chapters.

This book is the beginning of many conversations to come – we are just getting started – and we invite you to partner with us in creating conversations in our communities. These conversations can connect us in ways that break the glass wall that keeps us isolated from others. It can be empowering to learn that you are not the only one who has traveled this road, and while it may have been lonely up until now, it no longer has to be that way moving forward.

Layers

We can choose to honor our journeys. We can let go of the shackles of shame that keep us silent. And finally, we can build a community that is woven by threads of empathy, understanding, and hope.

Rachel Hercman, LCSW
New York
January 2020

Introduction

MY STORY

This work was born out of my own story of pain. During my twenties, I suffered from unexplained chronic illness and pain. Whatever made me ill left me feeling weak. I became allergic to everything and my blood sugar was out of control. I had pain all over my body that made it hard to function. As a newlywed and a young mother, I watched as my life slipped away from me. I had no energy to work, to be a mother, a community member, a wife, or a member of my family. I had always been the type of person who wanted to do everything on my own. My independence, control over my own life, and freedoms were central to my sense of self.

The sicker I got, the more I lost control. I watched as my grasp on the things that I cared about was loosened. I broke as all my strengths were stripped away from me. At the beginning of the end of my illness, I had little but the essence of everything that I loved and my Maker. It was in that space that I discovered who I really was.

Revealed by illness, I discovered gentleness. I nurtured empathy for myself and others. I learned about patience. I asked, "Why?" and looked for answers. With time and searching, I found some. I was being molded into a different person, someone who understood that the inner life of a person could be vibrant, even through suffering. I was learning that our lives can appear as a distortion of an inner reality, and that we were put on this earth to struggle. We live to love, to overcome, and to grow.

I was prepared to listen as I had never truly listened before. I was engaged in taking stock of what had brought me to the point that broke me and what I needed to do to heal myself. Only when I was ready to live in a different sort of mindset did my body heal. The steps that I took to rid myself of emotional pain made space for me to engage with physical healing.

I had spent the better part of five years keeping my suffering quiet, like a terrible secret. Few but my close friends and family knew the struggle of what I was experiencing. I was so ashamed of being "sick," as I was only able to see the world through the binary of able bodies and broken ones. At a certain point in the winter of 2015, I reached my limit. I tried to submit some pieces of writing to several blogs. I asked to keep those pieces anonymous. Though the editors liked my writing, they encouraged me to publish with my name. If I wanted others to pay attention to the message behind my words, I had to stand up alongside them. I was so afraid of what people would think of me if they knew that I wasn't the strong, capable person I wanted to be. I was terrified that people would pity me. I was still so ashamed and I didn't want anyone to know.

But I was sick of feeling alone. I was sick of feeling different. I had reached a point where I realized that I was keeping myself a prisoner in this state of seclusion. I was carrying the burden of my pain alone. It wasn't fair to me or my husband to keep these realities hidden. I wondered what would happen if I spoke my truth and let other people hear about my reality.

On the second night of Ḥanukka in 2015, I started a blog about my secret. I shared my anger, fear, and struggles. Ultimately, I ended my first post with this:

> Last night after we lit the Ḥanukka candles, I sat with my son in the shadows and watched the fire breathe. In those quiet moments, I sang his bedtime ritual, *Shema Yisrael, HaMalakh HaGoel,* and *HaTikva.* I witnessed the flames dancing to the music of whispered promises of redemption, inheritance of blessings, and the covenant of faithfulness.
>
> I invite you to join me on my journey of healing. Not just a healing of the body, but an invigorating of ability to see the good in the struggles that we all face. A reclaiming of the promises of our potential, and a prayer to live in the light.
>
> For now, may we all continue to find the strength to have faith in the dark.

As I hit "publish" on that post, my heart was pounding. Then the messages began to come. Within the first moments of publishing my essay, I was flooded with comments. My friends and family offered so much sweetness and support. I remember I just sat in front of my computer weeping while the notifications continued to ring. Then came the private messages: from friends who had no idea that I was going through a hard time and just wanted to reach out to me, from acquaintances who wanted to tell me they were inspired by my story, and from those who shared their own stories, not just of illness, but of all sorts of pain. Most of those people were like me, keeping their secrets close to their chests; I was the first person to whom they disclosed their stories. Even though I was a trained social worker, all of a sudden, I was offering support and a listening ear in a new way. This time it was personal. Through all these varied dynamics and exchanges, a new identity was forming.

From that moment on, I chose to operate under the assumption that everyone I came in contact with knew that I was struggling with chronic illness. This enabled me to release myself from the yoke of shame, the feeling that I had to maintain a secret that was suffocating me. I entered every interaction with the confidence that I was attempting to accept what God had given me with acceptance and humility. The meaning I created when I took control of my personal narrative emboldened me to live that life to the best of my ability. I resolved to embrace the positive personality and dynamic changes that illness brought on its tailcoats.

Two weeks after I published that post, I received a call from my mother. Someone she knew had seen my blog. After reading it, this woman had a feeling that she might know my true diagnosis and suggested to my mother that I speak to her son, who had experienced exactly the same symptoms. After our first, two-hour-long call, he told me radically new information. I went to a new doctor whom he recommended and who confirmed the new diagnosis.

That moment changed my life forever. I now knew what I was wrestling with and how to begin to fix it. Thank God, after months of hard work, I saw improvements. I hoped to be honest in my self-reflection, earnest in my *emuna*, and grateful for the tough lessons I received from illness. I reached out for connection and found healing. I never forgot that lesson, and so this work was inspired by my own journey.

THE LAYERS PROJECT

Until now, *The Layers Project* has taken the form of an online magazine. I launched the project when I was just coming back to myself. It started as a small photojournalism blog where I interviewed and photographed Jewish women. We discussed taboo or stigmatized topics that had yet to be explored out loud in the communal space. The blog following exploded when we touched on issues that women couldn't wait to talk about. We launched an online magazine a year later when it became clear that our followers had too much to say and we needed to make a space for them to express themselves.

My role in it is simple. I listen to the stories of Jewish women. I am present with them in their pain. I help them decide which parts are healing to share. I give them all the control; they get the final say on every word and every photo. I want them to feel that the way we tell their stories is exactly how they want to be portrayed. Then my part comes in. I present them the way I see them. Through my lens and through my own eyes, each woman glows in her own unique beauty, bravery, and resilience. These are ordinary women who live their lives in extraordinary ways.

Each of these stories tackles different life situations or taboo topics, but regardless of the specific circumstances of these women's experiences, the way they find meaning in their struggles and the way they express faith, doubt, and strength reflects so many readers' own individual struggles. These women teach us how to love through suffering and how to live beyond heartache. They teach us how to be sensitive to those who are different from us and they open our minds to realities we never knew.

Each woman who participates in this project has touched thousands of lives. I have received the most remarkable messages from women whose experiences were validated and felt like they were no longer standing on the outside, alone. I have heard from women who received support for the first time in their lives because they had shared a particular story with loved ones, who were then finally able to understand what these women had been going through. I have been contacted by many women who are eager to be empathic to their friends and neighbors, now that they can see difficult issues through new eyes.

The readers of *The Layers Project* have created a beautiful community of support and stigma breaking. Almost every single comment on our hundreds of posts has been loving and respectful. That is practically unheard of in the world of the internet. The women who stand up and the people who reach back out to them with support have created a tremendous community of healing, one in which I feel humbled to be included.

WHY TELL THESE STORIES?

As readers, it can be challenging to read a story that doesn't end in the traditional, happy, feel-good way. The stories in this book come to teach us something else. Sometimes issues, struggles, or problems don't go away. That is just a fact. But what can happen is that we can learn to live full, rich, beautiful, and happy lives, regardless. Pain and joy are not mutually exclusive. I tell these stories because within struggle is beauty. There is nothing as awe inspiring as human resilience. Life is not binary; exclusive to darkness or light. Pain does not need to overtake our lives but may be woven throughout, a reminder of the vulnerability of our humanity and the importance of cherishing every day, good or difficult, that may come.

The whole purpose of these profiles is the meaning-making. We all live with struggle. We muddle through it, wrestling with our challenges, sometimes pinned down by our pain, sometimes coming up for air, and oftentimes we are able to understand it and walk away a changed person. Pain can be a growth opportunity, but the work resides in making meaning of our experiences. We don't have to understand or know why things happen. We just have to make a decision that can help us process it. We need to spend time figuring out the story we tell ourselves about our challenges and whether that story serves us. We need to learn how to live with our hurt and still be okay, maybe better than okay. Maybe we can live with hardship and feel full of blessings, too.

I collect and write these stories because I know what it was like to think that the world around me was perfect, and I was the only one on the outside. I thought that everyone had it together: happy family of many children, successful career, perfect marriage, robust health (mental and physical). But it's simply not true. There is not a human on this planet who lives a perfect life. I believe that we are born to grow, and often, growth begins with struggle. I think that the more we can learn about how others cope – the more we can glean from their meaning-making and figure out how to apply those lessons to our own lives – the better off we are. I know that in a world that is becoming increasingly shallow, false, and full of facades, the way to move forward toward healing lies in sharing our rawness, vulnerability, and honesty.

THE ANATOMY OF A PROFILE

Every chapter of this book features a profile of a Jewish woman. The actual process for writing one of these stories is quite long. I connect with the woman who wants to share her story. She tells me a short synopsis, the key points. Then we meet in person or speak on the phone and we conduct our interview. With permission, the interview is recorded so that I can transcribe our conversation at a later date. We speak anywhere from one to three hours, depending on how long it takes each woman to share her story with me.

Then we meet (perhaps at the same time as the interview if it is in person) for our photoshoot. I do my best to make each woman feel as comfortable as possible, but as women, most of us are unaccustomed to being photographed alone, especially being captured in this raw and intimate way. I find that many of the women whom I profile have a difficult time being photographed. It can be so hard to have the lens focused on you. I struggle with it just like everyone else. It is hard not to nitpick every detail of the image. We are so accustomed to the airbrushed and overedited images we see on the covers of magazines that it hurts us to be so raw. I give the women being profiled total control over what we use. I show them the images as I take them, asking for their feedback and direction as to what they like and how they want to be portrayed. It is the women who are being featured who choose the images we use, not I.

The same rule applies to the text. I know deeply how one changed word or phrase can mean something totally different than what a person meant. After I transcribe the interview and shape it for chronology, narrative thread, and grammar, I send it back to the profile subject. She then has the opportunity to take out anything she wants and add in anything she needs. A word, sentence, paragraph, section – it is all up to her. In the text, you will notice that we kept the spelling of the Hebrew or Yiddish words authentic to the pronunciation of each individual. Jews from all over the world pronounce words differently. The glossary in the back of the book reflects two different denominations of spelling utilized by the women in this book. My goal is that when the profile is finished, every woman is portrayed in images and in words exactly how she wants to seen and heard. The opportunity to rewrite and reshape our narratives is incredibly empowering. It is a thrill for me, every time, to give that gift to someone. It can be life changing.

A fascinating part of this process was discovering that even if someone is prepared to share her story, that does not mean that she is looking to share every detail. The details we choose to offer are reflective of what feels safe or productive to share. The things we tell are connected to crafting our own narratives. You might read some of these stories within this book and still have questions. You might think, "But she didn't explain X." The truth is, none of us are owed all the details. These stories have been written deliberately. If there is something that feels like it's miss-ing, it wasn't for us to know. There are things the profile subjects can't or won't want to share. We all have things that we would rather keep to ourselves.

The voice of every chapter in this book is different, as it is specific to the person sharing her story. I do my best to retain each woman's uniqueness, from her perspective to her speech pattern to interesting phrasing. What you will read in this book is truly a reflection of each woman. One of my favor-ite compliments from my work on the *Layers* magazine was from a woman who told me that her best friend read her profile and told her, "I felt like I was hearing your voice and you were sitting in the room with me." I try to recapture that feeling every time.

These stories are meant to make you, the reader, feel as if you are sitting in the room with us. It should feel like someone you just met is telling you this personal narrative about who they are and what they have experienced in life. It is meant to feel intimate; I try to recreate eye contact with the sub-ject by using images and showing the woman's personality through the way she expresses herself. Aren't those deep, revelatory conversations the times that connections are bonded and friendships made? For me, those moments are some of the deepest joys that I have known as a human.

WHAT IT WAS LIKE TO WRITE THIS BOOK

I took on this project within the first month of my *aliya*. *Aliya* had been a dream of mine for many years. Illness both derailed the opportunity and also brought it to fruition. Only when our future seemed bleak were my husband and I able to reevaluate what we wanted out of life and look for a different kind of future. In a way, being ill brought me home.

As you can imagine, writing this book during our *shana rishona* of *aliya* was a challenging undertaking. I think perhaps it is a testament to how badly I wanted to do this work. While I was attempting to acclimate to a new cli-mate, language, culture, society, and life, I was also intensely working on this project to which I could not say no.

In order to tell the stories of Jewish women living in Israel, you have to know Jewish women living in Israel. Surely this book is limited by who I was able to meet in my first year here. Leaving the States behind, I also left behind my network of connections, curated over the course of my life. I arrived here almost empty-handed. I am so grateful to my online *Layers* community for helping to connect me to the women whose stories are shared here. I am also grateful to family, to new friends, and to profile subjects who became friends, who all shared their networks with me. I spent many days and nights stressing over how I would find women who would want to share what I thought needed to be said.

I found that working on the magazine had not prepared me for writing this book. These stories were far more complex than any I had worked on before. I would show up being prepared to tell a story on one topic and three more topics would unravel while I was listening. At first, I thought that I would organize this book by topic or theme based on the stigmatized, taboo, or painful issues covered in the stories: cancer, infertility, mental health, and others. That is how I organize my profiles in the magazine and it seems to work. But here it was a totally different ballgame. It felt ridiculous and reductionist to simplify a story into a single theme. These are real lives and real stories. They are complex and, dare I say, layered. Maybe I was looking deeper into what was already in front of me. By the time I started this book, I had done many, many profiles for *The Layers Project* magazine. I looked at these stories differently. They became longer, more intricate, and more nuanced than any I had ever written. I experienced a renaissance of my work.

Ultimately, I decided that in order to retain that sense of suspense that readers experience in the online format, I would not organize these chapters by theme. When you begin a chapter, there is no indication of what it will contain. We have included an index at the end of the book for those who would like to be aware of the type of content in a chapter before they read it. I absolutely understand that some topics may be triggering for some people, and some readers may be searching for a particular theme that interests them. My suggestion is to refer to the index if you would like to choose which topics to read and which to avoid.

I was surprised by my own emotional reaction to writing this book. When I wrote profiles in the past, I lived deeply and empathically in each woman's story during the week that it took to interview, write, and publish online. We worked intensely together and I sat with the pain that was shared with me. I believe that feeling is integral to give over someone else's story in the most authentic way. After publishing, the profile subject and I debriefed, and then I let it all go. I released her emotional life after sitting with it and meditating on it. I walked away from that pain, and somehow, came back to myself. It is always an intensely emotional experience for me, but one with resolution.

With this project, there was no release. I met with women, wrote, and ruminated over the stories for periods of months. I was writing in a vacuum. Gone was the rollercoaster of emotions, the intensity, and the letting go. No one knew that I was writing these stories, as I didn't share them with anyone but Rachel Hercman, my clinical editor, business partner, and close friend. I received no mass feedback or catharsis. Because these chapters were waiting to be shared, I never let them go. The emotional baggage of other people began to build in my own emotional life. I held on to much of it because it wasn't ready to be shared. I was working on it, crafting pain into stories that would help heal others. But in that process, I became overloaded.

I found that there were months when I was so encumbered by the emotions of others that I could not write. The chapters in this book were written in spurts. Weeks would fly by and I couldn't focus in order to get out what I knew needed to be written. Then I would have months when everything would come pouring out from my fingertips onto the keyboard. Beginnings, middles, and endings came flying out of me after storing them away and feeling them deeply for months. Even when the chapters were ready to be placed in the manuscript, I still couldn't let them go. Maybe only when my readers are ready to read will I be able to say goodbye to those journeys.

Surely, the path I took to get to the end of writing this work went in many directions. I collected stories from all over Israel, and in that way, this work gave me the opportunity to see the country during my first year here. My husband, Scott, who is my partner in all things, traveled the country with me, visiting places we had never been or had never seen together. In discovering the women of this country, I also discovered the land that had previously only lived in my dreams.

Due to the fact that I am an English speaker, my Hebrew is not fluent, and I speak no other languages, the range of women that I was able to interview was limited. In the end, most of the women I feature in this book are immigrants (or refugees) who have come to live in Israel. It was a humbling opportunity to learn from the lives they have built, hear their experiences, and understand how they define themselves in the space between the place where they were born and the place that they chose.

Rereading everything that I have written within these pages, I see a love letter to the Holy Land. She is revealed here in many of these stories: messy, needy, chaotic, fearful, glowing, gorgeous, holy, hallowed, missed, and beloved. These stories are unflinchingly honest about what it means to live here, often not having been born a *Sabra*. They showcase the joy and so much struggle of coming home, while feeling oftentimes like a stranger, often like a sister. We come here for many different reasons, but ultimately, it is the land and its people that pull us homeward.

I took a lot of time to consider the meaning and impact of exile and redemption, *galut* and *geula*. I was astounded by the opportunity to record, in my own way, a piece of the ingathering of the exiles, Jews returning to Israel after three thousand years in the Diaspora. I reflected often on my grandparents who survived the *Shoah* and what they would have thought of this gift that was given to me, in my lifetime. I spoke to women who were born all over the world, women who were born Jews, women who became Jews by choice, and women who discovered ancient lineages and returned home to their nation. I learned much about world Jewry, our history, challenges, and hopes for the future in this one year of meeting the people of this great country.

Ultimately, I learned that there are many types of exile. There is the exile of being kicked out of your birthplace, the exile of isolation and silence, and the exile of feeling like you don't belong where you are. Individual and national exiles blur in personal stories. Luckily, so do the blessings of redemption. Inherent in redemption is the promise of healing, a healing of things that pain us and keep us on the outside of what is sacred to us.

I know that God has blessed me with a personal redemption. He has brought me and my family home to our homeland, and we were additionally reunited with my parents and siblings who have settled here. He healed me from illness. He sent me on the path that led me to my work, my *tafkid*, my hope for the future. I pray that He blesses all of *Am Yisrael* with a personal and national *geula, bekarov*.

Within these pages in your hands are thirty-four real-life stories of challenge and triumph. These Jewish women, heralding from all over the world, have settled in Israel as part of the Jewish people. They exhibit awe-inspiring resilience, patience, fortitude, gratitude, and love. They also may experience anger, shame, fear, isolation, guilt, and pain. These experiences are not mutually exclusive, and together they form a picture of real life. These chapters contain meaning-making that all of us, both women and men, can learn from. The women profiled here are all different, each with her own perspective, life experience, history, and hopes for the future. It has been an honor and a privilege to listen to their stories, and it is humbling to share them in this format with you.

AKNOWLEDGMENTS

This book was a collaborative effort.

First, I need to thank Marla, who believed in this book so much that she pushed me to find the right publisher. She made me realize that even though I had made *aliya* on Tuesday and she pitched me the idea the following Sunday, the time was right to write this book.

Thank you to Yehudit Jessica Singer at Koren, who received the idea for this book with such warmth and excitement. Thank you to Matthew Miller at Koren, who sat with me and believed in the mission of this work. Thank you for taking a chance on me and having a vision for this project.

Thank you to the rest of the Koren/Toby Press team who worked on this book, Tali Simon, Nechama Unterman, and Tani Bayer, who engaged with this work with such sensitivity and attention to detail. I can't explain the relief of having the most caring hands tend to this labor of love.

I owe a huge thank you to Aryeh Grossman, who championed this book through the difficult Covid19 stages and whose belief in this work actualized the final push to bring it out into the world.

Endless thanks to Tomi Mager, who shepherded this manuscript from the beginning. Tomi answered all my millions of questions, soothed my anxieties, brainstormed with me, networked for me, and gave me the support to tell these stories. I am grateful for the insights, patience, and perspective.

Thank you to Rabbi Marianne Novak and Dr. Noam Stadlan, and Denise and Irwin Hametz, who have supported the vision of Layers for many years, and have now partnered in the vision of this project through their generous sponsorship that brought this book to life.

I would never have made it through this work without the support and guidance of my friends. I have so much gratitude to Nikki Schreiber who told me I could do this, kept me on task, helped me keep to my schedule, and gave me the confidence I needed to finish this work. Thank you to Shira Glass for being the first reader of this manuscript and giving me important feedback that shaped the final product.

To my old neighborhood friends in Fair Lawn, New Jersey, who supported my out of the box idea to start *The Layers Project* and stood by me while I stepped outside my comfort zone.

To my new neighborhood friends in Jerusalem, who nourished me when I struggled, made connections for me, served as sounding boards, read through these pages in final stages, cheered me on till the finish line, and nursed me back to myself when it was all over. I am more grateful to you all than you will ever know.

To my lifelong friends, for inspiring me in every chapter.

To Rachel Hercman, who clinically edited this book and talked me through its inception and every moment after. You are my official sounding board, life *chavrusa*, brainstormer, and close friend. It was such an honor to take our work to a new format and I feel so blessed to be able to have your insights on these chapters.

To my tribe, the women of *The Layers Project* magazine. To the women who have worked on the magazine, been profiled, written essays, or shared their pain anonymously – you are the bravest souls I know. To those who have read the stories and engaged in healing conversations, I am so humbled by the movement you have ignited to break stigma and support each other. You all have filled me with much hope and helped me personally and professionally to find meaning in my work.

To the women who are featured in this book. This work is a tribute to your generosity of spirit, your resilience, your bravery, and your vision that sharing your experiences might be healing for others. I owe all of this to you and feel so grateful to have made such beautiful new friends on this journey.

To my teachers, for shaping my mind and giving me the knowledge that the world is wide. Thank you for the technical skills, clinical skills, vocabulary, and Jewish values that you instilled in me. Every one of you is present in my writing.

To my in-law family: Mom and Dad, Marcie and Ron; Adam, Rachel, Hannah, Jacob, and Abigail, Grandma Fishman and Grandma Sheps. Thank you for your support all these years.

To my aunts and uncles, Holly and Robert Lankin and Harriet and Michael Hessdorf, for your unending love and involvement in my life and generous support of this project. Thank you for helping me get to the finish line and always believing in me and my work. To my cousins Andrea and Rebecca for teaching me to love literature and making me a reader before I was a writer, and Noah and Sara for their excitement and encouragement. I know that my paternal grandparents – my namesake Grandma Shirley, Pop Joe, and Micki Lankin, *z"l* – would have loved to see this work.

To my maternal grandparents, Oma and Opa, Marion and Herbert Achtentuch *z"l*, who taught me the importance of history, and why we need to record who we are and the places from which we come. They shared with me the value of language, how to live with an open mind, and how to love with an open heart.

To my siblings, Gavi and Noam; Josh and Jen; and Benjy and Bracha (and of course baby Yael). You are the people who bring me ceaseless joy. We are a soul family in every meaning of the word. You are my best friends, excellent editors, visionaries, dreamers, and cheerleaders.

To my *Abba* and *Ima*, Rabbi Dr. Eric and Jeanne Lankin, thank you for the imparting of values, validation, and love. You taught me to be empathic to others, to nurture myself, and to stand up for what I think is right. You taught me to write about what I know, and that there is no such thing as good writing, just good editing.

To my children, Ayelet and Dovi, your love sustains me through the most painful chapters. It is the highest honor of my life to be your mother. You fill my life with joy and meaning, and all this work is to make our little corner of the world a better place for you.

To my husband Scott, I could never have predicted how you would fill my sad moments with hope, make my painful moments softer, and make my successes sweeter. I am so grateful it was you by my side through it all. In this book, you are in every word.

To *HaKadosh Baruch Hu*, who truly heals the sick, who has a bigger plan for us than we can see, and who gives us every moment we have on this earth. Thank You for the lessons, for this life, for this work that I feel passionate about, and for all the love in my life.

Loss, Cycles, and Sisterhood

Neve Daniel, Gush Etzion

AS IF THEY NEVER EXISTED

When I was ten, my mother was pregnant and she didn't know that she was expecting twins. She went into labor at six months, and she left to the hospital and we heard almost nothing about what was happening. Back then, the feelings of the rest of the children in the family were not considered in the crisis of our mother and our new and tiny sisters in the hospital. Born very prematurely, the babies were in incubators and it was understood that the babies needed all the care and attention. No notice was given to the fact that their siblings were home worrying about our mother and these babies. We were not allowed to come visit, or even peek through the window. We never met those babies.

Perhaps the prevailing thought was that because my three siblings and I never met them, we weren't attached to them. Maybe it was thought that our lack of knowing them meant that we didn't feel towards them. But those babies were our sisters. We knew what being a sister meant and we were eager to cherish our new arrivals. But after one day on this earth, one of our brand-new sisters died.

The family and community pivoted all their energies and prayers to focus on the twin who was still alive. They named her Rachel Sarah. Still, we were not allowed to meet her. They didn't even take a picture of her. Rachel died

1

after a few weeks. Because her life was so short, our family was not required to sit *shiva* for her. So there was nothing, and we never had the opportunity to grieve for her. Both twins were simply erased from our lives as if they never existed.

For me, as the oldest girl, I carried this trauma with me into my adult life. When I grew up, I decided I wanted to be a maternity nurse and I worked with new moms, sometimes in the nursery. Usually, thank God, everything was fine. Both mom and baby were healthy. But once in a while, there would be a premature birth or fetal death and the trauma would resurface for me. It manifested in an explosion of emotion, every time.

Whenever I heard of babies born prematurely, it felt like I was experiencing the loss of my sisters, over and over again. I felt as if I could not move forward. I never had a healthy grieving process, so I was stuck in that never-ending cycle of fresh mourning. I would do whatever I could to help my patients and do my best to work with the parents of premature babies or parents who had just lost their children. I know I did my best to be sensitive to their pain. But it forced me to realize that I had never worked through my own grief.

THE BURDEN OF TRAUMATIC LOSS

When I was working in the field of maternity nursing, sometimes it felt like I was punishing myself. I don't think that when I went into the field, I was consciously aware of what it was stirring up for me. Consciously, it was much simpler. When

I gave birth to my firstborn and I was in the hospital bed holding her, I remember thinking that it was the best feeling in the world. I felt like I wanted to work with newborn babies professionally, because it felt so good to me to be with healthy babies. Maybe subconsciously, the feeling of the full-term baby in my arms was a relief. Frankly, it was odd that I wanted to go into the field, because I had zero interest in being a nurse. It was such a mismatched occupation choice because of my triggers and my lack of technical prowess. I was only willing to work in maternity or pediatrics. I was putting myself in scenarios that would trigger me all the time, yet all I wanted to do was work with the new moms and new babies. Perhaps subconsciously, I knew I needed to work through my unresolved pain to find resolution and peace.

In 1999, my mother realized that we had been living with this familial grief for all these years and that we had never mourned these babies. She decided that the babies deserved to be remembered, and that we all deserved the opportunity to grieve for them properly. She did something incredible, and put together everything that was missing all those years ago. She put headstones on their graves, made a big extended family reunion, and we all gathered around and flew to New York for the event. We held a graveside ceremony – it was the first time that any of us had ever been to the place where they were buried. We all wrote something to say to these sisters we had never met. We spoke to them and gave them the messages we never had the opportunity to give, messages of love and longing. We stood together and cried.

My mother made a scrapbook to hold every piece of memorabilia that she had from their short lives. There are no pictures, but their hospital bracelets, birth and death certificates, and copies of all our speeches are there. It was a beautiful tribute to their impact on our family.

We spent *Shabbat* together as a family. After we said *Havdala*, the huge stone that was sitting on me all these years was lifted. The triggers were processed. I carried that burden of grief for twenty years. Now I know I was subconsciously putting myself in situations where I could achieve closure. When I finally processed the loss of my sisters, I left the field of nursing and I never looked back.

ATTACHED

When we made *aliya* in 2002 on the first Nefesh B'Nefesh flight, I brought four children with me. I had an "*aliya* baby" during our first year of transitioning to life in Israel. After that baby was born, I wanted to have another child. It wasn't long before I got pregnant. I was excited and looking forward to growing our family.

In the middle of my second trimester, something didn't feel right. I went for a sonogram so that I could find out if everything was okay. The look on the technician's face told me something was very wrong. She said, "There is something not right." I thought she meant that the baby was in the wrong place, or had moved into a funny position. I thought it was something that was fixable. She didn't speak English so it was difficult to understand what she meant. She was using euphemisms because she didn't want to say out loud what she needed to tell me. Eventually, I got it. I had lost the baby.

I was in shock. Some people have said to me, "Thank God you have other kids." But it doesn't matter how many children you have. I lost a baby. The minute I saw that plus sign on that pregnancy test, I was attached. That baby was my child, and now my child was gone.

Everyone already knew that I was pregnant, so my loss was very public. I was wearing maternity clothes and showing. I couldn't quietly slip into a non-pregnant existence. I was also too far along to just pass the baby naturally. The baby was dead inside of me and I had to go to the hospital to deliver the baby. They gave me Pitocin to induce labor, and I had to go through the whole process of labor and delivery of this tiny child. It's impossible to describe the hours of stress and pain that one goes through to deliver a child that you know will never live.

During the delivery of the body, I hemorrhaged and needed a dilation and curettage (D&C) to clear the uterine lining. I lost a lot of blood. They put me on bed rest for a week because I was weak from all the blood loss and the physical trauma. I was experiencing things that a mom usually experiences when giving birth to a baby: delivery, hospital stay, my neighbors coming over and bringing meals for my family, and the physical ramifications for my body. But in my situation, my baby was not coming home with me. I was in so much pain.

SWEETNESS REBORN

At the time of my miscarriage, I was alone without family here in Israel. My neighbors were wonderful and supportive, but I needed the support of my sisters and mother. They, too, were feeling sad that they couldn't be here with me. They wanted to do something meaningful to send me the message that they were thinking of me. Together, my four siblings and my parents purchased a pomegranate

4

tree for us. We had just bought a house here in Neve Daniel, in Gush Etzion. We had no landscaping at our brand-new place. We were the first of our family to put down roots here in Israel and they thought that it would be really meaningful to give us a tree.

We planted the tree in our yard and today it is tall and lush and brings us beautiful fruit every year. For me, having one of the *Shivat HaMinim*, the Seven Species of the Land of Israel, growing in front of my home is symbolic of the beautiful life we have made here in Israel. It is powerful to have something living that memorializes someone we lost.

Later on, I found out that the pomegranate is a symbol of fertility. I was blown away by the connection between my loss and the fruits that are borne to us every year. This tree has given us many gifts. Most of all, it gives comfort for our losses and sweet reminders of the incredible life we have built here.

PRESCRIBED *SHIVA*

Because my miscarriage was so public, it changed the way I grieved for my baby. If I had a quiet loss, no one would have known. I would have been left to grieve on my own, alone again. It could have been like reliving the loss of my sisters. This time, I was forced to talk to people. I had one week of pre-scribed bed rest where I shared my grief with my neighbors, was visited by friends, and was fed, nurtured, and allowed the space for pain. My public miscarriage and subsequent bed rest gave me a period of time that served as a *shiva*. I grieved, I healed, I was given a tree that was living, and I was able to embrace it all so that I could live looking toward the future. It was a healthy process that did not leave me burdened again. It was the opposite of what I went through as a child.

I find that life can be cyclical and sometimes will present us similar scenarios until we can achieve catharsis and learn the lesson we are meant to learn. The healing that I experienced with my family twenty years after the loss of my sisters was the model I needed to process loss again when it was my child who was taken from me.

IT'S A BIG DEAL

When I was pregnant with the child I lost, two of my sisters were also pregnant. We were so excited that the three of us were going to be having babies together. As I watch their children grow up, I am reminded of the one who is missing. But somehow, as those children grew, I was able to separate my feelings. My loss stays behind in my pomegranate tree and there is no pain or resentment in seeing those babies hit their milestones and grow into people.

A few years after my miscarriage, I was no longer alone living here in Israel. Two of my sisters moved here with their families. It was wonderful to be reunited on this side of the world. One of them had a fourth pregnancy. She was also far along into her pregnancy, and the news was public. She was pregnant at the same time that my second-eldest daughter was pregnant with her first. They were due at the exact same time. They were comparing notes, talking all the time, and so excited to be doing this together. My sister is closer in age to my daughter than she is to me. They too are like sisters.

One day, my sister felt that something was wrong. She called me with her symptoms, because I used to be a maternity nurse, and I told her to go to the hospital immediately. When she got there, she was told that she had lost her baby. We were all devastated.

My initial reaction was, "We need to do something for her." I couldn't let her experience this loss by herself. At first, I was told, "We shouldn't make a bigger deal about this for her than it already is. It will make the pain worse." But I held my ground and said, "No. The pain is there. If we don't acknowl-

edge it, it will surely hurt more. We can do something for her to let her know we are there with her."

We tossed a few ideas around the family and ultimately we presented the idea to her. My suggestion was to do for her what our family did for me. I suggested that we go to the forest and plant a tree with Jewish National Fund in memory of the child she had lost. She loved the idea and that is what we did. We all chipped in and I went with my two sisters who live here in Israel to one of the JNF forests and planted an almond tree. Looking back, I feel as if I experienced cycles of loss until the lessons I learned were healing enough that I could pass on strength to others in their time of need. The women in my family – my mother and generations of sisters – have figured out together how to support each other and provide comfort and love through the pain of losing one of us.

GROWING UP

Soon I will be leaving the house where my tree is planted. I think the new owners of our home will enjoy having a pomegranate tree in their yard, and they will also appreciate the meaning of this species here in Israel. God willing, they will showcase the fruits of this tree on their *Rosh HaShana* table, too, and take *terumot* and *maasrot* from it, and I really am okay with that. We planted it, it's here, and it will continue to live and bear fruit for the people of this country. It doesn't have to be for

me. It brings me joy just to know it's there.

To me, this tree represents the child I lost. Now it is blossoming and continuing its journey of life. Like with a child, it feels so beautiful to watch it grow up and bear fruit for others.

REFLECTIONS

Questions to Consider
- What are your experiences with the bonds of sisterhood?
- Were there times in your life when you created your own ceremony around grief?

Words to Remember

"Looking back, I feel as if I experienced cycles of loss until the lessons I learned were healing enough that I could pass on strength to others in their time of need. The women in my family – my mother and generations of sisters – have figured out together how to support each other and provide comfort and love through the pain of losing one of us."

Group Discussion

Do families in your community who experience pregnancy or infant loss have access to resources for support and comfort? Which resources are available?

ॐ

Take a moment for yourself. What do you need right now?
Close your eyes and be in your own body.
Here is a breathing exercise to come back to yourself:

Breathing Exercise

Close your eyes. Breathe in through your nose, hold it for five seconds, and breathe out through your mouth on release. If holding your breath makes you feel uncomfortable, try it for just two or three seconds and then release. This exercise should help your body relax back to center.

Tzippi's Story

War, Love, and Memory

Nof Ayalon

After my parents passed away, I discovered a trove of letters and writings that shed light on my childhood memories. I learned a new backstory to the war trauma of my youth, showing my parents' perspective. New details and truths fleshed out the story that I had long remembered and revealed more about what my mother had shared with me. Though I was merely four years old at the time and decades have since passed, my memories of war are still so vivid. Because of these letters, I am able to share the bigger picture and explore a fuller sense of what happened to me and my family. It's been a lifetime of piecing together and assimilating the parts that have contributed to my narrative.

When I was a child, my father pursued his doctorate at the Technion and my days consisted of waiting for his evening return home from university. We lived in Haifa and my mother did her best to entertain two very small children while frustratingly confined to a tiny apartment. I was four years old and my brother was two.

During that time, my father created a project for each of us. As a published author now, it's fun to look back and remember that the first book I ever wrote was with my father when I was little. He told us to each pick a subject. I liked ships and my brother liked trains. When he left for university we half butchered, half cut out pictures of ships and trains and when he returned, we described our ideas and thoughts about the photos and he wrote them down as captions. I recently found these photo books that we wrote together. Holding those books in my hands, I could feel the sense of serenity of those times.

Our *mirpeset* looked out over the Haifa harbor and our days were punctuated by the sounds of fog horns from ships coming in to dock. I always thought the ocean was very mysterious, the fog banks either safeguarding or revealing big secrets. In Haifa, strong fog layers rolled over the sea. You could hear the fog horns, but could not necessarily see the actual ships. It was exciting when they finally revealed themselves after the fog lifted.

It was June of 1967 and my grandmother suffered a sudden stroke in Jerusalem. We immediately headed out to the Judean Hills and its city center, where she was being treated in an old British hospital. At the same time, rumors were spreading that Israel was once again on the brink of war. Yet, surprisingly, everyone seemed to be going about their usual business, while simultaneously claiming Jerusalem would be the safest of places to stay. No one dreamed that Jerusalem would be touched by war, let alone be the first city hit.

Feeling that Jerusalem would remain safe, my father told my mother to take care of her mother and said that my brother and I should stay with family at my uncles' apartment in Jerusalem. My father needed to go back to his classes in Haifa. As soon as my grandmother would be discharged from the hospital, the plan was to bring us back to Haifa, where we all would be safe and sound. When he got back to the Technion, classes were canceled due to the rumors of war breaking out. He decided to go to Kibbutz Beit Zerah, east of the Jordan river – near the point where the Syrian, Jordanian, and Israeli borders meet – where the war was anticipated to begin. His job was to help dig trenches for the children of the *kibbutz* to protect them from the barrage of fire. He thought that we would all be safe in Jerusalem.

My grandmother and my uncles lived on *Reḥov* Shmuel HaNavi. We were placed in their apartment for safety. As it happened to be, this street became the exact border of the war. Some of the first shots of the Six Day War took place on our street. Instead of being safe and out of the way of the war, we were directly in the line of fire.

BANANAS

On the morning of June fifth, my mother was shopping. She needed to go to the hospital to pick up some medication for her mother, who had been brought back to her home on Shmuel HaNavi after her stroke. She wanted to pick up some sweets for the Arab children whose fathers had been rounded up by the army for questioning before the war. She had grown up in Jerusalem and had many Arab friends and neighbors. She took pity on the children, and was thinking about them as the tension began to mount.

My mother was thinking about the Arab children of Jerusalem, and my father was thinking about the Jewish children on the *kibbutz*. What neither of them knew was that they should have been the most concerned about their own children.

So that day, the day that the war siren sounded, my mother was not home. I was at the apartment with my little brother, my grandmother, and my two uncles, *Dod* Moshe and *Dod* Baruch. The minute the siren started, *Dod* Moshe realized that his sister, my mother Sarah, was out in the city and was in danger. He was a cab driver and had his own cab. He immediately hopped in the car and went out to find her.

My brother Jordan and I were now home alone with my grandmother, who was immobile and recovering from her stroke, and *Dod* Baruch. *Dod* Baruch was a kabbalist who recited the midnight service *Tikkun Ḥatzot*, spoke minimally, and mainly *davened* all day. Our family is descended from a long line of kabbalists, starting with the Ohr Shraga. As it was, he was not the most grounded adult to have around in a time of crisis.

At four years old, I had no idea what the sirens meant. I opened the door and saw a flurry of activity. I saw neighbors running up and down the stairwells. Some were carrying mattresses, and others, bags of food. There was a frenzy outside and there was nothing happening inside my own apartment. I turned to *Dod* Baruch and said, "Shouldn't we be doing something?" He was mumbling prayers to himself and not addressing me. The non-stop siren was blaring. The neighbors were flying in the hallways. I told my uncle, "We need to go. We need to go where they are going." I looked around the apartment and saw a large pile of bananas on the table.

A week before the Six Day War, *Dod* Moshe was driving his taxi and stopped in an Arab village. He saw a Muslim woman who looked like she was in distress. He stopped his cab and asked her if she was okay. She told him that she was having a baby. He told her to get into the cab and he drove her to the hospital for free. While escorting her in, someone took his information. A week later, the woman's husband found my uncle and brought him a massive basket of fruit. I had just learned of this story an hour before this interview, during a call with *Dod* Moshe.

While I was searching the apartment, attempting to discover what I could bring with me to the place that the neighbors were going, I saw the leftovers of this fruit basket. I saw all our neighbors collecting food, so I grabbed as many bananas as I could fit in my arms and grabbed my two-year-old brother's hand. I told *Dod* Baruch, "It's time to go. Take *Savta* and we need to get out of here." This seemed to wake him from his trance. He tossed my grandmother over his shoulders like a sack of potatoes, and I led him down the stairs.

Everyone was passing us, running up and down in a frenzy. The sirens were blaring so loudly that our ears hurt. My uncle was climbing down the stairs so slowly because he didn't want to fall or drop my grandmother. The climb down felt like an eternity. I held Jordan's hand as tightly as I could. I would not let him go.

We were traveling to the bottom floor of the building. There was a shelter there that was a shelter in name only. It was used as a storage unit, where the leftover garbage was heaped into piles. There were old strollers, furniture, and castaways from people's lives dumped down there. There was no electricity. It had rats and cockroaches. Worst of all, there was no lock on the door. Everyone was stampeding in droves down to this bomb shelter. When I walked in, it was clear to me that no one had ever expected to need to use it.

KNOCK, KNOCK

On one side of the shelter, many of the religious people were praying. I wondered how they could see their prayer books in the dark. The only light came from small holes in the walls where a little light would filter through. *Dod* Baruch stayed on that side of the room. Perhaps it was a *minyan* of sorts.

On the other side of the room were what I understood to be "the loud people." They were the ones who discussed and strategized what we were going to do and also guarded the door. Because there was no lock, this group had pushed all the junk that was left in the shelter up against the door from the inside, blocking it so the enemy could not enter.

Outside the shelter was the front line of the war. My mother and *Dod* Moshe had found each other in the city and they had several things they had to do before they could make it back to the apartment building. They had to make sure another elderly grandparent got safely to a shelter, and they had to get medication for their mother. At one point, the cab was even shot by machine guns, so they abandoned the car and ran. They ran from doorway to doorway by the Mandelbaum checkpoint to get to the street of our apartment building. They held hands and kept running to try and return to us.

Back in the shelter, I was offered food by my friend from the building, Avner, and his mother. My mother always told me that I should not take food from strangers and so because I was four and I did not know Avner's mother Tzivia well, I refused to take food from her. I steadily fed myself and my brother from my stash of bananas.

I sat with my immobile grandmother and Jordan. I played with Avner, whatever little games we could come up with. We would peek through the holes of the walls to watch for the milk trucks that were bringing milk to sustain the Israelis under fire. Avner and I would open the caps of the milk bottles and lick the cream off the top of the milk. The adults were angry at us for ruining the milk for everyone, but they still let us do it.

It was hard to distinguish between night and day in the dark room filled with people. We had no radios, because apparently the enemy would pick up signals from the radios and bomb those locations. We had no idea what was happening on the outside. We just waited.

After a day or two, they decided to send someone from the bomb shelter to see what was going on outside. They picked a police officer named Uzi, because he had a gun. They decided that he would use some sort of code; he would knock in a special pattern when he was ready to come back inside the shelter. I remember it being a long stretch of waiting for Uzi to return. There were whisperings all around the room. It is my sense that it was the middle of the night when the knock came. The problem was that it was not the pre-arranged knock.

That's when the trouble began. Everyone in the shelter became hysterical. Was it him? Why was that the wrong knock? Was it the enemy? Because they needed to be quiet so that the enemy outside wouldn't hear them, they couldn't yell out, "Is it you, Uzi?" Someone said, "Maybe the enemy is with him and he needs to knock differently to alert us that he is not alone." It was so confusing and frightening. Even as a small child, I understood that we were all in danger and that even the adults didn't know what to do. If they opened the door, we could all be killed. If they didn't open the door, our friend and neighbor could be killed.

Thank God, they took a chance. They opened the door and it was just him. I never understood why he didn't use the code. Everyone breathed a sigh of relief. Then immediately, everyone in the room jumped all over him for information.

DON'T MOVE

I don't really remember which night my mother and uncle reached the bomb shelter. They traveled from cover to cover, overhang to door frame. Just as they got back to the apartment building, *Dod* Baruch, who had been praying the entire time we were in the shelter, heard my mother's voice through the holes in the wall. He stopped praying and started shoving junk away from the door to let in his siblings.

Just as the door opened, he rushed out to usher them inside. As he got through the doorway, a burst of shrapnel exploded in their direction. My mother was hit in the arm and the nose and *Dod* Baruch was hit in the stomach. After having not seen us for several days, my mother burst into the room and collapsed, with both my uncles right behind her.

My mother and *Dod* Baruch were lying on the floor moaning and there was blood everywhere. I was screaming, "*Ima! Ima!*" and Tzivia, Avner's mom, was holding me back from reaching her. It was *Dod* Moshe who took out the shrapnel from my mother's nose, and someone else took out the one in her arm. They used iodine to clean the wounds but still, she had those scars for the rest of her life. They also needed to take out the shrapnel from *Dod* Baruch's stomach. I remember the moaning and fear. This was the most traumatic memory.

There was a woman in the shelter whose name was Rivka. She was a Holocaust survivor and she suffered from mental illness. She had a nightly habit of going out into the street and screaming into the heavens. She did this for many years after the *Shoah*. As her son got older, instead of feeling more compassion for her, he felt that she was a tremendous source of embarrassment and he would hit her with a mattress beater as she screamed. He desperately wanted to make her stop. I remember how frightened I was in the shelter when she would moan and talk to Hashem out loud. The other people in the room would whisper to her, "Shhh Rivka, enough." I was always afraid of her and her pain.

Six days passed and the war was over. For the duration of the time we were in the shelter, my mom would smile at me from her semi-upright position against the wall. She would say things like, "Eat," and she gave me permission to eat food from Tzivia. At one point, *Dod* Moshe did something both brave and utterly foolish. He went upstairs to the apartment to get more food and a little portable stove so that he could make hot food for everyone in the shelter. There was a pregnant woman among us and she wasn't faring so well. He went to get the food so he could help revive her. Thank God, he made it back alive.

There was another pregnant woman amongst the families in a connecting shelter. She was so disgusted by sitting in filth all day and all night for so many days that she finally had enough and decided to sneak up to her apartment to shower. She never came back.

Meanwhile, my father kept trying to get back to us in Jerusalem. He hitch-hiked and found a full-scale battle at Latrun. He was sent back to Haifa and then tried to map out another way to enter Jerusalem. All the usual routes and roads were closed. He tried but could not come through. He went back to the Technion again and found out that my mother had called and checked in there. There was a rotating phone among the bomb shelters and he was able to get ahold of my mother. She told him everything was fine, but that he should not try to come to Jerusalem as it was only safe within the shelters and certainly not out on the roads. She did not mention that she or Baruch had been injured.

The last day of the war is a day that I will never forget. Everyone was very quiet as we made our way back upstairs. We found the door to our apartment open, and the whole apartment was covered in broken glass from the windows that had been blown out. On my grandmother's bed, there was an unspent bullet. Every single apartment on the street was covered in glass.

My father made it back to Jerusalem only when the roads were finally reopened. When he reconnected with us, he decided that Jordan and I needed some fresh air after being locked in the shelter for six days. He brought us to an empty dirt lot across the street from our apartment building. He thought that while the adults cleaned up the apartment, we could run around outside.

We began to run and within seconds, all the Israeli soldiers who were standing around the area began to scream, "Don't move!" We didn't know that there were landmines all over the field. My father screamed as loudly as he could, "Sit! Don't move! Freeze!" My brother cried hysterically but was too scared to move. I have never seen my father look so terrified. I thought he was angry with me. I couldn't understand what was happening. He screamed and screamed and screamed and we were paralyzed with fear. It took a long time for the soldiers to come, inch by inch, foot by foot, testing the ground to come save us. It took so long to reach us. This was extremely traumatic. The minute I thought I was safe, I was as close as ever to danger. Still today, seeing large groups of soldiers is a trigger for me, although at the same time, it is an amazing sight that makes me feel proud. They were my saviors. But some feelings of danger never leave you.

HAKOL BESEDER

After the war, we left Israel. I was six when I landed in the States. My father was a rocket scientist and before I was born, he worked on the Faith 7. My English name is Faith, after that rocket ship. Now he wanted to forget the war and forget the trauma. We moved to California and he continued to work in the space industry. We tried to forget it all.

But I couldn't forget. I had recurring nightmares of my time in the shelter. When I was a teenager, I flew to Israel every summer to visit my family that had stayed behind. I would go back to the same building and every trip I would refuse to go near the bomb shelter. The summer I was sixteen, I dated my old bomb-shelter playmate, Avner. He still lived there with his mother Tzivia and his siblings in the apartment beneath my family.

I asked him to help me with something. I told him, "I have to go back to the bomb shelter." "Why? There's nothing down there now."

"I don't know why. I just need to go back."

We brought two chairs and we went into the shelter. He sat on one and I on the other. I don't know how long I sat there. It was a long time. I closed my eyes and imagined I was back in the war, watching a ping-pong match between the people who prayed and the loud people who strategized. I reimagined all the characters huddled in that room filled with cockroaches and rats, smelled the fear, and relived the terrifying moments.

Avner said after a while, "*Hakol beseder?*"

I replied, "Yeah, it will be."

The holes in the walls had been fixed. Someone had installed a window that allowed a ray of light to come into the bomb shelter. In my mind's eye, I thought, "There's light here again." It wasn't so terrifying in the light. I was ready to stop those recurring nightmares of bullets and bombs, family members covered in blood. Electricity had been installed, and the shelter had been recently painted, too. It was completely empty of all that garbage and the leftover relics from the lives of other people. Now it looked like a proper shelter.

We were two people on two chairs. As empty as the space was, I did not feel alone. I was with my childhood playmate again and we had survived. It was time to make peace with that shelter. I did. After that, the recurring nightmares finally ceased.

ALL OVER AGAIN

I hated Israel. It felt like a terrible place for me to be. I always associated it with war. When I grew up and attended college, my feelings became mellowed and I actually became president of the Israel Action Council. Still, there was always a sense of otherness. I had an Israeli mother and an American father. We were the only religious kids in the San Fernando Valley. I felt like I never quite fit in there either.

Fourteen years ago, I told my husband that I wanted to take our family to Israel for the year. I had just given birth to my fifth child and he was six months old. We put everything we owned in storage and came to Israel for a trial period of a year. I felt I needed to give it another try. During the beginning of our trial period, I received a call from my younger sister in the middle of the night. "*Ima* is very sick. She has pancreatic cancer. She's not going to make it."

I departed on the next flight and left my family behind in Israel. After a month of caring for my mom, I told my husband that I wasn't coming back and that I would stay to care for her for the duration. During my second month there, my family decided to join me in California.

Because of that trauma in the shelter, I have a phobia of blood to the point where my family doesn't even use the word "blood" around me. Whenever I hear that word or see blood, I'm immediately transported to my mother collapsing in the shelter, covered in red. Now that she was sick, my mother was vomiting up blood – and worse, it would happen all the time. It was a nightmare. I took care of her, IVs and all, for nine months.

My mom passed away and we buried her here in Israel. We swayed, crying, on *Har HaMenuḥot*, the cemetery. As they lowered my mother's body into the grave, an IDF training exercise was in full session across the hill. As I was saying goodbye to my mother for the last time, I heard rounds of machine-gun fire, bullets, and explosions ricocheting through the valley.

All of a sudden, I was back in that moment as a four-year-old child, feeling like I am losing my mother all over again. I forgot where I was, and all I felt was fear followed by powerful grief. I reached out toward her body being lowered into the ground and shouted out, "*Ima! Ima!*" But it was too late. I would never touch her again. Someone held me back again. I could not get to my mother. For me, she was dying all over again.

A GOOD LIFE

Four months later, we were back living in Israel. One night I woke up from a dream. I turned to my husband and said, "The weirdest thing just happened. *Ima* came to me in a dream and told me to come visit her because it's her birthday." My husband responded, "That's odd, because your mother's birthday was last month. Not sure that it means anything."

The next morning, I called my brother in New York and told him about my dream. He said, "You know, we always knew that *Ima*'s birthday was in Adar, we just never knew which Adar. Maybe it was Adar *bet*? It's Adar *bet* now! Maybe it truly is her birthday. You've got to go to her *kever* today to see her. Call me when you get there and maybe I can say some *tehillim* with you while you are there."

I went about my day doing errands with my husband and toward the end of the day, we arrived at my mother's grave. After being there for a little while, I called my brother. When he picked up the phone, he had this weird, excited energy. I said, "What's wrong?" He told me, "It was so odd. My phone has had no battery all day. It was just dead. All of a sudden it came to life when you called. The phone rang without having any battery." His story seemed a bit odd but I just assumed it was something wonky with his phone battery.

Then I called my younger sister, Aravah, in California, to see if she also wanted to say something while I was visiting *Ima*'s grave. She missed my call but called me back a minute later. When I got her on the phone, she also had the same weird, excited energy that my brother had minutes before. She said, "It's so strange. When I missed your call, I called you back and it actually went through even though I'm not on any international calling plan. In fact, I've never been able to call Israel on my cell phone no matter how many times I've tried. I have no idea how we are on the phone right now." That certainly seemed weird too. But it was what happened next that I could barely believe.

My husband and I were standing in front of the gravestone. The sun had gone all the way down and it was now too dark for us to read the *Tehillim*. All of a sudden, I saw the words on the stone begin to glow. The engraving on my mother's headstone talked about the life of goodness that she led, growing up in Jerusalem and being a wonderful mother, grandmother, and wife. Now some of those words and letters were glowing. Ḥayim – life. Tovim – good. And the *lamed* and *yud* of *Yerushalayim*: li – me. Ḥayim tovim li – I have had a good life.

I turned to my husband and said, "Do you see what I see?" He replied, "Yes, there are words on her stone that are glowing!"

"Take a picture of the words glowing," I told my husband. He tried a few times but his phone camera stopped working.

I turned back to my sister on the phone and shouted, "Aravah, you are not going to believe what I am seeing right now." I could hear in the background that she was walking into her house and that her landline was ringing. Even though I was on the phone with her, she told me to wait and she picked up that other phone. I looked up at the gravestone and the only word that was now glowing was "Natan" from the phrase, "wife of Natan." My father's name was glowing.

Then all of a sudden, I heard my sister screaming on the other line. When she came back to the phone, she told me that our father had gotten into a massive car accident. His entire sternum was shattered into hundreds of pieces and there were many broken ribs. Once again, I got on the next flight. I stayed with my father, while he barely held on, for three months. I lost my father so soon after I lost my mother.

I believe my mother was sending me a message that day. First she told me in a dream to visit her and then words lit up on her tombstone. She wanted me to know she was okay and that my father needed me. She wanted me to know that she was watching us all.

MEMORIES

I call myself "the accidental tourist." It is hard to track how I ended up back here. I am back to where my mom started her life and I am continuing a life path she could have chosen, but didn't. Her life ended in California just as mine was newly transplanted in Israel. I didn't see it as a real option for me to stay in California. My parents were both gone and there was no one to go back to. Israel must have chosen me, because I don't remember doing the actual choosing.

My Hebrew name is Tzipporah, which means "bird." A bird flies and stops from time to time, to build a nest and rest. My English name is Faith, which can be solid or fleeting and I have had moments of both. When I build, I take on different projects. I have been passionate about creating a different image of Israel in the world through media. I have a column in a newspaper and a book featuring myself and two other women who identify differently in terms of political and religious views. We write together, hoping to build bridges across Israel's religious divide.

When I was a teenager, I came to Israel every summer lugging suitcases for my mother filled with wedding dresses for needy brides-to-be. My mother was the first licensed matchmaker in the state of California. She set up couples and even arranged for the actual ceremonies and parties. When I settled in Israel, I had enough dresses to start a bridal dress *gemaḥ*. Eventually I let someone take it over while I was grieving for my parents.

But I found another way to honor my mother's memory. I started a group of matchmakers called Points of Contact. It's a group whose raison d'etre is to set up religious singles in Israel and all over the world, with the intention of bringing together people who want to live in Israel. I have more than five hundred five hundred and sixty "Point People" who are responsible for setting up Anglo and Anglo-Israeli singles and connecting people from all over. I typically set up between four and five dates a day and will sometimes get calls at all hours of the day or night.

We already have Points of Contact babies. Our success doesn't always have to be measured by the *ḥuppa*, though. Sometimes just suggesting a match for a widower, or having a divorced woman go on a nice date after several years of not being set up, is a wonderful outcome. It is important to show people who are single that there are good people out there for them to date and that there are people working to find their match. A community has been created of Point People who have come from all walks of life. We are single-minded in our goal of "building Israel, one couple at a time." My own daughter got married through Points of Contact. It is a wonderful *zekhut* to do this work in memory of my parents. Additionally, to honor my parents, my husband and I have planted thirty-seven trees outside our *shul*. That was twelve years ago, and now those saplings have grown into a forest.

For me, resiliency stems from building others – building our homeland, constantly reshaping foundations, and continuing to take both the painful and beautiful memories and use them for good.

REFLECTIONS

Questions to Consider
- How have you sustained yourself through fear?
- How have you paid tribute to the memory of a loved one?

Words to Remember
> "In my mind's eye, I thought, 'There's light here
> again.'
> It wasn't so terrifying in the light."

Group Discussion
What does the modern State of Israel mean to you? What role does it play in your life?

ॐ

Take a moment for yourself. What do you need right now?
Close your eyes and be in your own body.
Here is a gratitude exercise to come back to yourself:

Gratitude Exercise
Reflect on one or more parental figures in your life.
Thank them for the moments when they made you feel safe.
Thank them for the times when they sacrificed to be by your side.
Accept them as humans, who can't always be there when you need them.
Appreciate the life lessons, challenging and sweet, that you have learned from them.

Living Outside Your Comfort Zone

Beit Shemesh

MILESTONES

Positive thinking and a positive attitude can get you very far in life. Not that you can do anything you set your mind to doing – I don't believe in that kind of fairy-tale thinking. While being very much aware of my abilities, I also know my limitations; I don't pretend that I can do something when I know that I can't. I think I need to be realistic about what I can and cannot do. Nevertheless, I do want to participate in things. Creativity and thinking outside the box, are vital parts of my existence.

I learned to solve problems this way from my parents. This is what they conveyed to me when I was growing up in Queens, New York. I am the eldest of six children. When I was born, I was not breathing and went into cardiac arrest, which caused brain damage. Ten months later, I was diagnosed with cerebral palsy (CP). I was in the hospital for nine days. Supposedly, everything was okay and they sent me home. They told my parents that there was a chance that I would have brain damage from the experience: there was a one-third chance that I would be typical, a one-third chance that I would be somewhat impaired, and a one-third chance that I would be completely

27

unable to do anything at all. I have no idea how a nurse could make such definitive statements without proof, but she did.

When I was ten months old my pediatrician could see that I was not hitting my milestones. He gave my parents a referral to a neurologist, who made a bold statement: "Your daughter is terribly impaired, both physically and intellectually, and you should consider putting her in an institution. She will be too difficult for you to care for at home." My parents were shocked at the audacity of the doctor to make such a prediction. My mother already knew that I was intelligent. I could play peek-a-boo and could respond appropriately. They were appalled by the doctor's rash recommendation and never considered acting on it. As I grew, they discovered that despite my being quite physically limited by CP, my intellectual abilities remained untouched.

When I was younger, my bedroom was upstairs in our house. As stairs were beyond what I could do, my father had to carry me upstairs every night. When I was ten years old, my parents decided to redo the house so that they could build me a bedroom on the ground floor that I could get to on my own.

When I started school, I began to use a wheelchair. But I only used it in school, because as soon as I got home, I would demand to be put on the floor so I could crawl. Being able to crawl was really important to me. It was great for me emotionally; I could be mobile on my own to a degree and I was able to play on the floor with my siblings and friends. Even when my physical therapists warned my parents that continued crawling would seriously damage my hips, my parents allowed me to crawl. They recognized that independently exploring my environment was crucial to my emotional and cognitive development. It was a trade-off. I almost dislocated my hip because of the crawling and I needed surgery to fix it. But I have never regretted that  choice. Consideration of my emotional needs has often come at the cost of my physical needs, and vice versa. When I entered fifth grade, I got my first motorized wheelchair. Now I had the independence at school that I had been used to having at home.

I went to a school for children who were physically disabled but intellectually typical. Thanks to my mother's persistence, the school agreed to test my IQ at age four and they were convinced that I would succeed academically in their school. It turned out to be an excellent learning environment. I look back on it and I think it was an important part of my education. I know that these days, mainstreaming is more prioritized, but I think that being with other kids with disabilities really helped my self-confidence. I wasn't the only one. I wasn't so unique. Whatever I lost from not being mainstreamed when I was young, that feeling that I was like everyone else made up for it. As a small child, that really laid the foundation for my self-confidence.

However, it was not a Jewish school. I was the only one who kept kosher, but that was not even the major challenge. The bigger loss was the Jewish education like my siblings were receiving in their yeshiva day schools. My parents hired a private tutor who met with me for an hour on Sundays, but it was not the same. When my younger siblings came home singing holiday songs and talking about the *parasha*, I felt left out.

GOODBYE, COMFORT ZONE

When I reached eighth grade, my parents decided that it was time for me to be mainstreamed into a regular yeshiva high school. I was really excited about the prospect. For most of my childhood, I had been part of a *Shabbos* group with my able-bodied peers from the neighborhood, and I had made friends. I was looking forward to joining them for high school.

It was a bigger challenge than I thought it would be. I was very behind in *limudei kodesh*. I was used to being considered a smart kid in school, and now I had so much catching up to do. It was a good lesson; I didn't need to be the smartest person in the class. It was humbling for me. And now I was the only one who had a disability in any way. I had to ask for help for everything that I needed. Except for once-a-day help in the bathroom, I didn't have an aide and I didn't want one. I wanted to manage on my own. I wanted to be like everyone else.

But I still needed help with everything – opening doors, taking out my books and putting them back, eating lunch. I did make new friends and I could ask them for help when I needed it, but it wasn't that simple. At first, I would latch on to one friend, teach her how best to help me, and then ask her exclusively. It was much easier for me to have one person who knew what I needed. Unfortunately, this would cause that friend to burn out. In the beginning, I cried a lot because it was so frustrating. I remember that my sweet European grandmother couldn't understand why my parents were "torturing me" by putting me in a school that couldn't take care of me. "Why couldn't you have left her in the school where she was comfortable? She was doing so well there..." she used to say. But I wanted to stick with it, even though it was hard.

I needed to change my strategy. I had to be considerate of my classmates' needs as well. I realized that there were limits to the help that I could expect from other people, especially if I wanted to keep them as my friends. I began to ask multiple people for help, as opposed to just one, and everyone was much happier.

People used to share with me their many ideas about how to make my life better and easier. Although I could sometimes understand their rationale, usually the idea wasn't applicable to me. Often in my childhood and in my life, I have had to fight to do things my way. I had lots of ideas about how to make my life better or how I could do things. But when you are a kid, people don't take your ideas seriously. Professionals wouldn't take input from a child. They always felt they knew best, regardless of the fact that I was living in this body and I was the expert on how it worked and what it needed.

At age ten, I had surgery on my hip and I needed to have a full-body cast up to my waist. The problem with that was that if you force my legs into a straight cast, they are going to fight against it. My muscles are very spastic and even with muscle relaxants, my legs strained against the rough plaster. At some point, I told my doctor that my heels were bleeding inside the cast from the friction. I could feel that they were cut inside the cast. It was very uncomfortable and painful. I even suggested, "Just cut a hole around the heel, and that would solve the problem." But the doctor told me that I was wrong, that my heels were fine and they weren't bleeding. He had put padding inside, and he knew that it was "all good." Eventually, my parents pushed back hard enough that the doctors agreed to examine my heels. They cut open the cast like I suggested, and lo and behold, there were bleeding cuts on my heels. This is just one little example of how often I was treated like I knew nothing.

Yet, in the end, with much perseverance geared toward making it work, I succeeded in school. I caught up in *limudei kodesh*. I worked hard and I achieved a lot. I participated in almost everything. If there was a trip, the teacher would drive my parents' van so that my chair could be transported. The school was very accommodating to me, helping me participate in any way I could. I was thriving.

KNOW WHERE YOU ARE

I can honestly say that I was scared to think about my future. I didn't think about it. I knew that in high school, I was still a child, and it was still typical for me to live at home and for someone to take care of me. I could still pretend I was just like my friends. What was going to happen when my friends started getting married? Was I going to get married and be able to live independently without my parents? I didn't want to think about it.

My father was always a very pragmatic person. I think I am like him in many ways. I am also optimistic like my mother. My mother thought that everything was possible.

My father believed that I could and would go far in this life, but I would need to be grounded and realistic about my limitations. Don't make too much of them, but don't make too little of them either. Know where you are. Then you can know where you can go. He always encouraged me, but he had his hand on reality.

He taught me to be okay with the fact that there are some things that I can't do. My family didn't make me feel that they felt sorry for me if there was something I couldn't do. They were teaching me acceptance and treated me with respect. When the family went on vacation, most of the time we did things that I could do along with everybody else. But there were times when we would do an activity in which I could not participate. If we went miniature golfing, everyone else would play, and I would sit in my chair and watch. But there was a trade-off; if my siblings got to play, then I got a special treat, like a snack that no one else got. The message was clear: Just because you can't do it, it doesn't mean that it is fair to deny your siblings the experience. There are going to be lots of times in your life when you are going to have to sit and watch. And it would be best for me to have to learn how to do that graciously. I really did learn that lesson with their support. So now, I generally don't feel sorry for myself if I miss out on something.

After high school, I did a year at Queens College, which was another adjustment. I went from being in a small school to a huge college. No one person was in the same two classes with me. I could have used an aide. I didn't have one, because I didn't want one. I was too proud.

Something that I have learned over the years is that true independence is not about what you can do physically by yourself. Independence is what you can accomplish from your own motivation and skills. It doesn't mean you have to do it with your own body. It means that something was done stemming from your own initiative, ideas, and direction. That is true independence.

After my first year in college, I wanted to go to seminary in Israel. My parents decided to take a sabbatical from teaching, to pack up the whole family, and move to Israel for the year. I was able to spend a year in seminary, living at home with my family in a nearby apartment in Bayit VeGan. Sometimes I would call my father to come pick me up at 11:30 at night because I was so immersed in the experience. He was willing to do anything to help me. Whatever I needed to do to fit in, my parents were there. They came on *shabbatonim*, *tiyulim*, or whatever I needed. It was a phenomenal experience.

I came back to New York with my family and I finished Queens College. I went to Columbia for a master's in counseling psychology. When I finished, my family and I were strongly considering *aliya*. At twenty-two, with a master's degree, I was ready for the next chapter of my life.

ARE YOU SITTING DOWN?

By the time I finished graduate school, I was thinking about what it would mean or what it would take to get married. My friends were dating and getting married and I thought for the first time, "Well, what is going to happen to me?"

Who was I going to marry? I was very immersed in the able-bodied world. I had no people with disabilities in my life at that point. Trying to think realistically, I thought, "Of course I would have to marry a man with a disability."

I decided that the only way this was going to work for me would be if I had a certain attitude about it. I couldn't afford to dismiss prospects out of hand. I didn't need to settle in the end, but in the beginning, I needed to be very open-minded. I couldn't afford to say, "No, he's not for me," off the bat. I decided this was my *hishtadlus*, and God would take care of the rest.

I was set up twice with men who had disabilities . One of them was completely not a good fit, but I liked the other one. He decided he didn't want to go out with me again, though. He also had CP and had limited mobility. He was worried about how we would function, the two of us together, with limited mobility. How would we ever be independent? Though I was disappointed, I understood.

Then a woman who had interviewed me for an article a few years earlier called my parents. She knew of a guy who lived in Toronto who had CP, who she thought would be a good match for me. The only caveat was that he was forty years old, and I was twenty-two. My immediate thought was, "No." Forty really was too old for me at that time. Nevertheless, I said that I was willing to entertain the possibility. I spoke to him on the phone a few times. He was a nice guy but was not for me. He wanted to date me, but I was not really interested. He called me and said, "I am coming to New York for a wedding and I would like to meet you in person." I thought of him as an interesting person, so I said yes. And who knows, something might come of it.

He called me a few days before he was supposed to come. He said, "I have a friend who is coming with me to the wedding, who has nowhere to stay for *Shabbos*. Could he stay at your house?" My parents' house was a revolving door for people who needed places to stay, so it wasn't that strange to me. My parents had no problem with it, so come Friday afternoon they were both going to come over. Then I was going to go out with the guy on Sunday.

I met him on Friday, and the whole *Shabbos*, I was ruminating over the fact that I knew the guy wasn't for me, so why was I going out with him on Sunday? I went out with him while my cousin waited for me nearby. The hour was enough. The best part of the afternoon was getting ice cream with my cousin afterward.

Because I was so distracted over *Shabbos*, stressing about my date on Sunday, I paid little attention to his friend who was staying at our house. But apparently, he was paying attention to me. About a week later he called my mother and said, "I want to go out with Malka. What do you think?" My mother was very excited. This great guy wanted to go out with her daughter! She told him that she would talk to me and I would call him back.

She came to my room all excited and said, "Malka, are you sitting down?" I laughed, of course I was sitting down! "Joel called, and he wants to go out with you." My first thought was – I know him already. I sat with him at the *Shabbos* table. I thought he wasn't for me. I said no.

My mother played it cool and said, "Okay, fine. You call him and tell him." She didn't try to convince me. She just left me his number. I said, "Mom, that's not how this is supposed to work. If you are the *shadchan*, you call him back please." But she stood her ground and made me do it. So I did.

Joel convinced me to go out with him. He said, "Malka, you are acting like I'm proposing to you, and I'm not. What does it hurt to go out with me one time?" I responded, "I don't want to be responsible for you paying all this money to fly from Toronto to see me." He said, "That's my problem, not yours. I can make that decision for myself. I would like to come one time to see you." I said, "Okay. But this time, you are not staying at my house for *Shabbos*."

We found him another place to stay. We went out on Sunday. Then he kept coming back every week, until the day before I boarded the plane to make *aliya* with my family. He had lived in Israel and had gone to school there and so the idea of living in Israel didn't faze him. We had been dating for five weeks and talked constantly on the phone. We kept right on talking after I made *aliya*.

He came to visit my family for *Sukkos,* and we got engaged.

BABIES

For the first few years, we lived in Bayit VeGan to be near my parents. By our second anniversary, we had two kids. As cerebral palsy is a neurological condition, it had no direct effects on my pregnancies. I had exceedingly normal pregnancies, as normal as they could be. I was uncomfortable like every pregnant woman, but I didn't have to change anything in my routine.

I made a decision in my first pregnancy that I would give birth by C-section. My doctor could not see a reason for it. I told him, "Pain causes my muscles to get tense. Being tense causes more pain." I just couldn't see how that was going to work for me. He tried to convince me to try having a natural labor, but in the end, he deferred to my self-knowledge.

I tried to find other women with CP who had given birth. My doctor tried to look it up in medical journals, but he couldn't find one thing on CP and pregnancy. My doctor wanted to write a journal article about me. In the end, my pregnancies and births were so uneventful that he had nothing to write. It was a wonderful thing.

It was a big *bracha* for me that my mother had three little boys when I was a teenager and young adult because it gave me a lot of experience with babies. It gave me confidence that I knew I could mother. I could rock a baby in his carriage; I could entertain him in a high chair. I knew how to take care of children from watching my mother. I knew what needed to be done. I understood that I could communicate with them, hold them on my

lap, comfort them. I knew that I could do it with help. I knew my limitations, but I also knew my strengths.

Joel had little to no experience with kids. That was actually good for me because I was the expert. He would listen to my instructions and it made us a good team.

The challenge with my children was contending with the fact that I needed an aide to help me. Babies are most responsive to the person who is physically taking care of them. They don't care that I am talking to them, they care about who is holding them. I worried that my children would bond to my aide and not to me. And they did, for a time. One thing I had going for me was that I was able to breastfeed my babies. I was able to nurse them until the age of one, and it was extremely important for me. It gave me a part in caring for them, nurturing them. It helped me bond with them. Once they became verbal, I felt that I "really" became their mother, to the extent that they would ask me to give them things even though they knew it would be the aide who actually physically did it. I became the most important person in their lives.

My children saw my disability as par for the course and generally didn't pay much attention to it. However, every once in a while, they would express an opinion. A few of the highlights: One *Shabbos* afternoon while I was playing outside with my three-year-old son, he said, "*Ima*, I want to go to the park." I told him that we would go when *Abba* woke up from his nap. "You know that I cannot take you to the park on my own." He complained, "Ugh…you can't do anything by yourself." And he proceeded to list all of the things I couldn't do. "You can't pick me up, you can't give me a drink, you can't help me get dressed, you can't give me a bath…" I went with it. "You're right! It's so annoying and frustrating, isn't it? We always have to wait for someone to help." Then he turned it around. "But you can talk to me and make me feel better, you can hug and kiss me, you can hold me on your lap, you give me a ride when I don't feel like walking anymore, you read to me, you tell Merli and *Abba* what to do for me." He paused (I smiled), and he continued, "Okay, we'll wait for *Abba*."

At age five, another one of my sons, who really spent a lot of time on my lap, said, "*Ima*, I know why Hashem made you have a disability." I was really curious and anxious to hear this one. "So that you would always have a lap for me to sit on." I laughed and said, "Aha!" We both giggled for a while.

Initially, we only had hourly help at home to help me accomplish the tasks I needed to do and to care for the house. But when we moved to Beit Shemesh, we had the space to have live-in help. We went through a number of aides before we could find the right fit. Once, an agency sent someone to our house for an interview. Upon entering and seeing our two small children playing on the floor, she asked, "Whose children are these?" That was the end of the interview.

Then we found Merli. She has been with us for more than twenty years. We are so blessed to have her caring for us. She has been here to help us raise our children and care for our home. She is a part of our family.

People always assume that because our children have a mother in a wheelchair, they do lots of housework. But the opposite is true. Things have always been taken care of for them because we had full-time help. They help out the way that all kids help out. But they have never been involved in or responsible for my personal care, like feeding or dressing me. Both my husband and Merli help me with those things.

All the support I have in my life has been such a blessing. *Baruch Hashem*, it has enabled us to have six children and one grandchild, who all lead happy, healthy, and full lives.

STRIVING FOR GROWTH

I made the choice to be home with my kids because I felt that in order for me to be established as their mother, as opposed to their caretaker being seen as their mother, I needed to be home and available for them. I felt strongly that I needed to be as involved as I could in their care. But I sacrificed my career. When you interrupt the momentum of your professional trajectory, it is really hard to get it back.

But in the middle of it all, for around ten years, I was very involved in building a complex of schools here in Beit Shemesh. It comprises four separate institutions: boys' and girls' elementary and high schools. I was part of the initial *amuta*, the non-profit board of directors. Before all this, there was no school here that I felt was a *hashkafic* match for my family. And so even though education is not my expertise, I found myself deeply involved in the work, including serving as the chair of the *amuta* for five years. We built the high schools, hired teachers, and fought with the *iriya* and *Misrad*

HaChinuch to get what we needed. It became a huge part of my life. We were always having meetings at our house, there were many phone calls, and in general, there was lots of activity. Once, one of my sons said, "*Ima*, I know that school is very important. But at night when we are home, it would be nice if you would talk to us sometimes."

Being so involved with the school positively affected my relationship with my kids' teachers. Instead of seeing a mother with disabilities and feeling that they need to treat me with kid gloves, they saw the competent woman who was in some sense their boss. It also gave me more of a say in my children's education, and that was a powerful tool in raising my children according to what I wanted for them.

Nevertheless, my approach with my kids is to teach them self-reliance. If they can do something on their own – solve a problem, create something, challenge themselves – I believe they should. Just as I had to learn about my own limits and abilities, I want my children to know themselves too. Although I could have fixed many problems for them at school because I was in a leadership position, that didn't mean that it was healthy for me to intervene on their behalf. They learned how to strike the balance on their own. They know when to ask for help, and when there is value in doing something themselves.

I always tell my children to go outside their comfort zones. Don't be afraid to go outside your box; that is the only way to grow and develop as a person. It builds self-esteem and helps you feel good about yourself. You don't have to do it all the time. There is also value in being in a comfortable space. But life is about balance for growth.

I have done so many things that I could have never imagined myself doing. My life is a testament to the value in pushing yourself to see what you actually can and cannot do. It's okay to fail. We all have limitations. But we don't need to live according to them. You don't succeed in everything you do, but you have to be willing to try. If you don't, you will miss so much.

REFLECTIONS

Questions to Consider
- How has having a an open-minded attitude helped you in your life?
- What are the limitations that others have placed on you based on who you are and the life into which you were born?

Words to Remember

> "It's okay to fail. We all have limitations. But we don't need to live according to them. You don't succeed in everything you do, but you have to be willing to try."

Group Discussion
When was there a time in your life when you pushed yourself outside your comfort zone?

ॐ

Take a moment for yourself. What do you need right now?
Close your eyes and be in your own body.
Here is an inspiration exercise to come back to yourself:

Inspiration Exercise
Identify three things that you want to work on:
Is it your drive, resilience, or perseverance?
Is it searching for more independence, accomplishments, or a focus on finding happiness?
Is it your attitude: striving to be more positive, inspired, or focused?

Shira's Story

I'm Not Giving Up

Arnona, Jerusalem

BINGE AND PURGE

My grandmother spent her life yo-yo dieting. While my father was growing up, it was difficult for him to watch her suffer. My mother also struggled with her weight and was teased because of her size. When my parents realized that I, too, was a chubby child, they focused on feeding me "healthy food." I would bring bags of cut-up carrot sticks and celery as a school snack, while my friends had junk food and baked goods. When the bullying about my weight started for me at school, my parents thought that further restriction would help.

By seventh grade, I was stealing money from my parents and giving it to kids in my class to buy me food at the corner store. I was also using stolen money to buy the snacks that my classmates would bring to school. I would spend twenty dollars on a bag of cookies. My parents eventually found out when a classmate called my mom to complain that I hadn't paid him five dollars for a half-eaten box of Tic Tacs. That ended my stealing to fund my habit.

The summer after tenth grade, I went to sleepaway camp. There was a girl in my bunk who had a terrible eating disorder and we all took turns "watching her" to make sure she was eating and not making herself vomit. One day it was my turn and I followed her into the bunk. We sat down on a bed together and she said to me, "I know you like boys. You have a very pretty face, and if

41

you lost weight, boys would like you back." That day she taught me how to binge and purge. That began a fifteen-year eating disorder.

When I went to seminary, I was finally no longer under the watchful eyes of my parents. I was spiritually fulfilled, making friends, and enjoying myself. No one was watching me or controlling what I was eating. I must have gained a lot. Before *Pesach*, I went home to visit my family because my grandfather became ill. My weight gain was a shock to everyone around me, and none of my *Yom Tov* clothing fit. When I went back to seminary, I began binge-ing and purging again to lose all the weight that I had gained. I knew I was expected to start dating when the year was over and the excess weight was going to make dating very difficult.

OBSESSED

During college, I kept up the habit. I went to my doctor one day when I began to feel ill. She told me that I had ulcers all up and down my esopha-gus from forcing myself to vomit all the time. She told me I needed to tell someone and get it under control. I finally told my parents, who had never heard about bulimia. They found me an expensive therapist on the Upper East Side of Manhattan who didn't understand my culture or background and after a couple of sessions, I stopped going. I told my parents I had stopped bingeing and purging all on my own and they believed me.

After college, I got a job in the city, moved out of my parents' house and into an apartment in Manhattan, and I finally felt like I was free. I was partying, working hard, and enjoying myself. With freedom, I gained more weight. It didn't bother me until one day I couldn't get up the steps from the subway. I looked at myself in the mirror and was unhappy with the way that I looked and felt.

I began bingeing and purging again. This time, I also tried to work out and tried every diet under the sun. I joined gyms, had personal trainers, and worked out. I had to be obsessive about counting calories for it to really work. I stopped going out with my friends. I spent my evenings sitting in my apart-ment reading through weight loss books, poring over food products, and fig-uring out my meals. I would say no to *Shabbos* invitations, too.

I always said that when I got married, the way I looked wouldn't matter anymore. I would never date anyone who had an issue with my weight. They would love me for me. I spent ten years in abusive relationships that never went anywhere.

Finally, in 2006 I moved to Israel. I was fit, at a comfortable weight for myself,, I was self-confident, and I knew who I was. Before the move, I had found the right therapist and finally stopped bingeing and purging. I had broken the cycle. I was happy with myself.

I met my husband. He was attracted to me and loved me for me. My weight was no longer an issue for me.

BABY WEIGHT

Within six months of our marriage, I was pregnant. We married "later" in life; I was thirty-one and he was thirty-four. We felt like we couldn't afford to have a getting-to-know-you period. Our first daughter was born a year and a half after we got married. I had a blood clotting disorder and we needed to be very careful and make sure that I saw a hematologist. I was put on a blood thinner for the entirety of the pregnancy and then taken off of it immediately before delivery. Our eldest daughter was born healthy and brought us tremendous joy.

Three years later I got pregnant again. I had a difficult first trimester with severe nausea, which was triggering for me. Vomiting without being in control was very distressing.
I had a miscarriage in the eleventh week of the pregnancy. We were devastated. We had already picked out a name for the baby. I had loved that baby.

I had also already put on weight. Very quickly I got pregnant again with my next child, our rainbow baby, and that compounded more weight onto my body. She was born healthy, thank God. Two and a half years later, my youngest child was born. Our son completed our family.

After four nearly back-to-back pregnancies, I was up a lot of weight and I was very unhappy about my body. I was a work-at-home mom with two toddlers and a baby, working American hours. I was getting very little sleep and giving myself almost no self-care. I was worried about several syndromes that, over the years, doctors had discovered lay dormant inside me, and they warned me that they could be triggered by weight gain. I was worried that though these disorders were currently gone, with the weight gain, they would come back.

I was the largest I had ever been. When I went to see my doctor, she suggested that I consider gastric bypass surgery. Perhaps that would be the solution I needed to manage my weight. Ultimately, my decision to get the surgery was made from a place of self-loathing. I went from looking at my legs as the tools that carried me from place to place, my arms as what enabled me to hold my children, and my stomach as the place where my babies grew to seeing my body just as lobs of fat and rolls of blubber. I was done hating myself and I thought that losing weight for good would be the answer.

HOW HAVE YOU BEEN FEELING?

I met with a top surgeon in Israel. He told me that to qualify for the surgery, I would have to gain more weight, and that he would be willing to do the procedure because I already had high blood pressure. I was worried that

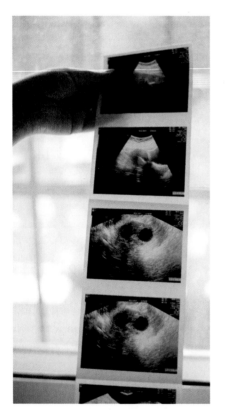

this procedure would probably be the only chance I had at a healthy life. It was right before the *chagim*, so I sequestered myself and gladly began to eat.

I had four months of pre-op testing to endure. There was a chest X-ray, stomach ultrasound, psychological testing, colonoscopy, meeting with my hematologist, and more. The list was endless. Speaking in Hebrew can be a struggle for me, so I asked my husband who was born here in Israel to set up all my appointments for me. It was too overwhelming to do on my own.

I went in for the stomach ultrasound, my first pre-surgery test. The technician asked why I was there. When I told him, he started lecturing me: "You don't need this surgery. You aren't a candidate." And then he paused and asked me, "How have you been feeling?" At this point, I was very annoyed. I just wanted him to do his job and I wanted it to be over. When it was over, he sent me on my way.

My family doctor called me the next day and said, "We got the results from your ultrasound. There is no need to panic, but we see that there are some spots on your liver. To see what is going on, we are going to send you for a CT scan."

I googled "spots on liver" and the first thing that came up was "cancer." At that moment I told myself that it was definitely not cancer and everything would be fine. But then I remembered how over the *chagim*, when I didn't go to *shul* because I was overeating and none of my clothes fit me with the added weight, I had paused and I had a feeling that everything wouldn't work out the way I had planned. I literally wondered to myself, "What if in the pre-op testing, they find cancer and I won't be able to get the surgery?" It was just me being catastrophic at the time.

I got the CT, and on November 15, 2017, my husband called me from the car. His voice had a frantic, almost excited energy. He said, "Babe, you need to get a babysitter." I thought he was going to take me out somewhere nice. But he had gotten a call from our doctor who said that we needed to come in that night as soon as we could (it was already after six p.m.). She would be waiting for us.

We walked into her office and saw that the doctor had been crying. She was our family doctor and saw all of us for many years, we were very close with her. She said, "It's really not easy for me to say this..."

I cut her off and asked, "Do I have cancer?"

And she said, "Yes."

I DIDN'T WANT TO DIE

My husband started to cry. The doctor had a stack of papers and her voice faded from my hearing. She told me, "There are a lot of things that you are going to need to do." She didn't know what kind of cancer I had and there were many tests that I was going to need.

The testing took a long time. I remember calling my husband and telling him, "I am going to die. They are just letting me wait and there is cancer growing all over my body. I have three little children at home. What am I going to do?"

That night, after more than three weeks of tests and waiting, we finally got the answer. They had discovered that I had a very aggressive form of non-Hodgkin's lymphoma. The cancer had metastasized in my liver, my spleen, and four bones. I went back to my hematologist, after thinking that I had seen him for the last time after my last pregnancy. I told him the whole story, and he looked at me with shock in his eyes. He said, "You know the gastric bypass that you didn't get is what saved your life, right?" I was already at stage-four cancer. I had subtle symptoms but I did not recognize them to be symptoms of cancer. Night sweats. Itchy skin. I know that if I had had unexpected weight loss, another symptom of cancer, I never would have said a word about it to a doctor. I would have celebrated it. How would we have ever known that I had such advanced cancer? My doctors were grateful that they found it when they did. They considered it early. It did not feel early to me.

We began the process of treatment. I walked into my doctor's office and was informed that I would be having a bone marrow biopsy that day. They knocked me out and did the procedure. That day was also my daughter's birthday and so that evening, I had twenty nine-year-olds in my apartment for a party. I struggled through the restrictions they gave me post-procedure. I realized that juggling treatment and my family life was going to be difficult.

THE BEGINNING

I had to tell the kids that I had cancer. I called my son's *ganenet* to help me. Our children were four, seven, and nine. I didn't know how to talk to them about this. They already knew something was up because things were changing. Family members were picking them up from school instead of their mom. I wasn't physically unwell and I was working, but they knew something was wrong.

Their teacher came over, and the kids were excited that she was in the house. She began to tell them, "Mommy isn't feeling well and there are going to be some changes. She might not be able to hold you, and she might physically look a bit different. She might lose her hair..." My eldest looked at me and said, "But people with cancer lose their hair. Mommy, do you have cancer?" I said, "Yes." That was the hardest moment of all of this. To tell my daughter, who understood what cancer meant, that her mom was sick. She was afraid. I was terrified for us both.

The first night of Ḥanukka was my first day of treatment. They were giving me a lesser dose of chemo and Zofran for the nausea. For the first part of the treatment, I was knocked out from the Benadryl that they gave me in case I had an allergic reaction to the chemo. I got through the first round of the medication and since I was doing well, they decided to give me the full dose. I had been there since eight in the morning, and at four in the afternoon I was finally finished. I got up from the bed and decided that I felt good. Everything was going to be okay.

I got home and I decided that I wanted to move. I had been in bed all day and I was feeling fine. I wanted to prove to myself that I was feeling fine. I got on the treadmill for a brisk walk for twenty minutes. I made myself a plate of food for dinner and I was all ready to eat when at that moment, the Zofran wore off. I put my plate down and ran to the bathroom and began to vomit.

That night my husband's family had a *Ḥanukka* party that we look forward to every year. All of a sudden, I realized there was no way I could go. I could not stop vomiting. But I made sure my husband took the kids. I was alone in the apartment.

When I first got my diagnosis, we asked our rabbis about what it means to change your name when you are ill. We were told that "when you change your name, you change your *mazal*" and so it was a good idea to add a name. I hoped maybe it would give me extra support through this fight. That first night of chemo, I was feeling so sick and I felt like things were not going to be okay. My husband and I decided that this was the time to change my name. At the party, our family gathered around without me, and with ten men present, they changed my name to Lior Shira Batya. We prayed that this change would bring extra light and healing into our lives.

When they came home, I was retching into a bucket in bed, looking horrendous. My kids began to freak out, and we did our best to calm them and tell them it was normal, that it was a side effect from the medicine, but things began to escalate. This was just the beginning.

SIDE EFFECTS

I went from taking vitamins to taking an entire shelf of medication. At every turn, they gave me more medication for the chemo, steroids, and meds to help with the rest of the side effects. My life revolved around medication.

We had so many scares – passing out after procedures, difficulty putting in PICC lines, spinal taps. Whenever we had problems, I was sent to the ER and then promptly moved out because I was immunosuppressed and it was flu season. The more chemo I got, the worse the side effects got. I had hand sanitizer in every corner of the house. I didn't go near my children; I didn't hug them or kiss them. If someone was sick, I would barricade myself in my room.

When my hair began to fall out, I went to our family hairstylist and told him that I was undergoing chemo and I needed to cut my hair short. I had decided to donate my long hair. As he held my braids in his hands, he was too emotional about my news to do the cut. His hands were trembling so badly that he cut himself. With tears in his eyes, he cut my hair very short. When I got home my kids were shocked at the transformation. Ultimately, super short was not enough. Every time I would run my hand over my head, my hand would be covered in short hairs. I went back to the stylist and told him, "It's time to shave it." When I got home this time, it was all gone.

My in-laws were incredible and were there to go through two rounds of chemo with me. By the third round, my parents were back in Israel and ready to help out. I remember I was in bed when they first came in and I was sleeping with a cap on. I took the cap off to scratch my head. I'll never forget how my father had to turn around and walk away. He couldn't see me like that. I didn't realize until that moment how hard it was for them, too. But they were there for me. My dad sat with me during long days getting chemo. My mom was there to take me at three a.m. for MRI appointments. It was a relief to have their presence and support.

I hate hospitals, and I had been doing so well thus far because I was able to get treatment at the day clinic at the hospital and then go home. I

could deal with all the awful side effects in my own space and sleep in my own bed. At the hospital, I couldn't eat the food. I had to share a room with someone who was very sick and it was so stressful to be trying to sleep next to them while they were receiving medical care. The first night I was there, someone came into my space while I was sleeping and took something from my area. After that, I did not sleep in the hospital again. I felt violated. I struggled through the difficult procedures and I couldn't wait for treatment to be all over and for me to be able to finally go home.

After three cycles, they did a PET scan and discovered that there was no longer any cancer in my body. The treatment had worked. But in order to finish the treatment and make sure it was all gone, I had to go through another three cycles of chemo. This time I knew that I was on my way. I was relieved and geared up to finish this process once and for all.

THANK YOU

Toward the end I was really struggling. I was fasting because I found that the side effects were easier to manage when I had less food in my stomach. That really triggered my buli-mia, and the nausea and vomiting didn't help that vulnerable feeling. The steroids made me angry all the time and always starving.

Someone asked me if I would go for gastric bypass surgery when I was finished with cancer treat-ment. I replied, "No, my body has been through enough." I need to learn to love my body and that is where I am today. I want to love my body as is. I have spent my life trying to be someone I'm not, by trying to make myself smaller to fit into someone else's definition of what I should look like.

It's really hard to take forty years of eating disorders, self-loathing, diet-ing, and societal messaging that convinced me, "You are not OK the way you look" – and reprogram my self-acceptance.

I want to embrace who I am.

There are days now when I look in the mirror and I can't believe I still look like this. There are others where I simply say, "Thank you."

I was not ready to leave this earth. I'm not done. I told my husband, "God is going to have to come take me. I am not going to go quietly into the night. I have too much to live for and I'm not giving up."

REFLECTIONS

Questions to Consider
- What has inspired you to fight harder to live the life you want?
- Who is the support system in your life?

Words to Remember
> "I have too much to live for and I'm not giving up."

Group Discussion
Women often have complicated relationships with our bodies. We are pushed and pulled by what society tells us is beautiful, by the amazing things that our bodies can do, and by how we heal. What do you think contributes to negative self-image?

❧

Take a moment for yourself. What do you need right now?
Close your eyes and be in your own body.
Here is a gratitude exercise to come back to yourself:

Gratitude Exercise
Thank your body:
  for your capacity to heal;
  for your strength and resilience;
  for waking up and giving you the gift of today.

Building and Rebuilding a Lifetime

Efrat, Gush Etzion

WHOLESOME

My paternal grandparents came from Rhodes, near Greece. My maternal grandparents were from Istanbul and Saloniki. They all migrated and settled in Egypt, because as traveling merchants they found work there. I don't know the dates of when they left their countries of origin or when they came to settle in Egypt. My generation didn't ask too many questions and my parents' generation didn't talk too much either. This is why I feel it is so important to talk about my past, to remember where I come from and where my parents come from. I feel it is my duty to pay tribute to those who are no longer here and to record what happened to my family. My grandchildren and future generations should know our history. I must leave a testimony to my family's existence.

I have nice memories of growing up in Cairo in the midst of a sizable and caring Jewish community. Friends and acquaintances would exchange invitations to share a demitasse of Turkish coffee, served with homemade jam. There was a certain elegance in that experience; the jam placed in a special decorated dish with spoons available all around the dish for any takers. These are special and simple memories of times long gone.

We lived in a mixed culture neighborhood and by all means, not a ghetto. Basically, life in Egypt was okay until it was not okay. Everything we needed was within our reach. Our *shul*, school, grandparents, aunts, and uncles were all nearby, a walk away from our home. Most of my memories of Egypt are of our family and the close bond we felt toward each other. Our daily lives were simple and lovely. It was the nicest time of my life, until it suddenly ended.

Though I am sure that in 1948 when the State of Israel was declared, things must not have been so favorable for the Jews in Cairo, at the age of five, I was not aware of it. My parents provided my brothers and myself with very sheltered lives, so as children we didn't feel the trouble. Afterward, in the course of my life, I did read about Jews dragged from their homes, beaten, and harassed. But I never heard about that from my parents; they never talked about it. The fact that the State of Israel was established was a definite thorn in the side of the Egyptian government and the Arab world.

Growing up, I fondly remember my father's love for Israel and his dream to live there. Local newspapers were not relating true and actual news. According to them, Israel was always doomed and vanquished. Therefore, my father religiously kept abreast of news about Israel, hunched over our radio trying hard to find the *Kol Yisrael* station and listening to its broadcasts at a very low volume so as not to make it known that he was accessing that station. I remember him whispering to my mother, "Esther, all is well in Israel. Let's not pay attention to what the newspapers' headlines say." However, his dream of going to *Eretz Yisrael* had to wait to actualize. I guess it was not in Hashem's plan for a while.

Our life in Egypt was a comfortable one. To the best of my recollection, we lacked nothing. Our needs were met. My mother was an excellent home-maker, seeing to all the needs of her family. She was in charge of the house-hold, with the help of a maid who did the laundry (by hand) and the heavy cleaning of the house, while my father, the breadwinner of the family, worked very hard as a textile merchant. He worked for a Jewish Italian firm and often traveled all over Egypt. His fluency in Arabic was a great asset for the work he did.

French and Ladino were spoken at home. At a certain point, when my paternal grandparents became elderly, they were living with us. At that time, even though nursing homes were almost non-existent, placing elderly parents in such facilities was not something to consider. I do not remember my grandfather much since he died shortly after they moved in with us and I was a small child. My grandmother only spoke Ladino and so the language was used at home to communicate and also as "a secret language." They spoke it when they didn't want the children to understand. However, with time, I eventually and secretly learned to understand it. I recall many funny instances where I should not have admitted that I understood what was being said.

I went to a local non-Jewish private school for girls, where 90 percent of the school was Jewish. Our studies were done in French. Our curriculum included weekly classes in Arabic. That was a requirement from the govern-ment, and it was how I learned to speak Arabic, which has stayed with me to this very day. My mother also went to that school and some of her teachers became mine. They thought it was amusing that my mother was an exem-plary pupil, whereas I was not.

We lived in a big apartment with large rooms and a long corridor separat-ing the living quarters from the kitchen and the family room. Each room had a balcony that was often used, never remaining idle. I remember how some of the shopping was done. A little basket attached to a rope would be lowered down from the balcony to the vendors who bellowed out their goods, vegetables and fruits. My mother would tell the vendor what she wanted and how much of it, and the vendor would place the required produce in the basket. The basket was raised and the goods were taken. The basket would then get lowered with the money for the purchases made. Being always fascinated with this process, I would run downstairs and watch the vendor working with his scale, weighing the produce with different shapes of weights. A flash of this memory comes to me whenever I go to *Shuk Mahane Yehuda* in Jerusalem and the vendors there apply the same weighing method.

Early in the morning, on a daily basis, fresh milk was delivered to our home in jerry cans. On his way back home from work, my father bought meat in a little store in a poor section of the town called "The Alley of the Jews." When my mother left the house, it was to visit one of her two sisters, her two brothers, my maternal grandfather while he was still alive, or friends. The family lived in very close proximity to each other. In short, life in Cairo felt wholesome.

But in 1956, everything changed. Our lives were totally turned upside down.

INK AND PAPERS

My father used to write letters to his brothers in Israel. They had left Egypt much earlier because they couldn't find jobs. Sometime before 1948, I vaguely remember waving goodbye to one of my uncles leaving by train from Cairo to Israel through the Sinai. That uncle settled near Tel Aviv while the other one who left before 1956 settled in Acco.

In 1956, things were brewing. Once, my father was writing a letter to one of his brothers with a blue ink pen, when the pen ran out of ink. Not wanting to postpone sending the letter, my father used some of the red ink he had on hand. Blue and red inks were always available in our home since my father was the *gabbai* at the local *shul* and did the *shul's* books at home after coming home from work. That letter was mailed as usual and no thought was given to it.

However, one day shortly after mailing the letter, there was a knock on the door. It was the police. Without any words of explanation, they took my father away. He was kept in prison for two or three days. We did not know if we would ever see our father again. I can imagine the fear that my mother must have felt while my father was being interrogated. The censorship bureau had intercepted the letter written both in blue and red inks. They suspected him of sending codes to Israel and spying for Israel. My father never spoke about what happened during the days he was taken prisoner. When this incident happened, I was thirteen, the eldest child in the family.

It was not long afterward that the government took over my private school. They expelled my teachers who were French citizens and French as a language was no longer used in the school. Government teachers were hired in their place. For a very short while I continued to go to school, but because my maiden name was "Israel" I was constantly being ridiculed and harassed. I did not want to go to school and somehow my father arranged for tutors at home so as not to interrupt my studies. I don't know if my many other Jewish classmates continued to attend school. Since the firm employing my father was owned by Italian Jews, it too was confiscated by the government, who then expelled the Jews who owned it. Consequently, my father lost his job. It was obvious that the Egyptian government had decided that it no longer wanted any foreigners living among them. That also meant that they didn't want any Jews.

These new policies boomeranged. The government realized that additionally the wealthy class of the country was leaving; the people with money, businessmen, and bankers were leaving town. And so the government closed its borders. That is when my family found itself stuck.

A coworker of my father, an Arab man who used to travel with my father on business, came to our rescue. He helped my parents forge papers so that we could leave the country. To this day, I do not know what names were given to us on the forged papers. I remember my father telling me once that long before the situation became difficult for Jews, he was advised to change his name from Israel to a name that would be less obviously Jewish, though my father already looked European with his fair skin and tall stature. But my father said, "I was born with the name of Israel and I will die as Israel." He never changed his mind. Maybe after all, his European appearance helped us escape.

I had no idea we were leaving Egypt. I remember being woken up by my parents in the early hours of the morning and being told that we were leaving that same morning. I started to cry and asked if the rest of the family, my aunts and uncles, were going with us. I was told that only our immediate family was leaving. I was so distraught at the idea of leaving my home and the rest of the family. What was going to happen to us and to them? We left for Alexandria within a few hours, leaving the house as if we were going on a vacation trip and would be coming right back. We left pictures on the walls and laundry on the lines. We left our home with one suitcase for the five of us and my father's precious violin.

Once in Alexandria, we went to the port. We were thoroughly searched in case we were smuggling money or jewelry. It was a frightening experience for me, but my mother was by my side reassuring me that everything would be alright. She must have been scared herself, but she tried to maintain a calming attitude for my sake and for the sake of my younger brothers. I imagine people somehow smuggled certain things. I do remember one young girl with her doll. I heard much later on, when we lived in Paris, that her doll had diamonds in its stuffing. I am glad that her parents were not caught smuggling their belongings out of Egypt – who knows what would have happened to them? People were desperate. Their money and their belongings were confiscated. Many resorted to smuggling whatever they could.

I have another memory of that day at the port. We were standing in line on the plank, waiting to get onto a boat that was going to take us to Marseille. There was a man in front of us wearing a very nice watch. The officer said that he couldn't board the boat with the watch. He asked the officer to please allow him to keep it, because it was given to him by his deceased father. The officer refused. The man removed the watch from his arm, placed it on the ground, and stomped on it, telling the officer that if he could not keep the watch, then no one else would have it either. That man ran such a risk. Fortunately, he was allowed to board the ship. We watched that incident in such a fright, fearing for his welfare.

We then found ourselves in the same situation. My father had taken his violin with him. The officer told my father that he had to leave it behind. My father pleaded with the officer to let him keep it. Speaking excellent Arabic, my father told the officer, "This is the violin that my mother gave me. She worked very hard to earn enough money to buy it for me. Please let me keep it." I wonder what did the trick; perhaps my father's pleading softened the officer or maybe it was my father speaking in the officer's native language. All I know is that we were all allowed to board the ship, with the violin in hand.

Besides the suitcase and the violin, my family and I carried with us some of the nicest memories of that instrument, such as hosting *melaveh malka* at our home. Family and friends would get together over refreshments and delicious goodies that my mother baked. My father and his friends would give little concerts – my father playing his violin, others playing the flute, the accordion, and the harmonica. It was so lovely. I am happy to have those beautiful memories. My father played that violin for many more years.

REFUGEES

As a result of the Sinai War in 1956, two European countries took in refugees from the Arab countries: Italy and France. Since French was spoken at home and our studies were in that language, given the choice, my parents asked the Hebrew Immigrant Aid Society (HIAS) to place us in France, so that my brothers and I could resume our schooling.

Our voyage to France was not a pleasant one. Our cabin, shared with other refugees, was at the lowest deck on the ship near the noisy engines. I remember my mother being seasick all the time. It felt like we were never going to make it. We were cooped up during the day (since we were not allowed to go to the upper decks), but somehow I found a way to sneak up in the evenings to breathe some fresh air and feel a little freedom.

For some reason, the boat stopped in Genoa, Italy, perhaps to refuel. By a miracle, my mother found her youngest sister in Genoa. It was an unexpected and tearful reunion. We had a few precious moments together before we headed toward our new lives. *Tante* Rachel and her family were waiting their turn to go to Brazil since, unlike the United States, Brazil and other countries such as Australia and South Africa did not require a sponsor for families seeking refuge. My *Tante* Mathilde and her family, and my Uncle Joseph, headed for Brazil as well, but we did not see them in Genoa. Our beautiful family was scattered around. Within a few days, all our relatives and the people from the community had left Cairo.

When we landed in Marseille, we were met by the HIAS who brought us to Paris. Life in Paris was very difficult for my family and me. We lived there for almost four years while we were waiting for a visa to enter the United States. We lived in a one-and-a-half-room apartment. And we knew that we were not wanted there.

Though we knew French, the culture was so different. Since we were refugees, my father was not allowed to work. I don't know how my parents were able to survive. I attended a public school and did not give it any thought at the time. We received an allowance from the HIAS for expenses. Our daily food came from a soup kitchen. Next to the kitchen was a facility where we got our clothing free of charge. After school, my father arranged for me to attend secretarial school. Much later in life, I found out that my father cleaned *shuls* in order to earn some money to pay for my extra schooling. At the time, I was angry about this extra school schedule. I was unhappy to have to come home from school and then have to go out in the evening to learn secretarial skills.

I must say, though, that those very skills helped me a lot later in life. I became a fast typist and stenographer which allowed me to have an easier time finding a job when I needed to find one when I got older. Thankfully, years later, before my father passed away, I told him how much I appreciated what he did back in Paris for me. At the time, I was not so appreciative. I also feel very good about telling my mother, later in life, how much I appreciated her teaching me to sew and embroider throughout my growing years. She taught me so well that many years later, I sewed my daughter's wedding dress.

The HIAS never offered to relocate us to Israel. While in France, my father wrote to his brothers, and my mother to her brother, inquiring about life in Israel. They told them that life was very difficult. "We are going through very hard times. There is barely what to eat. If you have a chance to go somewhere else, even though we know you want to come to Israel, go there and come to Israel later on, when things will be better for everyone." The dream to move to Israel would have to wait some more.

In school, we had an art class. I could not purchase the art supplies needed since my parents did not have the money for that. The teacher did not pay attention to my predicament; I was just a student with no supplies. But a girl in my class, seeing that I did not have the needed tools, offered to share her art supplies with me. I will never forget Sylviane's kindness and generosity.

As a class assignment, I tried my hand at drawing a tree. It was a rough trunk with gnarled branches. My teacher thought it was very good work and commented to me, "Sarah, you must be going through a very hard time, as you transmitted your feelings in your drawing." I did not know that I was expressing the feelings I had at the time. I wish I had kept that drawing to show my father, who was such a good artist. He drew family portraits that stayed back in Egypt, hanging on the walls of our home. My teacher kept my drawing for the school, showing it off in the hallway of the building. I should have kept it.

One day, Sylviane wanted to study with me for a test. I couldn't bring her to my house because I was embarrassed of our living situation. My mother had to do the laundry by hand and had to hang it in our tight quarters. I could not very well bring a friend over, so Sylviane invited me to her house.

Her apartment was in a very nice building. She and I made it to the foyer of the apartment where her mother met us. Sylviane introduced me to her mother with, *"Maman, mon amie Sarah Israel."* She immediately asked her daughter to come inside the apartment for a moment. Whether she meant for me to hear it or not, I will never know. But I heard the mother telling her daughter, *"Sylviane, prends cette sale juive hors de notre apartment."* That meant, "Get that dirty Jew out of our apartment." I did not know what to do with myself. I wanted to disappear but I stood there waiting for my friend to come back to me. Sylviane came back clearly embarrassed. I behaved as if I did not hear anything. My friend suggested that we go to a park nearby and do our studying there. Sylviane continued to be my friend. She was a true friend, despite her mother.

I never told my parents what happened. Though I hardly considered or thought of how hard life must have been for them, living like refugees, I guess I wanted to spare them this pain.

IMMIGRANTS

My father would periodically go to the HIAS to ask what was happening with our status. He had a great-uncle living in Florida who was our sponsor. One day, when he was ready to give up on going to the States and start applying to go to Brazil instead, the HIAS informed him that we finally received our visas. I think my mother was secretly hoping that we could go to Brazil where she could be reunited with her two sisters and her brother. But that was not Hashem's plan. We took a ship, the *Queen Mary*, to New York. The conditions were better than the previous ship journey we had taken from Alexandria.

We traveled to Florida, but that trip was a blur. My father's great-uncle met us and took us to a semi-furnished apartment in Miami. My father thanked his great-uncle for making it possible for us to come to the States and informed him that as of that moment, he would be responsible for his family and would not ask his uncle for any support. Luckily, I got a job right away as a filing clerk in a bank. My father got a job as a bartender. Jobs were scarce in Miami, at least for him. I remember him telling my mother that compared to the people coming to the bar and pouring out their problems, we had no problems at all. He felt so sorry for his customers.

Life in Miami wasn't a life for us. There was no Sephardic community at the time, and that was not acceptable at all for my father. He was a *shul* man all his life and was not about to abandon this aspect of his values. After a couple of months, he went to New York. Upon the recommendation of friends he knew from Egypt, he got a job as a warehouse manager at a big firm in New York City. He kept this job until he retired many years later. The company, owned by Syrian Jews, had full trust in my father; they saw how honest he was and that is what they were looking for in a manager. My father found us a small apartment in the midst of a Sephardic Egyptian neighborhood in Brooklyn. We all felt more comfortable in our new surroundings.

My parents needed me to contribute financially to the household, so I started looking for a job in New York City. I knew I could find a job that would be better than the simple one I had in Florida. I was seventeen, and with the secretarial tools I had acquired in Paris, I was confident that in a big city like New York, there would be a position for me. Still, I felt like a country bumpkin looking for a job on Wall Street.

I spent a whole day running around, responding to ads in the newspaper. In interview after interview, even after passing the typing and stenography tests, I was told that the only obstacle to my getting the job was my inexperience. In the last interview of the day, after being told yet again about my lack of experience, I started to cry. My interviewer was somewhat alarmed by my outburst and asked the reason for it, to which I answered, "I have been looking for a job all day. I pass all the tests required and am always told that I have no experience. I am only seventeen years old – how much experience do you want me to have?" I left the office after my interviewer told me that he had to consult with his supervisor. I felt very down thinking of having to do job hunting again the next day.

Still, even though discouraged, before heading home, I went to another office in Greenpoint, Brooklyn. At that time Greenpoint was in the middle of nowhere. The firm was a paper company run by a lovely Russian Jewish family, and I was accepted for the position on the spot. At last, I finally had a job. Once I arrived back home, my mother told me that I received a phone call from the last interview I had on Wall Street. I had been accepted for that job, but having accepted another job already, I turned it down. My tenacity in finding a job gave me a way to help my family financially. To this day, I am the same way. I do not give up easily. I try and try until, *barukh Hashem*, I am able to accomplish what I need to do.

Living as a refugee who had to leave everything behind taught me to have a special appreciation for material things, even for the littlest things. During the time I was helping my family, I saw how the house was furnished little by little. A coffee table came; a dinette set and a couch were bought. It was nice to see the house taking shape step by step and to see my parents happy. They had lost everything in Egypt. I remember having nice furniture in Egypt as well as all of our personal items. Whenever I handed my father my paycheck – he never bought on credit – something new would come into the house to replace the things we had lost. I was very happy to be of help and was delighted when my father would say to me, "Between you and me, we will build a new home in America." It must have been so hard for him to accept my help, but how could I not do that?

That is how I learned to appreciate the value of things, especially those that do not come so easily.

AMERICAN

The year was 1962. I had just broken up with a young American man who was introduced to me at my workplace. Naively, I thought it was serious but I guess I must have been too old-fashioned for him. Maybe he felt that there was a big cultural difference between us. Understandably, my family and I mostly socialized with the Egyptian community in Brooklyn. We spoke French at home and in *shul*. I totally understand why immigrants often live in closed communities. In some ways, it is easier to be with people who are from your culture.

One *Motza'ei Shabbat*, seeing how down I was feeling after the breakup, my mother called up two of my friends and asked them to come by and take me out. I thought that we were going to a movie in the neighborhood, but instead of going straight ahead toward the movie theaters, my friends turned left onto the main avenue. "Where are we going? The movie theaters are not in that direction," I said to my friends, who confessed that they had heard of a *melaveh malka* in a *shul* on that avenue. They did not want to tell me that ahead of time because they knew that I would not want to come along. At the time, I did not know about this type of function in a *shul*. I guess nowadays it is called a singles event.

I had to go along with them to the event, after being promised that if I didn't like it, we would leave. I was so shy; they were more outgoing. My two friends mingled in the crowd to socialize and I was left standing on my own, feeling like a wallflower. Then a young man approached me and said, "My name is Jack." That evening, I met my future husband. People often say that life is about the steps we make during our journey. Here, for me, instead of walking ahead, I turned left.

From the very beginning, it was always very easy to talk to Jack. I liked his voice. I always did. Despite my not-so-enriched English at the time, Jack made me feel at ease. He was American and was not religious. His family came from Russia and lived in Queens. Jack was in the Air Force in a special high-security-clearance program, learning Chinese to intercept messages and codes.

After dating for a few months, we decided to get married. Jack had to inform the Air Force of our plans. He was told that they needed to interview me because of his security clearance status. The interview took place in our house. After finding out that I came from Egypt and had relatives in Israel,

Brazil, and France, they said to Jack, "You either drop the program or drop the girl." Having so many ties abroad was too high a risk for the program. Obviously, Jack dropped the program.

We got married a year after we actually met. Jack respected my parents and the religious way I was brought up. From the very beginning, he told me that he would do as I wanted regarding our home and family, so we kept a kosher home and observed the *mitzvot*. We started our little family, we had a girl and a boy. We moved several times during our life together, as Jack became an officer in the Air Force. In 1972, while stationed in Lowry Air Force Base in Denver, he was informed that he would soon go to Vietnam for a year.

One evening in Denver, we attended a Zionist Organization of America (ZOA) meeting hosted in our community. From that very evening, my husband was bitten by the Zionist bug. He felt that the only place for Jews to live was Israel, despite the fact that he was always very proud of being an American. But he had to go to Vietnam, which he did. He intended to leave the Air Force once he got back to the States. But soon after his return from Vietnam, Jack was assigned to another base in San Antonio, Texas. We lived in Texas for the duration of this new assignment – three years. In the summer of '75 Jack dropped his air force career to make *aliya*. At this point, he had served for eleven years. It would take an additional nine years of service to retire with a pension. Nonetheless, we started planning our *aliya*. Family and friends thought it was kind of a crazy move, but our daughter was eleven

at the time and we did not know if she would be willing to make the move to Israel nine years from then. We could not take that chance.

I must say that personally, I was not too keen on the idea. After roaming around in my early years and finding that America was good to us, that it accepted us, whereas in Egypt and France we were not wanted, the idea of moving to Israel was a frightening and unsettling matter. But it was something Jack really wanted to do and I wasn't going to pull apart our family, not after what my family had gone through when we had to leave Egypt. For *shalom bayit*, and mainly out of knowing that Jack was right about Israel really being our home, I agreed to move to Israel.

During the year that we spent preparing for our *aliya*, we joined *Gar'in Yaḥdav*, an Anglo-Saxon group whose members came from England, Australia, and America. With the help of the *Sokhnut*, we planned to build a *moshav* in Gush Etzion.

We made *aliya* on August 25, 1975. Five years later, my father finally fulfilled his dream to live in Israel when my parents made *aliya*, too.

STARTING FROM ZERO

Once we got to Israel, we went to the Mevaseret Zion absorption center. Our stay there was short because the *Sokhnut* wanted our group to start living on the *moshav* as soon as possible. The *moshav*, which had no name at the time, sat on a hill surrounded by other hills. Except for the lights in our dwellings, darkness was all around. The only other lights to be seen were from our neighbors in Alon Shvut. The way to Jerusalem was a road that passed through Bethlehem.

Life on the *moshav*, which was eventually named Elazar, was interesting and very different. We all had to adjust to our new way of living. The members were supposed to work on the *moshav*, pooling the income they earned for the benefit of the community. Each family was allocated a *taktziv*, monthly stipend, according to the size of the family. The *moshav* was like a *kibbutz* except that there was no communal dining room and children slept in their family homes. Jack and I were not the oldest couple, but we were the couple with the oldest children. The rest of the families had very young children. Our daughter had to travel to Jerusalem since her grade in school was non-existent in the Gush. She never complained, but those early days on the *moshav* must have been very difficult for her. Our son, along with nine other kids his age, made up the first *kita gimmel* in the Gush. It was much easier for him. He had a *ḥevra*.

We stayed in Elazar until 1982. Because our kids were older than most of the rest of the children there, we felt that their needs were not being met and that made us decide to leave Elazar. We informed the *moshav* that we wanted to leave. Since we had grown fond of the idea of living in the Gush,

we tried finding a place in Alon Shvut, but the houses that were available were yearly rentals. I was definitely not prepared to move every year. I needed some stability, especially after not having had stability earlier in my life.

Since Alon Shvut was not going to work for us, we were considering buying an apartment in Gilo. One day after seeing a building project there, we found a postcard in our mailbox announcing that the Efrat project would be ready in 1983. We made a deposit on a plot of land on which our future home would be built. I am still living on this very same plot of land.

Once the houses were basically completely built, we were the seventh family to move to Efrat in March 1983, a week before Passover. Once again, we experienced dark hills and no paved roads. We were again starting from zero and I had a hard time readjusting to that.

With time, I loved Efrat. Each morning, I open the front door and have cool, refreshing air coming through the screen door into my home. I hear birds chirping. I have a cute little garden with flowers that I plant that give me such positive energy. I appreciate all the things that I have here and in a way, it reminds me of the time when my parents had to rebuild their lives in America. I feel rooted here and it has been an amazing experience to watch the growth of Efrat and the growth of the whole Gush Etzion area.

SHOCK

And then one day, my life was turned upside down. We had just celebrated our forty-fifth wedding anniversary by simply having dinner in town. Not wanting any special attention, I had asked Jack not to mention our anniversary to the restaurant, but he did. He was happy and he wanted me and other people to know it. A little cupcake with sparklers was brought over to our table. It was so sweet. We were plain and simple people, so happy, and in a very good place. Life was good and promising to be even better because in the not-so-far future, we would be finished paying off our mortgage. We had dreamt of traveling and now we would be able to do it. We would finally have a financially easier time, pampering our children and grandchildren without any worry.

For a long time, we had struggled financially. We were even forced to go to the States in 1986 for a couple years so that we could pay off personal debts incurred by starting from zero when we moved to Efrat. As soon as we accomplished that, we returned to our home.

A couple of days after our anniversary, in late February 2008, Jack took a friend to the airport in the very early morning hours and never made it home. He was found near his car after he dropped off his friend at the airport. He had suffered a heart attack at the age of sixty-eight. I was in shock. From one day to the next, my life changed drastically.

When it came time to bury Jack, my brother offered me money to pay for a plot for Jack in Jerusalem, but I refused his kind offer, saying that Jack loved the Gush and he would not want to leave it. Jack is buried in Kfar Etzion, and I have a plot next to him.

After the *shiva*, I spent a week in Modiin with my daughter and her family. My son-in-law brought our car over to Modiin from the area where Jack was found. The very sight of the car was an object of pain to me. I did not want to even go near it.

During that week by my daughter, all *Shabbat* I was thinking to myself that even though it felt impossibly hard to return to an empty house, I had to go home sometime. I could ask my daughter to drive me but then my car would still be in Modiin. And she would have to drive herself home too. Thoughts went through my mind. What was my life going to be from now on? Would I be depending on my children to pick me up so that I could spend *Shabbat* with them? Would I be depending on people for errands and whatever else came up? I felt that was not the way I wanted to live my life from then on. How would I live independently if I let that happen?

After *Havdala,* without saying a word to anyone, I packed my things very quietly. I announced to my daughter that I was going home. The hour was late, it was dark, and the roads were wintery. My daughter just said, "Okay."

I got in the car and drove alone for the first time, at night, back to Efrat. I was crying along the way. I was talking to Jack and I said, "Jack, you see? I am driving. I am going to be okay." I felt he knew how I was feeling because since coming to Israel, I had driven very little. Jack was always the driver since we always went places together. I could count on my hands how many times I had driven. To this day, I don't know how and where I found the courage that evening to go home on my own. I kind of felt that not only was Hashem watching me, but Jack was, too.

Barukh Hashem, I arrived home safely. My daughter was was worried about my traveling at night on my own and knowing how I must have felt. She didn't discourage me from my decision, but she had a friend waiting for me at my door when I arrived. She wanted to make sure that I was okay. Once I got out of the car, I broke down and cried like a child.

Scared and alone, I knew that I had to take that step. It may seem such a small step to others, but for me, it was a gigantic step into what my life was going to be. My daughter understood that too. I am so thankful to her that she did not try to stop me. To survive my present ordeal, I need to be independent. I knew I wanted to stand on my own two feet.

KEEP ON LIVING

I don't know how I managed during the first days, weeks, and months. That period of my life is somewhat of a blur to me. I was just existing day after day. My saving grace was that I had a job that kept me busy. I often worked late in the office, not wanting to go home to an empty and silent house.

I had to adjust to living on my own,

making a choice to go forward with life as best I could. Jack would have wanted me to do that. He always told me that I was strong and that I could do anything and everything, though I did not share his convictions. It was so hard to cook a meal for one, to eat alone, to sleep alone. It was so hard to sleep in an empty house. But I guess Jack was right. I could do anything if I put my mind to it.

Being independent means that I can do what I want to do, and to me, it means a lot. At this point in my life, if I want to do something, I do it. In the beginning, it was so hard for me to come to a decision on anything. It took time for me to take responsibility for decisions that needed to be made. I didn't want it to be the way it has been since Jack left this world. I wanted the two of us to grow old together, to enjoy the children and grandchildren.

Sometime after becoming a widow, people tried to set me up to remarry. One such *shiddukh* was with a man who had recently lost his wife. His family knew that he would be lost without his wife, that he would need a companion. I reluctantly agreed to meet him, even though I did not want to do so. I had very mixed feelings. I did not want to marry a man who was so recently widowed, especially after being told what a wonderful couple they were in their married life, and how much he had loved her. He needed a companion, and selfishly, at that moment in my life, I did not want to be that companion. I did not want to spend my life caring for someone else's husband. I felt I didn't need that kind of companionship. I did not feel like being burdened by having to cook if I didn't feel like it, by having to make a new life with someone else. To my great relief, the meeting we were supposed to have was canceled. I felt a heavy weight was lifted off me. About a year later, I heard that this man died the very same way his wife died. He may have died of a broken heart. Perhaps he could not live without her.

The years have passed. My heart is open to finding a partner again. I have been a romantic all my life and I still am.

I know it will never be like it was with Jack. I accept that. In the meantime, I am going forward in life the best I can. Though I manage my aloneness and I sometimes like being alone, I do feel lonely at times, especially when evenings set in, and when *Shabbat*, holidays, birthdays, and anniversaries are celebrated. Sometimes, while out to lunch with a friend and seeing couples all around us, I feel something tugging at my heart. I really do not think it is envy. It is just sadness about not being part of a couple anymore. Whenever I feel loneliness taking over, I push myself into doing something to make myself feel better. I read a good book, sew something for myself, do some embroidery, or call my daughter, my son, or a friend. I try not to dwell on loneliness.

With time, some of my friends have become widows themselves, and I do my best to keep in touch in them. I help them however I can, give them support, but never do I find myself preaching to them. They have to come to terms with their status in their own time and according to their own abilities.

Lately, as I get older, I think more about leaving Efrat after a lifetime of living here. I feel that perhaps it would be better or wiser to sell the home that I love so much and get a smaller apartment in Modiin to be closer to my daughter. It is a very big step for me, leaving the community and the good friends I have made over the years. But life is all about the steps we make.

Recently, my daughter and I took a trip to Paris. It was good for me to go back for the first time since I lived there as a refugee. Jack and I often talked about taking a trip there. It was not meant to be for me to go back to Paris with my husband. I saw Paris through different eyes, as Jack always said that I would. The first two days were spent going through memory lane, visiting all the places that touched my life and the lives of my parents and brothers. Afterward, we did what the tourists do. We saw different sites. Paris has a charm of its own. It was a good trip and I am happy that I went because now when I think of Paris, I think of the trip taken with my daughter and not of the Paris of long ago.

Once I read a quote in a book that made a tremendous impression on me: "There are wounds time does not heal, though it can reduce them to a manageable size." I think this is very true. We are not totally healed from our losses, but we manage them. I truly believe that Hashem gives us the strength we need and I thank Him every day for that.

Here I am, seventy-six years old, sometimes telling myself, "Sarah, where have the years gone?"

REFLECTIONS

Questions to Consider
- Consider your childhood: What were some of the wholesome moments?
- What have you built, or what are you looking to build, in your lifetime?

Words to Remember
"Most of my memories of Egypt are of our family and the close bond we felt toward each other. Our daily lives were simple and lovely. It was the nicest time of my life, until it suddenly ended."

Group Discussion
Many Jewish families have been refugees through history. What role does being a refugee play in your family history?

☙

Take a moment for yourself. What do you need right now?
Close your eyes and be in your own body.
Here is a relaxation exercise to come back to yourself:

Relaxation Exercise
Go to the place in your home that you love the most. Maybe it is a window with a view, a cozy nook, or a beautiful wall of images. Look around you and touch what makes you happy in that space. Remember how you got to that place and the comfort that it brings you.

Lisa's Story

Life Is Too Short for Regrets

Arnona, Jerusalem

HOW DID YOU KNOW THAT?

It was December 2004 and we had a couple of students from Hebrew University's junior-year-abroad program come stay for the holidays. We became close with them and one of them said, "My parents are coming for *Ḥanukka*. I would love if I could bring them for *Shabbat*." They came for Friday night dinner and we enjoyed getting to know each other. Toward the end of the meal, the husband said to me, "There is something gravely wrong with your husband. He is very, very sick."

This man wasn't a doctor. He just asked me to trust his gut. He had been sick himself and he just had a feeling.

My husband had been fighting sinusitis and hadn't been feeling well for two months. He had off-and-on fevers and had been trying all sorts of vitamins and antibiotics that weren't working. At one point, we even said to the doctor, "Hey, it seems like something is not working. Maybe we should take a blood test?"

So that Sunday morning we went to the *kupat ḥolim*. We got there right as they were finishing taking blood for the day. The nurse said, "Come back tomorrow." I told her, "Oh, no. We are doing this now." I took out one hundred shekels and I waited at the entrance of the clinic for the messenger who was coming to collect the samples. I gave him the money and said, "You do not move until I tell you to do so."

They took the blood. The messenger waited and collected the sample for delivery to the lab. My husband dropped me off at home and went off to work himself.

The phone rang. It was the doctor. "Lisa, where are you?"

"I'm home."

"Are you alone? Are you sitting?"

"Yes." (I lied.)

"I have to tell you something. Your husband's blood test shows there is something wrong going on. I don't know yet what it is, but he has no white blood cells and no platelets. You need to get him to the hospital immediately. I already spoke to the hematology department and they are waiting for you. Oh, and Lisa? On the way, don't get into even a fender bender. Because it will kill him."

My kids were eight and ten years old. I scrambled to get coverage for them. I got into a cab and by chance, I happened to know where my husband's meeting was. When he walked out of his meeting, he saw me. He said, "I'm going to die, aren't I? Am I really sick?"

I said, "Jeremy, how did you know that?"

He said, "I just had a feeling after the blood test this morning that this was it."

A *GIBOR*

We got to the hospital and they did a bone marrow biopsy. They told us that he had two weeks to live. They sent his results off to specialists outside of Israel and came up with a protocol to gently trigger his bone marrow to make some white blood cells and platelets so he could stay alive.

Picture a beautiful golf course covered in grass. Imagine there is one hole that was dug up and someone covered it with Astroturf. Visualize that feeling of walking and suddenly falling down that hole. That was me. My world crumbled beneath my feet.

Thankfully, I had a babysitter who basically moved into the house to take care of the children. I had to tell my kids, "Listen, *Abba* is sick and we don't really know what it is. And *Ima* needs to be with *Abba* in the hospital all the time to make sure that he gets the care he needs. You will have to stay here at home."

Jeremy was an absolutely brilliant man who grew up in a home of science, research, and knowledge. As soon as they began getting back some of the test results, he created a full disk of articles from specialists all over the world. They did a whole course in the hospital for his doctors, based on his findings. He was a true *gibbor*. And then they created a treatment plan. It was strong enough to save him, and controlled enough so that the treatment would not kill him before the disease did. He lived for eight more years.

They did all sorts of treatments. The first one put him in remission after two months. Then they realized the disease would come back. They took his bone marrow, cleaned it up, froze it, and wiped out his own bone marrow in his body. Then they reimplanted his marrow. Every step of the way felt like we were on the verge of disaster. They did it and he made it through. When he did a 10k run two years later, he had a better time than his doctors.

But then he got another disease. We went to Switzerland for treatment, because they didn't have it yet in Israel. It worked. And then one of the kids in our son's school had whooping cough. Our son got sick (he was a few months shy of getting the booster shot) and so did Jeremy. It nearly killed him.

A year later, we needed to do a second treatment as two rounds were needed to cure the disease. But his body was too weak for it. And that disease ended his life.

A MATTER OF DAYS

My kids were fifteen and seventeen. They were basically living alone while their father was dying, so I could be with Jeremy in the hospital. We had an amazing community who brought them food every day and checked in on them.

When they were sixteen and eighteen, he passed away. The Sunday before, the doctor told us that he wasn't going to make it much longer. It would be a matter of days. The boys came on Monday to bring Jeremy his *tefillin*. We were told that his lungs were filling with fluid and his body was not strong enough to pump it out.

The *rosh yeshiva* of our sons' high school made sure that someone was by our side the entire time, from the moment I called him and told him that Jeremy was going to pass away in a day or two. There was a rotation of the kids' teachers at all times in the hospital. I heard the *rav* say, "One of you is here with them until he dies and they go home." They were amazing.

Jeremy died just after midnight, and by three a.m. we were home. I told the kids to go to sleep. As an *onen*, you don't say *berakhot* or have religious obligations, so I just let them sleep in. At six in the morning, after very little sleep myself, I sent a text message to our closest friends asking them to call me when they got up.

We already had a plot in the cemetery from when Jeremy's mother passed. A few people came over and helped me get ready for the funeral. I didn't know what to do. But I did have a feeling of relief that my husband's suffering was over. My older son reminded me that he and his brother had never been to a funeral. There was lots to explain so they would know what to expect.

Thinking back on those eight years, I knew we made the best of them. We partied. We had terrible moments too, but overall we really had a good time together. We did something fun every single day, even if we were just at home. We accepted the reality of what was coming. Jeremy never spoke about being at our sons' weddings or becoming a grandfather. He knew that it was never going to happen. We both lived every day just for that day.

We both entered into therapy before the end. We were prepared for the eventuality. I was devastated. I had lost my best friend. But my grief had been processed over those long years. I was not looking to move forward. I just wanted to stay in one place for a while.

Jeremy told me in advance, "You have a year to be sad, and that's it. I don't want to look down and see you wearing black and not living your life. I want you to find love again and get married. I want you to enjoy your life and find happiness again."

MY FRIEND RIVKA

My life continued. It took me a while to get to a place where I could think about moving on and getting remarried. When the first year of mourning was up, I didn't feel finished, like Jeremy had wanted me to be. I was fifty-two, and I knew that I would meet someone and get married again one day. I decided to start dating even though I was not quite ready. Friends introduced me to some really nice guys. And I tried. Tea and talking, going out, while on the one hand being Lisa and yet, on the other, trying to figure out who tomorrow's Lisa was going to be. I knew what I was looking for, and yet I was very open-minded.

A couple of people suggested that I go out with a man named Moshe.

I knew Moshe. He worked with Jeremy and I had known his wife, Rivka. She and I met when I first became religious; she ran an organization for young religious adults living in Jerusalem. She took me under her wing and when I got engaged to Jeremy, I saw her and excitedly shared my news. A couple weeks later I saw her again, and she shared that she too was now engaged, to a guy she grew up with named Moshe. We both got married. Both our husbands were computer programmers and they worked together in two different companies. Over the years we were friends who would see each other at *smaḥot* and around town, enjoying exchanging parenting stories and living the Zionist dream. When we saw each other, it was like magic. One time we bumped into each other in the supermarket and we talked in the cookie aisle for over an hour. Jeremy and Rivka were also close, because they were battling cancer at the same time. She was blogging about her illness, and they would have meaningful conversations about the experience.

When we heard that Rivka had passed from breast cancer, I was so saddened and wanted to do something to help. I checked to see if I could make some food for *Shabbat* for the family, but everything on the list had been taken already. Jeremy told me there was one job still open. The family needed a *shomeret* to sit with Rivka's body in the hospital morgue over *Shabbat*. I went with a friend and we were there almost the whole day. We sat in a little hut outside the hospital, guarding her body. That night was the funeral, and

there were over one thousand people there. Jeremy was too weak to be able to attend, but I was there.

When Moshe was suggested to me as a possible date, initially, I just couldn't do it.

FIFTEEN MINUTES

Moshe's kids were twelve, fourteen, and sixteen when their mother passed away. After over a year, he began dating. He tried the best he could.

At the time, I was renovating a bathroom in my apartment. I was having a hard time making decisions about which tiles to choose, so the *kablan* sent me someone to help with the design. We became good friends. One day she said to me, "Lisa, you have to go out with this friend of mine." She told me that I should go out with her friend Moshe.

I told her, "I know him really well. I don't think I could go out with him." She pushed me to go out with him. Then at the same time, someone on social media also suggested that I go out with Moshe. I had multiple people suggesting him at the same time and encouraging me to go out with him. I was asked, "Do you want us to give him your number?" But we already had each other's numbers. I had called him that year to wish him a happy birthday.

I figured that since he knew me so well, if he was interested, I would have already known and he would have already called me. But they asked him, and he said, "I would love to go out with her."

I wrote to him on Facebook and said, "Hey, want to get together for coffee?" He responded, "Forget coffee, let's get dinner."

Fifteen minutes into the first date, I knew. Once I got over the hurdle of being nervous to go out with him, it was obvious to me that this was it. We sat for four hours on our first date. We talked about Rivka, and Jeremy, and God; you name it, we talked about it. We laughed and we cried and by the end, the waiters were cleaning up the restaurant around us.

We started dating in October and we got married in June.

LIFE IS TOO SHORT FOR REGRETS

We introduced each other to our children slowly. We did it in a casual way. They knew I was dating someone very seriously and I told them, "If you see something I don't see, you need to tell me right away. Your opinion really matters to me. If I am going out with someone you don't like, you need to tell me."

After my son spent some time with Moshe one night, he came into my room laughing. I asked him, "What was so funny?" He said, "*Ima*, let's be very honest, you are marrying the same guy twice. He's smart like *Abba*, he talks about the same things as *Abba*, and he even has the same beard as *Abba*!" We laughed together and I told him, "I guess I have a type! Smart and fun Jewish guys."

We very gradually blended our families together. We gave everyone the time and space they needed to come together. In January, there were big sales in the mall. I called up Moshe's daughters and invited them to come shopping with me. They were in the car in five minutes. We shopped and went out to eat and that was it. That day was a real cementing of our relationship. I fit in the right place at the right time for them.

We all have a great relationship as a family. The kids get along great too, and we all made the effort to bond. It is like a puzzle. We work hard to figure out which parts of the past we can bring into the present. It helps that we knew each other so well in the years before we married. Sometimes I'll be talking to the girls about something pretty deep and I'll say, "I know that your mom would have thought X." I am able to do that because she was my friend and I really knew her. When my son got engaged, we went to visit the *kalla's* family. When we left their house, Moshe turned to me and said, "Lisa, Jeremy would have really loved her family." He could say that because he knew him really well and he could share that with me. It is a really special and unique dynamic.

When we got married, there were three hundred people there, crying with joy for us. The people who love us just wanted to be a part of this *simḥa* after all the pain. We decided to do a "*ḥuppa* party." We had the *ḥuppa* and then a party with nosh at the First Station in Jerusalem. It was a Thursday morning at nine a.m. All the food came from the local vendors. The boys walked me down the aisle, we danced for two hours, and we met for lunch with the rest of our extended family. Moshe gave a beautiful speech under the *ḥuppa* about Jerusalem, about being broken and being whole, and how to put the pieces back together. There was not a dry eye in the place. It has been two years, and *barukh Hashem* we have built a beautiful life together.

Lisa's Story

I have zero regrets about the life I lived with Jeremy. We loved each other and rarely argued. It was never worth fighting. I buried him and I know that we lived our life together to the fullest. Honestly, life is too short to have regrets.

REFLECTIONS

Questions to Consider

- Do you feel that life is too short for regrets?
- How do you cope with grief?

Words to Remember

> "We accepted the reality of what was coming. Jeremy never spoke about being at our sons' weddings or becoming a grandfather. He knew that it was never going to happen. We both lived every day just for that day."

Group Discussion

Moving on does not mean letting go or forgetting. It can be simply an acknowledgment that there is more life to live. Life always moves on, even when we are not ready. When has there been a time in your life when you were not ready to move on? What brought you to the moment that you were ready? If you are still in that space, what would you need in order to feel ready?

ॐ

Take a moment for yourself. What do you need right now?
Close your eyes and be in your own body.
Here is a grounding exercise to come back to yourself:

Grounding Exercise

Look around you. Remind yourself who and where you are. Engage with your sensations. Feel what you are resting upon. Smell the aromas in the air. Notice the temperature in the room. Name the items you see. Let the stillness or activity in your space bring you back to your own reality.

Shlomit's Story

Returning to Where
We Belong

Natzerat Illit

LOST TRIBE

I grew up in Kolasib, India, a district of Mizoram. During the British rule of India, my great-great-grandparents were converted by missionaries to Christianity. Many years later, before I was born, one of our neighbors told my father about Judaism. He was interested in learning more about it, for it resonated deeply with him. He began to learn all he could about what it meant to be Jewish. In 1993, my parents fully accepted Judaism as their faith. In 1994, I was born.

The journey of my people is a long one. As converted Christians studying the Bible, they felt like there was something wrong with the way they were being told to observe and identify. When reading the stories of the exile of the ten tribes, we learned about the northern kingdom's banishment to the Diaspora. We learned about Menashe, the son of Joseph. In our tradition, we believe that our forefather's name was Manmasi. Following the history and trajectory of our people and how we ended up in India, we believe that we actually descend from the tribe of Menashe.

Our oral history shares that our people were exiled from our beloved homeland and then we traveled through Persia, Afghanistan, Tibet, China, and then on to India, where our people settled in the Indian districts of Manipur and Mizoram. Our ancient festivals are similar to present-day Jewish festivals, and so are our funeral rites and birth and marriage ceremonies. We have ancient songs passed down from generation to generation that share the stories of what we now believe to be the Exodus from Egypt and other biblical events. We have our own version of Miriam's Prayer after leaving Egypt, and we also have a song called "Sikpui Hla" that translates like this:

> While we are preparing for the Sikpui Feast,
> The big Red Sea becomes divided;
> As we march along fighting our foes,
> We are being led by pillar of cloud by day,
> And pillar of fire by night.
> Our enemies, O ye folks, are thick with fury.
> Come out with your shields and arrows.
> Fighting our enemies all day long,
> We march forward as cloud-fire goes before us.
> The enemies we fought all day long,
> The big sea swallowed them like a wild beast.
> Collect the quails,
> And draw the water that springs out of the rock.

Before my father began his research, he did not know that his family originally believed that they had Jewish roots. When he was learning more about Judaism, he contacted the Jewish community in Mumbai and learned about the *Benei Menashe*. After extensive historical family research and evaluation of our own practices and belief systems, he discovered that we were a part of the group identified as *Benei Menashe*.

Though our identifying as such has become highly political and disputed, we believe that we are one of the ten lost tribes. We believe that we descend from Jews, and that Israel is our homeland. Once we knew who we were, we had to begin our long journey back home.

DREAMING

Growing up in Kolasib, we had some difficulties. We lived among mostly Christian and Hindu people, who did not know about Judaism or what it was. They assumed that everyone was like them. When we had to fill out our school forms, we had to check a box to identify as either Hindu or Christian.

There was not even a box that allowed us to choose being Jewish. I would always choose "other." They forced us to go to school on Saturdays, and when I would not go because it was *Shabbat*, I suffered from that choice. I was punished because I would not go to school on *Shabbat*.

At home, we kept *Shabbat*, lighting candles and going to our *beit knesset* to pray. We kept *kashrut* at home. There was a man who is also *Benei Menashe*, who was originally from Mumbai, and he came to us after he made *aliya* to Israel. He would come visit our village and educate us about how to keep *halakha*.

My father was a policeman in Kolasib, and we used to live in the quarters of the police. Eventually, we moved to another community and our new neighbors knew nothing about our religion or practices. They would come around on Friday nights and listen to us sing *Shalom Aleikhem*. To them, it was a unique phenomenon.

We had friends in our neighborhood who were also *Benei Menashe*,

but they made *aliya* in 2006. When they left, we were alone in our village. We missed being with other *Benei Menashe*. The goal was always to make *aliya* and live in Israel. Since I was a child, my father would tell us that his dream was for us to settle there. He told us to learn as much as we could about Judaism while we were in India, and then we would move to Israel and start a new life there. He wanted to go as soon as possible. As a child, I always knew that my future would be in Israel. Living in India felt like temporarily living. We tried to make the best of living where we were. But it is not a fulfilling life to always be dreaming of being somewhere else.

ON HOLD

I did my best to study as much as I could. I would study with all of the *Benei Menashe* who would return to our village from Israel to teach us. I feel like in that process, we were bringing back traditions from an ancient identity.

We traveled to Manipur, a neighboring state of Mizoram, to stand before a *dayan*. I was twenty-one years old. We had an interview in which we

told him that we were *Benei Menashe* and that we wanted to be allowed to return to Israel. This began our process of *aliya*. We waited for three years to hear from them, to learn whether we were approved to move. We had no idea how long the process would take. We thought every moment after that initial meeting could be the moment that they would tell us to pack our bags and leave. We felt that at any second, we could be leaving for *Eretz Yisrael*.

In the meantime, I worked as a teacher in a school teaching math and science. But basically, my whole life was on hold. I was frustrated with the waiting. As a young adult, I wanted to start my life. I thought about dating and marriage, but everyone I was surrounded with was not Jewish. There were only six or seven *Benei Menashe* families in my village all together. There was no one who I could meet to even consider beginning that process.

I would go to *Benei Menashe* seminars in India and meet people like me, from all over. There would be around two hundred people who would come to these events. There are seven thousand *Benei Menashe* all together in India. There are three thousand who have arrived in Israel. We are a very small community.

We all were facing a long process. We were waiting for permissions for conversion, *aliya*, and relocation. We were waiting along with many other families, as our *aliya* was meant to be a group event. The *Rabbanut* in Israel had come at the beginning of the *Benei Menashe aliya* and approved that we are one of the ten lost tribes and that we have the right to return to Israel. Our process was in the queue along with many other families from India who were petitioning to go home.

After three years, we found out that our *aliya* was approved. They gave us two weeks to pack our entire lives and leave.

LEAVING

I was teaching in my village and we had a big exam coming up when we were informed that it was time to go. I had to scramble to prepare all the equations for my students to take their tests, even though I would no longer be there to give them the tests myself.

We had been living for three years as if our life would change any minute. My mother would always be prepared to leave right away, as if we would have to get on a plane the very next month. I would get fed up. I would say, "It's never going to happen." Waiting so long, it felt like the moment would never come. I really wanted to go, but living in an always packed room was very hard.

Israel was my dream. I wanted to move so that I could live fully as a Jew, keeping *Shabbat* and festivals with other Jews. I wanted a community. I wanted to walk around knowing that I believed in the same faith as most people around me. I wanted to live in a place where school, work, and all of life was built around Torah and *mitzvot*. We had no family waiting for us in Israel. We would make a new life for ourselves.

After we got the news, I felt shocked. I was frozen. I felt like I had no idea what to do. My parents gave me directions, and I ran around to pack and finalize all our paperwork. We had to tie up loose ends with our jobs. We were only allowed to bring three suitcases per person. We could not bring a lift with furniture, so we had to leave everything behind: our beds, dishes, books. I was so excited, but I was so nervous. All of a sudden, I had to say goodbye to everything I had known. But I also now had the opportunity to live my dreams.

I was sad to leave India because I had to leave my older brother and sister behind. My sister is married and my brother was late to make our flight, so he missed it. Now he has to do the process again, and continue to wait. We have been separated now for two and a half years. I hope they make *aliya* soon.

We have extended family on my father's side that still identify as Christians. They were happy for us that we could make our dreams come true, but they were very upset that we were leaving. They did not recognize that what we saw as our birthright belonged to them, too. My mother's side is not *Benei Menashe* and they were also very sad that we were leaving. I had many complicated feelings before I left India for my new life in Israel.

HOME

The flight was so exciting. They separated us into three groups and then again into another two groups. They made me a group leader, charged with helping my fellow *olim* navigate the process. I was very nervous about it and continuously asked the people in charge about every next step. I was frustrated that it was so complicated.

There were a bunch of flights that brought us all to Israel, around one hundred people. In my particular flight, there were twenty people who traveled together. I was able to be grouped with my family on the flight. Sitting on the plane, I was thinking about my sister and brother and leaving them behind. I felt so sad. Then I would get a wave of nervous excitement. I didn't know what life would look like in Israel and I had no idea what was coming next or where we were going. I had never been to Israel and had no concept of what life would be like.

The moment we touched down, I was filled with joy. When we came out of the terminal at Ben-Gurion, there was a whole group of people waiting for us. Among them were our neighbors who had made *aliya* before us, including my best friend and her parents, who were like grandparents to me. It was amazing to be reunited with people who felt like family and from whom we had been separated for so long.

I was crying and happy and so emotional to finally be in Israel. The reception we received at the airport was a true celebration. The whole group waiting for us was singing and waving flags, overjoyed that another group of *Benei Menashe* had finally arrived back home where we belong.

FOUND

After the airport, we went to Kfar Hasidim where they had a *merkaz klita* for *Benei Menashe*. We moved into a small apartment in a hostel. We had a main dining room where we all ate together. It was like *kibbutz* living; we lived and learned together. The food in particular was a difficult adjustment. Back at home, we would eat vegetables and rice, mostly. We would hardly eat meat. In Israel, the food was completely different. The tastes were nothing that we were used to. Our food in India was salty and spicy. Here, they served us things like schnitzel, rice, and cucumbers. It was much blander than we were used to, but eventually, we became accustomed to this new food.

In general, everything here shocked me. It was all so new. But I was so happy. I was thrilled to finally see the Land of Israel with my own eyes. It was fascinating to see all the different kinds of Jews. I had only seen Hasidim and Ashkenazic Jews in the movies. It was very cool to see Jews of all types living here.

It was the first time that I was living in a place where not everyone looked like me. I find that wherever I go, I need to introduce myself and explain where

I come from. Sometimes I can be frustrated by that because there seems to be a level of mistrust that we really are Jewish. It can be annoying to have to explain who I am. But sometimes it opens up a conversation with people who are truly interested in learning about our history and how it reflects on the Jewish people as a whole. Those conversations can be very nice and inspiring. Curiosity from a good place can be positive.

Often, before I introduce myself, people assume that I am from the Philippines or that I am a Chinese foreign worker. I understand. My facial structure is Asian and Indian. People are not as accustomed to seeing Jews from those places. I used to live in a place where everyone looked like me on the outside but lived a totally different life than what I wanted for myself. Now, most people I am surrounded by look different externally, but we believe and observe the same religion and lifestyle. I prefer to live like this. Here I feel free. The atmosphere matches how I feel on the inside.

We studied to begin our conversion process in Kfar Hasidim. The State of Israel recognizes our right to return and when we arrived in Israel, we were considered Israeli citizens. But we needed to begin our conversion to assure the *Rabbanut* that we are Jewish according to the halakhic standards of the State of Israel. Typical applicants have a one-year period that they must go through before they can convert. *Benei Menashe* have an expedited process of three months. We spent our time in *shiurim*, learning *halakha*, and preparing for the *mikve*.

They told us that it would be a long way home. We were a lost tribe, and years of assimilation and intermarriage in local communities (since we had been exiled) had almost lost us to history. Looking back on my family history, I understand how we became lost. But I have always known who I was and where I belonged. Now I see how we have been able to come back. We are now a found tribe and I saw that the conversion process was the final step in returning to our people.

The conversion itself was very exciting. I felt different when I came out of the *mikve*. They always told us that when we would come out of the *mikve*, we would have a new soul. I felt that newness, and I was ready for the next chapter of my life.

LIVING THE DREAM

After our *klita* process finished in Kfar Hasidim, we moved to Natzerat Illit. There is a small *Benei Menashe* community there. The 2006 and 2014 batches of *Benei Menashe olim* were settled there, and so we went there too. There are no more than 150 people living there. Even though it is small, it was amazing to live in a *Benei Menashe* community for the first time.

I went to *ulpan* in Maalot to learn Hebrew. We speak Mizo at home. I was in *ulpan* and *midrasha* for six or seven months. I lived there during the week and came home to Natzerat Illit for *Shabbat*.

They gave us a lot of time to acclimate. I found that it was really helpful in adjusting to our new society and language. I learned a lot during that time. I made many friends. I am not sure that I was prepared to enter Israeli society at the end of that process. But it was time.

Now I work in Natzerat Illit in a factory making computer technology. I love the work. My job is with the chemical process, working in a lab. I have a bachelor's degree in biochemistry from the college where I studied for three years in India.

I live at home with my family. My parents are having a hard time with the *klita* process because everything is new. They are happy though, making new friends and going to *shiurim* and living the life they always wanted. In some ways, it is everything they thought it was going to be, but other days it's harder than they imagined. My younger brother is studying in yeshiva and my little sister is studying, too. Everyone is busy, happy, and building their lives here, even if it often feels like a challenge. We are still waiting to be reunited with my siblings in India.

When I look toward the future, I am planning on going back to school to become a nurse. I am happy to start over with a new language and build a new life here. I feel like I am still building up my dreams. There is a part of me that knows we need to maintain our *Benei Menashe* culture, and yet I also see other spaces where we need to become more Israeli.

I believe that the return of our lost tribe is a part of the *geula* process. Our return is a signifier that something larger is happening across the world. I am grateful to participate in the ultimate redemption of *kibbutz galuyot*, bringing in the Jewish people from the four corners of the earth.

REFLECTIONS

Questions to Consider

- What was it like when you found a community where you felt like you belonged?
- Have you ever accomplished a goal that brought you great joy?

Words to Remember

> "We learned about Menashe, the son of Joseph. In our tradition, we believe that our forefather's name was Manmasi. Following the trajectory of our people and how we ended up in India, we believe that we actually descend from the tribe of Menashe."

Group Discussion

How much do you know about your own family's history? What chapter is most meaningful to you?

☙

Take a moment for yourself. What do you need right now?
Close your eyes and be in your own body.
Here is a gratitude exercise to come back to yourself:

Gratitude Exercise

Consider the things we all take for granted. Imagine what it would be like to lose those things – our homes, our belongings, our language, our access to our religion. Imagine what it would feel like to receive those things back, one by one. Envision a new appreciation for each component of your life.

Suzanne's Story

Healing My Own Way

Shoham

LOOKING FOR MEANING

I am a *giyoret,* and I grew up in the Netherlands. After my conversion, things were not going great for me. I was looking for a solution for the challenging things in my life so I took my Judaism seriously. I was looking for a sense of community.

I met a Jewish guy abroad while I was in the conversion process. I thought it was amazing and meant to be. He told me, "I am a religious person," and before you knew it, we were married and had kids. We moved to Israel together. I felt like I had won the lottery and being with him was my lucky ticket to a better life. I was seeing a lot of signs in everything. I was looking for meaning everywhere.

It turned out to be an unhappy marriage. I could never have imagined it would have turned out the way it did. I wanted to fit in, learn everything, and be everything, and so I accepted the way things were. We were married for ten years.

Our life felt very lonely to me. I didn't have friends and had lost touch with old ones. I felt I wasn't myself. I was extremely unhappy. My situation led me to believe that I was worth nothing and could accomplish nothing in my life. I had lost all my self-esteem. I was ashamed of the place that I had found myself in. I couldn't go back to my parents because I was afraid they

95

were going to say, "I told you so." I was so stubborn and I was led by ego. I didn't want to admit that I wasn't managing. I got a divorce and it was so hard. But the marriage was over.

GET YOUR LIFE TOGETHER

I left in the middle of the night. I had no money, and I only took what was mine and what I needed. I didn't want to keep anything else from that life I had there. I didn't want to bring those memories with me. My mom stepped in and sent me a credit card. She said, "There are twenty thousand shekels on this account. I want you to rent a place for yourself so you can get your life together."

We played camping in the new place for months. I borrowed a few thin mattresses from friends. I didn't want to take my old bed. I didn't want the towels. I wanted nothing. We sat on the floor and ate dinner on the floor. My kids were eight and six, and so I made the whole experience a game. I told them we were having a picnic. I didn't tell them the truth, which was that we had nothing and that is why we were living in a home with no furniture.

I learned to rely on friends, which was something new for me. I made new friends and began to lean on others to help us, like I should have all along. I really worked on my social skills and reviving old friendships. I learned that I could give, too, and that it would give me a sense of belonging.

We were living in an area where there were many old-age homes. We had no family here in Israel. I told the kids that we were going to "adopt a *saba*." We made a friend, an older man who we would go visit. We would make him coffee, visit him, help him buy his cigarettes, light Ḥanukka candles together. He had no one and we had so much support from our new friends. We wanted to pay it forward.

We volunteered in the *beit knesset*, setting up *Kiddush* tables every week. We went on every *shul* trip. We went camping with the school. For the first time, we were busy building an extended family and community. I wanted to give my kids the feeling that even though we were alone here, we were never alone.

I took a leap of faith and changed my career, even though my self-confidence had taken a hit from all the events of the past decade. I took an offer that a friend extended, to work at a hi-tech company that needed Dutch speakers. I became a salesperson and I was going to learn to sell. That job was the best thing I could have ever done for myself. I made so much money that it totally changed our lives. I had always had really bad finances. But one day I went to the bank and they told me to go upstairs because my account had been upgraded to premium. It was a glorious day. I got the chance to buy the apartment that we were renting and because of my new job, I got approved for a mortgage. I did everything right and by the book. I checked everything and double-checked. I didn't want anyone to take advantage of me. In the past, I felt that I would amount to nothing. I felt that I couldn't do anything, that I would be lost.

Now here I was, doing it all on my own.

WHAT I NEEDED TO HEAR

All along the road, there were people who were angels sent by God, who were there for me to help me. In one of these instances, when I wanted to buy my apartment, I had no idea if it was a good investment, or if it was worth the money they were asking. My worst fear was to be told afterward that I was stupid or that I should have known better.

I went to the *iriya* for some forms. I saw the dad of one of the boys in my daughter's class, who happened to own his own construction company. He was just there by accident. I told him that I was buying this place and I was stressed about the purchase. He said, "Want me to check it out for you?" He went with me to the apartment and told me that I would be making an excellent purchase and that I wouldn't regret buying the place. It was all I needed to hear. It was amazing to be able to buy my own apartment.

I was feeling on top of the world. I was driving my own car, a cute little Suzuki. I had a house of my own that was nice and cozy. It had everything that I needed. I was having the time of my life. I was single, but I was fine.

I was dating casually. It was fun, but I also knew that I wanted to get serious. The kids were small, but I knew that they would grow up and have their own lives. I should make my own. I went out for coffee with lots of religious guys. Then I met Niv. He had put up a random picture on his dating profile. He was clearly not self-conscious. He had beautiful eyes. His blurb on his dating profile said, "A simple person who wants a simple life." He was in hi-tech. He was honest about his height and age, which was rare. We met for a date. He was straightforward – no frills, no games. It was so refreshing.

I was supposed to meet someone else for another date right after our coffee and so I had to leave. He asked me if I had another date. I responded, "Yep." After that, he knew that I was always going to be truthful. That was exactly what he wanted. After our first date, he called his mother and told her that he really hoped that I was the one.

WHEN LIFE HAPPENED

I had my own money. I had my own car. I had my own stuff. I didn't need anything. I just wanted a partner. I was really empowered, but I was also lonely.

Even though Niv was great, I met so many great guys and I was distracted. He wanted to go out again and I kept pushing it off. He would drop little notes to me, nothing intrusive, just seeing how I was and saying hello. I liked that.

I agreed to go on a second date. We went for a walk on the beach for two hours. We both put everything out there. We talked about our lives and hid nothing from each other. He was so handsome. The way he walked was so confident, without being cocky. He was secure in his masculinity without having to prove it. He was laid back, which is still what I love about him. Within half a year, he asked me to marry him. It was quick, especially considering that we both had kids. We married, had a baby, and life happened.

The baby was sick all the time. My boss was being difficult. My daughter was admitted to the hospital and was sick for seven months. I was finding myself in a triangle of rides to the hospital, the kindergarten, and my work. Niv was doing all he could, but the baby was five months old and he needed me. My boss would say, "Well, I hope you make your hours this month. Your crises, there is always something."

I felt completely split between everything. My boss had let me know that I had reached the end of the ladder, that he would not be promoting me any further. I knew full well that I couldn't stay stuck in anything. I quit.

Now I had time for my children who needed me. I had a little room to breathe. I had the security and safety to nurse my children back to health, without dragging myself down to the ground. I had a year of paid leave to do whatever I wanted. I made sure my family was in straight waters again. Then there was time for me. I had forgotten about time for me.

FEELING SO ALIVE

I started to make some play silks for my son. I was using berries and onion skins and thought that it was so fun to make. I took a small course for a few hours and learned all about dyeing materials naturally and eco printing. I found it addicting. I have to stir a pot, and that is all I can do. I was able to slow down. I stir, wait, and see how the colors and bubbles are forming, waiting for a sheen, then reduction. The colors change. It takes its time. I can be in a hurry, but the process doesn't care. It takes whatever it takes. It doesn't care about my schedule.

It forces me to let go of the concept of time and control. I have control up until the point that I put the ingredients in the pot. Then it is not up to me. That feels magical. Dyeing fabrics naturally and eco printing are things that people have been doing for thousands of years. I get to be a part of the same process by choice. It requires me to go and submit myself to time flows that are ancient. I can make an eco-printed scarf and boil it for fifteen minutes and it will come out bland. It needs ninety minutes. There are all the small decisions that need to be weighed carefully to get a finished product. It's a whole different flow.

All the things that are making our lives easier are also ruining our sense of creativity. We need to get our hands dirty, stir a cauldron, light a fire. It is such a part of our DNA. We say, "Why do difficult when we can do easy?" But our human existence needs to create. We need to make things. The work is so satisfying for me. Having my legs scratched because I was running around in the bushes looking for plants, having dyed fingernails every once in a while, sweating because I am making things while I stand over the fire – these are all part of the process. I started selling my work. I built a whole business of eco printing and I send my creations all around the world. I get to make people happy with what I made from the heart. I put my soul into it because I am healing, too.

I am healing through the work, and it is making me whole again. The feeling that I had, that I was only in service of other people, is now gone. This work is for me. I get to decide what to put out into the world. I make things with my hands. There is an exchange of vibes and energy. I am connecting to other people through this work, and it makes me feel so alive.

SEASONS

Sometimes I struggle to collect plants for my work. I see a flower and it looks perfectly content being where it is. It didn't ask to be plucked. But I ask each

plant's permission. I only collect what I need; I don't want to take and not use. I aspire not to waste.

You see a butterfly in the forest. He doesn't care about the insanity of the world or what other things think of him. I try to be like that. I need to be a good person, to improve myself, to think about the needs of the earth. I have learned to appreciate the triangle of me receiving gifts from the fields and appreciating them, then making something that is healing for me, and selling it to someone who is healed by wearing it. I am more aware now of the seasons. I know what blooms when, where, and why. It makes me realize that I am a part of the same circle.

I used to be so hard on myself, about my marriage, being a mom, about work, building a business, needing to succeed. I learned the meaning of the seasons. I realized that I don't need to finish everything right now, that there is also next year. I feel that though I am not old, I am getting older. I am not the same anymore. My body is not the same anymore. I am learning to love myself the way I am right now, appreciating the wisdom that comes with age. I can live better, fuller, more vibrantly.

But there is also pain with it. We can't have more children. We would have loved to have had more. I have to say goodbye to that stage, but because I feel so connected to the seasons, I have found beauty in this new stage.

Every time I walk the route in the forest, I discover new things. I find new flowers and plants that I can transform from their current beauty to a lasting object that captures that moment in time. It keeps me going. It's a wonderful metaphor for the fact that one can find something new that is beautiful in every stage of your life. There is always something that can surprise you, something that can bring wonder into your life.

REFLECTIONS

Questions to Consider
- What does being independent mean to you?
- What have been the different seasons of your own life?

Words to Remember

> "I am learning to love myself the way I am right now, appreciating the wisdom that comes with age. I can live better, fuller, more vibrantly."

Group Discussion

What contributes to your positive sense of self-esteem?
What makes you feel centered and vibrant?

ℰ

Take a moment for yourself. What do you need right now?
Close your eyes and be in your own body.
Here is an inspiration exercise for further exploration:

Inspiration Exercise

What skills or talents do you have that you love to utilize in your life?

Do you feel like you have the space to engage with them as often as you wish?

What do you feel is working well for you right now in your life and your career?

What do you feel you need to further assess to decide whether it still belongs in your life?

Kerry's Story

I Choose Joy

Beit Shemesh

GONE

I had a wonderful childhood. I was loved and adored by both of my parents. When I was ten, I starred in the play *Annie* and I remember my dad sitting in the audience, waving and smiling at me, so proud. Our personalities were a great match – both extroverted and gregarious. We had tons of fun together.

It's a challenge to look back on my childhood and understand that my dad both adored me and abandoned me.

Because when I was fifteen, my father left. He didn't come to my high school graduation. He didn't walk me down the aisle at my wedding. My parents separated and he got remarried and had four kids with someone only a little older than me. This was before phones, the internet, or social media. He was gone.

It all fell apart when my parents decided to move to New York from Florida. My brothers had graduated from high school, and my parents were planning the next stage of their lives, and it just didn't work out.

So often, we hold on to what happens to us in our childhood. I'm forty-six years old and I'm done with holding on to it. I don't let it define me. I no longer walk around with the wound of being someone who was abandoned by her father. One of the biggest disappointments in life is truly understanding

105

how limited people can be. My dad had a lot of great qualities, like being generous, funny, and loving, but honesty and reliability weren't among them.

When I was twenty-four, I was about to get married. I decided to reach out to him before my wedding. I hadn't heard from him in eight years. I got him on the phone and he said, "Kerry, I am so happy for you. I am really glad that your life worked out so great for you. I made a lot of mistakes and I am trying to do better this time. I have a new family and I am trying to do better for them. My new son is just like your brother. My second son is just like your other brother. I have a daughter who is just like you. I made so many mistakes with my first family, but I am trying to do better with my second family. I wish you well and I wish you so much luck. Bye."

That was what he said to me – "I wish you so much luck. Bye." He sent me a *Pesach Seder* plate for my wedding. I didn't hear from him for another eight years.

I walked down the aisle with only my mother. Right before we walked down, I stood there alone with my mom, feeling excited and nervous. A wave of humiliation suddenly passed over me as I realized that my father was not on the other side of me. He had abandoned me. I stopped and I told myself, "You don't have to go there now, Kerry. Everything is good in your life. It is okay for you to be happy."

I find that healing often happens in a spiral. You can revisit the same place, but hopefully, you will be at a higher point. Now my life is full of blessings and joy. But sometimes I circle back to that place. I'll be at a bat mitzva and I'll see a girl hug her dad. I remember that once I had a dad who adored me, who hugged me. We had that relationship once, even though it ended. I have to remind myself that I am a healed and happy person. But that pain is never fully gone.

MOVING ON

I'm so lucky that I had my mom. My mom thinks I'm the greatest, wonderful in every way. She always built me up. In fact, I didn't really think of myself as having faults until I was an adult. That is how strong her positivity was. I knew I was the number one joy in her life.

The years after the divorce, where it was just me and my mom, were really rough. We were in financial straits, and it was an emotional crisis for us both. Our dynamic shifted. It went from me bringing joy to my mom because I was adorable, to us taking care of each other. We were the best and most reliable thing in each other's lives. We had to start over. We had an apartment in New York City and we were selling jewelry on the streets. But we were there for each other and we made a new life for ourselves, just the two of us.

At that time, I went to a performing arts high school in Manhattan. I always wanted to be a performer. I acted, sang, and tap danced as a child. But now my life was so difficult, such a departure from the joy and confidence of my earlier years, that I lost some of my acting ambition. A lot of my peers went on to become professional performers. The thing is, most people don't become a Bette Midler or Barbra Streisand. They become extras on Broadway if they're lucky, or they audition for commercials. I didn't like the trajectory that I saw for myself. It depressed me. So after graduating high school early, I left that track completely and decided to move to Israel.

It was at that time, in my early twenties, that I became religious. The experience was very healing for me. My brother once told me that I "became religious because of dad," and at the time I told him that was ridiculous. But years later, I realized there was truth to that. I was looking for more. I was looking for honesty, reliability, and community. I found that in the Orthodox community. There was a stability that came with the relationships that I made in this community. People have shown up for me in a way that has been healing.

When I married my husband shortly after becoming religious, that was a huge step in my process of letting go. I no longer felt that my family was broken. My husband is funny, creative, and idealistic, and he's incredibly loyal and reliable. When I met him, it was so easy. Everything just clicked and I knew I could trust him. In my secular friend circles, no one was thinking about marriage at age twenty-four, and they couldn't understand why I wanted to get married so young. But I wanted a fresh start. I wanted to settle down and make a new life for myself. I wanted a new identity, someone beyond the girl who was abandoned. I was creating my own family now. I had a baby ten months after our wedding.

In addition to wanting stability and wanting to be able to depend on people, I also felt a deep need for financial independence. I needed to know that I would be able to support myself. I wanted to determine my own financial destiny. I wouldn't be vulnerable to being stuck again with nothing. This was another part of the healing. It also tied back to a value I learned early on, from my mother.

When I was in nursery school, we went on a field trip to a hospital. The little boys came out with stethoscopes, and the girls came out with nurse's caps. My mom complained to the school about it. She then bought me a shirt that read, "Become the doctor or lawyer your mother wanted you to marry." I always remembered that. But before I really had a chance to start a career, I got married and started having kids right away. As much as I loved my husband and baby, I realized that I needed a career, too. Beyond wanting to support myself, I had all these other ambitions. Starting a family was healing and wonderful, but I also wanted to contribute to the world outside of my home. I decided to go back to school and become a chiropractor. We moved back to America so I could study.

It took five years and it was not easy. I had two more babies during that time. Juggling school and family, including three little boys, was incredibly difficult. There was one time I took final exams the day after giving birth. But I did it; I became a doctor.

In 2006, we returned to Israel. I was thirty-three years old and I was ready to come back and build the next stage of our lives here. We soon had our fourth boy.

DREAMS

I am an idealist with a sensitive heart. I have always wanted to make the world a better place in whatever way I could. As a chiropractor, it is my job to help people get out of pain. My work is to help people feel better, and it is deeply satisfying work.

Soon after our return to Israel, I heard that there was an all-women's production company that was putting on the play *Annie*. When I played Annie as a kid, it was my dream to play Miss Hannigan when I grew up. That dream withered during high school; I was so disillusioned with the profession, and with life in general. But back in Israel, with my family and career, there came a moment where I just let all that disillusionment dissipate. I love to act, and I am really good at it! I was in a new place in my life, in so many ways. I wasn't a totally different person, but I was an evolved and healed version of myself. I was able to integrate the things I loved about my childhood, my love of performing, and my new family and lifestyle. I wanted to say "Yes!" to life. I tried out for the part of Miss Hannigan and I got it.

It was so enjoyable and gratifying that after *Annie* I went on to perform in the *Wizard of Oz*. I incorporated tap dance into the shows, and then I began teaching tap dance privately. The performance scene in Israel just landed in my lap. It didn't initially hit me what these types of performances meant for women and girls, and why they are so important. But then mothers would come up to me after a show and tell me how much it meant to them and their daughters. They told me how little entertainment there was for religious girls, by religious women. These were women who could be role models for them and impart Jewish values and content. This spawned a second career. In 2009, Rebbetzin Tap was born.

With my husband's help, we went on to offer courses in tap dance and acting, as well as produce three musical DVDs geared to Jewish girls. I've given concerts at schools in the US, UK, and Israel. This branched into speaking to groups of high school and seminary students about blending creativity and religious life. When it comes down to it, it's not about performing. It's about me being me, sharing my exuberance for life, and imparting the message to Jewish women and girls that expressing themselves creatively, in their own unique way, is a vital part of life.

After moving to Israel and becoming religious, then starting my own family and becoming a chiropractor, this was the next stage of tending to childhood wounds. There was a hole in my life where my childhood love of singing and dancing once stood, and filling it has been immensely healing and gratifying.

TWISTED

But personally, my life was about to take another turn.

It was 2010, and one day I had a terrible blinding pain in my abdomen, which passed an hour or two later. I thought I had a stomach bug and went along with my business. It happened again a month later, the morning of a concert that I was supposed to be giving here in Israel. I called the organizer and told her that I wasn't sure if I was going to make it, spent the morning throwing up, and then eventually felt well enough to put my wig on and perform in the concert.

A couple of months later, it was *Erev Tisha B'Av*, and everyone in the house was getting ready for the fast. They were getting dressed and brushing their teeth, and all of a sudden, I couldn't talk. I felt like I was in zombie mode. I lay in the bathtub, applied hot water to my stomach, and wondered if I was dying. The hours kept passing with the pain not being relieved as it had before, and I realized I needed to go to the doctor.

The next morning, *Tisha B'Av*, the doctor suggested that I had a twisted ovary and they immediately did an ultrasound and sent me to the hospital. I went into emergency surgery right away.

Before they put me under, they made me sign a form that said that I would allow them to take my ovaries out if need be, and at thirty-seven years old, I was hysterical. I already had four sons, but I wanted to have more children and it was all happening so fast. I was freaking out while being whisked away. I was afraid I was going to die.

When I woke up from the anesthesia, the pain was gone. I was alive and they hadn't removed my ovaries. I was so happy that it was over. With time, I healed and I didn't feel traumatized while healing from the experience. It felt like God was good. I had experienced pain, and He fixed me. And now I could go on with my life.

Yet, there was a lingering feeling that there was something not 100 percent right with my body.

Soon enough, I had my first miscarriage.

BROKEN

I was teaching tap one day and I was around two months pregnant. I knew I was expecting but it was still early.

Before class, I got up to go to the bathroom and the fetus just fell out of me. That loss didn't crush me, because I knew that people had miscarriages, and it was early on in the pregnancy. I just told myself, "Okay, I guess you are not going to have this baby."

The next time around, it took longer to get pregnant, but I did. After four months, I was starting to show, and I told people that I wouldn't be teaching tap that semester.

I already knew that I was having a boy. I knew I might never have a girl, but I was comforted because for the first time, there were men who had died in our family and I wanted to name after them. I was consoled by reminding myself that we had a name all picked out.

One day, I was lying in bed and my water broke. All my births began with my water breaking and I thought to myself, "I'm going to lose this baby." We called the ambulance and as they loaded me into it, they assured me that I was going to be okay. I told them, "It's not okay. I'm losing this baby." They said, "Well, you don't know that for sure." I said, "Yes, I do. My water broke. This is it."

I felt that my first, early miscarriage was prep for this loss.

They confirmed at the hospital that the baby had no heartbeat. I then waited to give birth. I was shaking and shaking and shaking and the nurse threw water all over me and shook me out of my trance. The baby came out of me in the bathroom; the nurse cut the cord and I never saw that baby at all.

When I got home, I sunk into depression. I didn't know what depression was, and when I awoke in the morning, for the first time in my life, I felt like I could not get out of bed. Time went on and I told myself, "Okay, Kerry, you are going to mourn for six weeks, you are going to visit your mother, and then you are going to move on." I went to Florida and my mom took care of me. She made me food, we went to the movies – she nurtured me. And then the time had passed and I went home and resolved to be okay.

I started spinning, jogging, and doing different forms of exercise and I told myself that I was strong and I was healthy and that I would be okay. But really, I felt broken – body and soul.

THE CONTINUUM OF MOTHERS

I felt like something was physically wrong with me, between the twisted ovary and two miscarriages. I still wanted more children, but I felt that my body had changed, my fertility had changed, and I mourned for those things.

My husband and I decided that it was more important for me to stay healthy. I try to put away that feeling of "What could have been?" I didn't feel healthy physically and I had to make the decision that this stage had to come to a close.

I knew my fertile time was over. It was a huge loss. I never had a daughter. I never had the opportunity to name for the men in my family who had recently passed away. I lost the image of the large family I wanted.

I practiced a lot of gratitude because living in gratitude is healing. I appreciated that Hashem gave me the sons I do have. I decided that these children that I have are enough. My boys are enough. I don't need more to be happy.

I was in the hospital three times in a year and a half, and in my mind, I thought that something was wrong with my body. I had accepted that my fertility was over, but I had to remind myself that I was strong and healthy.

I got it in my mind that this three-kilometer loop in my neighborhood was the amount that a healthy person could jog. I started running, even though I wasn't in good enough shape yet to do it. I kept going, telling myself through every breath, "You are strong and healthy, you can do this, you are going to enter your forties, and you are doing this." I would secretly tell myself that I was training for a marathon.

Time pushed on, and when my mother had back surgery, I went to Florida to help her.

I am so connected to my mother. We take care of each other and I believe the idea that my life and my mother's life are on a continuum. I believe I am living the continuation of her life, and she is so proud of me for living with opportunities she never had.

It was devastating to me when, after the surgery, she was in agony and screaming in pain, even though it was considered a successful surgery.

A week after surgery she was in rehab, and she developed a blood clot. She said she wasn't feeling well and she had her blood drawn. I left for *Shabbos* dinner and when I returned there was an ambulance outside the facility. It was my mom being taken to the hospital. Her numbers were so low, and on the way to the hospital, she said, "There is something wrong with me," and I told her, "No, you are going to be fine." She responded, "Kerry, I can't feel my legs anymore." The feeling in her legs never came back.

CAREGIVER

My mother thought she would be able to take care of herself in Florida. We had a helper, but it wasn't enough. She was not okay there by herself. We made plans for her to come live with me in Israel.

The first three months we had no help, so my husband and I were in charge of everything for her care. Every three hours she has to be moved from one side to the other. Someone needs to take care of her sanitation needs. We have to feed her, make food for her, and even change the TV channel. She is paralyzed from the waist down. We needed to redo our basement and make sure we had everything she needed, like a bed, lift, and shower chair. It was a huge undertaking.

Now we have a helper, but it's still a tremendous amount of work. I am not the most patient person. But she is counting on me to make her life good. I feel like I make it good. If I invested more energy and time it would be better. But I invest as much as I can and that is how I live with myself.

I used to have a wall of guilt. But now I try and contain it, because she would be happy if I spent all day, every day with her. And I can never give her as much as she would want. When you are the number one joy in someone else's life, and they can't have a full life of their own, you can never give enough. But if she gets all of me, I lose the life I have made for myself.

My mother also gets so much joy out of me having a fabulous life. She enjoys everything I became: doctor, performer, friend. She loves it. It makes her happy to see that I can do things that she couldn't. She is proud of me and wants me to live my life, and be with her a lot too. I try to balance it all.

Shortly after my mom got sick, my dad had heart surgery, and then dialysis, and then a stroke. After the stroke, he stopped talking. All of these events happened to my parents within the span of a year and a half. Then I turned forty, and I began to understand the full measure of what was behind me and what was ahead of me. It made me reckon with what I wanted to do with my life.

I think there is a deep psychological connection between our psyches and what happens to our parents biologically. Mine were experiencing paralysis, stroke, diabetes, heart disease, and more, and it felt like it was a part of my genetic makeup too. I started wondering if the ages they got sick would be the ages that I would get sick. Would what happened to them one day happen to me? I was afraid that it would be my destiny, too.

Part of me was already there because I felt so physically broken. I was trying to pick myself up, but engaging with the reality of all the illness that was present in my life made me feel so sad and heavy.

THE RUNNING RELEASE

I used to see the *frum* women jogging in my neighborhood, and I would say to myself, "I don't want to feel the way I feel inside. I want to feel the way they feel when they are moving."

It was a commitment that I made to start running. When I run, it doesn't even matter how I feel when I start. It was a health imperative. I just couldn't be the person that I was. I didn't want to be my parents. I felt sluggish. I felt nothing. I didn't feel good. But I didn't care. I wanted to be a person who runs.

I self-identified as strong and determined. I was going to do it. And I would set new goals for myself till I was doing long-distance running. I would start, and feel sluggish, and motivate myself. And after an hour, I was just done.

I wouldn't even see it coming – I would have the deepest cry, a full-body emptiness. Because just then my physical being would match my emotional being. I was depleted of energy, finished, and couldn't take any more. I would cry and cry, about my mother, my father, my miscarriages, my body not working, life being so hard, and everything I've had to deal with. I would cry about all the sadness and challenges in the world, and how it was too heavy for me to hold.

On top of that hill, I would rally, and tell myself that I could do this. Slowly I would keep going, and the adrenaline would kick back in and an energy wave would come. Then I would feel good. My body was moving well. I was strong. Life was good. At the end I would be so exhausted, but it didn't even matter. I had proven that I was strong and determined. I had proven that I was healthy and that I would be okay.

Sometimes I lie in bed exhausted at the end of the day, and I let my body sink into the mattress. I begin my mantras of relaxation, trying to calm my body to sleep. My brain immediately goes to my legs and imagines them being paralyzed.

So I run because I can. I run because my mother can't. I train for marathons because I am strong and healthy and my mother is paralyzed. I have to remind myself that my legs work, and I am not my mother. I remind myself that she wants me to be healthy and that my destiny can be different.

CHOOSING JOY

I think a lot of people think that if you choose to live joyfully, that somehow invalidates or belittles your pain. I spent such a huge percentage of my life in the midst of trauma, and if I didn't choose joy, I would have been miserable half my life. For me, I'm naturally a joyous person with a bubbly personality. I'm always inclined to be joyful; it is who I am at my core.

I compartmentalize. I take the pain and sometimes I put it on the shelf. Then I grab what I call "*simcha* moments" – if I come across a moment of joy, I immerse myself in it.

In those moments I can put aside what happened to my mother and what happened to me, and I can get lost in the happiness I enhance for myself. I spend a lot of time developing my joy.

I am Rebbetzin Tap. I am a cheerful children's per-former, always encouraging both kids and adults to find their joyful creative spaces. I started a Facebook group called *Kol Isha*, where women post videos of themselves performing for other women to enjoy. I don't see a conflict between performing as a happy playful character, and having challenges in your life.

I feel like I am just choosing life, and allowing myself to be happy and ful-filled doesn't belittle my trauma or struggles. Making that choice allows me to heal myself. It doesn't help my parents, or anyone struggling, if I only feel sad. It might make me feel like I was honoring that person or loss by staying in a sad place. But it doesn't truly help them, and I would rather choose action.

In addition to being a chiropractor, I am a certified life coach, and all day long I speak to women about their health issues and emotional pain. I see that often, we get comfortable with certain emotions and ascribe meaning to them.

I would always come back to feeling lonely or not included. It was a safe space that was predictable, and I used to return there often. Then I would stop and realize that feeling didn't serve me. I did not live a lonely life, as my life is very full. I had to ask myself: Is that feeling true? Does it help anybody? Does it serve me? Do I need that feeling in my life? Maybe I could choose to feel a similar emotion like thoughtfulness, or caring, which would serve every-one much more than victimhood. Pity doesn't serve anyone, including me.

Just like my mom wants me to be happy, I also think Hashem wants me to feel happiness. I have decided that I too want that for myself.

In the end, my core is joy. I think my mission in this world is to bring others joy, too. I want to be a role model in that way. I want to show people that what joy means is the commitment to being loving every day, and doing *chesed* for others. It means that when there is anything that I can find that can make me laugh or bring me to a bubbly place, I grab it right then.

I am going to make the most of the best moments, even through pain.

Pain is so easy to find. It lies right at the surface of our consciousness. Sometimes we have to make joy for ourselves. And when we find it, we must foster it and develop it like a muscle. Because choosing that kind of life is a much better way to live.

REFLECTIONS

Questions to Consider
- What brings you joy?
- Do you practice creating joyful moments?

Words to Remember

> "I feel like I am just choosing life, and it doesn't belittle my trauma or struggles by allowing myself to be happy and fulfilled. Making that choice allows me to heal myself."

Group Discussion

What role does self-actualization play in your life?
What was a moment that you decided to choose to feel joy even through pain?

☙

Take a moment for yourself. What do you need right now?
Close your eyes and be in your own body.
Here is a guided visualization to come back to yourself:

Guided Visualisation

Close your eyes. Move your attention to each part of your body. Pay attention to the spaces that feel strong. Notice the places in your body that feel like they need support. Take a deep breath and breathe life affirming energy into those places. When you feel centered and ready, open your eyes.

Aviva's Story

Finding My Balance

Rehavia, Jerusalem

BURST

At my bat mitzva party, I remember feeling so happy I thought I was going to burst with joy. When I look back, I think it was more than an average person could feel. I have had many occasions like that. I was a hyper child with ADHD, so on average, I think I always felt a little out of control.

We lived in Antwerp, Belgium when I was growing up and I moved to Rehavia in Jerusalem as a teenager. I was a very unhappy teenager, and I felt like no one understood me. Around the age of fourteen or fifteen, I started cutting myself and smoking, and I developed anorexia and bulimia. I was thinking of ending my life. I was doing things that were pushing me toward the end. I was desperate for love and to feel something. I was cutting to feel physical pain that mirrored the pain I was feeling inside. I hated myself; I was uncomfortable in my own skin, I hated school, and I thought I had no friends. I felt like I was nothing.

I wasn't a good student and when you are a kid, that can really take a toll on your self-esteem. I hated school because I felt like I didn't have anything going for me. I wasn't talented. I was the opposite of extraordinary. I just wanted to escape all those feelings. Around that time, I began to have what I called "mini-episodes," where I would not be myself for a few hours. I would act strangely and then when I would wake up in the morning, I would be back to myself.

I was having a difficult time, so my parents decided to take me on a beautiful trip to Las Vegas. We stayed at The Venetian, saw concerts, and had fun. One night, we had a fight in the car and I got out of the car and ran away. I went to a random hotel that I saw. I was under twenty-one and I was wild, running around the hotel. The guards saw that I was a minor and disturbing the hotel, and they caught and detained me. My parents came to get me and took me home. It took me a few days to get back to myself. I was so "off" and they couldn't place what it was. Something was not right.

SELFISH

When I was seventeen, I went to a school for kids who were struggling. I was warned that if I didn't stop doing drugs, they were going to kick me out. I think I intentionally overdosed on the anti-depressants I was taking. Anyway, I felt that I was finished with school. I became so depressed. My parents decided that the medication I was taking to keep my behavior under control was doing more harm than good. I was continually taking many more pills than I should have. I would then tell an adult, get rushed to the hospital, and have my stomach pumped. This happened multiple times. Every time, it broke my parents' hearts.

At one point, I had taken some pills from the house that I thought were sleeping pills and gobbled up twenty or thirty of them. I lay down on my parents' bed waiting to die. After a while, I checked the bottle and called someone and realized they were natural supplements. Thankfully, all I got was a stomachache. That was the last time that I attempted to end my life.

Knowing that I had to get my problem with pills under control, my parents sent me to a rehab center for teenagers. When I met the other teenagers in the program, I was blown away by how difficult their lives were. They had parents who didn't care about them; they were terribly neglected and abused. It made me realize how much I had at home. I had parents who loved me and would do anything to care for me. I had everything I could ever want at home. I felt so guilty about what I had put them through. All the acting out and bids for attention were just selfish in my mind. I had only been thinking about myself. If I had been thinking about the bigger picture, I could have seen how hard it was for my family. I could have seen what I had been putting them through. I never went down that path again. I learned my lesson and I was able to turn my life around.

OFF THE CHARTS

Six months later, I went to a seminary that was recommended to me by my best friend. I felt like I was living a totally new life. I totally "flipped out." I became very religious and was living on a spiritual high. This new high filled me up with the answers I was searching for. It filled me till I wanted to burst. It filled me till I could no longer control the joy it made me feel.

I went to be a counselor and do *kiruv* in a school in Pinsk, Belarus. This was two years after I had been taken off all my meds, besides one for my ADHD. That particular treatment staves off your appetite, so I found that while I was working, I was hardly eating. I lost ten kilos in a month. The food there was disgusting and I was not hungry. But I also was not sleeping and I was hyper all the time. I was still engaged in my ever-increasing spiritual high. I was learning Russian and my brain was always busy. Eventually, toward the end, I lost control.

It's a bit hard to remember. That time feels blurry to me. On the way back home to Israel, I was starving on the flight. They gave me some kosher food and when I was finished, I asked for more. And then more. I was binge eating to fill the void of basically having not eaten in a month. When I got home, I couldn't stop eating. When my family saw me, they could tell by

the way that I was behaving that something was off. I wasn't myself. But they couldn't pinpoint what was going on.

Shortly after my arrival, my parents and I went to a wedding of someone we knew in Eilat. I was very wired, hyper, and energetic. My mom got me a massage, thinking that I just needed to relax. It was a horrible experience. I was so wired that I didn't want to be touched. Every time the masseuse touched me, I got more and more irritated. I was in sensory overload. The sensations, the smells – it was just too much. When I left the massage, I was wandering around the hotel and acting out of control. I was staying in a room with the bride's friends and all I remember is that the way that I was acting really scared them. I was not okay. I was acting in a way that I call "off the charts."

OUT OF CONTROL

There was a guy who I met in Pinsk who I had decided I was in love with. At the wedding, I was talking to his friends, trying to convince them that we were meant to be. I told them that I thought he was the *mashiaḥ*. I was feeling obsessive.

On the last night, I snuck into the bride's parents' room. I pretended to take a shower. In my mind, I did this because I wanted the bride's parents to be friends with my parents. But that made no sense. They were obviously already friends, as we had been invited to this wedding. When my parents tried to take me away, I got violent. I refused to leave. They knew that I needed treatment and they were trying to take me home to Jerusalem. Thank God, no one was hurt and they were able to get me safely to the car. All the way home, I was out of control. My mind was spinning. I felt like Neo in *The Matrix*. I felt like the world revolved around me, as if I was "the chosen one."

My parents dropped me off at my sister's house because she was supposed to watch me for the night before they could get me help. After everyone went to sleep, I decided that if I made a great, big noise, *mashiaḥ* would come. I took a huge mirror and smashed it into a million pieces out on the balcony. After that, I discovered a laptop in my sister's living room that had a video game on it. When the video game popped open, it said in big letters, "GO. RUN. NOW." I bolted out of the house and ran.

THE AFTERMATH

I was on the run. I asked to borrow someone's phone and then I stole it. I bumped into a man I swore was Eliyahu HaNavi and I jumped into a cab that seemingly came out of nowhere and decided that the cab driver was Eliyahu HaNavi, because he found me while I was wandering the streets of Jerusalem. I had him take me to the Old City to see my parents' rabbi. Instead of paying the cab driver I just gave him the stranger's phone. I figured since he was Eliyahu HaNavi, he didn't need any money. I laughed when he asked to be paid because it seemed so ridiculous to me at the time. Why would a prophet need money?

My father came and picked me up to bring me to my psychiatrist. My mind was playing endless tricks on me. I was saying the most random, upsetting things. I escaped the taxi but my father was able to catch me. When he brought me to the doctor, the doctor told me, "You are in the middle of a manic episode." I didn't believe him. My father was able to get our rabbi to help me, to convince me to take the medication they gave me to calm down. I took the pill they gave me. I do not remember what came next.

I slept for twenty-four hours. The following two weeks were just on-and-off sleeping, eating in a daze, and getting back into bed at home. I felt like a zombie for a long time. I had come off my high and now I was so low. I got to a point that felt like everything I wanted, Hashem didn't want for me.

I was given a bipolar diagnosis. It was so difficult for me to accept the diagnosis. It was soul-crushing because it felt so taboo. It was 2008 and no one around me was talking about mental health. People thought that a person who had a diagnosis of bipolar disorder couldn't live a normal life because it felt like no one would ever come near me. But I learned through therapy, and by following the protocol that my doctors set for me, that if I took care of myself I could be okay. If I ate, slept, took my medication, and engaged in self-care, I could be in better control of my mental health. I went to do the work and learned how to take care of myself. It was hard, but I made a lot of progress. I learned about what it meant to be diagnosed with bipolar and what it would take to be healthy and stable.

A year and a half after my episode, my sister encouraged me to take a cooking class. I can never thank her enough for that. We took it together and I was lifted out of the fog of anger and pain that I felt in the period after my episode. It re-engaged me in feeling passionate about life.

WHY BE WITH ME?

When I was twenty-one years old and had been stable for a long time, I decided that I wanted to get married. A family friend connected us with a *shadkhan* for people with physical and mental health issues. This *shadkhan* had heard of a guy who she thought would be a good match for me, but she was nervous to suggest him. She was nervous because he had sleep apnea. When we heard that the reason why she was hesitant to suggest him was because of his sleep apnea, we thought that it was ridiculous. Who cared about sleep apnea? It did not seem like a serious illness to us.

We went on a first date. I was promised that even though I knew what he had, he didn't know about my bipolar diagnosis yet. During the date, right away, I felt a spark. I didn't want the date to end. He asked me for my number when it was over and it felt like we had made an amazing connection. The second date was awful. He casually mentioned something that made me understand that he knew I had a bipolar diagnosis. I was shocked and then

furious. I shut down. I came home and was so upset. All I kept thinking was, "Why would someone who knows I am bipolar want to be with me?" Now when I look back on that, it makes me so sad. Why shouldn't someone want to be with me? Being bipolar doesn't define me. I am so much more than the diagnosis.

We continued to date. When our relationship progressed, I asked my soon-to-be future husband, "Why would you want to marry me?" He told me, "You take care of yourself, you take your medication, and you follow your treatment protocols. Your life is stable. You are wonderful, sweet, funny, caring, and you make me happy. Why shouldn't I want to be with you?"

We were married for more than seven years and we had two children. I haven't had an episode since.

ACCEPT THE TRUTH

This past *Pesaḥ* we were in Austria with the extended family.

One morning at eight a.m., I woke up to go to the bathroom. While I was in the bathroom, I heard a loud thud and I thought my daughter had fallen off the bed. I ran back into the room and saw my husband on the floor. He wouldn't get up. I called my brother-in-law who is an EMT. When they couldn't revive him, my husband was choppered to the nearest hospital.

When I got to the hospital the doctors told me that there was a 1 percent chance of his survival. I couldn't accept it. I couldn't believe it. I was in shock. To keep me going, everyone told me I had to believe that maybe he could wake up. Maybe there could be a miracle. I gathered my strength and committed to believing that he would wake up and that he could be okay. I went to sleep for the night.

The next morning, I was sitting on the balcony drinking water, waiting to go to the hospital to see my husband. My mother came and told me that he was gone. He had died from his severe sleep apnea. I didn't believe her. It took me a long time to accept the truth. I recall with bitterness how I scoffed at the idea of his condition being something serious. It took him from me.

The first time I really began to understand was my first *Shabbat* after it was all over. It was Friday night and the impact of the fact that I was suddenly all alone hit me like a ton of bricks. I was overwhelmed with anger, fuming at my husband for leaving me alone with the kids. I wondered whether there was something we could have done to prevent this. I was overwhelmed by the idea of raising our kids without him.

Now I am a single mom. The challenge of caring for my kids alone while grieving for my husband is difficult to put into words. It is such a lonely existence.

Practically everything becomes more complicated now. I now carry the job of two people, by myself. I can only be in so many places at one time before everything gets tangled up in a mess. The other day my son developed a high fever and because I had no other recourse, I called Hatzalah (Jewish emergency medical services). I don't have a spouse who can run out to the pharmacy, or help me bring our son to Terem, or stay behind to watch our daughter. The stress of trying to be in all places at all times makes my head spin.

The nighttime is the hardest with the utter loneliness of sleeping alone in an empty bed. I miss the feeling of safety and contentment that came with being married. I miss the knowledge that no matter what, there will be someone next to you to share the burden of life, to be there for you when you need help and love you as you experience the world together.

He was my best friend. I miss him more than I can explain and I wish that I could wake up from this whole nightmare and have it just be a bad dream. What I would give for the chance to do it all again! Unfortunately, for myself and my children, this is our new reality from which we cannot wake up. For now, I take comfort in my family and friends who are there for us. We lean on those who love us and are grateful for the amazing support we have received.

My daughter still cries for her father. She asks me, "When will *mashiah* come?" hoping that he will return when we all reach our ultimate redemption. In response, I assure her, "Soon. Very soon, my love. Keep believing and you will see him again one day."

Love conquered all the obstacles that we faced. Now, even through the shock, I have been stable and getting all the therapeutic and familial support that I need. At the end of the day, I am getting through life because of my will to live and my *simhat hahayim*. I love living and I love the life that Hashem has given me. I know that I have so much to live for – my children, my family, and my friends. I am living for myself, and for all the future potential that is inside of me.

My life took a turn I did not expect. But I am so proud of the fact that I am making it work. I am caring for my kids and investing in myself. Looking back on my coping mechanisms from my youth, I see how far I have come. Every day, I choose to step one step in front of the other and keep living with joy and laughter. I am happy to be me, everything that I have been and everything that I am. I love traveling and enjoying life. Humor is medicine to me. I live past all the pain through the medium of joy.

REFLECTIONS

Questions to Consider
- Have you ever found a way to live with joy even through pain?
- What are the steps you take to support your own mental health?

Words to Remember
> "I live past all the pain through the medium of joy."

Group Discussion
Is mental illness stigmatized in your community?
What steps need to be taken to provide support and acceptance for individuals and families who are struggling?

✍

Take a moment for yourself. What do you need right now?
Close your eyes and be in your own body.
Here is a grounding exercise to come back to yourself:

Grounding Exercise
Think of a time when you experienced *simḥat ḥayim,* joyful living. Notice the images that come to mind. Explore the details – what you hear, smell, and touch in that moment. Who is there with you? What about that time brought you joy?

My Family, My Identity, My Country

Ofra, Shomron

AFRO-LATINA

My identity is complex and layered, and my cultural history, home life, community, and choices are multifaceted.

My family has a long and storied past. My grandmother was born in the United States in the South and converted to Orthodox Judaism at the end of the 1800s. My grandfather was an Egyptian Jew whose family we believe originally came from Ethiopia. Together they had eight children; my father is one of the youngest. He was born in the New York area in the 1930s and when he was a small child his parents got divorced. He was living with his father who stayed up North when his mother came and kidnapped him and his siblings and brought them to live with her down in Tennessee. Tennessee in the 1940s was highly segregated and they worked as indentured servants. Today, my father is in his eighties. His experience of being a black man in America is vitally foundational for us.

When my father was eighteen, he ran away from home and started a new life back in New York. His time growing up in the South scarred him and shaped him for the rest of his life. He is a man to be reckoned with, someone who deeply identifies with and is passionate about the experience of black people in America. He felt an obligation to make sure that I was deeply connected to the black side of who I am through history and community.

My mother used to speak Spanish to me at home. She was born and raised in Panama; her mother's family were Jews who left Spain after the Inquisition and her father's side were Jews who came from India. We are Sephardic from all sides.

My parents met in Panama. My mom was working as a bookkeeper at the only kosher restaurant in the city. My father learned to speak fluent Hebrew from his father and so he was chatting with the Israeli owner of the store. The man got excited and mentioned, "I have a girl for you!" He then introduced my mom. My parents corresponded for a while. At the time, my father spoke no Spanish and my mom knew just a few words in English. When they spoke on the phone, they would have translators on standby. But they both learned to communicate in the other's language and they decided to get married. My father was in his forties and was a member of the Orthodox community in Hollywood, Florida. My mother was in her twenties and moved to Florida to marry him.

My mother grew up unaffiliated with Judaism because there was a significant amount of anti-Semitism in the village where she was raised. Because they couldn't find her parents' *ketuba* and because she had so little Jewish education (she later found out much more about her family's genealogy), the rabbis made her do a *giyur safek*, a conversion just in case.

The place where I was raised did not reflect my cultural history. I was born an Orthodox Jew in a typical Modern Orthodox community in America. People I meet now often wonder, "Where does she come from?" or "How

did she become Jewish?" They wonder because of the color of my skin. But I grew up like everyone else around me. I received the same education, went to the same *shuls*, and have relatively the same upbringing. My family history is how I look and where I come from, but my upbringing also plays a powerful role in who I am.

GROWING UP DIFFERENT

I grew up in Hollywood, Florida and for most of my childhood, we were the only family of color in my entire community. My ethnicity has always been a part of me, whether I have noticed it or not. I believe that children are sponges – they soak up what is offered to them. I didn't notice that I was different until it was pointed out to me.

When I was in kindergarten, I was regularly pulled out of class for a reading class for gifted children. A little girl who was a good friend of mine innocently asked the teacher one day, "Why is Yaffy being pulled out of class for gifted? Everyone knows that black people can't read." When I came home and told my parents what she had said, they were enraged. That was my first introduction to racism and the concept that I was different than all of the other Jewish kids in my class.

I remember first noticing that my hair was different than all the other little girls. I had thicker, curly hair. My mom, who is Latina, happens to have very fine silky hair; she really struggled with knowing how to do my hair. It caused a lot of conflict. I was always jealous of my friends who had silky straight hair because no matter what they did to their hair, it would just dry, be fine, and they could move on with their day. My hair was always an ordeal, and there was no one in my life who was equipped to know how to do it well, teach me to do it well, and to make me feel good about it.

I identify as an Afro-Latina woman. Being biracial, I tend to identify more with my Latina heritage, but it is my blackness that takes up a lot of space in my life and really affects the way people see me and what I see in myself. Growing up in South Florida, there were tons of people who were black and Latino. Being biracial and religious, I find that my blackness is often focused on. People never questioned how I could be Latina and Jewish. There was no conflict there. But people often questioned how I could be black and Jewish.

The deep pain of my father's experience with racism and the pride that he feels in the strength of his heritage were things that he worked hard to impart to me. Growing up in South Florida, people assumed that you spoke Spanish because there is a very significant Latino population there.

It was comfortable for me to be Latina and I was free to speak my mother tongue.

Growing up, I never felt like I had to define myself or prove myself. I was born *frum*, in the community where I was raised, and I felt validated and included. It was only when I traveled to other communities that I felt like my existence needed to be explained. But there was never a question of who I was in my town. All the racist experiences that I have ever experienced in my life were always outside my home community.

As I got older, I came to realize that most of the people I grew up with barely acknowledged my blackness. They saw me as the same as them – white Ashkenazic Jews. They rarely saw me as a person of color. I choose to believe that it came from a place of inclusion, as I am a person they have known their entire lives. But I wonder if someone else of color, who was new to them, would get the same reception. Because I was not being raised in an African American or Latino milieu, it was what I shared with my peers and fellow community members – a set of values, religious observance, Jewish education, and a general attitude toward life – that became paramount in my identity.

ALIYA

In my community, it was expected that I would go to Israel for a year to study Torah. Initially I wasn't sold on the idea for a multitude of reasons. It is expensive, I wanted to study medicine which is a long process, and since I grew up *frum*, I didn't think I needed any help in that area. Ultimately, I got assistance and encouragement from many incredible people in my life, and I decided to come to Israel for my year in seminary after high school. Then I decided to stay, and I made *aliya*.

To this day, my friends from Florida and I laugh that I ended up moving to Israel. The community I grew up in is Zionistic so I was raised to love and support Israel. Personally, though, I never wanted to live here. But I had a phenomenal year at my seminary and we lived and learned with Israelis in my program. The traveling and the experiences that I had during that year opened me up to realize that this country was so much richer in meaning than I could have ever understood from my vantage point in the States.

For me, living in Israel is experiencing life on a deeper level. While no place is perfect, there is so much beauty and wonder here that is unique to this space. I fell in love with this land, much to everyone's surprise, and decided that this is where I want my future to be.

INTERRACIAL

I was lucky enough during my time in Israel to cross paths with the amazing guy who one day would become my husband.

I grew up with almost no friends who were people of color like me, and so I always assumed that the likelihood of my husband being "like me" in an ethnic sense was slim. While this posed no problem for me, part of me always wondered: At the end of the day, would someone who was not like me be interested in being with me?

Nadav and I met and we started our relationship half-way through our time in seminary and yeshiva. He comes from a multicultural background as well; his father is from Indiana and his mother is French-Algerian. He was born and raised here in Israel. It wasn't until months into our relationship that it dawned on him. One day he turned to me and said, "Yaffy, we're an interracial couple!" I laughed, because it took so long for this to occur to him. For me, this was something that had been extremely obvious since the first time I ever sat with him in public.

As we dated longer, Nadav also started to see what made me hyper-aware when we walked around together. More than half the time we were out in public, people would stare. They did double-takes and sometimes even stopped us to inquire about who I am and where I come from. For me, it was more

annoying and frustrating than upsetting. It was the first time that I was ever properly living outside my childhood community. While Israel is a melting pot, people were often confused by my skin color, mixed features, and fluent English. Many assumed at first glance that I was Ethiopian. Others thought I was Indian, Phillipino, Brazilian, French, and the list goes on. People get creative when they try to envision where I'm from.

For me, living in Israel as a multiracial woman doesn't feel any different than it did in America. There may be more Jews of color commonly walking the streets here than one will typically see in a *frum* community in America. Today, I am used to being stopped by total strangers. Thankfully, it is happening less and less. I'm hoping that it is because the population of Israel is becoming more multicultural, and there is such diversity in Jewish people who are returning home.

DRAFTED

From the first day that we met, Nadav was already talking to me about going into the army. The ongoing conversation we would have about the army became a major part of our relationship. He would say, "When I go into the army my goal is at least to become a *katzin,* an officer, if not more. We'll see what happens." From the beginning, I had an idea of what that would mean for us.

After two years in post-high-school yeshiva, Nadav was drafted into the IDF. The yeshiva he attended is known for military excellence. It was a perfect match for Nadav because he shares that mindset and he always wanted to be drafted to an elite unit. He was invited to try out for *Givati*'s special forces unit and he was accepted to their highest level of combat service. We were both really happy about that, but what it meant was that his training was going to be very grueling and twice as long.

We dated for three years and most of that time, he was in the beginning of his army service. On a surface level, I didn't struggle. But we never really had time together. His being in a combat unit meant that we didn't have the opportunity to speak for days on end. At one point in his training, I didn't hear from him for almost three weeks. Being in special forces also meant he wasn't able to come home, except for *Shabbat,* and even that was not always a given. For most of our relationship, we would see each other at best for four weekends out of the month. In the worst case scenarios, we would see each other only once during the entire month. If we were lucky and he was released home for *Shabbat*, we would have to switch between his parents' houses. But most of our time was spent with other people and we rarely got a moment together without family or friends. Even when he would get home once we were married and we had a *Shabbat* alone, he would be so exhausted that what he really needed was sleep.

For a lot of that time, people pitied me. My American friends could not understand why I was dating someone who was gone all the time. They could not relate to understanding the importance of army service or to the fact that I saw my boyfriend once or twice a month, for a few hours at a time. They could not understand how we were able to have a relationship. My Israeli friends thought I was crazy for being an *olah*, but they understood the sacrifice for those of us who are left alone while our significant others are in the army. They felt bad for me, a young person with no family in Israel, and Nadav away. I was alone.

When we got married, Nadav was already a commander in the army and had been accepted into officers training. After our wedding, we had ten days when he was off from work and we had time together. But when he returned to the army, he was gone for a long time. We struggled with that continued pattern as we began married life.

I don't feel sorry for myself. I came here at eighteen years old, and I made *aliya* at nineteen. I had no concerns or responsibilities for anyone but myself.

I consider myself fortunate; I was able to move to this country for which so many have died. *Aliya* was such a simple process. I was so moved by that fact, and I knew that I should do what I could to give back, in gratitude.

I often think that if I had been born at an earlier time in history, I most likely would have had a really difficult life. Being born in America, I would have been a slave in the South like my ancestors. My whole life would have been a struggle. Even if I was born just fifty years earlier, I would have been fighting against segregation and lynching, and for my own civil rights. I think about all my family members who lost or came close to losing their lives (my father included) for freedom for black people in America. I think about all the people who laid down their lives and made sacrifices there, so that a person like me could be free.

Now living in Israel, I feel the same way. Moving here, thank God, was so easy. I just filled out a bunch of forms and I was ready to receive citizenship and the rights to be a Jew in my homeland. This country's history is just as much a part of me as my ethnic history. Growing up learning Israeli history, you know that the blood of thousands of Jews is spilled all over this country, so that we can live here and have a sovereign state. That didn't happen by accident; it happened through sacrifice. I need to do my part.

WHO WILL?

Most people who grow up here contribute to society in one way or another. When I decided to move here it seemed obvious to me that I, too, would do my part. I chose to do *sheirut leumi*, national service.

When my husband's mandatory three years of army service was ending, he was invited to participate in officers training. This meant that he would be signing on for more time in the army so he could extend his service. We had to consider what it meant for us as a couple. If he didn't sign on for more, he would have been out of the army a few months after we got married. We deliberated for a short period, but ultimately decided that we wanted him to go for his dream and that we could handle more separation for the sake of a bigger cause.

There were some practical benefits. We were living on a combat soldier's salary and since my husband isn't a *ḥayal boded,* a lone soldier, his salary was rather small. His original monthly salary in the army couldn't even cover our rent. Signing on to be an officer meant he would finally receive a proper salary that would give us some financial breathing room. We would have certain tax benefits and receive discounts in stores and restaurants all over the country. But at the end of the day, those things only sweetened the deal. They didn't make it easy, and they weren't a reason to support my husband in this. Ultimately, I felt like we could do this, that this was a moment when I could make a sacrifice for the country I love. Someone has to take on this responsibility; why shouldn't it be us? If we don't do it, who will?

The time of year that I feel most emotional and connected to all those in the IDF is on *Yom HaZikaron*. Nadav went into the army right after Operation Protective Edge, the big war in 2014. I remember the night that we met, he was with a whole group of his friends. He introduced me to them. We bumped into one of them again after the war, and his friend had lost half his unit in the fighting. That moment was a big eye-opener for me.

My first *Yom HaZikaron* in Israel, I didn't even know Nadav. I don't think you need to be an army wife to feel connected to the day. I was so emotional even then. But now, on *Yom HaZikaron* I feel a deep connection to every single one of those soldiers we are mourning. Now it feels as if every family mourning their losses is my family.

It is not that there are no other people who could do his job. But if every young married wife decided that she didn't want her husband serving because she wanted him home with her, and refused to let her spouse serve, that would be a problem. Not everyone needs to, or should. But for me, I knew that I could. If I could, then I should. Who am I to send someone else's brother, son, or husband off to war, while I refuse to send my own?

Now we have been together for almost six years and he has been in the army for four and a half years of that time. It has taken up a huge chunk of our relationship. I joke that our marriage is made up of three parties: me, Nadav, and the army. They have had just as many rights over him as I do.

ALONE

I don't know all the things Nadav has done in the army. I didn't spend my days wondering or thinking about whether he was safe. I would have been a walking mess if I constantly contemplated all the potential situations and dangers. I needed to be strong for myself and for him. I didn't let myself think about it because I knew that if he was in a dangerous situation, there would be nothing that I could do. Thankfully, war did not break out while he was on active duty.

I thought that I was dealing just fine with Nadav being away. But now I think that I was only fine on the surface. Marriage can be trying in general, but it is especially challenging when you never get to spend time together properly. Being an army wife, especially a combat army wife, isn't always a walk in the park. There are a lot of things that made life difficult, like the fact that he wasn't physically there to help me through the challenges of life. For example, once in the middle of the night I woke up severely sick and stayed that way for days with a high fever and virus that probably would have ended sooner if I had someone to help me take care of myself. He also wasn't there any time I required my partner to be present. The most difficult was not having him there at the end of a really rough day to be an emotional support. It was hard to miss him so much. But I was not crying myself to sleep every night. At the same time, maybe I wasn't spending time every day thinking about the negatives, but deep down I know I was struggling.

I do not have any biological family here in Israel. I have amazing friends, but we weren't living in the most accessible area for most of my friends. Emotionally, I often felt pretty alone. It was very isolating for me to be living a reality that most of my friends, family, and peers didn't understand. They couldn't genuinely relate to it.

Nadav will serve in *miluim* until he is forty-two or until we have six children, as is the rule for army reserves in Israel. We have been married almost three years. I look to the future and hope that we will have normal jobs that allow us to spend time together. I want to feel secure. I want to know that he is home, that he is here, and that he is staying. I want to feel secure in the knowledge that he won't be pulled away from me at any second. War could break out at any moment here in Israel. There is no certainty for me. If war begins, my husband is going. I pray that he will always come home.

IMAGE SHATTERED

In the last year of Nadav's service, we went to America for a family crisis. Thankfully, Nadav's commander was able to give him time off. The commander's own wife had been through a medical scare that year and he too had to take time off from the army. Our trip happened to fall out right before the *ḥagim*, and there were only seven or eight workdays in the month of September. That month was the longest amount of time that we had spent together consecutively in two years. All of a sudden, I saw what I was missing from our relationship.

Nadav and I never had the regular life of a married couple, not until a crisis brought us together. Now I felt for the first time what it was like to be married. It shattered the image of the life that I had been living. It was not enough anymore. Once I knew what it was like to be with my husband for thirty straight days, I couldn't go back. For the first time, I got what my friends were talking about, and why they felt that what I was doing was so crazy. My emotional life caught up to the image that made them feel sorry for me – the sad little army wife, eating alone and crying herself to sleep. I could not wait anymore for his service to end.

The day that Nadav was meant to get out of the army was July 18. On July 17, late at night, my father called to tell me that there had been a sudden death in the family. We had just moved all our things into a new apartment and our life was already a mess when we got that call. We bought tickets to fly back to the States again.

Our flight was the day that Nadav was supposed to be finished with the army. We had all these plans of how we were going to celebrate, and everything just went blank. Nadav was supposed to cut his *ḥoger*, army identification card. It's the very end of the discharge process that soldiers go through when they leave the army. It is meant to be done at the base. You take pictures and have a whole celebration. We did it on the dirty streets right outside our apartment. Nadav cut the card and I snapped two photos. Someone came to pick it up and bring it back to the base. That was it. He was discharged. It was over. Then we went to sit *shiva*. After more than four and a half years, the highly anticipated discharge of Nadav from the IDF wasn't anything like we had envisioned. It was almost ignored completely between all the things going on for us that summer.

SURROUNDED BY LOVE

One of my favorite Jewish quotes is, "This too shall pass." And so it did. The summer was full of heartache surrounding our loss, but we made it through, and stayed with my family in the States until the *chagim*. We came home for a month to sort out the mess that was left behind.

We had already planned our next adventure. We packed up and headed to the airport for our belated honeymoon and post-army trip that we had been planning for the last five years. We had slowly saved up for a big backpacking experience since we got married and our efforts paid off. We were privileged to spend several months traveling in Panama, to visit my mother's family, and all the way down to southern Argentina by bus, by car, or whatever else was the most cost-effective for young two backpackers.

We were about to reach the pinnacle of our trip. Before we reached the location we had been looking forward to the most, something drastically changed. We went to sleep Saturday night after finalizing details of how to get there and when we woke up the next morning, I felt the strangest compulsion to be back in Florida. I felt I needed to be there that very moment. I told Nadav we needed to leave right away. I couldn't explain why, but I just knew it.

Nadav understood that I was serious, it wasn't like me to make such rash and sudden conclusions. After going back and forth for a few hours, my incredibly understanding husband agreed to purchase tickets and start our way back. We made it to Florida early Friday morning and I immediately felt a deep relief that I had never experienced before.

We helped make Shabbat and settled in. All the while I was confused about what my intuition was warning me about. And then the answer came two weeks later.

My father had been battling cancer on and off again since I was ten years old. And occasionally he was hospitalized for treatments. I had been used to cancer being a part of our lives. Two weeks after we came back, my father was released home from the hospital just in time for his favorite holiday, *Pesaḥ*. We made two *Sedarim* surrounding him with love and singing, and the very next day, my father's *neshama* left this world.

We were shocked and heartbroken. Although I couldn't have known it at the time, Hashem led me back home just in time to spend the last days of my father's life with him. He was surrounded by my mother, Nadav, myself, and some of the people he loved most in this world.

After *shiva*, *shloshim*, and Shabbat, Nadav and I eventually had to return to Israel. We came back to finally build our lives and new home, together. We took the love and wisdom my father imparted to us and used that to guide us forward.

There have been painful, challenging, and many sweet moments that we have lived in the last few years. We can look back today and be thankful for all the things we have gone through as a couple and the beautiful place the journey has brought us. We have learned that life is unpredictable. We are looking forward to a continued life full of love.

REFLECTIONS

Questions to Consider
- What does it mean to you to sacrifice for something larger than yourself?
- How does your identity play a role in your life?

Words to Remember

> "This country's history is just as much a part of me as my ethnic history. Growing up learning Israeli history, you know that the blood of thousands of Jews is spilled all over this country, so that we can live here and have a sovereign state. That didn't happen by accident; it happened through sacrifice. I need to do my part."

Group Discussion

How does your family history affect who you are and the choices you have made in your life?

Take a moment for yourself. What do you need right now?
Close your eyes and be in your own body.
Here is a gratitude exercise to come back to yourself:

Gratitude Exercise

Think of the generation in which we were born. We have much to be grateful for: a vibrant Land of Israel in which to visit and live, and the many Jewish communities all over world that are thriving. Consider what it is about this time period that is an improvement on generations past. What opportunities are available to us now? How are we able to express our Jewishness more fully than those who lived before us?

Leah's Story

Surviving the *Shoah*

Raanana

JUST ENOUGH

I was born in Czechoslovakia in a little city called Cop near the Carpathian Mountains. I had a wonderful childhood. We lived peacefully alongside our non-Jewish neighbors and we were not harassed. My father had a good business and we were comfortable. We had several Orthodox *shuls* nearby and a good community, and we were not treated differently because we were Jews. There were eighty Jewish families in our town. We went to the local public schools and received a Jewish education on *Shabbat* afternoons. We had a nice, happy lifestyle. I was the fifth of eight children and I loved my home. I had five brothers and two sisters – three older brothers and one older sister, and one younger sister and two younger brothers.

My father had the biggest oven in the whole neighborhood and he was a great cook. We had a summer kitchen and the massive outdoor oven. Every Friday my father would stir up a big fire in his oven and our Jewish neighbors would drop off their *chulent* pots to cook in the heat of the leftover coals all night. There would be at least ten or fifteen pots full of food. On *Shabbat* morning, all the ladies and children from these families would come and pick up their pots to bring their lunches home. We had a big dog, but no one was afraid of him because they all knew him. My house was full of people, noise, and love.

My mother was the queen of the house. Everyone knew that if food came from her house, it must be kosher. She did everything properly. She grew up in a small town and my father fell in love with her when he was drafted into the Hungarian army and he was stationed in her town as an officer. She was seventeen when they got married.

We were not poor, and we were not rich in wealth. We had just enough. But we were rich in our home life. My favorite times were Friday nights, when we would sing and dance and enjoy each other. There were so many children and we had so much fun.

Before I was born, my city was part of Hungary. It was that way until 1920, when it was claimed by the newly created Czechoslovakia. Briefly, when World War II began, it became part of Hungary again. Every time our land switched hands, it affected where we went to school and what languages we spoke. In 1938, when I was ten years old, the Hungarians started occupying our area.

Between 1939 and 1944, we lived at home. My father had heard rumors about what the Nazis were doing to Jews all over Europe. He and my mother decided that before the Nazis invaded our city, we would try to escape. He came home one day with horses and a big wagon and told my mother to pack up all she could. They were planning on running deep into Hungary to escape the impending danger.

We packed everything and loaded it up into the wagon. Our family was all together. My two older brothers were home from the army. After a day of travel, we reached the border. But when we got to the crossing it was too late. The borders were closed. The soldiers threatened to kill us all on the spot. We were terrified and obeyed their orders. We returned home.

We traveled back to our home in Cop and when we got there, we saw our non-Jewish neighbors lingering outside the house. They were waiting to see if we would return or not. They were waiting to loot our property. It was disgusting. The next day, the Nazis invaded Czechoslovakia. It was March 1944.

The first thing they did was take away Jewish work permits. People who worked in city hall, the post office, and more, were replaced with Hungarian workers. Then they took away our business licenses. My father had a delivery business; he had four wagons with rubber wheels like trucks. He would pick up goods from the train station and deliver them to local businesses. Most of those businesses were shut down when the Nazis arrived.

Then they took the Jewish students out of the schools. They took all of the children, from first through fifth grade, and stuck us all in one room. They sent two adults to sit with us, just to babysit us. They didn't teach. The older children, including myself, were responsible for teaching the younger children.

Next, we were forced to wear yellow stars on our clothes. Every Jew who left his house was forced to wear one. If you were recognized out in the street as a Jew without a star, you were punished. Our lives had changed so drastically and we were miserable. We didn't know that more misery was on the way for us.

THE GHETTO

It was the end of *Pesaḥ* 1944. The Nazis grew tired of policing us. The SS officers banged on our door. They asked us, "Are you packed?" Packed for what?

We had no idea where we were going. They knew how many children there were supposed to be in our home. We packed as much as we could and we were told to meet at the train station. We packed our clothes, pillows, and blankets. I had with me a fur coat, a siddur, a change of clothes, and a nightgown. They loaded all the Jews into cattle cars. We traveled twenty-four kilometers till we reached Uzhhorod, a nearby city. They brought us to a brick factory that they had turned into a makeshift ghetto.

The Nazis told us that we would stay there until they were ready to send us somewhere else. We didn't know what to feel. We were all living outside and used what we had to make shelters. We were all being housed in the same location. They gave us a roof and we used blankets and sheets to section off private spaces for each family. There were eighty families staying together. But then they began bringing in families from other locations around Europe, like Poland.

I learned to speak Yiddish in the ghetto. My *bubby* always spoke some Yiddish at home, but not too much. I knew a phrase here and there. Now I befriended some girls from Poland who didn't speak Polish, though they did speak Yiddish. They taught me their language so we could communicate.

I was one of the "older" girls who were responsible for all the children of the ghetto. We needed to keep them occupied and clean. The children were infested with lice. There was no water for showers. They were scared. They were hungry. It became our job to remove the lice from their hair. I rubbed petroleum through their heads and picked out the lice. Then I would give them makeshift showers. We also taught them what we could, but mainly it was to distract them.

Two of my older brothers had already been in the military. Now they were forced to trade their rifles for shovels; they were sent to dig trenches for the SS soldiers in a labor camp. My father was assigned to be a kapo, a Jew who helped manage the ghetto. He did his best to get people what they needed and to help them.

We ate soup that we were given every day. We got extra food when people left the ghetto on work permits. Sometimes the townspeople would toss food into the ghetto, too, like salamis and loaves of bread.

We were there for six weeks. When the Nazis told us they were ready to move us, my father said that it was okay. We needed to go. It was not sustainable to live there like that. It was a horrible life and we couldn't go on much longer. We didn't know what would be waiting for us on the other side of the train. But we knew that we couldn't stay in the ghetto any longer.

CATTLE CARS AGAIN

We were uprooted again on June 6, 1944. They loaded us back onto the cattle cars. They had to push us in, but we thought that anything would be better than the ghetto. We were stuck in these tiny cars for two and a half days. There was no food or water. It was torture. It was hell. Several people tried to jump out of the cars and landed on the tracks. I don't know if they all survived the fall. There was a man in the corner of the car who stopped moving. We thought he was sleeping. When we went to inspect, my mother pushed us away from him. She didn't want us to see a dead man.

We were packed in the car so tightly that we had to take turns sitting down. There was a little window high up in the car and we tried to look out the window to see where we were going. We tried to shout for help. When we got to stations, we cried and begged for assistance or water. None of the people at the stations would approach the cars to help us. They were terrified of the soldiers.

When the cars finally stopped, we had no idea where we were. Everyone was told to get out. It was night and the whole place was lit up with bright lights. There were massive gates hovering over us. There were wires everywhere, electrical wires that would electrocute you if you touched them. Some people touched them because they didn't know. Some people touched them because they did know. We didn't yet know the fresh hell that was Auschwitz.

We were told to put our bags on the side. Then we were lined up in front of a man who seemed to be sorting the families into different sides. This man was Dr. Mengele, the infamous Angel of Death who experimented on and tortured Jews. He was the man who decided whether you lived or died in Auschwitz. We all stood in line and as we got closer to him, we tried to understand how and why he was separating us.

The men and women were separated. They took my mother and my younger siblings to one side. My father said to me, "Go with your mother. She might need help with the younger children." I was sixteen at the time. An SS officer grabbed me by the neck when he saw me going with the mothers and the children. I told them I was sixteen. He told me that I was old enough to work. They sent me back to the other line, where my sister Joli was waiting for me.

Mengele had his hand in his sweater. He was directing people toward the lines with his thumb, pointing it in this direction or that direction based on his assessment of how useful you would be to him. My mother and my younger siblings were sent to their death. We didn't learn what happened to them until afterward. They were stripped down and brought to take showers, but instead of water streaming from the showerheads, pellets of gas were dropped inside. They were gassed to death and their bodies were cremated. When I think about their deaths, it is very hard, so very hard.

My grandparents, *Bubby* and *Zayde*, had been in the ghetto with us. But when we were all loaded into the cattle cars, the elderly were taken to a separate car. We didn't see them on the journey. We never saw them again.

SMOKE

The Hungarian Jews were the last community to be sent to Auschwitz. By the time we arrived, the camp was so overloaded, their systems started to fall apart. We were stripped, shaved, and showered under the eyes of the guards.

We were the only ones to not have been tattooed in Auschwitz because the Nazis didn't want us to know how many people had gone through the system. They tried other forms of numbering but the whole system collapsed when it was overloaded. My arm has no tattoo on it. I was never meant to live long enough to need it.

I was able to keep the sturdy shoes that I had brought. They had no other shoes for us. They had all been taken by previous prisoners. I was stripped of my dress that my sister had made for me and given a random uniform that was able to be found. There wasn't much left to be had by the time we got there.

There were more than one thousand people in one barrack. We were stacked on top of each other. They gave us horse blankets and nothing else. There were four or five women to a pallet. If one person wanted to turn over in the night, all the others needed to turn too, because there was no room. There were thirty-two barracks of Hungarian Jewish women – 32,000 Hungarian Jewish women working as slaves to the Nazis.

That first morning in Auschwitz, we stepped out of the barrack and I wanted to find my mother. I was crying and vexed and had no idea where she could be. I had not seen her since we had been separated the day before. The Jewish woman who was in charge of the Hungarian block saw me crying. She said, "Why are you crying already? You have only been here one day! I have been here four years! I built these barracks for you!"

We thought she was crazy. What was wrong with this woman? What was she talking about? Then she said something so cruel. She pointed to the chimney stacks of the crematorium. We had no idea what they were. A cloud of thick black smoke was wafting from the stacks. She said, "You want to know where your parents are? That smoke is your mother and father."

I became hysterical. I started to run but a soldier grabbed me by my hair and threw me back. My head hit a gate and I lost consciousness. When I woke up, my sister told me that we were just separated from my mother, that this crazy woman didn't know what she was talking about. We learned soon enough that this crazy woman knew exactly what she was talking about. I saw bodies with my own eyes. I saw piles and piles of dead bodies being taken out of the gas chambers. I wouldn't wish that sight on anyone, not even my worst enemy. No human should ever have to see that.

My sister Joli and I were first given the job of sorting the belongings of the transit victims. While Jews were being taken to be gassed, selected, or sorted, their belongings were left on the side. Our responsibility was to go through the luggage – the clothes, valuables, and goods – and sort them. Decent clothes and personal items went to the German people who had been displaced by the war. Gold, jewels, and money went to the Nazi banks. Alcohol, fancy items like watches, or delicacies went to the SS officers as rewards for their work. Bloodied, torn, or destroyed clothes went to the inmates.

Every night we had to be in bed by seven o'clock. We usually didn't go to sleep until midnight. During those night hours, we got to know our fellow prisoners. Every girl and woman had a story. We learned about where they were from, their families, and what they left behind. Those connections helped pass the time. By four o'clock in the morning, we had to be up for roll call once again. We had to wait in the freezing cold for the SS to come and count us. They knew exactly how many of us should be waiting. Sometimes they would make us wait many extra hours. We could wait from four to ten o'clock in the morning by the time they would come to count us. We could not move a muscle until they had come. Those moments were sheer terror. You never knew if you would make it through alive.

NOT WITHOUT ME

At one point in Auschwitz, our job was changed. We became responsible for delivering meals around the camp and so we saw a lot of what was going on in the camp. One day, Joli and I noticed a girl inmate walking by us. We noticed her dress. That was my dress! It had been taken from my luggage that we were forced to abandon. I knew that it was my dress because we didn't purchase clothing from a store. We made our own clothes. My sister was an excellent seamstress and she made me that dress.

I walked up to the girl who was wearing my dress and I told her that it was mine. She said, "Why should I believe you? How could you know that this particular dress is your dress?" I told her that if she opened up the shoulder pads of the dress, she would find the earrings that I had hidden there. I had hidden them because my mother had heard rumors about earrings being ripped out of women's ears. Trying to save my ears and the earrings, I hid them. Sure enough, when we opened the shoulder pads, they were there. I didn't keep them long. I traded them for a piece of bread to stay alive. Shortly after that, we found my sister's dress on another inmate. Joli's ring was sewn inside the hem, where we had hidden it.

Whenever our group of inmates was asked, "Who would want to volunteer for a work assignment?" my sister would tell me to raise my hand. If you worked, they didn't kill you. If you hung around doing nothing, you would be erased. We never knew when, where, or how. People would just never come back.

In September they told us one day that they were looking for 220 strong young girls to work in a camp called Reichenbach. It was a subcamp of the Gross-Rosen concentration camp. They needed us to work in an airplane factory. We volunteered, but they didn't pick us. An old woman told Joli, "No matter what, when they ask you if you can work, you must say, '*Jawohl*,' yes, I can work. That will keep you alive."

We knew we needed to get in with that working group. They started listing identification numbers, but our numbers had not been called. Five women who hadn't been picked, including myself and Joli, snuck into the line. We had been in Auschwitz long enough to know what happened to people who stayed there too long. We knew that if we stayed, we would have died there. I don't know how, but they counted us among those that were chosen.

We left Auschwitz. They took us somewhere and gave us clean clothes. In the afternoon, they put us back in cattle cars. There was a bit more room to breathe. They locked us up in the car and opened it two to three times a day while we were traveling. We stopped in Krakow and then they brought us to Reichenbach, which was brand new.

Even in the cattle car, we were treated more humanely than we had been treated in Auschwitz. By the time we got to the factory, we were given soup and a piece of bread, which was far more than we had in the first camp. They gave things to us because they needed us to work. They gave us more food, and they gave us warmer clothes. We worked from six in the morning to six in the evening, twelve-hour shifts each day.

In order to get to and from the factory, we had to walk 3.4 miles every day and every night. We were given horse stalls for sleeping. It was far more comfortable than the barracks we had in the first camp. There were thirty-two women to each small barrack. We did the same thing that we did in Auschwitz, stayed up till late all hours of the night talking. We talked about who was waiting for us at home and what we used to cook. Then I would get too hungry and tell them to talk about something else. Joli was the key to my survival. It was never easy, but having her with me gave me hope that we would be okay. She was my link to home, my past, and my future.

One day in the factory, one of the Germans thought that my sister was pretty. He put an extra ration of apple on her desk. She cut it in half and gave half to me. She was thinner than I and I told her that I didn't want to take her apple. She needed it. She told me, "I am not going home without you. Eat the apple." So I did. I was not going to let her go home without me.

ALL WE WANT IS HOME

Near the end of the war, we heard it coming. There were bombs and planes flying overhead. We heard from the Germans that the Russians were near us. They were coming. The SS men were hiding in shelters and left us to be outside, exposed to the bombs raining down from the sky. We tried to run since we weren't being supervised, but the Germans came after us and brought us back.

In March, they told us they were going to close the factory. They sent us on a march toward an unknown location. When we were walking we came upon an empty theater, and we slept there for the night. When we were there, someone from the factory came back for us and said that they needed some women to come back to the factory to pack it up and close it all down. So I went with my sister and a friend back to continue to work. It seemed like the best option at the time.

When we finished with that work, they asked us who could sew. We were expert seamstresses and volunteered for more work, so we could stay alive. They took us to another camp called Langebelau. We were meant to be fixing military clothes. Our consolation was the fact the place was warm, after a long winter. Because we knew how to sew we were able to repair torn uniforms and still remain useful and therefore, alive.

In May of 1945, the time had come when the Russians were right near the camp. They were coming. The Germans loaded us all into our barracks. They locked the door. They tied electrical wire around the building. We were stuck.

We sat together in fear of what was coming. Any second we could be freed or bombed from above. The Germans had escaped; they were all leaving and left us behind. We were left with no food or water for three days. Then one day we heard people coming. There was a big boot that kicked the door. Then I heard the most wonderful words I ever heard in my life: "Hitler is kaput! You are free. Get out." We hugged each other and laughed and cried and could not believe our ears. It was over. It was time to go home.

When we were set free from the barracks, the world was scary. We didn't know who to trust. The Russian soldiers were nice until they were drunk and they were drinking vodka half the time. They opened up the Germans' food stores for us and we had everything we could have wanted – cheese, bread, milk. I took material from their stores, too, so I could make new clothes for myself. We had access to their sewing machines. All we wanted was to go home.

We and several other women connected with three Jewish Polish men who were on the men's side of the camp. The men went into the city and took over a doctor's villa for us to use. They brought back food and the women cooked it. We were there for three weeks, but all we wanted to do was go home.

We took some of the material in red, white, and blue, the colors of the Czech flag. We made a large flag. Then we began to walk. There were no trains, as everything had been bombed by the Americans and the Germans. We walked for three months to get home. At one point we got picked up by a Czech truck that was heading to city near Cop. It took us to the train station, but yet again we discovered that the station and the tracks had been bombed.

As we got closer to home, every Czech city had a soup kitchen set up by the Red Cross. We were able to eat there. There were always people trying to locate their loved ones, asking, "Have you seen this one? Have you seen that one?" Everyone was looking for someone.

At one point, we met a woman who said that she had been at the train station in Cop. She was sleeping on the railroad and had nowhere to go. She said she had met a man who was kind to her and said that she should come to his house. He offered to give her his bed while he stayed elsewhere. She said, "I thought he was an angel." I asked her, "What was his name?" She said that she couldn't remember.

She went home because she said she might have something that she could check to find out his name. When she returned, she said, "I found his name! It is Avraham Weinberger!" I said, "That is my father!" She told me that this man had been coming to the train station every day, for six months, waiting for his children to come home. He too was asking everyone, "Have you seen my children?" He was at home, waiting for us. I hadn't even known he was alive. He had been in Auschwitz all that time. He was forty-eight years old, and he was a strong man to have survived. The Nazis had capped working at forty.

He had worked in a factory in Monowitz, near Auschwitz. He was abandoned in the hospital and eventually got stronger and was able to travel home. He was the first one to make it home. He had been liberated from Auschwitz six months earlier than us. He had been waiting for all of us to come home. He stood at the train station every day, praying we would return.

Someone had seen us and reported back to him that we were on our way. We got to the house in the middle of the night. The first thing my father asked us was, "Where is your mother?" We told him, "You know. You don't have to ask us."

Our two brothers Zoltan and David returned home as well. Our other brother Maurice was shot by a German officer on his daily shooting spree, at the age of twenty-three. He never returned home.

REBUILDING

We lived in Cop for a short while. It was never the same. We were treated poorly by our neighbors and we knew we didn't belong there anymore. It couldn't be home anymore. We had no home. The Czech government resettled us in a beautiful apartment for a few months. Zoltan, Joli, and myself went to live close to Prague, in Litomerice, until 1949.

My brother's best friend, Andor Klein, returned home from the war too. I remembered him from before the war. Now he started coming over to see me, taking me out on his motorcycle and going on dates. My father said, "Marry this man. You better take him; he is the best we have. If you choose him, he will treat you right and you will have a happy life."

My father was right. I was eighteen when we got married. After the wedding, we wanted to go to Israel. First we went to Paris and then we were going to go to Marseille. Next we were supposed to travel illegally on a ship to reach Israel. But the Hebrew Immigrant Aid Society (HIAS) was making plans for us to get resettled. They didn't want to send us illegally.

We needed to be examined by doctors before we boarded the ship. The doctor who examined me asked, "Did you know that you are pregnant?" We had no idea. We were told that now we could not go because the ships were illegal, and they would not take pregnant women. We would have to stay in Paris. We stayed in Paris as refugees for five years. My son Maurice was born in Paris. I learned French in classes they set up for us. I already knew Hungarian, Yiddish, Czech, Polish, and Hebrew. Soon I was to learn English, too.

About two years into our time in Paris, we got a notice from a relative of ours who was living in Cleveland, Ohio. It was my husband's uncle, a chaplain in the American army who was visiting Paris. We reunited and he moved us out of refugee housing and got us a beautiful apartment. He was sponsoring visas for us to come to Cleveland, and while we were waiting, we had a nice life because of his help.

Eventually, we went on a boat to New York. We had a comfortable journey; I felt like a princess. We had first-class tickets bought for us by our uncle. We got to Ellis Island and passed through immigration. We then took a train to travel to our new home in Cleveland.

Andor and I were married for sixty-two years. Most of that time, we lived in Cleveland. After Maurice, we have two beautiful and wonderful daughters, Susie and Hedy. My hus-

band learned a trade and was a very skilled electrician with his own business. My sister Joli soon joined us in Cleveland as well. Many other family members joined us there, too. We had a beautiful clan. My two oldest brothers who survived the war moved to Israel. My father remarried and also lived in Israel. My husband had several siblings living in Cleveland. I lived there for sixty years. We have many grandchildren and many great-grandchildren.

When I was eighty-two years old, a few years after my husband passed away, I decided that it was time for me to move to Israel. I was the oldest person on my *aliya* flight, and I was met by family at the airport. I began a whole other journey.

SPEAKING NOW

All the time that I was raising my children and my grandchildren, I kept this story to myself. I never spoke a word of it. I felt that it was too painful. The losses were too great. I could hardly utter the names of my lost loved ones. I lost my mother Sara, my younger siblings Yossel, Shmiel, and Fradyl, grandparents, aunts, uncles, and cousins, all in Auschwitz.

But my children were asking. My grandchildren were asking. And so when they asked me to share my story on *Yom HaShoah* two years ago, I agreed. I gave a speech and told my story for the first time. My daughter was in the audience, and it was the first time that she had heard most of the details. I didn't want to hurt the kids. We have lost so many people. It was very difficult to live with the aftermath. But they were asking where our family members were. Maybe I waited too long. These stories need to be told. I am ninety-one and I am telling mine now.

A message from Leah's granddaughter, Pnina
When Bubie told her story to Shira and I, over *Sukkot* 2019, she was verbal, vibrant, and remembered even the smallest details of her past. Just three months later, her health severely started to deteriorate and she is no longer able to communicate with us.

We are so grateful to have had the opportunity to listen to Bubie's story, some of which we heard for the first time. All our extended family will cherish this testament for years to come.

A message from the author
On January 12, 2020, our beloved Leah left this world. With tremendous gratitude for the story that she shared with us, I humbly ask that you offer a prayer for an *aliya* of the *neshama* of Rachel Leah bat Avraham *z"l*.

REFLECTIONS

Questions to Consider
- Who told you about the Shoah? How old were you and how did that impact you?
- How has sisterhood played a role in your life?

Group Discussion
How can we preserve the memories, testimonies, and truths of the Holocaust in an age of rising anti-Semitism?

≈

Take a moment for yourself. What do you need right now?
Close your eyes and be in your own body.
Here is an inspiration exercise to come back to yourself:

Inspiration Exercise
Think of a moment from your childhood. Does this memory bring you joy or sadness? Can you remember the smells, tastes, and sounds of that moment? Is there anything that your adult sensibility can reframe or add to your understanding of that experience?

Noam's Story

Fighting for My Country

Mevaseret Zion

THE BONDS THAT CONNECT US

My parents were both born here in Israel.

My father's parents were born in Israel too; their families were from Iraq and Germany, with my grandmother's parents escaping from the *Shoah* and making it to Israel in time for my grandmother to be born here in 1939. Like many others, they lost family in the war.

In the wake of the *Shoah* there was increased violence against Jews in Iraq. Jews were among the top tiers of society, education, philosophy, and government, but the drama between Israelis and Palestinians in Israel turned many Iraqis against their Jewish neighbors. In 1947, the government of Iraq announced that *aliya* to Israel was illegal. Even being a Zionist became illegal. In 1950, the Israeli Knesset passed the Law of Return, which stipulated that any Jew could return to Israel and receive citizenship, and in 1951, the Iraqi government opened up *aliya* to Israel under great financial restraints. Israel airlifted more than 130,000 Iraqi Jews to Israel in Operation Ezra and Nehemiah. My family was among those who signed up to build a new life here in Israel.

My *saba* came first in 1951 without his family and settled in Atlit in a *maabara*. He came from the city of Kut in Iraq. His father was a rabbi and

159

the rest of his family were merchants. They joined him in 1952 and they all moved to the *maabara* in Rishon LeZion.

My *savta* and her entire family came in 1952 from the city of Hillah, Iraq. Her father was a very well-known healer and according to my *savta*, he was known as someone with special powers. They settled in the *maabara* in Rishon LeZion, which is where she met my *saba*. He went to build roads and she worked as a seamstress in a clothing factory.

The first words that my *saba* learned to say in Hebrew were, "I want to be a soldier." Though he was sent to build roads, he was insistent that he wanted to draft into the army. Eventually, the army relented and allowed him to draft into the Artillery Corps. He served his country in that capacity for thirty years.

I was the first in my family of my generation to serve in the army. My *saba* was in awe of my service and of the fact that I followed in his footsteps. I always looked up to him and saw him as an example of what it meant to fight for our country. Now I was dedicating my life to the service of our country, and he was so proud of me. Our bond was so strong that I was one of the last people he recognized before he passed away.

LIFE NEXT TO GAZA

I was born in Jerusalem but when I was three, we moved to Nahal Oz, which is a *kibbutz* right next to the Gaza Strip. It was 1995 and at first, it was peaceful. For a child, a *kibbutz* is a dream environment, a perfect place to live. I have a sister a year younger than me and we were best friends. We were always together and always with the rest of our friends. We would walk ourselves home from kindergarten; there were no cars driving by, nothing for our parents to worry about. My brother is five years younger than me, and I would go and pick him up from *gan*. We were living in our own little peaceful bubble. I knew that I was safe, and I was – until I wasn't.

I don't think I ever actually felt unsafe, but I don't think I am typical in that way. It is just the way that I was made. You could ask my sister or friends and they would have a totally different answer. When everything started, I was in first grade. I know that there were lots of kids on my *kibbutz* who utilized the therapy services that were provided, but I never needed them. I think it was because of the way my parents handled the impending danger. They never made me feel frightened. We always had a plan. I trusted that things were going to be okay.

Life was relatively calm on the Gaza border between 2001 and 2005. But then the *hitnatkut* happened – the disengagement of Jewish settlements from Gaza – and that is what changed everything. There was an army base right outside the *kibbutz* and while I was young it was very small. Perhaps there were five tents in total. But after the *hitnatkut*, it became a full, massive army base. They were building non-stop to accommodate all the soldiers being rushed into the area. All of a sudden, you could feel the army presence everywhere.

That year was my bat mitzva, and my celebration was a month before the *hitnatkut*. You couldn't enter the area without express permission from the army if you weren't a resident. We had to send a list of our guests to the army to get permission, but it was not a quiet time in the area. Many of our guests did not come. We went from living in a quiet, idyllic *kibbutz* to being in the middle of a buzzing military zone. Our beautiful life was disturbed.

I was never a very emotional person and I always felt safe. I felt like I knew what to do in case of danger and I trusted that the army knew what they were doing, too. Ultimately, their presence was to protect us from incoming rocket fire, as well as from terrorists crossing the border eight hundred meters away and entering the *kibbutz*. I always saw the troops and felt them around me and that added to my sense of safety.

My parents also had a large impact on how I dealt with those tumultuous times. They educated us about what to do in an emergency, where to run, and what the protocol was. The *Misrad HaBitaḥon* built bomb shelters in every home on the *kibbutz* so we could run to a place that would keep us safe. There was never any talk in our home about leaving the *kibbutz*. We were standing our ground.

In the summer of 2006, when I was fourteen, the Second Lebanon War broke out. Though the fighting was in the North, we in the South were still reeling from unending rocket attacks on our communities. We were averaging fifty rockets a day, with sirens ringing non-stop. We were struggling to live our lives and then we would turn on the TV and see almost none of it reported on the Israeli news, let alone in the international media. There was a war going on somewhere else, and our suffering was basically ignored.

It made many of us feel small and unimportant.

When I was in high school, my family moved to Kansas for my mother's job for two and a half years. We were gone during Operation Cast Lead, in the winter of 2008, when the IDF went into Gaza following constant missile threats and terrorist activities in Gaza. It felt much harder to be away during times of distress in my community. I felt so far away physically and mentally; I was in such a different place. When you are far away, you are always worried about your neighborhood and friends.

When we came back to Israel, I had already graduated high school. My family moved back home to the *kibbutz* but I never really joined them. It was time for me to do my part and serve my country.

FIGHTING TO FIGHT

I spent a year after high school participating in a program called *mekhina*, which is a leadership program that prepares you for drafting into the army. They are physically and mentally preparing you for the best and most meaningful service. They helped me discover what my strengths are and they helped me get to know myself and look for the best placement. I went there not knowing what I wanted to do in the army. I wanted the extra time to consider where I should be. Having been exposed to soldiers almost every day of my life, I knew that I wanted a meaningful service. Being so connected to my *saba*, I knew I had to make it a priority.

Because I was coming back from the States, I missed my initial screening process, which is a day-long examination and interview where all potential soldiers are matched up with potential positions. Since I had missed it, they were not really helpful to me in terms of finding where I belonged.

With time, I decided that I wanted to go into a combat unit. I didn't just want to fight, I also wanted to be a commander. *Mekhina* was the first opportunity for me to assess my own leadership skills, and I found them. And I didn't just want to be a commander. I wanted to be a commander and have the most influence that I could, in order to affect the quality of my soldiers' service.

But the army turned me down. They weren't willing to put any effort into helping me get where I wanted. They stopped listening to me. In order to draft into combat at that time, you had to pass a series of physical and mental tests over a very intensive forty-eight hours, and they wouldn't give me that opportunity. It became a bunch of bureaucratic nonsense. So I switched to my Plan B and got into the IDF Spokesperson's Unit. It is the unit that provides information to the news, media, and more. It is a very small unit and many people wanted to serve there. It is a great unit and exclusive, but it was not a combat unit.

I drafted in July of 2010 and went into three weeks of basic training and then three months of the Spokesperson's Unit training. I began my service and it took a few months before it really hit me – this is not what I want to be doing and I shouldn't be here. I went back to fighting to switch to a combat unit. It took six months and a lot of advocating for myself, but finally, I got a yes. They were going to let me switch and finally I felt like I was moving in the right direction, to the place where I needed to be serving. It just had to happen.

At that point, I had been serving for a year, and now I had to go all the way back to the beginning. I went back to basic training; I got a new uniform and new shoes. My commanders had been drafted after me, meaning that I had spent more time in the army than the people who were teaching me. But I thought it was great and I thanked God. I was patient through the frustrations and I was single-minded in getting to my goal. This is what I wanted to do and I was going to do what it took to get there.

MIXED UNIT

I was calm through basic training and I succeeded. I knew this just needed to happen. I had been drafted into a unit called *Caracal*. It was the only infantry battalion that was mixed: one-third men, two-thirds women. It is the most intense service available for women in the army. They offered this option to me and I was thrilled to take the opportunity. The IDF wanted it to be a unit of mostly women because it is the only place where women can serve in the infantry.

At first, the gender dynamic felt odd. The women all chose to be there. We knew where we were going and we were grateful for the opportunity to serve as boots on the ground. But many of the men were disappointed with their placement. Heading toward combat, they had expected to serve among only men. I think that in the beginning, some of them felt like working alongside women devalued their placement. They had been taught that a real army experience means fighting alongside men and there can be a lot of machismo that comes with that idea. It made some of them feel that we were a weaker unit because there were so many of us women.

It took about two weeks for the dynamic to shift. For men who were taught that women are the weaker gender, it could be really upsetting to go home after a long week of training and feel wiped and exhausted, knowing that there were women training alongside them who did just as well as or better than them. The idea that men are stronger and better soldiers quickly dissipated when they were bested by the woman training next to them. The guys I was training with told me that they needed to get rid of those thoughts for their own egos.

In my unit, when a female soldier performed a task or trained better than her male counterpart, at first it might have been really hard for the men in the unit to accept. But it happened all the time and something shifted. We developed mutual respect. We came together as a unit and worked together. We all worked toward the same goal. We stopped seeing each other in terms of gender and started focusing on teamwork. It became more personal than gendered; it was now about who was good at what because of aptitude, not because of being a woman or a man. As we came together as a team, we used each other's strengths to further our missions. That is when we found the power of a mixed unit.

Oftentimes, I found that the men and women in my unit were thinking differently. The way we approached missions was different, too. We each brought our skills and uniqueness and together we got the job done. I found that women sometimes brought creativity to our missions, coming up with unique ways to minimize losses and maintain as many priorities as we could. I also found that female soldiers had great time management skills. These skills became really meaningful when managing a team – we always needed to choose the right course of action, and there were always things that needed to be given up.

I am pretty strong, but the male soldiers in my unit were physically stronger than the female soldiers. They could carry more, and for longer. But as women, we strategized amongst ourselves to do what needed to be done. In general, on these mixed teams, we helped each other. We filled in each other's gaps with our own personal, physical, and mental strengths.

LET ME LEAD

We trained for eight months and then my fellow soldiers went to patrol the Egyptian border, as that was the mission of our battalion. I went with a small group of soldiers to the commanders course. It was four months and at the end of the course you become a squad commander, with nine to twelve soldiers beneath you. I then went back to basic training with those soldiers for another four months to help train them. I taught them everything they needed to know and went through drills with them. Then I went to the officers course.

It was four months of a basic officers course and then another four months of training specifically for infantry. The second part was very intense. There were three hundred soldiers in the officers course – two were women, and one of them was me. It felt natural to me, though, because this is where I had been aiming all along.

For a lot of the male soldiers, who were coming from all-male infantry units, it was their first time meeting a woman who was training to serve exactly at the same level as them. At first, they were skeptical of the two of us and we had to prove ourselves again and again. I felt like everything I did had to be perfect; I couldn't mess anything up. I felt like I was being watched by my commanders more than the male soldiers. It felt like they were trying to find a reason to kick us out of the course. They didn't approve of a woman doing this "man's job" – they thought it was weird and that it wasn't right.

I didn't earn everyone's respect by the end of the course. I think some of my commanders let me finish it because they couldn't catch me making a mistake, but they didn't think I should have finished. They didn't believe in women serving in combat. It was just that I didn't do anything to justify them getting rid of me.

Now I went back to basic training again, this time as a platoon commander. I had four squads beneath me that consisted of forty-five soldiers. We did it all again for eight months. This time, when we were finished, we all went together to protect the Egyptian border. It was time to fulfill our mission.

WHAT IT MEANS TO SERVE

Finally, on the Israeli-Egyptian border, we got to work. We protected the border, we stopped drug deals, and we patrolled the area. About half the platoon on base was made up of women, but I was the only female platoon commander. I was the highest-ranking woman on the base and I was there for four months.

Then I was given a new platoon of men only. They had gotten some soldiers from a different unit and it was an experiment to see if they could transfer. We were together another four months and it was definitely an interesting experience. I don't think they minded that they had a female leader, but they were almost done with their service at that point and they were eager to be cool with each other and finish the job they started.

At some point during this time, Operation Protective Edge began. Our missions became more intense, and we were often off the base. We were gone for longer periods of time. But for me, it was not only about what was happening with my soldiers. I was also thinking about my family and friends. My parents were at home in Nahal Oz and our home was a war zone. All my friends from my officers course were leading their soldiers on missions inside Gaza. If I ever slept, I would wake up every day praying that I wouldn't see the names that I knew listed on the news. But sometimes I did.

When you lose a friend while you are serving, there is not much you can do. I would put the phone down and go to my soldiers and do what I had to do. I couldn't go to their funerals because I had to stay at my station. I lost four friends in that war, as well as many other people whose names I knew and whose faces I had seen. It was extremely tough.

I called my family as often as I could, but it was really hard. My dad was in charge of all the agriculture for the *kibbutz*. He had the army in his fields, trampling on his crops. But they discovered a terror tunnel in one of those fields, so thank God the army was there. The war ended after fifty days, but those days left a significant mark.

FROM SCRATCH

I don't think I ever chose to stay in the army, exactly, but I stayed. I didn't want to stay at that point – I was exhausted and my contract was ending. But I was offered the position of deputy commander of a company in *Caracal*. It would mean that I would have to go back to basic training another time and I couldn't stomach doing it again. I asked for a position in one of the companies already stationed along the border, but they didn't have any roles open for me.

At that time, a rumor was going around about a new battalion that was being started and I decided that this was where I was going to be. If I was going to go back to basic training all over again, at least I should start over with a new place and new people. I went to some interviews and I was chosen to be the deputy commander of the first company that drafted into the new battalion. It was the craziest, most exciting thing I have ever done. This position was the most influential one that I had ever had.

We were starting everything from scratch. I was pretty much on my own and we kept facing so many challenges. We were given the name *Arayot HaYarden*, the Lions of Jordan. It was our mission to guard the Jordan border. It was more intense than the Egyptian border, because it included some parts of Yehuda and Shomron, a more complicated area.

We started basic training but we were lacking commanders, sergeants, drivers, and more. We didn't have people to drive food to our soldiers in the fields. We didn't have commanders to lead our soldiers. It was my job to find soldiers to fill these roles, and it was difficult to find people to step into these positions because we were not an all-male unit, and we were new. Morale was down.

At some point, we took soldiers from basic training and told them, "We need you to step up. You're the commanders now." It worked, because these soldiers really wanted to be there and make a difference. So we built the unit together.

I was there eight months and my contract was ending in August. I was also engaged to be married. I had met my soon-to-be husband in my commanders course several years earlier and now we were planning our wedding. I was torn,

167

but I felt like it was time for me to go and move on with my life. I had a very meaningful army service. I felt satisfied and ready to leave, though I stayed an extra month or two until all the roles were staffed and everyone settled in.

Two days before the end of my service, I changed my mind about leaving for good. I wanted to go on a break instead; I decided I wasn't ready to be officially finished with my service. I took eight months off, which is the longest they could give me, and I got married. I did the Israel Trail from Mount Hermon to Eilat with friends. I decided what I wanted to study and I went to register for school. But I realized it was April and I wasn't starting school till October. What was I going to do with my time?

I called my brigade commander and asked him if he needed help. I went back to do some administrative work in their local office. When I served in these roles, I was always the highest-ranking female officer on base. My higher-ups listened to me and my opinions because they believed that I saw situations and strategy differently than everyone else. I had a unique perspective and they respected that. I took part in many brainstorming sessions. A month after I came back, my battalion commander came into my office and said, "I need you to become the company commander starting next week." Usually, you need to go through a course to be a company commander, but no one had time for that. It was far from the administrative work I had planned to do at that point, but I took it and I was ready to be there, on the condition that I would leave by August.

I went back to my old company where I had been deputy commander and I knew mostly everyone. I jumped right back into the water. It was a mess, but it was exciting. I felt I was valued and needed and the impression they gave me was that I couldn't be replaced.

I ended up staying through August, and then through September. I left the army on October 27, and I started school on October 30. On Thursday I was sitting in my office as a company commander, and on Sunday morning, I was a student in Calculus A.

LIFE AFTER THE ARMY

I studied industrial engineering and now I'm in my last semester of school. My husband is serving as a company commander on the Gaza border, near where I grew up, and we now have a two-year-old son.

Reflecting back, I think my husband was as supportive of my army aspirations as anyone could be. I was a higher-level officer than he was at some points, but he stood by me at every opportunity, came to spend *Shabbatot* with me on base, and was proud that I had achieved my goals.

He is now home every other weekend, and my son and I rarely go spend *Shabbatot* with him. Now that the situation is flipped with him on base and me at home, I finally see how hard it was for him. A cool part of our relationship is that we really understand each other's military experiences.

The army experience requires you to be one hundred percent focused on your mission. It's hard to be torn, thinking about people you love back home. My husband's schedule doesn't allow him to help out or to be around whenever we need him. The army's schedule must be prioritized over our family schedule. Even if he wants to be there for us, right now, he can't be here every moment we need him. What that means is that most of the time, I run our household alone. Sleeping alone isn't the hardest part – the tough part is having all the responsibility on my own.

I am a student, I work full-time, and I am mothering our son. I am grateful for my manager, who really appreciates what I am doing. One day she gave me an evaluation, and I was expecting her to tell me that I could do better, because I felt so jammed with life. But the first thing she said to me was, "I don't know how you do what you do." I felt so heard and validated. It was so eye-opening for me, because it helped me realize that this stage of my life is much harder than when I was in charge of an entire company of 120 soldiers in the army. My time is not my own. If I need to take time for myself, I need to buy it in the form of babysitting.

But my son has given my life a new purpose. He is the center of my universe. My army service taught me to keep doing what I need to do at all times, no matter what. Being a mom has taught me that I need to take a step back and set my priorities right. Sometimes that means taking a break from school lectures when I need a break. I constantly need to decide what I need to give up, because I can't do everything. I learned that in the army, too.

There is a lot of self-sacrifice in my life right now, but I am loving it. I am happy knowing that I did my best and had the most meaningful service that I could. I am happy to support my husband in furthering his army experience. I love raising my son.

I feel as though, throughout my life, I have actively chosen to take the road less traveled. Life at this point could have been much easier if I had

chosen to live near my parents, not go to school, or not work full-time. My choice of staying in the army as long as I did also impacted the trajectory of my life. If I left earlier, I might have accomplished much more academically and from a career perspective. But I felt that I had something meaningful to accomplish, and that my personal life could wait. Now I have a bigger purpose to fill and I am eager to discover the opportunities waiting for me, just outside my comfort zone. I am sure they will be another great adventure.

I always worry about the safety of my family, but I don't let it define me. I have random thoughts that come and go, but I am still able to sleep at night because I have faith in the systems that are set up to protect us. Last night, the whole night, the sirens were blaring near Gaza, where my husband and parents are living. I wanted to either be there or to bring them to me. I still feel like I want to protect them. I want to know that they are safe. But for now, I just need to have faith that peace will come again to my homeland.

REFLECTIONS

Questions to Consider
- Have you ever been discriminated against in the workplace because of your gender?
- What does it mean to you to serve your country and your people?

Words to Remember
> "I still feel like I want to protect them. I want to know that they are safe. But for now, I just need to have faith that peace will come again to my homeland."

Group Discussion
What does female leadership mean to you? What does it look like in your community of choice?

ஜ

Take a moment for yourself. What do you need right now?
Close your eyes and be in your own body.
Here is an inspiration exercise to come back to yourself:

Inspiration Exercise
Consider all your talents. Identify your strengths. Are you good at delegating? Organizing? Inspiring? Strategizing? Mobilizing? Listening? Imagine how you can offer your gifts to your community. Where are the spaces where your efforts are needed? Who can you help? How can you make where you live a better place to be?

Lauren's Story

The Pain of Waiting

Modiin

EACH MONTH THAT PASSED

When I was a little girl, I often I imagined my adult life. I would be married with kids, and have a house with a white picket fence. I always assumed that things would go just as I had imagined them. I have been so lucky in my life, thank God, things have worked out for me. I haven't had many disappointments or much turmoil. My parents raised me in a loving home. I had a wonderful upbringing filled with love, went to college and met my husband at a reasonably young age. I am happily married and assumed that I would have kids as soon as I wanted them. That's where the story starts, because it didn't play out that way for us.

When we had been married for around two years, we decided it was time to get off of birth control and start trying to have a baby. Some of our friends had already started having kids, but we were both very early in starting our careers and we wanted to take the beginning of our marriage to get to know each other better. We wanted to develop a strong foundation for our lives before we had kids.

When I went off the pill, I assumed that I would get pregnant that month. It never occurred to me that it would take any longer than that. When I got my period that month, I remember feeling such a profound feeling of disappointment. I remember thinking to myself, "How could that not have worked?"

Everyone told me it could take between six months to a year to get pregnant so I decided not to worry and resolved to try again the next month. When I got my period again in the second month, I experienced those negative feelings all over again.

I started reading fertility books and trying to figure out when I was going to ovulate. I did whatever I could do that was within my control to make it happen. I wanted to take a proactive approach. The third month passed and I got my period again. I started to ask myself, "What if there is something wrong with me?" My husband is very laid-back in general and he reminded me, "Sometimes it just takes some people longer than others." He tried to get me not to stress about it.

Four months went by. Then five months. And each month that passed became harder for me. I was becoming more convinced that something was wrong.

WHEN IS IT GOING TO BE MY TURN?

Every month when I went to the *mikve,* I dreaded seeing the *mikve* attendant. I didn't want to see her anymore. I didn't want to be there. I wanted to be

pregnant. As the months ticked on and we were still not able to get pregnant one month, I had to go to the *mikve* yet again. I did my best to keep it together while I was there. As I was about to leave, the *mikve* attendant said to me (mistakenly, I'm sure), "See you next month."

I made it to my car. As soon as the door was closed, I burst into tears. I didn't want to be there next month. I wanted this cycle of wanting and disappointment to be over. Sure enough, I saw her again the next month.

At that point, I began looking into special *brachos* to say at the *mikve* as a merit for having a child. I was searching for a spiritual way to make this happen. But nothing was connecting. I'm a pretty type A person. When there is something I want, I work really hard to make it happen. But this felt like it was completely outside of my control. It was in Hashem's hands. That was such an internal battle for me.

All my friends who lived in my neighborhood seemed like they were just living their lives and moving forward without me. We lived in a *shtetl*-like environment, and everyone had babies and strollers. It was all that anyone would ever talk about. Every *Shabbos* meal, there was someone present who was either pregnant or just had a baby. Every week we were going to someone else's *bris mila* or birthday parties for someone else's kids. I wanted to be happy for them all. But inside, I was breaking. I kept wondering, "When is it going to be my turn?"

People started making stupid comments to us. "What's taking so long? Why don't you have a baby yet? What are you waiting for?" Every single time I heard a comment like that, it was heartbreaking. It was so cruel, because I would have to come up with a smug or funny response. No one wanted to hear the truth: "We are desperately trying and nothing is working, if you really want to know."

I hadn't told a soul outside my marriage what I was going through internally. My husband and I were dealing with it on our own. Everyone around us was busily getting pregnant and having children, and we felt so isolated and in a place all by ourselves. The word "infertility" was so taboo. No one was talking about it in our circles. No one was talking about it in the community at all. We carried this secret that felt so shameful, all alone.

SPIRALING

I went to my ob-gyn to discuss the fact that it had been so long and I still wasn't getting pregnant. She was very unkind to us. She said, "There is nothing I can do to help you. You probably have an issue. Good luck." She said she couldn't find anything wrong with me from her internal exam. She didn't know why I couldn't get pregnant.

I felt lost. No one I knew had gone down this path, to my knowledge. It felt like me and Zvi, my husband, against the world. He was so incredibly supportive and we held each other up during that time. But we kept getting reminders of what we were missing.

That year on *Simchas Torah*, I stood in *shul* during *Kol HaNe'arim*, a prayer for the children. They called all the children up to the Torah, and each stood beneath their father's *tallis*. When they started singing *HaMalach HaGoel*, a song that is classically sung as a lullaby to children, I couldn't be there anymore. I left the sanctuary in tears. I felt empty and filled with loss over what I wanted to be carrying inside. I felt so "other." These feelings pushed me to make an appointment with a specialist. In all the research and reading I had done, the phrase "reproductive endocrinologist" kept coming up. I found someone in my area and scheduled an appointment.

I was not expecting to begin treatment right away. I was so unprepared to immediately, the next day, begin the process of conceiving in what felt like an "unnatural" way. The doctor was rattling off different things we needed to test for, and the names of invasive tests and procedures. My head was spinning. It happened so quickly and I had such an overwhelmed, spiraling kind of feeling. It just felt like, "What is this crazy path we are going down in order to have kids?" This was just not what we thought our lives were going to be at all. It was so hard to take it all in.

We thought we were going to have kids like everyone else in the world, in a natural way. But here we were with test tubes, schedules, and blood tests. It was so much information to take in and such a weight to carry. Yet we both agreed that we would do almost anything to become parents.

We felt so lucky that our insurance company covered our specialist appointments and treatments thereafter. We were initially very worried about the cost of fertility treatments. It caused us a lot of tension and friction. We knew that it could be a huge financial burden. At least that part would be less of a burden. But we had only begun.

NO END IN SIGHT

I was sitting in a hospital gown, on the table in the doctor's office, freezing. I couldn't stop crying. All I kept thinking was, "What is wrong with me and my body, that I can't do what God intended my body to do in the typical way?" I felt so bad about myself. My head kept telling me, "It's not your fault. You didn't do anything wrong." But my heart was screaming at me, "What is wrong with you? Why can't you just get pregnant?"

They did test after test to see if there was something clogged or blocked inside of me. They told me I had unexplained infertility. That diagnosis is good for nothing, because it doesn't help figure out what is wrong. They don't know why you can't get pregnant. You just can't.

They had to test my husband's sperm to confirm that he was fertile. It was so awkward and a horrible experience. No man wants to go through that. He came home feeling so uncomfortable about the experience. We were fighting two feelings of wanting to do everything and anything to have a baby, and having to endure so much physical and emotional pain to get there.

His tests came back just fine, so we started fertility treatments for me in earnest. I would have to go to the doctor's office at five or six o'clock in the morning for blood tests. We were waiting to see when my hormone levels would be just at the right time to begin. I was started on Clomid, which stimulated my ovaries to produce more eggs. We were told to begin to try, and that this could be it and I could get pregnant. When I got my period again that month, we were devastated.

We had to skip the next month because my ovaries were hyperstimulated and we weren't allowed to try. It felt so cruel because all we wanted to do was move on with the process. But they told us it was dangerous and of course we didn't want to risk my health. I ended up back at the *mikve*. Again. The next month we did another round of Clomid. It was again unsuccessful.

We met with the doctors who told us we needed to go to the next step. It felt like there was no end in sight. We had been getting treatments and testing for several months and it was so hard to understand why Hashem was not granting us the gift of a child. What would we have to do to make that a reality for ourselves?

TABOO

Because things were getting more complicated, we decided to finally tell our parents. The testing and treatments were becoming more invasive, it felt like we might need financial help to continue treatment, and it was getting too hard to carry the emotional burden alone.

Watching their reaction was almost harder than having to go through it ourselves. Parents want their children to have everything they need in life. When that doesn't happen, it can be so painful for the parents. When we sat down with each set of our parents, they were so supportive, kind, and said all the right things. But you could see behind their eyes that their pain for us was so profound. It was too much to bear.

Later that month there was a blackout in our neighborhood and we needed to go to Zvi's parents' house for power. I needed to begin my progesterone shots for treatment that night. I was mortified to have to endure it in my in-laws' house. I had to stick the needle into my behind and it was so painful that I screamed so loudly in pain when it was injected. It added insult to injury that I wasn't in my own space. I was ashamed of needing to go through this process. I felt so vulnerable. It was a part of the path that we needed to go through, but it was horrible.

I was artificially inseminated when I was ready. When I was on the table, I kept thinking to myself, "This is so unnatural, but if this is the only way that we can have a baby, then we have to do what we have to do to make it happen." Yet the experience made me feel uncomfortable with myself. I didn't understand why this is what my body needed to make it happen. It made me feel abnormal and I hated that feeling. It's hard to qualify what it means to not feel normal. There were just those feelings of self-deprecation: "Why me? Why like this? Why can't I be like everyone else?" I wished I didn't have to go through this.

At times we talked about what we would do if we couldn't conceive. Would we adopt? Not having kids was not on the table for us. It was not the way we envisioned our life going. It was such an adjustment to have to look at our future through different eyes.

I felt isolated because I didn't know anyone going through this besides for myself. I didn't know that it was so common that it could almost be seen as typical. Had people been talking about it more, I know I would have felt more comfortable to talk and share. I think that would have helped me go through the process with less shame.

I had a very small and close circle of friends. As close as we were, sex was not something that we talked about. When you think about pregnancy, you think about sex. That was a taboo topic in our community. Maybe I wasn't mature enough yet, or maybe I didn't feel comfortable talking about it. While we were going through infertility, I was too embarrassed feeling that I was the only one in the world going through this.

Our first indication that maybe it was more common than we thought came when we saw many *frum* couples in the waiting room alongside us, at six a.m., for those tests. Seeing them go through the same tests and timelines that we were on helped us feel a sense of community. Maybe we weren't alone, after all.

CONFIRMED

After insemination, we had to wait a week or two. The waiting felt like an eternity. One Sunday, we were on the way to yet another friend's kid's birthday party. Just thinking about it was torturous for us. Right before we walked out the door, the phone rang. The nurse said, "Your blood test came back positive. You're pregnant."

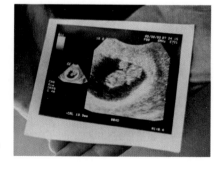

I burst out into tears. I felt a thousand emotions at the same time. The first thing I did after I gave Zvi a hug was to sit down on the couch and take out my *Tehillim*. I had never felt so thankful to Hashem for anything in my entire life, as I did at that moment.

The nurse told us that 90 percent of the time, it really is a pregnancy, but it could also be a chemical pregnancy. I had to come in for several days to have my numbers measured. With each blood test, my numbers were rising. This was our moment. It was confirmed. We were going to have a baby. Thank God, nine months later, our daughter Kayla Eliana was born. We named her Eliana because it felt like Hashem truly answered our prayers.

I always have believed that there are ways that Hashem runs the world that we as humans will never understand. The deep *emuna* that I needed to have, that Hashem runs our lives in the best way for each one of us, is important. It taught me a lot about my own faith and my belief in myself and in God.

As a couple, though it was so challenging while we were going through it, infertility also created an incredibly strong bond between us. It is something we have forever. In hindsight, I can appreciate that supporting each other through this major life hurdle and coming out stronger on the other side was a great thing for our marriage.

I don't know if there is anything else to make of it. People go through all sorts of pain in the course of their lives. I am not sure that we can ascribe a reason. In my case, this is what Hashem wanted from us in order to have children. We had to go through this test. And we did.

WHEN LIFE MOVES ON

Because I couldn't get pregnant on my own, I obviously didn't need to go back on birth control again. Four months after our baby was born, Zvi walked into our apartment with fried chicken from the supermarket. I gagged.

I looked at my husband, laughed, and said, "Zvi, I'm pregnant."

He responded, "No, you're not. You can't be pregnant."

But I knew. The next morning, I took a pregnancy test and I was right. I was pregnant again. My older kids are fourteen months apart. It is the biggest *bracha* I could imagine. Apparently, it is very common to have initial infertility, and then be able to conceive after a first baby is born. I didn't know that till after the fact. We were beyond thrilled. A few years later, we had one more child.

We are so grateful for the times that we live in, and for the doctors who were there to help us. In the scheme of life, we now thank God have three children, have made *aliya*, and moved on with our lives. But while we were going through infertility, it felt endless. We could not see the end in sight.

Everyone's story is unique. For some people, conceiving can come really easily. For others, it can be really hard. Both paths are okay. There is nothing wrong with you if you are having problems conceiving. That is the way Hashem made our bodies. He also made the doctors and the medical procedures to help us have children.

Once my eldest was born, the shame of our experience melted away. Sometimes in life, we go through chapters that feel like they are the end of our world or that they will define us for the rest of our lives. But then that chapter ends and a new one begins. Life moves on. I look back on those years, and still that pain can come back to the surface so quickly. Tears come to my eyes just talking about what it was like for us. Yet, on a day-to-day basis, it doesn't define my life or how I mother.

We always think we know that everyone else's lives are perfect. I used to see someone with a baby and assume the baby was conceived without intervention. But we have no idea how other people's lives play out or what their emotional life is on the inside. When we talk to other people, we like to fill the space of the silences with small talk. But we really need to be careful when we make comments or ask questions about having children. We need to consider how the person is going to receive that thing you said. Think through the possibilities of what that question might mean to the other person. Don't talk just for talking's sake. You never know what is on the other side of that answer. It's not your business to ask about when or how someone is having children. Unless you are being invited into the conversation, it has nothing to do with you. It is a couple's choice to disclose the how, where, and why of their decision-making process or experience.

For me, it was so freeing to relinquish the shame, to learn that my experience was common and that there were other people in my community just like me. I am grateful for the gifts of my children and my husband, and I am grateful for the support I have had. I cherish the pleasure of raising my children. We are always looking toward the future.

REFLECTIONS

Questions to Consider
- What sustained you in moments where you felt like you didn't have what you needed?
- Have you ever felt shame because your life was moving at a different pace than that of your peers?

Words to Remember
> "We always think we know that everyone else's lives are perfect."

Group Discussion
One in eight couples struggles with infertility. Is infertility considered shameful in your community? What can we do to bring it out in the open and normalize the experience?

✍

Take a moment for yourself. What do you need right now?
Close your eyes and be in your own body.
Here is an affirmation exercise to come back to yourself:

Affirmation Exercise
I respect and validate my own feelings.
I am kind to myself.
Calmly and with hope for the future, I acknowledge feelings that may be unresolved.
I am here to be in the moment, as I am right now. And I am okay.

Sewalem's Story

Waiting for You

Be'er Yaakov

LEAVING

I was born in Wegera, a small village in Ethiopia. My mother is a Jewish woman, and my father a Christian man. My mother was orphaned as a young child and was raised by her extended family. Over the years, her family made *aliya* to Israel. Her aunts, uncles, and cousins traveled on foot through the Sudan. Some members of the family didn't survive the trip and died on the treacherous journey.

My mother always wanted to make *aliya*. She wanted to be reunited with her family and finally come home to the Holy Land. She told my father that she wanted to immigrate to Israel with him and their children, but he did not want to go. He did not feel any connection to the land and his family was living in the village where they had been living. He told her, "If you want to go, go alone. Leave the children here."

Secretly, my mother took a picture of all her children to the embassy in Gondar and applied for our *aliya*. When my father found out that she was planning to leave him and take all of us with her, my parents divorced.

As the day got closer, more of our family in the village found out that we were leaving. There was a lot of sadness and tension. The day came to leave to Gondar, where the Jewish community was, to begin our *aliya* process. My sister was ten, I was six, and I had a two-year-old brother as well as

187

another brother who was two months old. I also have an older brother who was twelve at the time. My mother's plan was to take all the children with her. But my big brother did not come with us. It was decided that he would stay behind because he was the oldest child, and he was needed to help the family in their work. My mother was planning on sending for him at a later date, but she did not know that they would soon close the Ethiopian *aliya*. That was sixteen years ago. Still, to this day, we are waiting to be reunited with my brother.

LONELY AND LANDING

When we were ready to begin our travels to Israel, we left Gondar and traveled to Addis Ababa, the capital of Ethiopia. The people in the Jewish community that we were leaving made a party for us celebrating our *aliya*. They wanted to say goodbye to us. We didn't understand what it meant to leave, to say goodbye to our father, our family on our father's side, our Christian neighbors, and all of our extended family.

We went on a plane for the first time to travel to Israel. I remember that we were told not to look toward the ground and that if we did, we might fall. I was so afraid to look out the window. Now, I feel sad that I didn't get a last glimpse of Ethiopia as I was leaving or a first look at my new home in Israel.

Immediately, things felt different. The food was like nothing I had ever tasted before. That was the beginning of the adventure and the adjustment to a new life. I was very little at six years old. I know that my mother was so excited about *aliya*, but she was so sad about leaving her eldest son behind. She reassured herself that it would be easy to bring him over after we got settled in Israel. Unfortunately, that was not the case.

We made *aliya* at the same time as my mother's sister. She came with her husband and her children. My father could have come with us, even though he was Christian. They would have kept our family together. But he did not want to come and he respected his parents and didn't want to leave them behind. My mother was lonely. My name Sewalem is made up of two words: *sew*, which means "man," and *alem*, which means "world." The name means that every person is an entire world. My mom was hoping that her children would be her whole world.

The plane we took had a group of Ethiopian *olim* traveling together. I recall that when we landed, they took us to the mall. We were given a talk and had a meeting. They fed us a meal, too. The food was weird. We had been eating only natural, local foods in Ethiopia, and here in Israel, we were given what seemed like junk food. It took a while to adjust to the difference.

This was just the beginning of our new lives.

ABSORPTION

In the first stage of our *aliya*, we lived in a *merkaz klita*, an absorption center for Ethiopian *olim* in Mevaseret Zion. I remember it as being a really fun experience. I took an *ulpan* class, and then for first and second grades, I was bussed to school to Modiin and then Beit Shemesh. I enjoyed school and did well.

Unfortunately, after we arrived in Israel, my mother became very ill. She had several different health issues; I am not sure what they were. My mother was hospitalized and during those times, we were at home alone. At one point, she was in the hospital in Jerusalem for over a month. The oldest sibling at home was twelve. We all took care of each other and had no one else watching or caring for us. When she was home, she was both our mother and our father. We are all good children, and we did not cause any trouble.

Things began to get better when she was feeling well. She was very happy to be in Israel because in Ethiopia she felt like she belonged, but she was an outsider. Here in Israel, she felt like this was where she was supposed to be. She also had her whole family here and that really helped support us. We were able to cook at home in the *merkaz klita*, so we were able to cook our Ethiopian food again. We had missed our injera.

We were in the *merkaz klita* for four and a half years. We were waiting for our father to send authorization that we could go through with our conversion process. Starting in 2003, it was put into law that when you come from Ethiopia, it does not matter if you can trace your Jewish identity or not. Either way, you must convert to make *aliya* and be considered Jewish here in Israel.

Since he was in Ethiopia, it took time for my father to send permission for us to undergo the process. It is not possible to go through the process if there is not an agreement between the parents. We had to send a letter and wait.

The conversion process itself was not long, but it took time to collect the authorizations. My mother could have gone through the process for herself and converted alone. She could have moved out and found a new place while we were waiting. But she waited to go through the process as a family. She wanted to do it with us and didn't want to be separated from us. In the meantime, we enjoyed life in the *merkaz klita*. We had youth groups and we did well in school. We spoke Hebrew on the outside and Amharic at home.

In 2006, we were able to complete the conversion process. I recall the feeling of standing in the waters of the *mikve*. In other families, the parents have to get remarried according to *halakha*, by the *Rabbanut*. Because marriages from our home country are not recognized by the *Rabbanut,* my mother was listed as single on her identification forms.

Four years into our absorption, we heard the news that my father had passed away. We found out several months after it occurred. My mother had heard at the time, but she did not tell us right away, and there was no *shiva* or grieving process. I had always said, "When I grow up and I finish my studies, I will go visit him." I didn't remember much of him but I felt sad. I remember being close to him. It took me a while to understand the reality of this loss. It was hard to internalize it. I was so far away. In the end, my mother should have been listed as a widow on her forms.

Now I just think about my brother, who was left alone with my father, and who is now without any of his immediate family at all. We are a family divided.

REMINDERS

After our conversion process was finished, we moved to Be'er Yaakov. We were reunited with my mother's sister, who had been living in Tzfat during her family's absorption process. I do not understand why they split up our families. At this point, though, they had moved to Be'er Yaakov and were waiting for us to join them.

We don't live in a large Ethiopian community, which can be difficult because my mother doesn't speak very much Hebrew. She understands us when we speak to her in Hebrew, but she mostly speaks Amharic. My mother was able to buy a house and we have been living there since 2007, for twelve years now. I still live at home with my siblings and my mother.

Growing up here in Israel, I feel like I am being constantly reminded that I am Ethiopian, though I find that where I immerse myself makes a difference. In some places of the country, people have accepted me for who I am. In others, they always remind me that I am different. Very often people make us feel like we are not smart because we come from Africa. I choose to have a strong internal voice that tells me that if I study hard, I will do well and I will be independent and successful. That is the voice that I choose to accompany me. But it is terrible. It is terrible to see the difficult circumstances of other Ethiopian immigrants because they feel so discouraged by the negativity and racism that they give up.

Thank God, in most places I felt accepted. I had positive experiences during high school in *ulpana* and in *sheirut leumi*. Yet, throughout my life, I have seen examples of racism that were painful for me.

For example, when I was doing my *sheirut leumi*, I was a supervisor for an *ulpan* class for new immigrants from Ethiopia who were in eleventh and twelfth grades. The *ulpana* where I was working tried to integrate the girls from the Ethiopian *ulpan* class into the rest of the school by putting Ethiopian students and other students together in the dorms. The idea was that if we all lived together, the new immigrants would acculturate and learn Hebrew.

I was shocked by what I saw. I didn't think that something like this could happen. But some girls wrote on their dorm request forms, "I don't want to be placed with girls from the *ulpan* class." I wondered, "What does that mean that you don't want to be with anyone from an entire class of girls? Just say what you mean. You don't want to be with Ethiopians."

It can happen that sometimes people don't get along. But when you are discriminating against an entire class of people, as opposed to struggling with personal differences, then you have a problem. The staff of the school should have held themselves responsible for fixing this problem and educating these kids to know that this kind of discrimination is not okay. But they took these requests "into consideration." In my opinion, racism is not something that you ever take into consideration. As an educator, it is your responsibility to teach them to be better than that.

Mentoring these young Ethiopian women was amazing. I really loved them. These girls were responsible, smart, and very serious. They even learned Hebrew before they arrived. They came here ready to succeed and now I can't wait for all of us to make a difference here in Israel and contribute meaningfully to society.

STATUS

When I was in tenth grade, I joined a movement that advocates for Ethiopians who are trying to immigrate to Israel. There are people who have been waiting for eighteen or twenty years in Gondar and Addis Ababa. It seems that the *Rabbanut* here in Israel is not willing to recognize them as Jews and refuses them entry. There are families who had children of a certain age, who were told that the parents should go ahead to Israel with the younger children, and that the older children would follow. Later, they closed the Ethiopian *aliya* and refused to let these children enter the country to join their families. Not all stories are like this, but there are many where the parents are here in Israel and the children are left behind and stuck in Ethiopia, waiting.

The State will not currently even bother checking my brother's status. They won't check if he is Jewish. He has all the same paperwork that we did. He has paperwork that shows that he is our brother and the son of my mother. But the State of Israel says that it is impossible for him to be our brother because he is too old and my mother is too young. They say it would be impossible for him to have been born to my mother, because it would mean that she would have been very, very young when he was born. But that is how it was in Ethiopia. She was a young bride and a young mother. They are not considering the cultural context from which we come.

So he is waiting. He wants to come; he has a family of his own now. We thought that at least, they would give him permission to enter the country to visit us when my sister got married. But he was denied. He couldn't even join us for a family *simḥa*. We prayed that he could come visit our mother, who is ill, but he was still denied. Being seperated from her son is very painful for my mother and very much affects her ability to get better. She is in much distress over not being able to see him. If only they would let my brother into the country to join our family, my mother can live in peace.

My mother has three grandchildren: two from my brother, and one from my sister. She always says, "If I don't see something with my own eyes, I don't believe it." It is hard for her to accept that she hasn't met two of her grandchildren.

Though my brother cannot come here, we are allowed to go there. My mother is too sick to travel, but I went back to our old village to see him. Three years ago, I went to volunteer in the community and visit with my brother, meet his children, and see our extended family on my father's side. It felt like a visit to the past.

GOING BACK

In the beginning, it felt like everything about Ethiopia was beautiful, but foreign. But then I began to remember. I saw our old house and it seemed so small. I wondered, "That door is tiny – how did we get in and out?" There were whispers in the village that I had returned. They kept saying, "The daughter has arrived…"

I was able to see my father's mother, my grandmother, once again. I got to see all my uncles. They recognized me and were thrilled that I had come back. My grandmother was so excited that I had returned, and she was sad that my father was not alive to see me, too. My grandfather had died two years before I came and that was upsetting because I would have loved to see him. My uncles don't live in the village – they are doctors in the cities, true scholars. But my grandmother lives with her daughter in the same village that I lived in as a child. My brother is still in the village with his family, too.

I was so emotional over seeing my brother again. He was also very emotional. It was hard for me to cry in front of my family that I had left behind, so I cried at night when I was alone and no one could see me. My brother was with me for a whole week. He dropped everything, including his agricultural work, to be with me. While I was there, he made a *brita* for his three-month-old daughter so I could be there for the celebration. After the party, I went to visit my father's grave. It was not like graves here in Israel. There, it was just a hole. I felt very emotional. But I was too flooded with emotions to cry at that moment.

It was very moving to meet my niece and nephew. They were scared to come close to me because I was a stranger to them. Even my brother's cows were frightened of me. I didn't feel at home in Ethiopia. My brother was still my brother, but I also felt the distance. Life there seems so hard. I don't know how my uncles managed to succeed; they are a doctor, an engineer, and a physics teacher. My brother is smart enough to be any of those things, but he decided to stay and farm the land that our father left him.

I was happy to come home to Israel at the end of that visit. When I landed, I was convinced that I would travel to Ethiopia every year to see my family there. Now three years have passed and I have not yet returned. One day I would like to bring my little brother to visit; he is nineteen now. We have a plan to fly together, God willing, when we can. He was so little when he came to Israel, and he is curious about where we came from.

My older brother continues to wait to make *aliya*. He has been saying to me, "When do I come? When do I come?" It is so hard for me to explain to him that we don't know when. The last I heard, his case is closed. I fought so hard for him to come. I brought so much proof – pictures and documents – that he is one of us. I don't understand why they won't allow them to come. I pray that one day, at my wedding, he will be here. We will fight to be reunited until he is allowed to come home.

BRING HIM HOME

I have many dreams. Right now I am studying bioinformatics. But later on in my life I want to study to become a psychiatrist. I don't know when it will happen, but it is what I want because of everything I have seen and learned about the impact of this arduous *aliya* process and how it impacts mental health. I want to learn about the brain. I want to study medicine. I want to research. I have seen so much pain and I want to help people feel better. I want to help people feel whole again.

I want to have a family. I

would love to raise my children as religious Zionists. I would love to offer my children a mother and a father and give them that experience that I didn't have growing up. I grew up without a father, so I know what it can be like. I want my kids to have everything. I want a partner for myself, too.

My main dream is that I want to be able to reunite my mother and brother. My mother's health is not an easy situation. I really want all of us to be together again. The fact that my mother and brother have been separated for so long has had a negative impact on my mother's physical and mental health. If I could make this dream of bringing my brother to *Eretz Yisrael* a reality, it would feel like I was successful in my life. It would feel like it was enough.

We have participated in many protests. We went to meet the members of the Knesset to talk to them. Our actions did ultimately bring changes because there were a few *aliyot* from Ethiopia in the last few years. My students' siblings were able to come and we went to the airport to welcome them.

We have written articles telling the stories of those left behind. We send them the newspaper clippings and try to continue spreading the word. Right now, though, *aliya* from Ethiopia is closed. Every time it is opened, it closes again. There are approximately eight thousand people in Ethiopia waiting to make *aliya*. One of the issues considered when an *aliya* application is filled out is whether there are family members in Israel. I am ready and waiting to fill out those forms for my brother, but I can't because currently there is nowhere to submit them. The office is closed.

It takes strength and heart to come up against politics and bureaucracy. This is a frustrating and sad process. Each person in the Knesset, if they were separated from their sibling, would do anything in their power to bring them home. I am not going to stop fighting for my brother until I have brought him home.

REFLECTIONS

Questions to Consider
- Have you ever had to start over from scratch?
- Has policy and bureaucracy affected your life?

Words to Remember

> "I choose to have a strong internal voice that tells me that if I study hard, I will do well and I will be independent and successful."

Group Discussion

When in your life have you come up against odds that felt impossible to beat?
What inspired you to keep going?

ઓ

Take a moment for yourself. What do you need right now?
Close your eyes and be in your own body.
Here is a resiliency exercise to come back to yourself:

Resiliency Exercise

Remember the moment of your greatest hardship. Review the details that you remember in your mind. See if there are moments where you can reframe the challenges. Perhaps there are moments of struggle that became opportunities for resilience. Retell your story to yourself with this new, empowered perspective.

Living to Thrive

Bayit VeGan, Jerusalem

TO BE HEALTHY

During my entire childhood, we viewed our house as a temporary home. We always knew that we would one day make *aliya*; it was always in our parents' grand plan. With every piece of furniture we owned or bought, we would consider whether we would keep it or sell it before *aliya*. When we made home improvements, it was not so much for our own enjoyment but to make the house more attractive for the time that we would put it up for sale.

My mother always says her tagline is "Man plans and God laughs." Before I was born, my father had a brain tumor and nearly died. His recovery was considered a miracle, even by the doctors who saved him. I grew up knowing that every day he lived was a precious gift. He and my mom told us how "tumor humor" got him through the really tough times. He continues to use humor as a tool to deal with challenges in life and encourages us to do the same.

When I was a child, I heard all the stories of what my family went through before I was born. These stories were presented through a lens of laughter, jokes, and having achieved victory over "the demon of cancer." Unfortunately, my father experiences some consequences from the tumor and treatments that cause him to be chronically ill (after a brief lull of full health that lasted for a few years after his initial diagnosis). Yet he keeps up his humor and never complains. He is a quiet, gentle man, but a fierce fighter inside and he never gives up or gives in to challenges. He is so grateful to be alive to see us grow and thrive and has always been there for our family no matter what.

When my father was sick and we were younger, his parents were always around to take care of us. And when he was well, they were also around so that my parents could take a vacation now and then. They spent every *ḥag* with us and we were often together for *Shabbat*, too. They helped our family succeed in so many ways. Now they are elderly and ill and my father has dedicated his life to helping them in their time of need. This is why my parents are still in the house they plan to sell one day, living with some of the furniture they viewed as temporary.

They instilled their love and yearning for Israel in all of us. One of my brothers came here to Israel for high school and served in the IDF as a *ḥayal boded*. Now he has made a home for himself in Ariel, working as a police officer. My oldest brother moved to Jerusalem with his young family.

I joined them two years later. We have more siblings back in the States and I am praying for the day that my parents can join us here, too. It's been so

hard to be separated from them. While it is hard for our family to be split up, we are learning such a beautiful lesson from our parents about respect and gratitude. Our time together will come at the right time.

Around the time that my father was beginning to have recurring symptoms from his illness, I was in fifth grade and my class was taught a nutrition curriculum. The content and materials really pushed the concept of healthy eating too far. Naturally, having given a lot of thought to health in general, I was very motivated to be healthy. But I took it even further. I cut out everything that would be considered "fatty" from my life. It wasn't that I wanted to be skinny, it was that I was so traumatized by the material and afraid of the health risks associated with becoming fat. I felt desperate to be healthy. As I began to restrict my food, I began to lose weight. Before long, I was no longer at a healthy weight for someone as young as I was.

I noticed that when I began to lose weight, I started to get attention from boys in my grade. Looking back, I recognize that these friendships began at an age-appropriate time, likely not connected to the fact that I was losing weight. But in the moment, that correlation was made and noted. I "got skinny" and boys started talking to me. Over the years, my fixation on eating and being skinny grew. I tried to lose weight so I could fit into my bat mitzva dress, because that is what women do. They lose weight to fit into their dresses before a big event. But my health was slowly unraveling, spiraling out of control.

When I went to the doctor for a checkup, I was told that I was not at a healthy weight. I didn't believe them. Wasn't I doing all of this so I could be healthy? They told me that my weight was far too low for my size and age. They knew about the way that I was eating. I was diagnosed with anorexia, and my team – doctors, parents, teachers – set out to help me recover.

CYCLE OF HELL

I was barely in school for all of eighth grade. I would go to doctors who recommended a method that encouraged eating as a family. The idea was to always eat together, and that everyone would partake of a variety of rich foods as a way to normalize eating. I was not sent to rehab or put in a hospital. I was still okay enough to be home. But it was rough. I went to twice-weekly visits with anorexia specialists, and sometimes my mother even had to come to school to eat with me.

During this time, my mother and I would fight like cats and dogs. It was such a difficult process to eat the way that they wanted me to eat while fighting the anorexia that lived in my head. In the end, the healing process bonded me with my mother. Her perseverance and refusal to give up on me saved my life. Till this day, I consider her to be one of my best friends.

I would go to doctors and they would weigh me. But I wasn't gaining weight like they wanted. At a certain point, my stomach started to reject the food. I couldn't hold down the ice cream, the protein shakes, the pasta. I would vomit at least once a day. I was not doing it on purpose. I did not want to throw up. I really wanted to get better. But my stomach just could not contain what I was putting in it. What we didn't know at the time was that I have anxiety-induced irritable bowel syndrome (IBS). When I become really anxious, it feels like there is a wrench being thrown around inside my stomach. I physically cannot eat. That led to a cycle of hell.

I would sit and cry about how badly I wanted to eat, how much I wanted to get healthy – really healthy, not an imagined healthy. I was ready to begin to heal from my anorexia, but the thought of that would make me more anxious. When my anxiety took over, I could not put food in my mouth. I was lost in a cycle of being anxious because I wasn't gaining weight, or because my parents were upset, or being afraid of not getting healthy, or just being afraid of life in general. My severe anxiety made everything so complicated. I developed panic attacks and phobias. Till this day, I am phobic of vomiting. It is so triggering for me.

When I was in ninth grade, after a year of trying to hold down enough food and gaining just enough weight to "feed my brain," as the doctors put it, I was finally diagnosed with anxiety. I was put on medication and a more focused therapy, stressing less about my eating and more about dealing with my anxiety. I learned that my brain just doesn't make the chemicals that it is supposed to make, and that medication and therapy can fill the gaps. I was able to heal and recover. I was finally able to stop the cycle of hell. But two years later, the summer before twelfth grade, my anxiety relapsed.

FOR THE BEST

I was enrolled in an incredible coding program that summer. I was at the high point of my life thus far, meeting new people and learning these awesome skills that I had become so passionate about. I was gaining self-confidence and practical knowledge that I could take into adulthood.

I also broke up with my boyfriend and it was definitely for the best. I had dated him for three and a half years and it was time for me to focus on myself. I finally had the time to think about my needs. But still, the breakup was really hard for me. The change started up my anxiety again. To make things even worse, I had held on to some toxic friends for far too long. The anxiety-induced vomiting began again. The same old cycle restarted. I was miserable and vulnerable.

When my suffering got more intense, a "friend" texted me something hurtful and shaming about my condition. That was a turning point for me. I ditched her and the rest of the toxic people in my life who were bringing me down. The very same day, I made some new friends who are still there for me today, through my ups and downs. It was *min hashamayim,* coordinated by the heavens. Sometimes the most difficult moments can bring the best things and people into your life.

My family knew what to do to help me recover again. We did intensive, focused therapy. I got better. My family and friends were behind me. My school took my experience seriously, too. They didn't look down on me or say that I was just spiraling out of control over a breakup. They understood that these transitional moments and loss of friendships can be so hard on a teenager. They treated me with respect and accommodation, which I will forever appreciate.

This experience brought me closer to my family. These moments were so formative. They taught me how to care for myself and how to empathize with others.

NO RESPECT

When I got to seminary, I continued to see a therapist. All around me, girls were struggling with eating disorders. Many girls were restricting their eating as a form of control in their new environment. Others were bingeing on food, knowing that they were expected and "allowed" to gain weight. Many pictures of girls eating were tagged with #sem70, as in the seventy pounds you gained when you went away to Israel for the  year. The glorification of disordered eating really disturbed me.

My anxiety was still difficult to manage. I didn't go to class as often as I should have. I just felt like hiding under my covers. I was overwhelmed by the transitional moments and wrestling with the decision of whether I should be making *aliya* on my own. I was trying to figure out who I was and who I wanted to be.

I think of my anxiety as a boiling pot of water. Sometimes it spills over because the flame is too high. I try everything to keep it from spilling over. I try to lower the flame; the heat is whatever is triggering me. Sometimes it continues to bubble and spill over. Sometimes it abates and the water – my emotions – remains at a simmer, all staying in the pot under control.

Every time I felt down or overwhelmed, I would get back up. I would talk to my friends or my mother. I dealt with the overwhelming feelings by taking one day at a time. My head became clearer. I felt empowered to make decisions and take a more active role in my life.

I decided to stay in Israel, make *aliya*, and do *Sheirut Leumi*, national service, for a year. I made *aliya* in August 2017 on a charter flight. My mom met me here and helped me settle in for my first two weeks. We opened my bank account and dealt with all the bureaucracy. I accepted a *Sheirut* position in Petah Tikva.

When my mother left Israel, I moved into my apartment. I arrived at my first day at my new job. When I walked in, they said, "Who are you?" They had lost all my paperwork and my placement had slipped through the cracks. I told them, "I made *aliya* two weeks ago and I am registered for *Sheirut Leumi*. I need a job, or I am homeless." They pitied me. They nicknamed me *Miskeina*, which translates to "poor thing." They didn't have a job for me, but they let me stay in the *Sheirut Leumi* housing. They gave me two hundred shekels out of the eight hundred shekels that I was supposed to get every month. They were also supposed to give me lunch every day and as I was short on cash, I was relying on that benefit. They told me, "You spoiled American, you think you deserve to get lunch?" I was bewildered. I had signed up. They had offered me a position and because there was a change in administration, everything got messed up.

My *rakezet,* the person who was assigned to be there for me emotionally during this process, told me, "Just go back to America, where you came from. Who needs you?"

I felt so alone. If I had been a lone soldier, I would have had so much support behind me. There are organizations dedicated to the well-being of those soldiers. There's a safety net of support. I had no one to advocate for me. There was a new, small organization that was made up of some former *Benot Sheirut* who understood the challenges. They tried to help but they were not equipped to deal with the big issues I was having. At least their validation was helpful.

People don't know that *Benot Sheirut Bodedot* exist, that there are young women, eighteen to twenty-four years old, who are here without their parents and doing national service. As a *Bat Sheirut Bodeda*, you get eight hundred shekels a month from the *Sheirut* program. You are entitled to five hundred shekels more from *Misrad HaKlita*, the Ministry of Absorption, for making *aliya*. You are not entitled to the discounts that soldiers get. While lone soldiers get discounts at restaurants, supermarkets, and even spas and hotels, there are none for *Benot Sheirut Bodedot*.

The country relies on the women who do national service. *Gan* is so inexpensive because it is staffed with women doing their service. A key reason why hospitals work semi-properly is because there are *Benot Sheirut* doing a great deal of the work behind the scenes. Tourist attractions, rehabilitation centers, at-risk youth programs, and more. They all rely heavily on *Benot Sheirut*.

In the job that I am doing right now, I make applications and devices for organizations and government offices that need these interfaces but cannot afford to fund them. We are working with some of the most vital organizations in the country, serving the most vulnerable populations. We are the grease in the wheels that helps the country run, most often behind the scenes.

We give heart and soul to our jobs. We volunteer because we believe fully in helping the country. Sadly, we get very little respect.

HEAD ABOVE WATER

Last year I was sick for a week. I was so lonely. I was alone in the apartment. I just needed my mom to care for me. I was only twenty years old.

I realized that I needed to get back into therapy. I found a good therapist who gives discounts to *Benot Sheirut*. We began to do some art therapy. She would encourage me to draw my feelings, and I would draw images of myself at a crossroads. What was I going to do after my service was over? What was I going to do with the rest of my life?

I loved the job where I ended up doing my service after the one in Petah Tikva fell apart. I even signed up for two years. After working for eighteen months, I took a quick trip to America to see my family. Coming back to Israel after visiting America was one of the hardest things I have ever done. I was just so miserable. I missed my family so much and I felt so alone here. I was working so hard and I felt like no one understood my situation. In

my misery, I texted my rabbi from seminary and he responded. "When you made *aliya*, your sails were flying in the wind. Now you have to pedal and keep that boat afloat. There will be easier times with wind ahead, and now you just need to keep pedaling."

He was so right. I just needed to keep my head above water. I decided to focus on the next steps, looking at my life in a bigger picture. I always thought that I would be a computer programmer. I've been passionate about coding since I was a teen. But during this second year of service I wasn't a coder anymore. They recognized that I have other talents, like public speaking, activism, and design. So now I do UX and UI design, social media, marketing, and public speaking.

Going forward, I am planning to do a year of *mekhina* at Hebrew University. I want to feel prepared and work on my academic Hebrew, and *mekhina* will give me a nice slow transition. *Mekhina* is paid for by our national service and we get a small stipend. It doesn't cover everything, but it helps a bit.

I run a blog, *Living That Bodedah Life*, for Nefesh B'Nefesh. It's a platform for *Benot Sheirut Bodedot* to share their stories. I also run my own blog, *Adventures with Avital*, chronicling my personal experiences since *aliya*. Young women just like me experience things like bed bugs in their apartments, sexual abuse in *Sheirut Leumi* jobs, mental health struggles, and coworkers taking advantage of them. It is really important to get the truth of our experiences out there.

I am so passionate about advocating for people like us. I have a meeting scheduled with the head of the entire *Sheirut Leumi* program to talk about how they can make it better for all of us, not just *Bodedot*. He came to my work and I popped up and introduced myself as an advocate for the needs of *Benot Sheirut*. His assistant told me that one day I'll probably be one of the *olim* invited to light a candle at a special event because of my advocacy. I've set my mind to it. I just have this powerful desire to help people, to change the world. I am just one person with very lofty goals. I am still trying to not let my anxiety hold me back. There is so much that I want to do. That in itself, ironically, is an overwhelming thought.

THRIVING

Sometimes it feels like in life, you have to be a big important person in order to get people to listen to you. I am a young person. I have so few resources at my disposal, besides for my passion and attitude. Right now, I am so passionate about women in tech. It is not just about educating women to be in tech. There are tons of people out there who are already educating women to code and design. That is not what I am worried about. What I see is missing is what keeps women in tech. There is a huge dropout rate because it can sometimes be a toxic environment for women. We need to help women to be confident, to get up and talk, and to advocate for themselves. I want to empower women to stay in the field and thrive.

We need to learn to assert ourselves. Oftentimes at work, women come up against a whole host of problems, such as men taking credit for women's ideas, sexual harassment, and inflexible environments that make it difficult to have a family.

I've had amazing mentors who encouraged me to be strong and confident, to embrace the kind of leadership that is inclusive and that raises up everyone around me. They encouraged me to speak up for myself and include that exclamation mark in my email! They have told me to be fierce, because I am, and to be brave and live with the knowledge that I don't need to be perfect. I don't care what other people think of me and that lets me be myself. I can accept failure as part of growth. Mentorship is so important. It is really hard to be what you can't see. I am always seeking out women who inspire me and who can teach me.

For now, I am taking one stage at a time. I let my passion propel me forward but I am careful about my pace. My dedication to my self-care allows me to thrive. I find time for my art. I eat well and mindfully. Most importantly, I make time to laugh, both with myself and with others. I find the humor even in the tough times, just like my dad. My life is imperfect, and complicated, and full of potential. I can't wait to see what I do next.

REFLECTIONS

Questions to Consider

- How important was your relationship with adults when you were a teen?
  Were they able to support you?
- What are your hopes and dreams for the future?

Words to Remember

"I don't care what other people think of me and that lets me be myself. I can accept failure as a part of growth."

Group Discussion

What role has mentorship played in your life?

Take a moment for yourself. What do you need right now?
Close your eyes and be in your own body.
Here is an affirmation exercise to come back to yourself:

Affirmation Exercise

I am strong. I can weather the challenges that come my way.

I am smart. I can create the reality that I want for myself.

I am patient. I can wade through the tough stuff to get to the other side.

I have hope. I believe that my future will be bright.

The Power of the Mind-Body Connection

Tzfat

LET ME CHOOSE

I was born and raised in Venezuela. I am a Latin girl by every definition; I am passionate, and I love music, the beach, and dancing. I grew up in a secular Jewish home, but at the age of eighteen, I had an amazing life-changing encounter with the Lubavitcher Rebbe. I always say it changed my spiritual pH.

When I first got to Crown Heights, I came in jeans and a t-shirt. I came to explore New York before I went to university. I wanted to have fun. My brother who lived there couldn't host me for the week. My mother was already on her *baalas teshuva* journey and had begun learning Torah. She told me about a rabbi's daughter who could host me, and I stayed in Crown Heights with this girl who was super ultra-Orthodox. The only thing we had in common was that we both were female.

At that time, my father was very ill and my sister had just broken off an engagement. Someone offered to take me to visit the Lubavitcher Rebbe. I had heard that he gave blessings. I had no idea what a *tzaddik* was and I had never seen someone who embodied spirituality on a deep level. I had no dictionary that would help me understand the soul or a higher life, although I considered myself a spiritual person. At the time, I was only interested

211

in psychology, philosophy, and astrology; anything Jewishly spiritual was remote from me.

I was always looking for more. I would ask myself, "Is this all there is?" I felt that there had to be something else out there. I didn't know to call what I was looking for "God" or *hashgacha pratis,* but I felt there was something more. I am an introvert, and I was never a person of small talk. I needed deep conversations about the universe, parallel lives, or even reincarnation.

When I met the Rebbe, I felt a rush of something. I couldn't understand what it was. He told me that I should have *hatzlacha* at Machon Chana. One thing led to another and I realized that it meant going to a yeshiva for girls and I thought to myself, "No thank you, I am way too busy and I am not interested. Nice try. Not now." I heard so many myths about what it meant to become *frum* and I wasn't interested.

Yet, I felt like I had zero clue what it meant to be Jewish. I thought to myself, "Even if I don't keep this lifestyle, I need to explore it." The Jews in Crown Heights looked so happy and I desperately wanted to know what their philosophy of life was. They seemed to have a purpose and I wanted to know what made them tick. I'm Jewish too, so I thought, "I need to understand if this lifestyle would work for me."

Out of deep curiosity, I went to one *shiur* at Machon Chana. It was a class on the *Tanya* and I stayed for one class. I came back for another and another. By the end of the week, impulsively and intuitively, I decided that I needed to stay there. My father was so worried that I was going to marry a guy with a beard and *peyos,* and my mom was in tears. I said, "Mom, I'm not going to get married. I am just learning."

I stayed. A year and four months later, I was offered a *shidduch.* He was a guy who had just come from Israel, a former officer in the army who studied political science and history of the Middle East. He was very worldly. They gave me his information as if I couldn't say no. I thought we would meet, say hello, and say goodbye.

The minute he walked into the room, there was something about him that pulled at me. It wasn't love at first sight, but I immediately knew I would marry him. We got married four months later in Israel. It was an utter shock to my family and I too was surprised by my decision to take this next step. He was learning in Tzfat, and had become *frum* at the same time as I did. We decided to stay here in Tzfat for the year. When the second year rolled around, we already had a child and were pregnant with our second.

I came to Israel with no language, newly married, already having babies, new to running a household, and in need of a job. I was in a completely new environment which I didn't know how to manage. I was completely alone, with no family or friends, and feeling lost. I would get dressed in fancy clothes every day, which made me feel like an outsider among the people in my community who would dress very simply. I didn't want to give up who I was or what I liked just because I was in a new environment. But I felt like I didn't belong and that I struggled to fit in. I was from a different world. I think that is when everything started taking a toll on me.

DANCING BETWEEN TWO WORLDS

I didn't quite like where we were living. My husband had a job, I had some work on the side, and I was busy with the kids and the house. I was always a perfectionist and I wanted things to be the way I liked them. But I didn't have things the way I was accustomed to them. Never mind that I grew up

with household help and that I was currently living a simpler life. Life here, in this space, was just a huge adjustment. Even the smallest things, like shopping, were different. Coming from my Latin Sephardic home, when you asked for apples, you got a big basket of apples. I asked for apples here, and they asked me in return, "How many do you need?" It was just a totally new mentality.

Here I was, running a home, pregnant, paying bills, managing a budget, working, and cooking. Before, I had barely known how to boil water and never did *sponja* in my life. I felt I was constantly between two worlds. I didn't want to let go of who I was, but I was committed to the lifestyle we had chosen. I hadn't become *frum* because I didn't like who I was. I did like myself. I became *frum* because I was seeking meaning and answers. Now I had to balance all these parts of me. I made a commitment to myself to never forget who I was and who I am, to never relinquish my personality, and to bring those vibrant parts of me wherever I go.

The Rebbe told me that Nathalie was also my Hebrew name. I think he knew that it fit me, and I needed it to continue to be rooted in myself while I was *chozeres b'teshuva*.

I felt like I constantly had to dance between two worlds, being myself and being in a place that was slowly forcing me to become someone else. I tried to make my home look (almost) like Miami Beach, with white leather couches, white flowers, and a crystal table. It really retained the look of a South American home. But I had so much anxiety about preserving it – that style, that personality. My kids were always perfectly dressed in fancy clothes, but it wasn't natural for the environment that we were living in. I just always felt like an outsider. I needed to find my own way of doing things so I could be myself and still be a part of something beyond myself.

Because I became *frum*, I was always questioning, "Is this something I believe in and connect to, or is it something that is being pushed on me?" I needed to make sure that what I was doing was authentic to me, without compromising *halacha*. Whatever I do, I feel compelled to add my own signature touch. Even my weight plays a role in that dynamic. I think it's protecting me. Emotional eating is something I developed at an early age when my parents got divorced. I was nine years old and trying to cope.

My weight protects me from feeling too much. It becomes a wall between myself and someone else. It offers a boundary between the way that I look and the rest of the world. When I became *frum*, I became concerned with being "too much." I was afraid to be too attractive or attracting. Beauty was not valued in my new space like it had been where I came from. I was ashamed of being too much. Maybe subconsciously, I ate so that I could be heavier, which I thought would "diminish my looks" in the eyes of others. Maybe it would make it easier for other people to accept me, even though I was still different from everyone around me. Or maybe being overweight makes me too much, still. It's an issue for me. It obviously still serves a purpose and a *tikkun* because it is still here.

I'm a very sensitive person. I feel too much. I am sensitive to energy and other people's feelings. Being an empath and an introvert can be powerful, but it is also very draining. I have learned to make better boundaries for myself. The journey from empath to codependent is very short. I can now say that I have healed from that struggle of being drained by others' emotions, but I will always remain an introvert.

DOOR ALWAYS OPEN

There is a part of me that feels like I always kept the door half open, never fully committing to my life here. It was, however, the perfect place to raise children. I have nine children, *baruch Hashem*. It is quiet, as there is no rushing here. It feels like an ancient way of living. My oldest child is twenty-five. My youngest is seven. Five girls, four boys, no twins, one husband.

Because of my anxiety about living an authentic life, maybe I opened the door to what happened in my family. My children are so comfortable looking for what feels authentic to them, that it opened up many other possibilities. Four of my children have chosen not to be religious at this point in time. I am not sorry that my children are not *frum*, because I know that there is always a possibility that when they begin to look for their truth, they will open up to their upbringing and search for it. I am sorry for the fact that *frumkeit* is often taught in small, restrictive boxes that make it harder for many children to relate to it. This generation doesn't fit into any small boxes. Children are always crying out for truth.

I feel like the fact that my kids aren't *frum* is a part of their struggle to find truth where it lies for them. Of course, I wanted all nine of my children to turn out exactly the way that I wanted them to be. I wanted the perfect family with the perfect *frum* kids in the system, happy, and committed. But what we want is sometimes not what Hashem wants, and I feel blessed because what is really important is the connection that we share with our children. We can always be a safe space for them. They can always feel comfortable coming home.

I learned very early that my kids are not a continuation of me. They can't be what I wasn't, and I can't give them what I don't have. I give them the best of what I know. I try to help and guide them. I am there for them 100 percent of the time. Life taught all of us that if we want something, we need to work for it. We can't have everything we want all the time. At the end of the day, when I am questioning myself as a parent, I remember that my children have told me, "The first person I will call when I am in trouble is you. The first place I want to run when I am feeling bad is home."

I tell myself that I had children so that I could be a part of their chosen lives and be there for them as best I can. I may have dreamt of being like a perfect family billboard, but I want to create independent kids, and that means that our family won't match that perfect image. To us, though, our kids are everything. They are all deep, spiritual, beautiful, kind, and loving. Whatever they do with their lives, we are going to be there for them.

That isn't to say that it doesn't take a toll on me and my marriage. My husband and I had to do a lot of work to get to the point where we could accept all our differences. Growing up, my mother was very authoritative in the home. I felt it was too much, so I tried to be the opposite. I was very lenient at home. It wasn't that I didn't want to be like her, I was just running away from any conflict or confrontation until I very quickly found what felt like my middle ground. I took a more engaged approach; I talk to my kids about what is going on. I ask them about their feelings and ideas. We talk about the hard stuff, and I am not afraid to have tough conversations. What I am afraid of is becoming numb and doing things just because everyone else is doing them.

Life happened. We had lots of *shalom bayis* issues. I had many community struggles. The first major rift came when I decided to accept my child and to not be ashamed of the ways he has deviated from our community. At that moment, I owned the fact that I have nothing to be embarrassed about. So often, I find that we are punitive with our children because of what the *rabbonim* are going to say, or what the community will say. How are we going to be looked at as a parent? We worry that "they" are going to think that we are failures.

I got to the point where I said, "I didn't plan this. No parent plans that their child will live a different lifestyle than them. There is someone else who runs the world and has a plan. I have done my best with the tools I had and the energy I had when I had it. If I would have known better, I would have done better. This is what my child has to go through on his own soul journey."

Once I started embracing my child where he was, regardless of what the community thought, I felt a lot of loneliness. I felt that my community didn't understand my choice. People probably feel like I am often opening Pandora's box. Maybe it stirs something in their souls because this issue reflects on everyone. There is so much we need to do in our communities and schools; both are making it difficult for children who are searching or struggling to stay. Something needs to change. It can't be that so many children are leaving the *derech* and getting caught up in drugs, alcohol, and any kind of addiction because they feel isolated and don't have answers for what they are going through.

WHAT IS HAPPENING TO ME?

In my professional work, I am a spiritual life coach. I help people find purpose and meaning through emotional management. I have spoken to thousands of women as individuals and in groups, both in Israel and abroad. I address life issues and try to provide some tools to help people live authentically and successfully.

Four years ago, after returning from a speaking tour in Miami and Mexico,

I came back home and decided to create a daily blog in Spanish called *Fresh Water for the Soul* (*Agua fresca para el alma*) to offer spiritual inspiration.

I use coaching tools, positive psychology, and stories from all sorts of people, and I incorporate *Chasidus* and *Kabbala*. I sent one post to a group of fifty people, and it just exploded. It was the right thing at the right time – or what I call synchronicity. I love blogging and connecting with others. It brings out all the different sides of myself and I feel I can help people.

A year ago, I was invited for a public speaking tour in Panama and Mexico. I talked about real issues, like intimacy, self-worth, what really goes on in the *frum* world, and how we need to address these issues. I spoke about how fungus grows in dark, warm spaces and how we can eradicate so many problems by just exposing them to the air and light. I talked about how we, as a Jewish community, need to talk about important things and stop sweeping them under the rug. I focused on our important role as women and leaders.

But when I came back from that talk, I was very anxious. My back started to twinge in pain. I ignored it. I remember being on the plane and feeling like I pulled out my shoulder when I was moving my suitcase, but I just chalked it up to working too hard. I just wanted to get home.

I have always had back pain, anxiety, migraines, and more. Whenever I feel overcome with pain or hardship, I often get another wave of energy to keep going. I always ask myself, "Where does this energy come from?" I think people think that I seem so strong and capable and that I can manage everything. Most people don't even ask me how I am doing, because they just assume that I've got it together. I don't always have it together.

When I got home, it was three weeks before *Rosh HaShana*. My house was a mess and I felt so overwhelmed and drained, like I had zero energy. I did what I know how to do best, which was to strain myself until I collapsed. I was working and working, cooking and cleaning, and catching up on everything. I just kept pushing myself. I pushed too hard.

BAD TO WORSE

During this time, my two eldest daughters returned home after a trip and three years away in the Tel Aviv area, where they worked.

My eldest son came for *Yom Kippur*. He had a very traumatic experience in the army and he had developed epilepsy as an adult. For two years, we didn't know that he was struggling. I found out from someone else that he had epilepsy, but I didn't want to push him to tell me how he was doing or whether he was following his protocol. If he wasn't telling me, he wasn't ready yet and was clearly working through something. When he told me he was coming for the holiday, I was so excited. He also mentioned that he wanted to fast. I was thrilled. Maybe this meant that he was considering reconnecting again? Maybe he was ready to engage in spiritual work? What I didn't know was that fasting is contraindicated for the medication that he was taking. Fasting is dangerous.

On *Yom Kippur* morning, I went to *Shacharis*. I came home around *Mincha* time because I started to get a migraine. All of a sudden, I heard this loud scream. It was like a moan. My other son came running into my room shouting for me. I went into my older son's room. He was seizing. The moment of seeing that seizure was the most frightening thing I have ever witnessed. I jumped on his bed and turned him onto his side because I was afraid he would choke on his saliva or swallow his tongue.

When I jumped and pulled him to safety, I felt something painful in my back. I told my other daughter to hold my son still and had another child call an ambulance. Five minutes later, it arrived and they took him to the hospital. At that point, I was already walking while holding on to the wall because I was in so much pain. My family asked me what was wrong with me and I said, "I don't know. I guess I hurt myself when I lunged forward to help him."

I was getting ready to go visit my son that night and as we got in the car, I realized how bad the pain was. Then we got a call that my son had another seizure. After we hung up, I felt something tighten in my back and the pain intensified even more. My husband had to pull me out of the car and help me to bed. I was bedridden from that day for seven full months. I got out of bed only two months ago.

The first month was bad. The second was even worse. I could barely turn over. I couldn't shower. I couldn't go to the bathroom. I couldn't go to the *mikve*. My husband and I were so afraid of what was happening to me. I didn't know what was going on. Was I depressed or anxious? Was I shutting down? Was I dying? I thought I was going to die in my sleep. I couldn't even write. I couldn't concentrate. I was just lying in bed like a zombie, thinking that my life was over. And in a way, it was.

SUBCONSCIOUS

That *Yom Kippur*, life was just taken from me. I began to ask, "What did I do wrong?"

Only someone who has lived with this kind of pain can understand what this kind of suffering can do to your life. I used to cry from how badly it made me feel, from the amount of energy that it took to hold myself up when I wanted a cup of water, and from the frustration of seeing the house fall apart once again. What it took to make myself a cup of coffee when no one was home! Sometimes I would just have to lie down no matter where I was in the house because I couldn't continue.

It became a situation where my mind was playing games with me. I knew that something was happening but I had no idea what it was. I was just caught between my brain and my body and trying my best to hold on, even though I had no hope.

I was endlessly lonely. I would cry that no one was talking to me, but then I would talk to no one. I told no one about what was going on. I didn't want anyone to know what was happening, but I also wanted everyone to know. I pushed everyone away. I was such a perfectionist that it was devastating to think that someone would think that I wasn't perfect. They could say, "Oh, she actually can't manage." It was tapping into my deepest vulnerabilities.

My amazing daughter had come home a few months before her sister, who had also been away for the previous few years. She was the one who helped me manage the house and take care of the other children. I don't know what would have happened without her help.

I felt like I was losing everything I was. It made me wonder, "If I have lost all of this, who am I?" Doctors gave me a diagnosis that meant that my back was out. I took all kinds of medicine that didn't seem to help. A few months ago, my husband went to America on a speaking tour and he stayed in Crown Heights. He told his host family what was going on with me and his hostess called me. She suggested I stop all my treatments. I had not been taking narcotic pain killers and either way, nothing was helping. I had done disc suction, two epidurals, Pilates, and more at the suggestion of my doctor.

This woman told me about a diagnosis I had never heard of, Tension

Myostis Syndrome. I learned that TMS causes real physical symptoms that cause pain and discomfort in the body, but it is not due to any pathological or structural abnormalities and cannot be explained by diagnostic tests. The pain symptoms or other biological changes are caused by mild oxygen deprivation via the autonomic nervous system. The theory behind the diagnosis is that this is a result of repressed negative emotions and psycho-social stress.

To put it frankly, we are talking about real physical pain that is caused by emotions that we are keeping inside and refusing to acknowledge to ourselves. It is about emotions that go against our belief system and that are unacceptable to us, and so we repress them. We can't acknowledge them, so we swallow them. The negative feelings can range from guilt, shame, rejection, resentment, rage, and trauma. Sometimes, because of a desire for perfectionism, or to be wholly (and holy) good, the fact that we have any flaws or imperfections, make mistakes, or experience normal human limitations serves as fodder for negative feelings that lead to physical pain.

Imagine that the brain knows what is unacceptable to us. It knows things that have happened to us, or truths that are unspeakably painful. It knows how much it would hurt us emotionally if we had to deal with those truths. This theory suggests that the brain believes that distracting us with physical pain will prevent us from having to engage with those painful truths that it thinks would be shattering to us. Forcing those unacceptable things into our subconscious, the brain thinks that it is protecting us by distracting us with physical pain.

When we are triggered to the point where those issues begin to creep back into our minds, the brain hits the trigger button, cuts off oxygen to parts of the body, and the pain erupts, distracting us once again. Once I understood these concepts, they deeply resonated with me.

DARK PLACES

There are people I like to call "anger machines." They do not filter or temper their anger. I have a few people like that in my life. I feel as if I am the opposite. If I feel angry, I just put it away, tie it up with a neat little bow and repress it. I label it and stick it in a good, sturdy box in my mind. I don't talk about it. I don't want to get angry and act like I'm *meshuga*. I don't want to look like that.

I am afraid of feeling so angry that I will feel crazy. My need to control everything and to make sure everything is perfect is what drives me. Feeling angry makes me feel out of control. I always have a fear of looking crazy, because when I see people who are angry, they look out of control to me. I know that I have never learned how to channel anger in a healthy way. I am afraid to be angry, but then I am furious that I can't express it. This cycle so clearly ties into this new understanding of my symptoms.

In my family and in my marriage, there had been a cycle of anger, expressed and repressed. For so long, I chose to walk on eggshells and keep the negative feelings to myself, maybe even hiding them from myself so I didn't have to engage with them. If we would have a fight at home, I would hush my husband and make sure that all the windows and doors were shut so no one would know. I did this so that we would seem perfect to the outside world.

About nine years ago, I started not caring about what other people thought about me and I was able to begin to free myself. I disconnected from toxic people who were bringing me down. I recreated my marriage and made things so much better with us. I worked on my relationships with my kids. I did things that were non-traditional and even deemed radical by some. I owed it to myself to make myself better and work on myself and my relationships. I was learning to accept myself in my darkest moments. Sometimes in those dark moments, we make it seem like we don't deserve anything. We don't deserve love. We deserve to be relegated to staying in bed, not being able to live our lives. We don't deserve the control that we so desperately crave. We can't be trusted with it.

Just a few months ago, I was in one of those dark places. I felt like I was dying slowly. There were nights when I went to bed and didn't want to wake up the next morning. I begged Hashem to take me. I couldn't suffer anymore. I begged Him to take me or help me heal. I don't know if the emotional torture or the physical pain was worse.

When I was finally able to grasp the concept of this new diagnosis, I realized how much of what I experienced finally made sense. My chronic pain was always connected to emotional discomfort and negative feelings. I can look back and track every time the pain started or got worse, and see that it was connected to a major life stressor that caused me immeasurable emotional pain that was too hard for me to deal with. My son being sick, for example – the fear, anger, and unacceptability of that reality was immense. Maybe my brain thought that I couldn't handle it. Maybe it put me to bed, thinking that it would be easier for me to deal with back pain than to deal with what was happening with my son. Maybe this was the answer I was looking for.

HEALING

I began following the treatment protocol for my mind-body work. The premise of recovery is that we need to uncover the subconscious issues we are defending against. We need to acknowledge that the real pain we are experiencing is caused by our emotional distress. We need to break the pain cycle by deconditioning ourselves from expecting pain in certain circumstances. We need to fully get in touch with our emotions and our body to make sense of what we have been experiencing.

For some, recovery can be an immediate process. Once the brain understands that its defense mechanism isn't helping and that these issues are no longer subconscious, but fully conscious, sometimes the brain just returns oxygen to the locations where it had been cut off. The pain is relieved and you are free to resume living. Other times, it can be a more complicated process of therapy, journaling, deconditioning, self-talk, patience, and more.

I began the process. I began journaling and writing about what I was feeling in my body and in my emotional life. I practiced self-talk, reminding myself that I was angry, maybe at my husband, community, son, daughter, or myself. I acknowledged what was true for me. I thanked myself for the awareness of the reality of what I was going through, and I befriended my pain.

Once I began the process, I began to see improvement. I was able to get out of bed. I began to resume my life. I was able to be a mother again. I am now taking care of my home and I have gone back to work and speaking. Carefully, I have begun my life again. My anxiety makes it hard to trust my body. I don't know how to make plans anymore. I don't know how my body will react from one day to the next. I am continually afraid that I won't make it, that I won't get up from bed. How can I explain last-minute cancellations? How can I tell people that I am not reliable anymore? This anxiety is a part of the recovery work. Every day, I choose to trust and be patient and kind to myself.

This morning I couldn't get out of bed because I was so anxious. I had a full day of meetings. I want to believe I can do it. I'm doing it right now. But still, it frightens me. I tell myself that I am not my pain. I am learning to trust my body again. I am trying to learn to trust myself again, and trust that I can live up to my own standards and even if not, I am still fine. The most important part is to keep going. Sometimes the anxiety of thinking, "Maybe I won't be okay tomorrow," makes for a difficult night. I wake up in the morning feeling exhausted, like I didn't sleep at all.

The load that I carry in my life is immense. It is full of blessing. But the pressures that I carry are intense: to seek truth, live authentically, and to be excellent in all areas, for all and everything. The conflicts that arise when raising children can be complicated – *shidduchim, parnasa*, living with purpose. What do my children want for their lives? Will they be okay? I bear so much weight from anxiety and the pain of doubting myself. I have financial pressures. I have the desire to live, do, and be more.

I signed my own contract with the life I wanted to lead. Now I am in it and it is throwing at me the lemons that life throws. I didn't expect them. Now I need to integrate those lemons into what I wanted to be and expected to be. When I started committing to being in my truth, then the somatized pain began. Maybe it felt too scary or too intimidating. I think I am afraid of my own power. Sometimes I feel like I have to contract and minimize myself. But I am learning to treat my emotions like guests; they visit and they leave. I do not need to make myself smaller for them. Instead of holding on to them, I can just release them.

But here I am, speeding up my life in a more present way. I am not running to a future vision that I have, but I am living every day as it comes. I am honoring the mind-body connection. I respect my pain, both physical and emotional.

This recovery process has been very healing. The journaling I do surprises me all the time. Sometimes I read back what I have written and I am surprised. I didn't know I felt that way or was thinking about that issue. It is amazing what lives in our brains without us being aware of it. My perfectionism tells me that I am going to write about what happened to me today. But then I read back what I have actually written and I discover old memories, issues, or pains that have popped up in my writing.

Once I started doing this healing work, something clicked in me. I felt synchronized. I felt like I was accepting that I was living with chronic pain for now and it was telling me something deeper. It was alerting me to things I wasn't dealing with. When it started working, I felt the healing begin. It was amazing to discover how sometimes we have the potential to heal ourselves.

Living in the space of authenticity means owning my story. It means using my story to reach higher, instead of being stuck within. I am deep in the work right now. I have always been doing this work, but now that my body is in the picture too, I have to work harder. Once I intellectually connected my physical pain to my emotional pain, I decided that I needed to change. I can't bottle myself up anymore.

We are whole entities and we cannot separate our minds, souls, and bodies from each other. Our bodies are going to show us what our souls are not talking about. They are going to carry what our hearts refuse to accept. We have to connect them and we have to befriend them. It is the entirety of who we are.

Everything is different now. I was one person before and another after. The way I view the world has changed; all my relationships have changed. I am becoming gentler and more forgiving to myself. Maybe pain came to heal me. It came to teach me how to heal. I accept myself as a flawed woman. I err and I fall, but I always get back up. I accept myself, my family, and my feelings, and I work toward becoming my better self every day. We can choose how to live this life that Hashem has given us. It is easy to believe that stress can hurt our bodies. Why is it so hard to believe that our resilience can heal us?

REFLECTIONS

Questions to Consider

- What was it like when something you planned didn't work out the way you imagined?
- Have you ever tried journaling as a form of meditation or self-discovery?

Words to Remember

"Living in the space of authenticity means owning your story. It means using your story to reach higher, instead of being stuck within."

Group Discussion

In Jewish communities of all types, perfectionism is often a strong value. We need to appear perfect on the outside, and struggles of all kinds can be swept under the rug. We need to break down this stigma of being "not good enough" and acknowledge that no one is perfect. What ideas do you have about how to break the stigma?

Take a moment for yourself. What do you need right now?
Close your eyes and be in your own body.
Here is a body awareness exercise to come back to yourself:

Body Awareness Exercise

Connect your feet to the ground. Feel how solid the floor is beneath your body. Pay attention to your your muscles and bones, the feeling of energy flowing through your body. Notice your breathing – deepen your breath till you feel comfortable and release any discomfort that you may feel with the out-breath.

Journey to My Judaism

Rassco, Jerusalem

A RELIGIOUS CRISIS

Both of my parents are history teachers. My mother spent many years teaching about the *Shoah*. As an eight-year-old, when I would go to her study to see her, her office would be covered with history books and images from the *Shoah*. We grew up as Catholics, living in France, and we did not have any family that was touched by the *Shoah*. But she would tell me that it was very important for me to learn about the war so that I could really understand the history of France and the history of Europe. As a small child, I already knew about concentration camps, extermination camps, and where they were located in Poland and Germany. I could name many of them by heart.

I couldn't understand why so much of history was focused on this one people and trying to destroy them. I just kept asking why. What is it about these people that makes them different or unique? I grew up in a small city called Tours and I didn't know any Jewish people, so I had no answers.

When I was eleven, I had a religious crisis. I didn't know why we were Catholics and questioned why I needed to believe in those tenets of faith. I began to read the Bible and engage with the story of the Jewish people. From the beginning, their story resonated with me and I began to feel that perhaps these people were somehow my people. By the time I was twelve, I knew that I wanted to convert to Judaism. As a student of history, I knew all about conversion and the power it has played through the centuries. I had books about Judaism that I read and studied. I knew you could convert, but I didn't know how.

When I was thirteen, I moved to Strasbourg, France. There was a large Jewish community there. For the first time, I had Jewish friends. All of a sudden, I was exposed to Jewish life. Church and state are not separated in Strasbourg, so people are more open about religion than in the rest of France. Religion is prioritized in a way that is not questioned.

As a teenager, it was hard for me to navigate the social components of my interest in Judaism. I didn't want my Jewish friends to think I was overeager to learn about their lifestyle and customs because I didn't want them to think I was weird. One of my Jewish friends invited the whole class to his bar mitzva, but another one only invited his Jewish friends and I was so upset. He told me that I wouldn't understand what was going on, that it would be boring for me. I was offended, because he was a good friend and I wanted to belong to these people.

I saw their lives on *Shabbat*, how they paused life and focused on family and children. We had that in my family too, but for some reason it seemed a bit different. I wanted to know more.

WHY NOT?

Between the ages of fourteen and seventeen, I let it go. I was a teenager and I had other stuff to focus on. When I was eighteen, I had a Jewish friend who was becoming *ḥozer biteshuva*. His experience piqued my interest in Judaism again. For me it was fascinating, because in some ways it felt like he and I were on the same track. I told him that I wanted to convert, and his reaction was basically, "Why would you want to do that?"

I moved to Paris for college. I started my first year of law school and simultaneously I began to study to convert. I wrote a letter to the *Rabbanut* in France, stating that I wanted to convert. Their response was something like, "It is really hard to be Jewish and you can be a really good person by keeping the Noahide laws. You can stay a part of your family, and get a part of *Olam HaBa*."

I responded by saying, "I don't want the *sheva mitzvot benei Noaḥ*. I want more." They gave me a very long list of books to read, and told me to come back in a year.

I decided that I would begin to keep *Shabbat*. I was not studying for law school on Saturdays and I struggled to keep up with my coursework for conversion and school. My parents were really worried. They told me, "You cannot keep *Shabbat* when you need to be studying!" I responded with, "Why not?"

It didn't hit them that I was really converting until I told them that I was keeping *Shabbat*. They didn't really know what it meant and it was made harder by the fact that we were living in different cities. They weren't really upset, but they weren't convinced that it was a good idea. They were supportive, but they didn't fully understand what was happening because we didn't grow up as a religious family.

I was really excited to learn but I was also feeling a bit lonely. I couldn't talk to my friends in law school about my conversion process, because they wouldn't understand. I wasn't a part of the Jewish community fully, so they couldn't understand either. They were not a big community. Some people were supportive and some were not. Some invited me right away to their house for meals and took care of me. Others saw me every week, every *Shabbat,* for more than two years, and ignored me.

Living a Jewish life was growing on me but becoming a part of a community was a big culture shock. It was also a Sephardic community, which took some time for me to get used to, since the Jewish people I had known back in my hometown were Ashkenazic. Everything I believed was normal was suddenly not normal and all the things that were strange to me suddenly became the norm. Because I was converting, I couldn't really say anything if there were things that didn't sit well with me or if I was struggling. I was still an outsider. My faith was in the community's hands, because anything that you say may be used against you and prevent you from converting.

TESTED

It was so hard and I was so lonely. No one really understood what I was going through. I was different wherever I went. When my college friends would invite me out on Friday nights, I couldn't go. At a certain point they stopped asking me to hang out. How many times can you ask when someone says no? I couldn't date anyone, either. I couldn't date my non-Jewish peers because I was converting. And I couldn't date Jews, because I wasn't yet Jewish.

The process was not going as fast as I wanted. The bureaucracy was inefficient and tested my patience. There was a lot of waiting, being made to wait some more, lost paperwork, and running around.

When I was twenty-one, I was finally allowed to take the handwritten test from the *Rabbanut*. It was 280 questions in three hours. They asked questions about *Shabbat, kashrut, Yom Tov, nidda*…they want you to know everything. I finished and I had to wait two months to get my results. I successfully passed.

They said they would contact me for the next part. They never did. I waited a week. Two weeks. Three weeks. Finally, I reached out to them and they told me that I was supposed to have

called, even though it says on the letter they sent me with my written test results that I was to wait for them to reach out. When I finally got them on the phone, they said, "You need a date for the *Beit Din*? We have tomorrow available."

The next day, I found myself in front of the *Beit Din*. I didn't know what was supposed to happen. They asked me questions about *Purim*, what *parasha* we were reading, and other things like that. It lasted ten minutes and they were really nice. They told me that I was ready to go to the *mikve*, and that I needed to choose my Jewish name. I told them I wanted to be Esther because I was born on *Purim*. They didn't believe me that I was born on *Purim*. After a whole back and forth, they conceded that I did indeed know my own birthday.

I had to pay a lot of money, which no one had ever mentioned before. It was extremely expensive. I had to pay "administrative fees." I met with rabbis three times during the three years of my conversion. The *Beit Din* I met twice. I paid without fully grasping what those "administrative fees" were. Then I was ready for the *mikve*. It was a traumatic experience.

MAZAL TOV

I had braces at the time. No one had noticed up until I was in the waters. I dipped once, completely naked, in front of the *balanit*. Then you are supposed to dip three times, in a robe, while the rabbis stand above you watching.

Between my second and third immersions, seconds away from finally becoming Jewish, they stopped me. "Wait, you have braces? But that is a *ḥatzitza!*"

The *balanit* fought them. "She cannot take them off! She has had them for a long time! She's fine!" I was standing in the water in a robe. I felt I was about to cry. I had worked so hard. I had no idea what to do next.

"You have had them for a long time? Over a year? You are not taking them off soon?"

"Yes. Yes. Yes."

"Okay, dip a third time, and say all the blessings now."

Dazed from the back-and-forth, I quickly said the *berakhot* and got out of the water.

"*Mazal tov*, you are Jewish."

I threw on my clothes and rushed out of the *mikve*. I just wanted to get out of there. I ran to the subway.

All the way home on the train, I had all these realizations about how my life was different now. Each restaurant I passed, I said to myself, "This one isn't kosher. That one isn't kosher." I felt that I was different. Just that day, these surroundings had seemed normal. I had been one of them. All of a sudden, I realized that I was not a part of these things anymore. It was bittersweet.

WHAT NOW?

That evening I met up with my mom, who was in Paris for work. I told her, "I just converted today." She was happy for me, but it also came with, "Okay, well what is life going to be like now?" which I thought was a fair response.

I went back to my Jewish community. Some people knew that I had completed the process and some people didn't know. The president of the *shul* knew and he congratulated me. The rabbi did too. I felt different, but also exactly the same. I felt confused about what my role in communal life would be now. I didn't want to be "the girl who converted."

During the summer, I went to Israel for the first time for three weeks. I went to a learning program that was wonderful. I had wanted to know what it was like to learn Torah, and I loved it. I wanted to come back, but I was in the middle of my master's degree at the time and I needed to finish it. I was about to start my fifth and final year of studying (three years for my bachelor's in law and two for my master's).

I came back to Israel in 2013 and stayed to learn for a year and a half. It was hard because I didn't know any Hebrew yet. I learned Hebrew, Aramaic, and improved my English at the same time. I began with *Gemara*, but also transitioned into learning many other texts, also all at the same time, including *Ḥumash* with *Rashi, Gemara, Nakh,* and *halakha.* Everyone expected me to manage and I had no idea what I was signing up for. I was the only French girl there. No one could relate to my background. Most of the women I was learning with had come after high school, had supportive parents, grew up in America, and were raised with a strong Torah education. My parents were not happy that I left France, that I didn't take the bar, and that I was in Israel. They told me I was making a mistake, that I was wasting my time and hurting my career. But they supported me even though they didn't approve. It was hard to explain to them what I was doing here. I couldn't tell them what I was learning and why I was so excited about it. They wouldn't understand. I just told them I was having a great time and finding it meaningful. But that was the extent of it.

I was making a ton of friends. For the first time in a long time, I didn't feel lonely. This new experience of being part of a community where I felt I belonged made me realize that France was not the best place for me to be Jewish. It wasn't just the anti-Semitism. It was also that where I had come from was not as open as I wanted it to be. I was becoming so serious about learning, but the place where I came from was not accepting of women learn-

ing on the level that I was striving to reach. I also realized that the rabbi who I had been associated with while I was converting was no longer interested in supporting me. We were no longer in touch.

As a convert, you don't have a support system. People don't understand that. They don't understand that even when you are so serious about your religiousness, or serious about who you are and your identity, if something goes wrong, you don't have a safety net. I have been Jewish for seven years now and I have a good group of friends. But at the end of the day, my family is not in the country, no one can help me with bureaucracy, and I really am alone in this.

THRIVING THROUGH FAITH

I realized that people have so many misconceptions about conversion and converts. Many are welcoming and kind. Others can be condescending and judgmental. I feel like I have to justify myself all the time and that I have to be perfect all the time. I always have people in my life (who are Jewish from birth) checking on me, making sure that I am doing things right even if they themselves don't keep *halakha* perfectly. No one has to check on me. No one has to make sure I am doing my *mitzvot*. I know what I am doing, and that is between me and God. My observance isn't anyone else's business.

It's not always easy to have faith in God. On my journey, I often felt very lonely and disconnected from my surroundings and it was not always easy to feel God. As I started *davening*, my faith has deepened and through prayer I feel closer to Him. Twice a day, I talk to God. It's just me and Him for a certain amount of time, without any interruptions. I learned where I can insert personal requests and prayers. My time spent *davening* always seems to exist outside of time itself. It is a period of time to relight the flame. I know He is listening. I know He runs the world and that He has a plan for me. He is not my employee. *Davening* is not an ATM; it's not a magic formula where I'll receive all the answers clearly explained to me. But still, *davening* brings me feelings of clarity and closeness to God, and it strengthens my faith.

Through learning Torah, I also found another way to connect and increase my faith. As I learn to serve Him better, I understand how and where to focus my *avodat Hashem*. It allows me to get a better understanding of what it means to be a believer and how one can truly believe. I grow with it, flourish, and keep my *emuna* strong.

I was here in Israel learning from 2013 to 2014, with the plan of making *aliya* right away. It didn't work out because my parents said that if I left France for good, I would be on my own. I could not be on my own, so I didn't stay. I went back to France for a year, but eventually I received my parents' support and made *aliya* in January 2016.

My year in France was a total mess. I was unemployed for the whole year I was there. I was dealing with depression. I was living with my parents and it was becoming very intense. They realized that no one could keep going at the rate I was going. They were worried about me and I was worried about them and myself. It was awful.

They accepted my plan, because it was a plan. They were eager to see me thrive again. I went to *ulpan* for five months. I found an apartment. Then I found a job. Then I found a new apartment. Then I found a better job. Things just started working out for me. I was happy and stable. I felt like I was in the place I was supposed to be, and I knew how I was supposed to be.

My parents have come to visit me once a year since I have been here. They love it here. Put them in the Old City and they could be happy for days. As historians, there are unlimited things for them to see. They are planning their next trip already.

I KNOW WHO I AM

I am dating now and it is really hard. Even if I believe that I'll find the right man at the right time, it is still challenging. As a convert, everyone puts you in a box. I am not the kind of girl you put into a box. People don't know what to do with me. Some guys go out with me and find out I am a convert and break up with me because of it. People don't know how to introduce a convert. You don't say, "This is my friend. She is a convert." Don't make a big deal about it and make it into an issue. If it is an issue for someone, fine. But don't lead with something and make it a problem when it doesn't have to be.

For some, my being a convert is a concern because my family isn't Jewish and they will have to deal with that. Or they say I am not serious enough, or

I am not religious enough. People want to have all the answers before they start dating. But that is not how it works.

For some, when we start dating, at some point my conversion is too hard for them to deal with. For others, the fact that I am an avid reader striving to learn at a high level, combined with the fact that I am religious and want to have an active role in my observance, and that I have a strong work ethic – it all becomes too much for them. I am not a simple woman, and I have worked hard to define my identity. I will not compromise who I am.

I built the life that I wanted. I live according to how I believe a Jewish woman should live her life. I find that many of the men that I date have had their identities formed for them by the structure of the community in which they were raised. But I never had that. How I understand myself and the way I have configured my life is very deliberate. I made all those choices. I am constantly evolving and updating my identity according to the new things I learn and experience.

I always ask, "Where am I going? What do I want? What is the right thing to do?" That is the best way I know how to grow.

REFLECTIONS

Questions to Consider
- Have you ever struggled with questioning where you belong?
- Have you ever dealt with feelings of otherness?

Words to Remember

"I am not the kind of girl you put into a box."

Group Discussion

How are converts treated in your community? What can be done to further the goals of inclusion and welcoming them into the fold?

&

Take a moment for yourself. What do you need right now?
Close your eyes and be in your own body.
Here is an inspiration exercise to come back to yourself:

Inspiration Exercise

Choose something in your life that you wish to accomplish. Consider these points:
- What do you need to acquire to make it happen?
- What do you need to do to get to the place you want to be?
- What would be helpful for you along the way?
- Who would be a helpful support system during the process?

Devorah's Story

Face to Face with God

David's Village, Jerusalem

THE MONTH OF MAY

I have lived a fulfilling life. I have a wonderful large family. I have a great marriage. I have my PhD and have achieved much professional success. I have many things to be grateful for. But there was a period of my life when everything turned upside down, and I was being led down a new path that would drastically change the future of my family.

In 2012 my husband was deployed to the Middle East as a part of the space program of the United States Air Force. We were living in Beverly Hills, California. At the time, I had an eight-month-old, a three-year-old, and a sixteen-year-old at home. Our other children were already grown, living out of the house. After my husband left for his deployment, everything started to fall apart.

One day, my sixteen-year-old daughter collapsed at school. We were told that there was something wrong with her heart. Her heartbeats were irregular and we began a grueling cardiology exploration process. Because my husband was deployed, I was not able to call him on my own. I had to wait for him to call me. I was taking it in stride, hoping that it would all be okay.

Shortly after, my baby daughter started having issues with eating. I was nursing her but she was constantly throwing up. Every time I would feed her, she would pull at her hair. She was clearly in pain. Why would someone

239

that young be in so much pain? I took her to the pediatrician and the doctor said that perhaps it was reflux. But something wasn't adding up. Finally, the last straw came when she had a severe allergic reaction to a smell. I was cooking in the kitchen and all of a sudden, she couldn't breathe. I rushed her to the ER and suddenly the doctors realized that something much more serious was going on.

The doctor determined that they needed to do a procedure where they would have to put the baby under anesthesia so they could scope her esophagus to explore the issue. Because her allergies were so severe and the risk was so high, they needed my husband to come back from the Middle East for the procedure. We sent seventeen Red Cross messages because the Air Force kept denying our requests. The doctor was adamant that my husband needed to return home.

His flight from Qatar came into LAX the morning of her procedure. Typically, because of the danger, you would need to take a military aircraft to get off the base. But because of the urgency and timing, they didn't have the luxury to do that. Instead, they had to drive my husband to the airport in an armored vehicle through the town where he was stationed.

After the procedure, the doctor approached us and said, "Mom, you were right. Her insides look like a ninety-year-old person, and her esophagus, colon, and intestines are filled with white blood cells. Every time she eats, it causes those areas to bleed out." She was diagnosed with a disease called eosinophilic esophagitis (EoE), meaning that she's allergic to 99 percent of all foods. It put us in this bind of, "How do we feed our daughter?"

That was all in the month of May. The bad news didn't stop there.

SOMETHING IS NOT RIGHT

Another of my daughters had received word that she and her husband would have to move to England with the US Air Force. She was planning to stay with us in Beverly Hills for two weeks, while her husband and all their belongings got settled in England.

My baby had finally settled down after her procedure. We found out that she needed specialized formula that you could not buy in stores. It would have to be specially made for her in a lab and shipped to us. It was completely uncovered by insurance, and they would only cover it if she needed it by feeding tube. But she was willing and able to drink it, and there was no way that we were going to put in a feeding tube if she didn't need it. The formula was so gross, it was like chalk. But she was so hungry that she drank it like it was the best thing in the world. She continued to gain weight and was starting to heal. Now that our baby was healing, my husband was getting ready to go back to the Middle East. But then Mother's Day morning came. Everything changed once again.

My daughter who was visiting came into my room. I thought she was coming in to bring me a present. She came crawling into the room. She couldn't walk because her leg wouldn't stop swelling. Quickly, we rushed her to the hospital. The swelling was moving up her body and the doctors had no idea what was going on. Shortly after they did some tests, my daughter was diagnosed with lupus and kidney disease.

All of her belongings had been shipped to the UK – cars, furniture, clothes, personal belongings. She was twenty-three years old and newly married, and her husband was away setting up their new life in England. The doctors told her there was no way that she could go join him. We had to work with the government to get her husband's military orders canceled and be placed back at a US base so he could rejoin her and have all their belongings shipped back to the US. All the while, we were fighting for her life. That was the end of May.

In the middle of June, my husband and I share a birthday. That year we wanted to go out to lunch and we were planning to take the whole family. As we were figuring out where we should go, I began to cry. I told him, "I am too weak. I don't know why, but I am too tired to do this." I was planning on going nowhere. I had no energy and I had no idea what was happening to me all of a sudden.

The next day I went for a run around Beverly Hills, like I normally do. I got to a street corner and the next second, the whole street started to spin. Something was not right. I called my doctor and I told him, "Something is wrong with my brain." He laughed at me. I knew I needed an MRI. He humored me but he didn't think there was anything wrong with me.

Earlier that year, this particular doctor had diagnosed me with reflex sympathetic dystrophy syndrome (RSD), which means that my brain gets pain messages all day from the body. The only way to reverse it was to be put to sleep twice a week in the OR to send medicine through the spine to the brain that would trick the brain to stop sending the messages. I was losing my ability to use my right foot. All day long, the nerves were going crazy. I had already gotten my last injection and was back on my feet and back to my regular life. The doctor didn't think anything else could be wrong. But I went instantly to get my MRI.

When he got the results, he called me immediately and told me to come into his office. He said, "Your MRI results are not good. You have a chiari malformation in your brain. Part of your brainstem is hanging out of your skull."

STILL SMILING

He continued, "There is no way for your cerebral fluid to flow properly because it is blocked. You are going to need surgery. But there is only one doctor who can do this." My doctor had trained with the surgeon who pioneered this surgery. My doctor assured me that he knew firsthand that this surgeon was so skilled that he could also build an airplane by hand and by memory. I figured if he could do that, he was going to be able to do a good job when it came to fixing my brain.

I went to go meet with this surgeon in Beverly Hills and he confirmed that I needed the surgery. He told me that the chiari was really serious and that he needed to shave down my brainstem to create space for the cerebral fluid to flow.

After the months of May, June, and July being full of my kids' crises, now it was my turn. I had my surgery on August 3. I made them wait till August because I wanted to travel and get away with my family, just in case my surgery didn't have a good outcome and this would be the end of my life. We went to Virginia Beach with my kids. I had been through so many things already. Still, everyone else in my family was more concerned than I was.

When they admitted me to the hospital, the nurse came up to me and asked, "How is it that you are still smiling? I am looking at your chart and you are so sick!" I told her, "I don't think I will have the best outcome if I let this get the better of my attitude."

The day of the surgery came and the entire waiting room was filled with my family. Even up until the point that they wheeled me in, I was still feeling positive. My family was crying. I told them, "I know I will come out of this thing okay. But if my purpose is fulfilled and it is my time to go, Hashem will take me. But if I still have work to do on this earth, I will come back."

Surgery lasted six hours. When I woke up in recovery, I didn't recognize any of my family. They were strangers to me. One person at a time came in and I looked at them like I had never seen them before. I didn't know how to say words like "cup." I couldn't string together sentences anymore. I lost all the ability to gather my speech properly. I couldn't turn on the water or brush my teeth. I couldn't even walk.

When I got out of the recovery room, every day I worked on speaking and walking. They would tell me that I was too tired to work on it, and that they would come back the next day. I begged them to keep working with me. I was determined to be myself again. I was working so hard that I was getting to the point where I could go home and have rehab in my house.

I was home for two days, but I was not familiar with my surroundings. I didn't really know where I was, and I did not recognize my house. I was not functioning well enough to take care of my baby. I was relearning how to be an adult.

One morning, I was lying on my bed and felt that my pillow was soaked. I told my husband but he didn't know what to do. I called the doctor and said, "My pillow is soaked, but we can't tell where the fluid is coming from."

The doctor didn't even say goodbye. He just slammed the phone down. The next thing I knew, he was knocking on our door. He had run nonstop to my house.

He found me in my bedroom and told us, "Her brain is leaking."

THE VOW

My husband and the doctor loaded me into the car and rushed me back to the hospital. I really didn't think I was going to come out of this one alive.

I needed an emergency lumbar drain. They needed to put a drain through my lumbar to collect bags and bags of brain fluid. It had to be the right amount and it is measured while you are hooked up to a machine 24/7. The pain was something that no human being should have to go through. I was on the highest level of pain medication that a person can take without their heart stopping. My brain was swelling.

Eventually I had to tell Hashem to take me out of my body. There was no way that I could endure it any longer. I was almost delirious because the pain medication was so high. I just checked out of living. I was basically gone from consciousness; the only thing that was coming out of my mouth were verses of *Tehillim*. I was reciting them by heart. Even the doctors couldn't understand how I was saying all of these verses. I said nothing else coherent but those passages of prayer.

I was there for more than two months. Every day they collected entire bags of my brain fluid. My family never left me alone; they rotated with each other for every shift. One night I told my husband that I couldn't take it anymore. I told him to take care of our children, and that the pain was no longer bearable. We cried together. It felt like this was the end for me. My doctor said that any more medicine would make my heart stop.

I told Hashem, "If You feel like I have done everything that I am supposed to do, take care of my children, and take me. But if You think I am supposed to do anything else on this earth, give me another chance. Now I am like Job, given so many tests, but please, release me from this. If You are going to heal me, step in now, because this is too much."

I made a vow: "If You heal me, I will let the world know who You are, and serve You all the days of my life. I will teach my children Your ways."

After that, things slowly began to turn around for me.

SHUTTING DOWN

I could start holding my head up again. The leak was repaired, the fluid started flowing properly, and my brain stopped swelling.

They told me I could go home and do rehab in the comfort of my own space. I was still learning to put things back together – how to put on my socks, how to turn on the water, how to comb my daughter's hair, how to give her a bottle. I had physical, speech, and occupational therapy. Because I was a highly functional woman with a PhD, it seemed as though my therapists and doctors assumed I didn't need the intensive therapies, that I would figure it out. But I really needed all that help. It was so frustrating that they didn't seem to understand that.

One day at home, I went limp as a dishrag. I was so lethargic that I couldn't stand up on my own. They rushed me to the doctor again. This time they found that all my organs were shutting down. The medicine they had given me to keep my brain from swelling was too much. There was no cortisone in my body from the steroids. They had to try and reverse the organ failure. I have a blood disorder called G6PD, which means that your red blood cells stop getting oxygen if you get the wrong medicines. Apparently, this medicine they were giving me was the wrong kind.

We had to fight to revive me from this whole mess. Every time I felt like

I was trying to get ahead of this, there was something else that came and knocked me down again. But during this whole time, never once was I angry with Hashem. I never asked, "Why me?" I just felt that this was something that I had to walk through. It wasn't just me; we were all on a journey and my illness touched so many people. My neighbors would cry when they saw me and tell me, "You are nothing but a miracle." They saw me at my absolute worst. But Hashem kept healing me. People started calling me "Miracle."

In the depths of my illness, I kept repeating Psalm 23, "The Lord is My Shepherd." I truly believe that I lacked nothing. I believe Hashem blessed me with so many things: wealth, family, education. I have dedicated my life to giving charity and helping people through my work. I've raised my family. I've done my best to keep kindness in my heart and to treat people fairly. I believe He said, "I know I can trust you with these things. Now it is time for a new test."

Without health, it is hard to appreciate these blessings. Somehow, through illness, I gained a new gratitude for what Hashem has given me. Without Hashem, I am nothing.

WHO CONTROLS THE WORLD?

It took me around a year till I was mobile and myself again, and until I had learned all the things I needed, completely and comfortably.

After I was back to myself, we needed to heal as a family. We decided

to go to Arizona to learn Torah day and night and decided to convert to living as Orthodox Jews. We became well versed in Torah. We became immersed in the Chabad community there. We chose Arizona because we felt it was close to the feel of Israel. We were learning in the desert, which provoked our soul-searching. We were on a journey and we could see where we were going, but I couldn't yet see the whole picture. We had been religious for a long time, but at this point we really dove in and committed to our observance.

Our spiritual journey began many years ago when one of my older daughters was born. I had a 50 percent chance of making it out alive and it seemed like she had a zero percent chance. She was born at twenty-six weeks and the amniotic fluid had become toxic. When they coded me in the hospital, they ran with my bed to the OR to save my life. I had a 107-degree temperature and my daughter had flatlined. On the way to the OR for the emergency C-section, I spoke to God. I said, "If You allow her to live, I will not fail to teach her Your ways." That was the first big step in our religious journey.

Fast forward twenty-seven years. After she was diagnosed with lupus, they told my daughter that she would never be able to have a baby. They showed her all the scans and proved to her that it was medically impossible for her to carry a child. She kept this a secret to herself.

One day we were together and I told her, "One day you are going to have a son." She began to cry and told me that the doctors had told her she would never be able to have children. I don't know why I said what I said. I just said it. It just came to me.

Three years ago, she wasn't feeling well. She went and took a pregnancy test and it came out positive. Two days earlier, she had been to the doctor and they had told her again that she would never be able to have children. Now she took another pregnancy test to be sure. Then another. The doctor wouldn't believe it. They did another test there, and found that she was in fact pregnant. They told her that she was going to have to abort her baby because it wasn't safe for her to carry the child. She said no. She went through the pregnancy – first month, second month, third month.

One morning she woke up and there was blood everywhere. I've never seen someone lose that much blood and live. It looked like a murder scene; everyone was screaming and panicking. The EMT said that there was no way that the baby could have survived. The doctors in the ER said the same thing. There was no way the baby could be alive. I told my daughter, "I don't care what anybody says. Your son is fine." Sure enough, in the ultrasound they saw the baby was sitting happily inside his mother, sucking his thumb. He was born several months later. I was just in LA for the birth of her second son. She's doing amazing as a mom.

My baby daughter is almost eight. She is finally able to eat some real food. Up until she was six, she was on baby formula. Now there is no more bleeding out. Her colon looks good, and she is healthy and thriving.

Looking back on all this gives me perspective. When you have been living through miracles, how can you not trust and believe that Hashem controls the world?

LET'S GO

Each experience I went through increased my *emuna* more and more. In my prayers, I don't go a day without asking God to bring me closer to Him. I tell people that at the end of the day, we can be as religious as we want, but Judaism isn't a religion. It's a covenant; it cannot be broken. That is what makes us distinct.

I think my name Devorah suits me. The biblical Devorah was a mother, a judge, a warrior, and a leader. I led my family here to Israel. After my recovery, I came to Israel on a solo trip. It was a getaway. I knew that I was searching, but I hadn't yet found what I was looking for, and I came for two weeks to see if it was here.

The first moment I got here, I said, "I'm going to live here." I think it is the energy of this place. I immediately wept when I got to the *Kotel*. I had

never felt this way before. That trip was in February 2018, and I came back to Beverly Hills in March. My husband said, "You have followed me to many places and I did say you could pick the next place." So I just packed up my stuff. My two younger kids said, "Yes, *Ima*, let's go."

We put in the paperwork, but I was ready to leave as soon as possible. We got here May 29, just a few months after my trip. I hired a full-time *ulpan* teacher for us. Now my kids are fluent in Hebrew, due to a completely immersive experience.

We had a whole long saga with the forms for *aliya*, but we weren't discouraged. We've been through too much to get upset about bureaucracy. Yesterday they called, and said, "Devorah, we want you to know that the week of *Pesaḥ*, you will all be approved and you can go to the consulate to pick up your *aliya* visas."

Another covenant is sealed. We are officially Israeli citizens. We can't wait to keep on living our lives here, in good health and faith.

REFLECTIONS

Questions to Consider
- Think back to a time when you were in crisis.
  What kept your faith that you would get through it?
- Who do you support in your life?

Words to Remember
> "I don't think I will have the best outcome if I let
> this get the better of my attitude."

Group Discussion
In your experience, what role has perspective played in moments of crisis?

⳹

Take a moment for yourself. What do you need right now?
Close your eyes and be in your own body.
Here is a grounding exercise to come back to yourself:

Grounding Exercise
Begin a body scan exercise by moving your thoughts away from any agitation or stress you may feel. Notice your feet and slowly work your way up through your body: calves, knees, thighs, stomach, chest, arms, hands, shoulders, neck, and then all the way to the top of your head. Sense that you are present, that you are whole, and that you are safe.

Janet's Story

Fighting for You

Gilo, Jerusalem

VISA

I was born in Odessa. In 1971, after my fourth year studying in university to be a chemist, I went to Vinnytsia, a small city near Kiev. I went to do my practical work at the chemical factory there. I also had relatives in the area who I went to visit. They had a neighbor named Mikhail who came to visit them. He had studied electrical engineering with them.

We started talking about Judaism and Israel. Growing up in Odessa, we had a traditionally Jewish household. In the USSR, you were not allowed to practice Judaism. But my father was the son of a *dayan*. My great-grandfather on my mother's side was a *shoḥet*. My father knew Hebrew and would read us the *Pesaḥ Haggada* every year at our secret *Seder*. We did not keep *Shabbat* at home, but my father would not smoke on *Yom Kippur*. We would keep other holidays at home, quietly. We had a strong tradition of Judaism but we did it with closed doors and windows. No one could know. If anyone found out, we would have problems.

When a movement of mass exodus of Jews from the Soviet Union began, we wanted to leave Russia. In 1967, I remember listening to the American radio stations that told us the truth about what was happening in Israel during the Six Day War. The media in the Soviet Union told us that Israel was losing and many other lies. After that, the USSR broke diplomatic ties with

Israel, discrimination against Jews increased, and state-sponsored atheists persecuted Jews and denied us the right to practice our religion. We knew that it was time to go. We knew that Israel was the place where we wanted to build our lives. We believed in Zionism and we believed that we belonged in Israel.

In 1968, 231 Jews were granted exit visas to Israel. In 1969, 3,033 Jews were allowed to make *aliya*. Up to 1973, around 163,000 Soviet Jews were granted exit visas to leave the USSR and make *aliya*. Prior to that, the USSR had hardly let anyone leave, declaring that it was treason to want to move somewhere else. It was not easy to get those visas. You needed to have family already in Israel, and they needed to sponsor your visa by inviting you to stay with them.

By the time we were eligible to apply for an exit visa, the USSR had imposed a diploma tax. The claim was that it was a way for the people who wanted to abandon the State to reimburse the State for the public higher education they had received. The fee could sometimes be astronomical. The purpose of the tax was to limit emigration and prevent the intelligentsia, the people with high levels of education, from leaving the country. My mother and I had to pay this tax. We found someone we could borrow the money from, and eventually the State of Israel would pay him back for helping us to immigrate to Israel.

Families all around us were leaving, some to Israel and some to the United States. We didn't know what was going to be for Jews in the Soviet Union. We didn't know that it would get worse, but we also knew that it would never really get better.

GOODBYE

At this time, I was dating Mikhail long-distance. Both our families applied for exit visas to Israel. My family and his family got permission to leave the country the first time we applied – everyone except Mikhail. He was in the Russian army, conscripted after his second degree in engineering. Because he had higher education as an electronic engineer, he became an officer. He served from 1968 to 1970. They told him that to leave, he would have to wait six months after his discharge date so that he would "forget any military secrets." He was confident they would let him out much sooner.

We decided that I needed to go with my family. I needed to take the opportunity I was given to get out when I could. When you applied for an exit visa, you were branded as a troublemaker. Job opportunities were taken away from you; the KGB would surveil you. It caused a lot of trouble. If you got the visa, you took the chance.

We wanted to get married before I left. We couldn't have a legal marriage because all our documents were being held by the visa office. We got together with two friends and a ring. We had no *ḥuppa*. Mikhail said, "*Harei at mekudeshet li.*" It was a sad wedding. It was 1972 and I was just about to leave. But I wanted to help him if I could. If I had the status of his wife, it would be easier. I would have more influence to do what was needed to help reunite us.

We spent twenty hours together on a train from Odessa to the Czechoslovakian border. We believed we would be together again soon. I would do whatever it took to get him out.

I waited on the border for three days while they checked our luggage. We had shipped some things before we left, like pillows, blankets, dishes, and clothes, so we slept on our suitcases and chairs for three days until we were allowed to pass through the border. We took an airplane that was organized by the *Sokhnut* from Vienna. It was a full plane of Russian Jews, flying during one of the peaks in immigration.

The *Sokhnut* sent us to an *ulpan* in Naharia for six months. Then we went to Givatayim, and later to Netanya. I started working in a factory and lab as a chemist. My diploma and all my documents were recognized as a master's in chemistry and teaching.

Mikhail's family came a few months after us. They went to stay with friends in Be'er Sheva. Shortly after, we began to make plans for how we were going to get Mikhail out.

LETTERS

Mikhail and I communicated via letters. At least I had letters. He wrote to us about the provocations against Jews and how he was so glad and grateful that we were out of the country and safe. He couldn't say anything outright because his letters were being screened and they would have thrown them away if they had found something "politically incorrect." We became good at reading between the lines. There was less of a chance that something would have happened to me, because I was far from the reach of the KGB. Mikhail felt good that our families were safe, while I was stressed because he was still very much in harm's way.

Even though all his family had gone, he still had some friends left in Vinnytsia and quickly found new friends, too – the Jewish activists in Kiev, Moskva, Vilnus, and other places. He became a Jewish activist. Because of this activity, the KGB surveilled him constantly and he was interrogated at least once or twice a month. He lost his job because he had applied for the visa, and he was forced to pick up whatever menial work he could find. He had to live with another Jewish family, because no one would rent to him. It was too dangerous for anyone to be involved with Mikhail Mager.

He helped other Jews, and he learned and taught Hebrew. He was concerned about other Jews' court cases, and published information about them. Sometimes the KGB tried to involve him in those cases (at least as a witness), but they never got any useful information from him. Mikhail was patient. He believed that he was going to be able to make *aliya* very soon.

In Israel, I connected with the Russian department of the Ministry of Foreign Affairs. They were very kind and interested in helping us. They helped me get phone connections to Mikhail. Aside from enabling us to have personal conversations (which was very important to us), it was a channel that we could use to inform the world about Jewish activism. I began sending letters abroad to the United States and England. We were trying to get Mikhail's name out there so that his name would be put on the top of the list to receive a visa. This was the Israeli strategy because we thought that if the Soviets knew that the world knew about specific people, it would be harder to hurt them.

During this time, Senator Henry Jackson was working on the Jackson-Vanik amendment in Washington. He was working together with Jewish activists in the US who were trying to help the Soviet refuseniks, the ones who were refused visas, to get out of the Soviet Union. These people were very concerned about the well-being of the Soviet Jewish community and

the serious human rights violations and emigration restrictions that were being placed on them. The goal of this amendment was to place economic trade sanctions on the USSR and other countries that restricted freedom of emigration. They planned to strangle the Soviets financially until they let the Jews go. It was a slow process to pass the amendment, but we watched their progress eagerly.

After a long time, I decided that sending letters upon letters was not enough. The Foreign Ministry gave me the addresses of organizations that I needed to contact, but we needed more. I was so frustrated that the process was not working fast enough. I decided that I needed to leave Israel to meet with people of authority directly. We needed them – the senators, congressmen, and members of parliament – to apply pressure. Economic pressure had worked before for other refuseniks. The Soviet Union would lose face if the world powers demanded the freedom of the USSR's own people. The USSR depended on the world for trade, and being economically suffocated would force them into a dire situation. Additionally, being harassed to free specific people just made them look bad. They did not like to look bad, not in front of their own people and definitely not in front of the world. I was connected to many organizations that helped Soviet Jews, including the National Conference Supporting Soviet Jewry, Union of Councils for Soviet Jews, the Student Struggle for Soviet Jews, and the Thirty-Fives (Women's Campaign

Protest at Russian women's game

for Soviet Jewry). I was encouraged when they all offered to help me publicize our plight. Maybe their support could help free Mikhail.

HELP ME

There was a movement here in Israel that was dedicated to helping get Soviet refuseniks out of the Soviet Union. They had meetings at the *Kotel*, protests, and hunger strikes. But we needed more. I hate to say it, but during that time, whenever I met someone, I would think to myself, "How can this person help me get Mikhail home?" I was singularly minded to reunite us. When your husband is stuck, you do what you have to do.

On my many trips abroad, I was accompanied by the person who represented the organization that had brought me. They took me to universities, to Parliament, to Congress, to the Senate. I worked to advocate for the Jackson-Vanik amendment. They brought me to communities, schools, and synagogues. My first trip was to England: London, Southampton, Leeds, Cambridge, and more. Then they brought me to the States, and I traveled coast to coast. I went from Omaha to Denver, Des Moines, Atlanta, San Francisco, Washington, Boston, New York, New Jersey, Detroit, and more, rallying support for Mikhail.

I spoke everywhere I went. I studied English in university in Odessa, but I didn't speak it. The first time I was to give a speech, I thought that I would speak in Russian and someone would translate for me. But a very good friend, Michael Sherbourne, said to me, "You need to speak your *tzebrochene* English, because it needs to be your story, from your mouth to their ears." So I got up to speak.

It was terrifying. It was difficult for me the whole way through. But I told my story. Once I was on the radio, and they said, "You're on the air," and I had to fight my way with my broken English to share what was happening to Mikhail. Once, I was even on *Good Morning America* in New York.

We made thousands of postcards with all the information about Mikhail on them. We disseminated them and asked people to mail them to Russia. We had people making phone calls, protesting, and writing letters of support, all asking for Mikhail to be freed. I asked people to write letters directly to Mikhail in Vinnytsia to lend him support and give him courage. I asked people to write to their congressmen and senators to request intervention on Mikhail's behalf.

In May of 1976, I was quoted as saying, "I know that letters and publicity help, but we must work fast. I don't know how much longer he can stand it. He has no home now, no family, and the KGB is constantly watching him. I have a husband and I don't have a husband. For his parents, it's the same. For two months I haven't been able to get through to him on the phone (of course with the KGB's 'help'). He may be arrested but we've had no information in all these weeks." The truth was, as time passed, I became more and more concerned for his life.

SYMPATHY

Time continued to pass. It was increasingly difficult for both of us to be alone. We were missing out on so much. His parents were not getting younger; I was not getting younger. Our two families were stuck.

I didn't believe that other people could be so dedicated to helping someone else. But the support was so strong and people were so committed to helping us bring Mikhail home. They made me feel like I was not alone. I felt sympathy from all the people I met. I was a Jewish girl from Russia and Israel and I was welcomed into every community I visited. They were warm, and each time they made me feel like they were on my side. I asked them to help, and they did.

It was 1977 and congressmen sent letters to the Kremlin, asking for the release of the refuseniks. Each refusenik was given a particular congressman who would advocate on their behalf. For Mikhail, it was Congressman Bill Brodhead from Detroit. The Detroit community "adopted" Mikhail and his case. When Mikhail began hunger striking as a form of protest, many in the Jewish community fasted for a day in solidarity with him. I met with Congressman Brodhead in Washington. He was deeply familiar with our case and he even went so far as to introduce me in the gallery in the House of Representatives while he made a plea for Mikhail's life on the floor of Congress, urging US legislators to help us free him and the other Jews who were being held hostage by the Soviets.

We heard that Dr. Mikhail Shtern, one of the Jews who was standing trial after being accused of "poisoning children" in Vinnytsia, had been released. My husband had worked to support his cause. A friend of mine told me that

257

day, "I know the Russians. Once they let someone go, they take someone else in their place." Sure enough, the next day we heard that Anatoly (Natan) Sharansky had been arrested, charged with treason for giving a list of 1,300 refuseniks to the American government. He would spend nine years in Soviet prisons. Soon his wife Avital was brought to America to petition on his behalf. She and I met in New York. The people who I was with said, "You need to leave New York now. The priority must be to get Sharansky out of jail. He is in far more danger now." Of course, I understood this. I was afraid that the same would happen to my husband, so I left and kept petitioning for help in other states.

HOMECOMING

I was always involved in fighting for Mikhail. Being busy and feeling like I was useful helped me maintain hope that one day he would be allowed to come home. My place of work was so kind to me; they let me fly all over the world and kept my position for me while I was gone. I fought for almost five years. I missed having a family and having children in those early years of my life.

During this period, Mikhail had visitors from abroad who brought him news and hope, though of course, I could not go to see him. They told him everything that I was doing for him. They brought him books for studying Hebrew, news clippings, and letters. He always felt like he was about to be freed.

Toward the end, his phone was cut off by the Soviets. The KGB released a statement, "We have him in our hands and will do what we will with him." When I heard this statement said about my husband, it chilled me to the bone. I expected the worst.

Then one Friday morning, I was home in Netanya when at six o'clock, there was a loud banging on my door. It was Mikhail's mother, screaming, "How could you sleep all night? You should have been praying in thanks!" I understood that she meant that my Misha had been given permission to come home.

I did not have a phone at home yet. An hour after he had been given permission, someone from the UK got in touch with him and he told them his news. Michael Sherbourne called Mikhail's parents in Be'er Sheva and they came to Netanya to tell me the news. It felt too good to be true. I started to cry. I cry now thinking about that redemptive moment.

My husband has told me that in that moment, he felt nothing. He was just calm. He was called in for a routine interrogation with the KGB. Then they just informed him that his application for an exit visa had been approved.

He had to be calm; he knew how to behave with them. He was always play-ing "the game," as he had been doing it for five years. There might have been repercussions if they jailed him or hurt him, so they couldn't do whatever they wanted to him. But they told him he had to leave in five days, otherwise the visa would not be valid. Typically, a person was given at least a month to prepare for emigration, but it was five days or nothing for Mikhail.

In order to send his things, he needed to put them through customs and that would take about a month. He asked if he could have three weeks to go to Kiev to send his luggage. He was granted permission for that because interoffice policies between the KGB and customs officials were too compli-cated. It was easier to let him stay to ship his things. This was good for him because he had time to wrap things up in his support of other refuseniks in the area. His mother cried, "What are you doing? Leave this country as fast as you can!" But he had business to finish up.

When we were reunited, we were in heaven. I was given special permission from the Foreign Office to be taken straight to the plane. No one was allowed to go to the just-arrived plane, but they knew I could not wait another second.

When Mikhail came to Israel, he was calm. I was shocked at how relaxed he was. For months afterward, I watched him. Whenever someone asked him a question, he would give a delayed response. He was thinking all the time. He had been trained to be careful about his responses. He was still stuck in the mindset that his demeanor and his answers could make a life-or-death difference. He looked different to me. We had both aged in five years.

Shortly after he landed, we were walking together when he stopped some-one and asked in Hebrew whether he could light his cigarette. When I met Mikhail, he knew just a little Hebrew! I was shocked.

Our relationship was just as wonderful as before. We were hungry to live our lives together. Months after he arrived, we finally had a *ḥuppa*. It was a wonderful celebration. Three weeks later, he began work-ing at Hadassah Hospital. He began as an engineer and a few years ago, he retired as the head of the medical equip-ment department.

The world was so happy for us. We still keep in touch with many of the people who advocated for us. I invited everyone who was in Israel who had helped us to come to our apartment in Ramot to celebrate with us.

We got on with regular life. Yet, this experience is still with us. In the beginning, we were able to continue our advocacy for other refuseniks, but after a while we needed to stop. We needed to move forward. I needed to forget everything; it was too painful for me. The memories are exhausting. It has been many years now, and we still commemorate our experience. Every year, we invite other refusenik friends and family to our sukka. We remember old  times, the difficult ones as well as the wonderful memories of reuniting with each other.

Today, we have three kids and six grandchildren, thank God. Yesterday, we celebrated forty-two years since we were finally able to have our *ḥuppa* here in Israel, forty-two years since we were reunited. They have been years full of love and happiness.

I thank God for everything: for helping us before and for everything we have now, for our wonderful family, friends, children, and grandchildren, and for being able to live in the best place – Israel.

Special thanks to:
Irene Manikofsky (*z"l*), Washington, D. C.
Lillian Hoffman (*z"l*), Denver, Colorado
Michael Sherbourne (*z"l*), London
Glenn Richter, New York
Rachel Kalman, London

And to special ladies who made *aliya* to Israel:
Rae Sharfman
Enid Wurtman
Evelyn Ross

REFLECTIONS

Questions to Consider
- Have you ever had to step outside your comfort zone? What helped you succeed?
- How do you measure resilience? When do you need it the most?

Words to Remember

"It was a sad wedding. It was 1972 and I was just about to leave. But I wanted to help him if I could. If I had the status of his wife, it would be easier. I would have more influence to do what was needed to help reunite us."

Group Discussion

Jews all over the world were involved in helping free the Jews who were Soviet refuseniks. What role does your community play in helping oppressed communities of Jews around the globe today? What can be done to get more involved?

Take a moment for yourself. What do you need right now?
Close your eyes and be in your own body.
Here is a journaling exercise to come back to yourself:

Journaling Exercise

Write down or review in your mind the following:
- What does freedom of religion mean to you?
- Do you feel safe where you live?
- On whom can you rely when you need help?
- How can you stand up for what is right when you see injustice?

Living with Love and Faith

Beit Shemesh

I KNEW

It was July 2012 and I had been feeling unwell. I was going back and forth to different doctors and trying to find a reason for feeling so tired. I started feeling useless. At age thirty-six, I could not accept that I was just going to be exhausted for the rest of my life. I felt I was too young to be complaining about how tired I was. I had some mid-cycle spotting, which for me was a huge alarm. I was bloated and swollen. I could tell that something was just not right. I had been hoping so badly to be pregnant and have a sixth baby.

It was a Thursday and I was panicking that something was wrong. I had made an appointment with a gynecologist who I had never met before. He had the next available appointment, but it was on Sunday. I am a licensed physical therapist and I was reading through all my anatomy books, trying to find an answer as to what was going on. I felt these balls the size of melons in my abdomen. I was trying to figure out what these things could be. They weren't kidneys. Could it be intestines? I came to the chilling conclusion that it must be related to my ovaries.

I had never thought about ovarian cancer before. My father was a survivor of stage 4 colon cancer and I had always known that I was at a higher risk. But it was breast cancer that really worried me my whole life. My paternal grandmother had died of breast cancer at a very young age. I had never heard of the BRCA gene (a gene linked to cancer suppression) or understood the links to other cancers.

I was lying on the floor feeling my stomach and I told my husband, "I think I have ovarian cancer." And he said, "No, no, don't say that. Just wait and see what the doctors say."

It was pretty clear as soon as I got to the doctor. He did an exam and then an ultrasound and then said, "You need to go to the emergency room." I was alone for the appointment, my husband was working, and my five kids were home alone. At this point I knew. I could tell by the tones they were using and how urgent the situation seemed to them.

But still, at first, I couldn't comprehend how serious the situation was. I called my husband, who had just arrived at work after a long commute, and asked him to turn around and come home to stay with the kids. I then drove myself to the ER. They gave me another ultrasound and a CT and it was clear to them. It was serious. I definitely had cancer.

GET IT OUT

In the meantime, we decided not to tell anyone in the family until we knew for sure what was going on. My brother Eli called me that day. He wanted to bring his wife and kids over to our house to visit. I couldn't lie to him. I wasn't home. I told him where I was and what was going on. He rushed to the hospital to be by my side. It was a huge comfort to me.

We all decided that I needed to tell my parents. Once my dad found out, he kicked into high gear. He started asking all his contacts and doctor friends, inquiring into candidates for the best doctors and surgeons. My dad found the top oncologist and gynecologist surgeon. My husband and I showed up the next day, which was Monday, where he operates. He was about to go into surgery. We stopped him in the hallway and I said, "Please, please, can I see you today?" He told me that he had surgery scheduled for the next three hours, but if I waited, he would see me afterward. I felt a huge rush of relief. He could have just said, "No, make an appointment with my secretary." But I think he could see in my eyes how much I needed to be seen right away. He was so kind.

I showed him the results from the CT and ultrasound. What we were dealing with was apparent to him – it was advanced ovarian cancer. His plan was to perform a hysterectomy and oophorectomy and remove everything in between.

I begged him, "Please, if you can leave my uterus and maybe an ovary, please try and do that because I really want to have more children." I was obviously not with it. I didn't realize quite how serious it was. He told me that if there was any chance of saving them, he would, but he knew already that there was zero chance.

I told him, "I don't think I can wait another *Shabbat* with this cancer in me." He did me another kindness. He said, "Thursdays are usually my day off, but I will operate on you this week." It was *Erev Tisha B'Av*. But he understood that human feeling of needing to get this cancer out of my body.

I was scared, but I have always been the kind of person who had a lot of faith. I don't remember crying or telling myself that I was going to die. I had no intention of shutting down. It was a major abdominal surgery. I woke up in instant menopause. I had a tube going down my nose into my stomach, which was really unpleasant. I also had a catheter, tubes, and oxygen. It was scary waking up like that. But I was so happy to have the cancer gone.

KEEP ON

I was so thankful. I felt like the doctor had saved my life. He told me, "We got the cancer. We got it all out." I was relieved.

He made a *shiddukh* for me with my new oncologist. They told me, "We are going to do chemotherapy now, but you are really lucky. This chemotherapy is just meant to be a mop-up job because there is no evidence of disease in your body right now." It made me feel really good, like I didn't really need that chemotherapy, but we were just going to do it for peace of mind. In retrospect, I know that it was not true.

I told myself that I was like my dad, and that I was going to beat this. I began chemotherapy and my mom moved into our home to help take care of our little kids. I was really okay. I felt like I didn't have much to complain about, because at that point, beyond the nasty side effects of the chemotherapy drugs – nausea, fatigue, and hair loss – I was feeling okay. I was tired, but I could walk around, run, and still exercise. Being mobile made me feel like I was alive. I could walk down the beach. I could take my children on short outings and participate as a mother and wife and friend. I buckled down on my writing, being positive, and helping fundraise for cancer organizations. But with a devastating blow, the cancer came back in less than one year.

Considering how serious everything had been, I had remained so upbeat. I was convinced that everything was going to be okay. I had been through the tough stuff – the surgery, the challenging chemo, being bald, the recovery. And still I had maintained my faith that when I finished, I would be done with this cancer business. But that wasn't to be.

I started having a feeling that the cancer was coming back. My oncologist said, "You know, it's very difficult after a cancer diagnosis. People are always worried that every pain is cancer. You need to go and live your life and be cancer-free." I told him, "No. I am sure the cancer is back."

They did a CT and they saw that I had some fluid in my pelvis. He said, "It's probably nothing, just go and enjoy your life." But I couldn't let it go. Unfortunately, I was right. They tested the fluid and it was cancerous. They did a PET scan and discovered cancer in my liver and my chest wall. It was already stage 4 and from then on, life seemed fragile and fraught with disaster and constant ups and downs, including more bad news.

I was scared. That diagnosis felt like a death sentence. I still refused to believe that I was going to die, though. I would think, "Not me. I am going to continue to find treatments and I am going to stay alive."

RUN OUT OF OPTIONS

From that point on, my life has been just searching for new treatments. I did another surgery, this time working with an overseas medical institution. They tried to come up with a new treatment. The idea, if it had worked, was to create a designer chemotherapy for me. Unfortunately, it didn't work. The cancer continued to grow in me. I was treated with chemotherapy again in 2014, and it initially worked. I used a grueling regimen of fasting before, during, and after my chemotherapy infusions to starve the cancer. I achieved full remission again, which was unheard of. But the cancer came back a third time.

I was accepted into a study where two-thirds of the patients were getting a new drug, PARP inhibitors. When the cancer progressed, we fought with the drug company to tell us whether I was getting the medication or a placebo. Disclosing that information was in the contract I had signed, but they reneged. After much grief, we strong-armed the drug company into revealing the truth. Unfortunately, it turned out that I was getting the placebo.

Eventually, I had the opportunity to take another medication as a mainte-

nance treatment, but that one didn't work for me either. The cancer came back anyway. At this point, every once in a while, I would get this horrible feeling, "Oh my God. I could die." It was a terrifying feeling, but then would I tell myself to snap out of it. I would tell myself, "You need to be a mother for your children. You need to keep going. You need to find more treatments and get better."

Last year, I was overseas getting treatment for half a year. Thanks to the generosity of my loved ones who paid obscene amounts of money, I was able to receive immunotherapy and a specialized type of radiation. In spite of the love and generosity, the cancer grew out of control.

I have four daughters and a son in the middle. Each *simha* is another step that I might not have been there to see. We have celebrated two bat mitzvas and a bar mitzva since I have been sick. For the girls' *smahot,* I was still very active. Even though I had cancer I didn't feel like a sick and dying person. For my son's bar mitzva, I started making all these plans, ordering things and making reservations, and then we realized: I was too sick to be doing this. I wouldn't be able to be at a hall to celebrate this *simha.*

We canceled everything. We made it more of a *Shabbat* bar mitzva. All of my immediate family was here and we ate all the meals together. My son invited all of his friends and it was a very spiritual occasion. It was more than cool; it was fabulous! The entire event was about my son. He and his friends sang and danced and even played soccer. We ate delicious meals. My amazing and loving friends provided beautiful cakes and platters of fruit and vegetables for *Shabbat Kiddush.* It was all about him  and we really were able to celebrate together. Though I was in a wheelchair, I didn't take a second for granted.

At a certain point this past year, we were at the end of the road. There was no treatment left for me. The doctors here in Israel said, "Sorry, we have run out of options."

Being told, "There is nothing else we can do for you," and being sent home felt like the end. But my parents encouraged me to leave Israel and try other things and said, "If you don't go now, right now they are telling you that you will die." We wouldn't accept that this was the end. My father found a clinic in Turkey that treats cancer with a method I hadn't tried and we were hopeful that it could change my prognosis. Thank God, I've been doing it for seven months.

TREATMENT, HOPE, AND FAITH

When I got to Turkey, I was in terrible condition. I had a belly that looked like I was nine months pregnant, because my abdomen was filled with fluid. My spleen was filled with cancer. My scan showed a horrible picture. My body was overcome with cancerous tumors. My downfall was the cancer in my left hip joint. It has made it difficult for me to walk and that is where my intense pain is now.

The flight to Turkey is an hour and a half. For the first round of treatments, my dad and I spent eleven days there and returned home for eleven days. After consulting with the doctors, we decided I would not spend another *Shabbat* in Istanbul. Instead, my treatment cycles consist of three days in Istanbul, five days home, and then three days in Istanbul followed by a break of twelve days. I get to go home for *Shabbat*, which is such a precious time for my family and I to be together. I travel back and forth. Luckily, that's possible due to the geography. The treatment seems to be helping me. But my quality of life is disrupted by the traveling.

After two months of treatment, I did a PET scan here in Israel. It showed

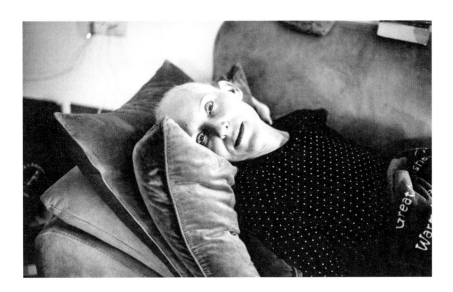

a 70 to 80 percent regression of disease. It was my first time receiving good news in years. I feel that even though it's so difficult, I need to continue. Perhaps it could put me into a remission where I could have quality of life and enjoy my children for years to come.

One part of me doesn't want to believe it and just wants to give up. The pain is intense, and it would be so much easier to give up and allow myself peace – the forever kind. Pain is a horrible thing, and can make you say horrible things. This pain makes me understand how brains go to dark places.

Strength-wise, it feels like I am no longer immediately dying of cancer. Obviously, I need treatment to keep reducing the cancer, but I am no longer in bed, incoherent, and relying on pain medications from minute to minute.

We are hoping that this is real, but you can never know. I have been burned so many times by so many different treatments. So now, I just rely on my faith. I believe that whatever happens is for a reason and I pray that Hashem should please not let me be in pain, and let me get out of bed and run again.

To me, that would be everything.

EVERYDAY GIFTS

I am thankful for every minute of every day. I continually say thank you to Hashem in my head. When I am in pain, I just cry. I say, "I can't do this anymore." The relief from the pain medication is a miracle from Hashem.

With stage 4 cancer like this, it's very unusual that I have made it this far. I am a persistent patient. I'm exceptional! I refuse to give up. I keep going regardless of what doctors say. They say, "There is nothing else we can do for you." But guess what, I'm going to find other things you can do for me. I'm going to find other options.

My instinct is to be happy. I am not always happy, and cancer can lead me to misery. My roots are my name, Ahava Emunah – love and faith. That is my essence and how I really feel. I hope that people would remember me in that way. I pray that no matter what happens, my legacy will always be love and faith which truly equals happiness. I always have love and faith in my heart. Remember that I did this to stay alive for my children so that they could have a mother who will love them on this earth. I did this to teach them to have faith. Hopefully, that is a legacy that I can leave.

It's easy to say these things when one is vibrant and mobile. It's a much bigger challenge when it's accompanied with pain and feeling your mortality. It becomes a bigger test. Knowing that there are people who love me and are praying for me gives me strength to go on.

When I sit in my living room on the couch, I get to look out into the yard. I see the trees swaying in the breeze and the birds on my neighbor's roof. I just think to myself, "I am lucky to see another day." I can still enjoy Hashem's creations. I went out into my garden when the sun came out a few days ago. I was able to see a tortoise egg and some of our first flowers blooming. I wish I could do that every day. It makes me feel very blessed, like it is a gift.

ALWAYS HAVE HOPE

We all suffer on this earth, whether it is illness, infertility, or financial or emotional troubles. Everyone has something that makes them hurt and question. Being alive is scary. We are here for a short period of time and we hope to make an impact.

I have been listening to a lot of *shiurim* about what comes after death. I am not scared of death. The scary part is what will happen to the people I leave behind. How will my death leave an endless impact on my children?

Hopefully, I will have given them everything they need before it's my time. I feel like I have close relationships with my children, each in their own way. I feel like that is because I have learned when to hold them close and when to let them go. I hope I'm doing the best I can for my kids. They are everything to me.

Life is unpredictable and there are no guarantees. The gift of my cancer is that I had the time to appreciate my blessings, my relationships, and all that Hashem gave me. When you are in a dark place, there is always a spark. Ask yourself what you can do with that spark. Can you make it bigger? Can you make it into a flame? Can you make it into a fire? That light can lead you out from the tunnel of darkness.

There is always hope for things to get better. Always look for the potential. As you inhale your last breath, still hold on to that hope.

Message from the author

I was preparing to leave Ahava Emunah's house after we took the photographs for this story. She raised her face up to me and with a sweet smile, she said, "Shira, I can't wait to see this book on my shelf. I am so proud of you." My heart broke in that moment. I realized that I could not wait to tell her story. I wanted her to have *naḥat* from receiving responses to her story being told. I was afraid that she would not live to see this book published.

When I got home, I sent her a message and asked if I could publish her story first, on *The Layers Project* magazine. I suggested that we could use this method of online storytelling to raise money for her treatments. She was thrilled and agreed. We shared her story in February of 2019. It was read and commented on by thousands of people who were touched by her incredible spirit and powerful story. People donated and a movement continued to grow. There were so many people praying every day for our friend's healing.

But soon the treatment in Turkey ceased to help. It gave her an extra year; Ahava Emunah lived to see her daughter's bat mitzva, her son's bar mitzva, a graduation, a dance recital, and much more. But on August 8, 2019, surrounded by her beloved family, she left this world.

In his eulogy at her funeral, Ahava's husband David said, "Ahava Emunah had her first big surgery on the seventh of Av, and it was the beginning of her journey. She fought every single day of the seven more years that she lived. She died on the seventh of Av. Seven is a divine number, meaning completion or *shleimut*. So Hashem gave her that time to complete her mission and she did, exactly to the day."

Ahava Emunah's father spoke at her funeral as well. He quoted the very last paragraphs that we have printed above, the words that Ahava Emunah shared with me and now with you. He finished by reading the last line of her chapter: "There is always hope for things to get better. Always look for the potential. As you inhale your last breath, still hold on to that hope." As her words echoed throughout the large, packed room, he informed all of us standing and listening that she had indeed breathed her last breath still holding on to that potential for hope.

Join me in praying for an *aliya* of the *neshama* of our holy friend, Ahava Emunah bat Chava Ehta *z"l*.

REFLECTIONS

Questions to Consider

- Do you see yourself as an optimist, a pessimist, or somewhere in between?
- When you're in a dark place, what brings a spark of light?

Words to Remember

> "When you are in a dark place, there is always a spark. Ask yourself what you can do with that spark. Can you make it bigger? Can you make it into a flame? Can you make it into a fire? That light can lead you out from the tunnel of darkness."

Group Discussion

So many of us have known and been close to people who have been diagnosed with cancer at some point in their lives. What was that experience like for you personally and what were those flickers of light that led to hope?

❧

Take a moment for yourself. What do you need right now?
Close your eyes and be in your own body.
Here is a grounding exercise to come back to yourself:

Grounding Exercise

In a sitting position and with your eyes closed, put your feet firmly on the ground. Feel the support of the chair beneath you. Let it anchor you to your present. Notice the pressure of the seat on your body. Take in a deep breath and open your eyes again, focusing your attention back to your reality.

From Feeling Otherness to Finding Home

Be'er Sheva

SOMETHING BIGGER

My father is a material science engineer, originally from Nigeria. During his career, he headed up labs for different large tech companies. His work brought our family to multiple parts of America and other parts of the world. We first moved internationally when I was turning twelve years old.

We had been living in Huntsville, Alabama. It was an interesting place to live. There was a small tech hub there including engineers working for NASA. It was pretty southern culturally, and we lived in a predominantly white neighborhood. I think there were only two other black kids in my school (other than my brother). It was okay for the most part and I didn't have too much trouble. There was an obvious difference between me and the other kids in my class, but there were quite a few kids of other nationalities. I was able to have friends and have a pretty good life. I was raised mostly amongst white kids and when we would spend time with other black families, their kids would notice that I spoke differently or used a different accent than they did (I never developed a southern accent). They would ask me, "Why do you talk like that? Why do you talk like you're white?" Conversely, I have had white people say to me, "Wow, you are so well spoken."

I would respond, "Well yes, I speak English and I live in America." I was fed up with that obvious racism.

I was pretty excited when I was told that we were moving out of the country. I had been in Alabama for most of elementary school and I was definitely ready for a change. I didn't feel super comfortable where I was. I looked forward to a new adventure, something bigger. And that's what it would be – I had never even heard of our new country. Before we left, we went to Florida to receive cultural training for our new living environment. The only person in our family who had ever been there was my father. The training was a pretty useless experience, though, and we learned nothing of practical use there.

That summer, we moved to the Philippines. The training did not prepare us for what to expect. Once again, I found myself in the minority among my peers. Maybe there were one or two other black kids in my school, but I was surrounded by the very unfamiliar culture of southeast Asia, in the middle of a major metropolis. Back then it seemed like a lot of the people in the city had never seen black people in real life. They might have seen someone like us on TV or in movies, but that was the extent of it. They were eager to interact with us in person.

I was able to ignore a lot of the attention that came our way because of our race. I would go out with friends or my family and there would be a lot of staring, pointing, and comments. People weren't aware that what they were doing was inappropriate. My mom would go out shopping by herself and she would get so much weird attention that she would feel really uncomfortable. There was a culture of whiteness equaling beauty and wealth, with an abundance of skin whitening products available on every corner. She would notice all the blatant shock, or perhaps curiosity, at seeing a black person, and she endured all the microaggressions that came her way. I guess when I was with friends, it was easier for me to ignore it.

We all spoke English because we went to an international school. Either way, many people in the Philippines spoke English. There were kids in my school from all over the world. We weren't allowed to wear uniforms because it was a school for rich families and dignitaries and there was a concern about students being identified and kidnapped. We were there during a somewhat politically unstable time. For example, there was a pretzel shop at the mall down the block from my house. One day, radicals put a bomb in a trashcan there. There were quite a few riots in the area, too.

It was quite an experience, educationally, and personally. I was certainly afforded a lot more adventure than most twelve-year-olds get to experience. I don't even know if I had time to consider my own feelings. Things were so intense and yet so much fun. I grew up very quickly there. It was just the beginning of the journey.

CULTURE SHOCK

Next we moved to Mexico, to a town called Guadalajara. It was six hours away from Mexico City. It was very mountainous, pretty, and it was extremely calm compared to the city where we had just lived. It was all European style. I went to an American school there, which meant that I could apply to an American college afterward. Half of the schooling was in English and the other half was in Spanish. I was able to learn Spanish there. Again, there were very few black kids in my school, maybe one or two in the whole school. I noticed my otherness and but it didn't hinder us from living our lives and having fun.

After Mexico we moved to Atlanta, Georgia, when I was finishing tenth grade. I remember being excited that I would be in school with other black people. I wondered what it would be like to not be the only black kid in class. I was also excited to finally live in the calm security of the United States.

I arrived in Atlanta on September 9, 2001, two days before the tragic terrorist attacks on America. I wasn't able to register for school and my dad was not able to enter the country at the time we had planned. Already, my perception of what it would be like to live in my home country again was challenged.

When I did finally start school with kids who look "like me," I began to realize that it was much easier to leave America than to move back. The cultural differences as a teenager were vast. The cultural shock was huge. I had nothing in common with the other kids in my class. I was like a foreigner to them, and they to me. No one was mean to me, and they tried to befriend me, but we just couldn't connect. I switched schools in my senior year, with not much change. The schools themselves were behind academically, so I rarely went to school and still received all As and Bs. I only made one close friend in high school. She is still my best friend today.

After high school, I went to college in downtown Atlanta at Georgia State University and I studied abroad in Granada, Spain, for my last semester. I received a bachelor's in Spanish and international business. I started becoming much more religiously observant in college. When I graduated, my best friend and I moved to the Pico Jewish community in Los Angeles. I lived there for three years.

I don't know if I ever felt like I belonged in any space where I had lived up until that point. Things got better in LA, but I was still uncomfortable. I didn't feel like I stood out too much, but I didn't totally fit into my community there, either. While living there, I was working in a few different places. I was teaching in a Chabad preschool, working in the office of a Chabad House, and sometimes I would work in a popular kosher *milchig* restaurant that my friend owned.

There was a customer at the restaurant who thought he had a good match for me. I wasn't serious about dating even though it was "time for me to date," and I didn't think I would be interested in anyone who this particular guy would know. My friend took it upon herself to look into it for me. She did a ton of research and called all his references. She thought it was a good idea and said that I should go on one date with him, at least to check it out. I agreed.

We went out and I was pleasantly surprised that it went really well. In the end, he was the one for me.

BREAKING STEREOTYPES

Being in an interracial marriage is interesting. We get a lot of questions or even confusion about us being a couple. It is much more common to see interracial couples these days, but we still sometimes get interesting publicity because we fascinate people – a *frum*, Chabad, interracial couple. In a way, it's cool because our relationship challenges a lot of misconceptions, preconceived notions, and stereotypes that people have about race, religion, and relationships.

We had our wedding in Crown Heights in front of 770, the Chabad headquarters. It drew a crowd of people we didn't know, Jews and African Americans alike, who were excited about our union. One lady yelled out, "You go, girl!" in the middle of the ceremony. That made me smile.

I appreciate that us being together demonstrates the diversity of the Jewish community.

We wanted to get our marriage off on the right foot and so we enrolled in a *kollel* in Morristown, New Jersey, and stayed for two years. While in New

Jersey, I was able to earn my master's in international relations and conflict resolution. It was a great community and we loved yeshiva life. Ultimately, though, I was looking for a place that felt like home. Though it didn't fit the bill, the people there were very loving and accepting of our family and we created many close bonds. I enjoyed working there and meeting the families and *bochurim* there. I miss them and still talk to some of the people there.

In Chabad, the standard is to do *kollel* for one year and after two years it was time for us to move on. We were thinking about where we wanted to be, where we wanted to go, and what we wanted to devote our lives to doing. We had a new baby and we felt so free because we weren't really tied down by much. We felt like we could do anything or go anywhere. It was a turning point in our lives and we knew it.

We were thinking about different communities in the States but nothing seemed quite right. We had both been in Israel before we got married and we both knew that we wanted to ultimately end up in Israel. We thought it would be a great place to have a family and find a community. Hopefully, it would be more our style. We asked ourselves, "What better time than now?" We decided to make *aliya*.

BLESSINGS OF DIVERSITY

We shipped our stuff to Israel and we went to visit my parents in Atlanta for two months. When we landed in Israel, we stayed in Modiin with friends for another two months and we spent our time going to *ulpan* and checking out communities. We moved to a small *yishuv* for two years and lived in the *charedi* part of the neighborhood. There was a lot of infrastructure, so I didn't need to leave the *yishuv* if I didn't want to leave. It was affordable, but I felt a bit isolated. We didn't really feel like part of the community.

Our friends told us about a new community that was being put together. They were looking for people to be a part of a seed group to build a community, starting in Be'er Sheva. We went to check them all out and we really liked them. We decided we wanted to join this group. We loved the people and Be'er Sheva was awesome. Everything about this place and community felt really different. We traveled back and forth trying to find an apartment and interviewing for jobs. It took a few months to put it all together.

Most of our adjustments moving to the South of Israel were positive adjustments. Everything is very close by and easily accessible. The city is so diverse that I don't feel different here. In other places where I lived in Israel, kids would stare at me and talk about me visibly. Here, the diversity makes me no longer feel "other." I am just like everyone else.

Recently, a kid came up to me to ask me a question. Rarely in my life has a kid just walked up to me. Usually kids are afraid of me because I look different. But this kid just walked right up to me. I looked at him and he asked, "Hey, do you have a phone I can use?" It was such a normal and pleasant interaction. I was just another typical, safe adult on the street. That was cool.

I have a black friend who was walking on the street here in Israel when some lady came out of her apartment and asked him to help her move something inside her home. He was floored, because in America, no one ever came up to him and asked for his help. Here, he was seen as being the same as everyone else. I loved hearing that story.

RAINING ROCKETS

It is not always easy to live in the South. The bureaucratic system is a nightmare and not having strong Hebrew makes it even more difficult compared to Jerusalem, where everyone speaks English. People are really nice and helpful, though I often feel like a "dumb American," but that is the least of my worries.

The rockets are the most difficult part of living here. It became much harder once my son became aware of what was going on and the fact that the sirens mean danger. We recently had a round of rocketing where we live.

My son was traumatized from that experience. Now, if he hears something that sounds like the siren or a rocket, he jumps.

We don't have a shelter in our apartment. Most of the older apartments don't have one. There is a public bomb shelter across the street, but with kids, we really can't make it there in time. Instead we go to the stairwell because it is fortified. It isn't as good as being in a shelter, but it is better than being in your apartment with no fortification.

When I go to take a shower, sometimes I pray, "Please God don't let there be a siren while I'm in the shower. I really don't want to get to know my neighbors like that." During "rocket season" every little noise makes me jump. I walk to work every day and I always wonder if a rocket will come while I am walking, or when my kid is on the van on the way home from school. The last time the rockets were non-stop, they canceled school for two days. They figured it was safer for the kids to be at home. It is already hard to juggle the work/life balance without also having to worry about terror raining from the skies.

It can be pretty scary to hear the rockets flying above your head. You can hear the Iron Dome catching the rockets as well. You know the immediacy of the danger right above you. But I am not crippled by this fear. I believe that everything is in the hands of Hashem and I know that the Iron Dome is incredible technology. We take the proper precautions to go to a safe place when the sirens go off, but at the end of the day, it is Hashem's world, and all we can do is do our best to take the right actions. I trust that He will keep us safe.

We have a plan about which parent grabs which kid, and we have a "go bag" with everything we might need in an emergency. We have our important documents there in case, God forbid, a rocket hits the apartment. We try to stay as calm as possible for the kids. We remind them, "We have the IDF. We have the *Kipat Barzel*. Everything is fine. It isn't nice that people are doing this, but everything is fine. Once the siren is over, we will go back inside our apartment. We are going to go to sleep. We are safe."

My son still has questions. He asks, "Why are they shooting rockets? Are these bad people? Why would they want to do that?" I get it. It doesn't make sense. How could he understand why anyone would want to terrorize innocent people?

I tell him, "Some people are misguided and others tell them that it is okay to hurt people and that hurting people is a good thing to do. In reality, it isn't a good thing, and they are being tricked. It is really sad and we should pray for them."

Ultimately, I think the trade-off is worth it. In every place you live, there is always something. No place is perfect. I know because I have seen a lot of the world. For me, the rockets are scary, but I feel like we have a lot of protection and there are things we can do. When I lived in Alabama, we had tornadoes. We hid in shelters and followed protocol, just the same as we do here. In California, we had earthquakes. In the Philippines, we had destructive typhoons in the rainy season. In Mexico, we had drug cartels in the North. Every place has advantages and disadvantages. Here, I feel the advantages win out by far. We will not be scared away by rockets. The beauty of our life here is too precious to abandon.

PEACH AND BROWN

In my past, I often felt like a passive actor, like a background character. I felt that things were just happening. Now I feel more like an active player. I am doing things for a reason. The otherness doesn't bother me that much anymore. I bring all of what makes me unique to impact my family, community, career, and country. I am trying to be an example by living and being comfortable with who I am and focusing on the positive.

The most otherness that I feel is connected to race. I purposefully make sure that I have friends who are also religious Jews of color. We get together as families and encourage friendships among our children. My kids need

other Jewish friends of color so that they don't feel alone, like I did. They have other kids of color in their classes and schools, though not necessarily other African Americans. My son is not the only "brown kid" in his school. I also make sure to teach my son about my family and our heritage. I teach him about African American and Nigerian culture. I make Nigerian food at home.

He knows he is different. We talk about it openly. He tells me that he is "peach and brown" because his father is peach and his mother is brown. I want him to have some of the cultural things that I grew up with, specifically things that are African American or Nigerian American. He is missing out on these things because he is growing up as an Israeli.

I want my son to know that difference isn't a bad thing. I want him to know that difference can be special, and that he should embrace all his differences and be proud of them.

I know that when we first got engaged, my husband asked other interracial *frum* families a lot of questions. He wanted to be educated about raising bi-racial children. He wanted to know what he should be considering and about what he should become aware. He heard stories about instances where white fathers who are out with their black children, or vice versa, are often mistaken for being strangers to those children. On first glance, people don't always realize that he could be their parent. It makes him nervous. He has learned so much about what it means to be black, both in America and here in Israel. We have to teach our children about how to respond to police officers as a young black man. For example, a black man needs to not make any sudden movements around police. He needs to speak a certain way and make sure the officer can see his hands at all times. These are things that white parents don't often have to tell their white children.

When I moved back to the States when I was young, I was treated totally differently by authority figures like police officers. I would get stopped all the time and get asked, "What are you doing here? Why are you standing here?" when I was just waiting for my mom to pick me up.

Israel isn't America, but we need to be cognizant of these things in our family life.

HOME

These days, I feel a very deep sense of calm and stability that I never had before. I feel a sense of purpose much more. The place where I live is the place that feels like home. I have a community that feels like my people. I worked for an incredible organization that is all about developing this homeland, planning for future generations, and bringing us all an unmatched quality of life. I have now co-founded and run a social impact business here called Aleph to Zee digital marketing agency with a social aim to train ultra-Orthodox Jews in the South of Israel in analytics-based digital marketing. All with the help of supportive organizations such as Nefesh B'Nefesh and Eretz-Ir, who believe that we immigrants can make a big impact on Israel. One day, I would love to start a project or a company connecting the innovative people of Israel and the brilliant people of Nigeria, sharing all of our talents with each other.

I finally walk around and don't feel totally alienated. In my life, this is so unusual and it feels so exciting. My greatest hope is that from the beginning of their lives, my kids will always carry that feeling of belonging.

REFLECTIONS

Questions to Consider
- Have you ever moved to a new community?
  What were the challenging and rewarding moments?
- Is safety a consideration where you live? How is that mani-
  fested?

Words to Remember

> "Every place has advantages and disadvantages.
> Here, I feel the advantages win out by far. We will
> not be scared away by rockets. The beauty of our
> life here is too precious to abandon."

Group Discussion
What are your safety concerns regarding living in or visiting Israel?
Have they stopped you from making *aliya* or taking a trip?

ஃ

Take a moment for yourself. What do you need right now?
Close your eyes and be in your own body.
Here is an inspiration exercise to come back to yourself:

Inspiration Exercise
Taste and smell are two of the strongest senses for memory. Think of
the foods in the places where you lived as a child and where you live
now. What ingredients are used? Reflect on the spices and tastes of
your culture. How does the flavor of your upbringing affect your tastes
today? Is there a way to fuse the cuisines of all the communities and
countries where you have lived?

Rebecca's Story

The Pain of Being Alone

Ramot Menashe

STARTING A FAMILY AND COMING HOME

I have polycystic ovary syndrome (PCOS). I had a feeling with my first child that it would be hard to conceive, so it was not a surprise when we experienced infertility and had to go through the treatment steps. I had a failed intrauterine insemination (IUI) and a chemical pregnancy, and it took a long time to qualify for in vitro fertilization (IVF). Finally, after waiting for a long time, I was able to get pregnant. This process really set the stage for our experiences in trying to have children.

The next time around, I wanted to try and get pregnant right away. I was scared. There were so many "what if" questions in my mind. I got really lucky, though, and I was able to get pregnant naturally when my son was seven months old. It was completely out of the blue and we found out on *Pesaḥ*. I was so thankful. Everything felt easy. The experience with conceiving my first really made me more grateful than I even thought I could be. They are seventeen months apart, which made it hard, but also so much fun. I have no regrets.

At this time, we decided that we were going to make *aliya* to Israel. In the back of our minds were the questions, "Do we want a third child? Should we go for it?" The idea of wanting one more, but not being sure if we would get it, was hard. My PCOS doctor said that if we were going to try, we should

287

do it before I turned thirty-five. She said that after that, it would be harder for me. Because we had a little time before then and because we were moving, we waited.

Our *aliya* was amazing. We moved to Kibbutz Ramot Menashe. After World War II, my grandparents – who had survived the Holocaust – established this *kibbutz* with a few of their friends from Poland. My grandmother worked in the laundry and my grandfather worked with the sheep. We are the third and fourth generations  of my family to live on this *kibbutz*. It is so beautiful, so lush, and a great place to raise a family. It brings me so much pride to live here. I grew up in Boston and I used to come here to visit every summer. I remember walking around when I was a kid and wondering, "What would it be like to raise my family here?" This place brings me happiness. I feel grateful that I can recognize that, because now that I live here, I can think of this place as my own, too. When I look around, I just see home. We were accepted so quickly and received so much help when we arrived. But I wish now that I had been more open with the people here about what was happening to us.

THIS IS NOT GOOD

We were here for about six months when we both decided that it was time to try for our *Sabra*, one more child to complete our family. I had a feeling like I did with my first child that it might be hard. We started trying naturally in January and in March, I was really late with my period. I got a positive pregnancy test, but something didn't feel right. It was bad timing because a few of my good friends had just told me that they were pregnant, and then a few days later I miscarried the pregnancy.

I called the medical service asking what I needed to do and they told me to come in to be seen. I must have waited too long, because I didn't get the information I needed from the doctor. She seemed to not believe me that I was miscarrying. Maybe it was a miscommunication because of the language difference. I felt so down and confused.

A month later, I went back to the doctor and she confirmed that my blood tests showed that I had been pregnant. In the scans, she saw my right fallopian tube. Since you are not supposed to be able to see the tubes on the scan, she said to me, "I am not certain. But it seems to me that you had an ectopic pregnancy, and it miscarried on its own. If you do get pregnant again, you have to come to see me right away so that we can check it out." Once you have one ectopic pregnancy (in which the embryo usually attaches itself to the inside of the fallopian tube, an unviable pregnancy and very dangerous to the mother), the chances of having another are higher.

Right before *Shavuot*, I had a really late period. I was wondering why it was taking so long. I finally got my period and it was a light bleed for a few days. Eleven days later, I had more spotting which I thought was really weird. I ended up taking an ovulation test and it came out positive. That should have been impossible for me. My cycles are always inconsistent.

I took a pregnancy test and it came out positive. I remember thinking, "This is not good." I just had a feeling that there was no way that this could be a good sign. The timing of everything just didn't work. I went to the doctor and she confirmed the pregnancy. I went back a few days later for another test, and I was told that my hormone levels weren't doubling like they should have been. I didn't feel pregnant. I knew that either I was going to miscarry or it was ectopic. I wouldn't let myself believe that it was viable.

The doctor said, "Wait until you are in pain, and then go to the hospital." I was waiting for the pain to start, but I didn't know what kind it would be. I didn't know how to make that call. The internet was not my friend in that moment. It was terrifying reading about other women's experiences and the horrendous pain they felt. There were stories about fallopian tubes bursting and all sorts of other horrors. My kids were with me when it began. I felt pain on my left and right sides. I had a friend who had been an ER nurse back in the United States, and she helped me figure out when I should go to the hospital.

I remember the intense pain and bloating I experienced during that *Shavuot*. I have these beautiful pictures of my family and I from that holiday, but I can't look at those photos anymore. All I see is the uncertainty and fear that I felt in that moment.

I opened up to one friend. We were walking around and I remember telling her, "I am either waiting for the most extreme pain I have ever felt, or I am waiting to miscarry a child." I hated being in that moment. There were not enough tears.

WORDS SPOKEN AND UNSPOKEN

I was done waiting for the pain to happen. I went to the emergency room in Haifa and it was so horrible; it felt like it was an out-of-body experience. It was packed with people and I was by myself. I thought they would check me and let me go home. I met with the gynecologist on call. She knew only Russian and Hebrew. Unfortunately, they didn't teach me the names of women's body parts in *ulpan*. The doctor and I had no way to communicate about what I was experiencing. Finally, she took a look and was able to understand the situation.

I didn't know they were admitting me to the hospital. They did blood work. It was obvious to them that something was wrong. They kept bringing me for scans and having someone explain them to me in Hebrew. I really did not understand what was happening. I also couldn't understand why they couldn't bring a translator to explain these findings to me. I was at a loss. I just wanted to be understood. They took me upstairs and put me in a bed. I asked, "How long am I staying in this bed?" They told me it would be one night.

I was there for four nights and five days. It was one of the worst experiences I have ever had. The first night I was there, I was able to speak to another patient even though she didn't speak English. She was Muslim and lived somewhere up North. She was the only person I came in contact with during this ordeal who cared enough to ask if I was okay. She was clearly in pain too, but she took a moment to inquire how I was. I told her, "I am not good."

I had to remove my mind from the situation. I read two books while I was there. I waited for the doctors to come in the mornings. It was the only time during the day that someone would speak to me. There was no other exchange of words.

I could have really benefited from speaking to someone – a social worker or anyone else who spoke English, just someone to come and talk to me. I was so lonely and scared. Every day there was an ultrasound "to try to find the pregnancy" as well as blood tests twice a day to see if my HCG hormone was rising.

The second-to-last day that I was there, I went to have the ultrasound and finally, someone spoke to me in English. I had tried very hard not to let myself believe that I was pregnant with a viable baby. Once you have those images in your head, they are really hard to take back. This ultrasound tech said, "Who knows, maybe tomorrow we will see the pregnancy in the right place." I was so mad that he gave me this false hope. I was being realistic with myself. There was a 99.9 percent chance that I was not in a good position, and now this guy made me feel like maybe it would be okay.

I went back to the bed and started to weep. It was the first time I cried since I had arrived. I didn't need someone to give me hope when it wasn't there. It was going to hurt me no matter what. It wasn't going to be okay. I wish I had never heard those words.

WHAT ARE YOU GOING TO DO TO ME?

My husband was so sick during that week. He had strep and I had the car in Haifa. He couldn't come see me in the hospital.

The day before they released me, a doctor came in to try to explain things to me. "All the evidence points to the fact that it is an ectopic pregnancy, even though we can't prove it. We want you to terminate the pregnancy." He didn't explain to me how it was going to happen.

I asked, "What if I am not ready to do that?"

He said, "There are many people in your situation who end up in real trouble, with ruptured tubes. If you end the pregnancy, you are likely to save your tube rather than have it rupture."

I had to think about it. The nurse came in. She was very cold and barely spoke Hebrew. No English, either. She took out the shot and I said, "Hold on! Wait a moment! I need to understand what you are about to do to me!"

I wanted to know what was going to happen to me. She dismissed me. I refused the shot until they could bring someone to explain it to me. Another doctor came in and explained in English that I didn't have a choice. They had to terminate this pregnancy that wasn't a real pregnancy. I still have a hard time saying that out loud. I wanted to know what was going to happen to my body during and after. I wanted to know what my options were and what it all meant.

I let the nurse give me the shot. It was so degrading. I lost it. I cried for three hours straight. All those thoughts of "Is it real?" flooded my brain. I felt so alone. I come back to this moment a lot. I think that if I had some human contact it would have made a difference – someone to hold me, hug me. But I had nothing. I don't understand how they could have let me cry like that, ignored for hours. I was sobbing. I couldn't control it. The loss was too immense. My confusion and fear were overwhelming.

At one point I remember thinking it was finally going to be okay. I got up to go to the bathroom and there was a cleaner in the room. When I came out, she said, "What is wrong with you?"

The nurse walked by at that moment and told her what had happened to me. How she could have disclosed my medical information I'll never understand. It was such a personal and painful truth. They both just dismissed me, as if what had happened didn't matter. It was the ultimate slap in the face. I couldn't stop crying. I was so alone.

KEEPING IT ALL TO MYSELF

I got released from the hospital on a Friday. My parents were landing that morning to come and visit us for a pre-planned trip. I hadn't told anyone that I had been pregnant, not even my parents. I didn't tell anyone that I was in the hospital, either.

I was scared. I still had this idea in my head that you aren't supposed to tell anyone that you are pregnant at the beginning of the pregnancy. I was confused about when it was okay and when it wasn't okay, and it didn't feel right. It felt like I would be violating something important if I disclosed what I was experiencing. Now I wish I had told everybody, or at least close friends.

When I did share later on, friends told me that they would have come to see me, that they would have been there for me. Now I know what a mistake it was for me to keep it all to myself. How I could have used their support.

I didn't want people to feel bad for me. I also didn't want to bring other people pain, too. But later I realized that so many people have gone through so many things. Other women have gone through ectopic pregnancies and could have been there for me. I regret keeping it to myself. For shame that I did.

I think that maybe, deep down, I was also keeping it to myself because on the off-chance that the pregnancy turned into a baby, I would have that moment of happiness in sharing my news. It didn't come and I was miserable.

I came home to the *kibbutz*. I walked along the paths and saw the fields, grasses, and trees. They made me feel calm. They made me feel at home. There is something about being here on the *kibbutz* that brings me a sense of belonging and clarity. Looking at the hills brings me a quiet, restful sense of relief.

THE IMPACT OF BEING UNDERSTOOD

Initially, I told my parents I had a cyst and that was why I was in the hospital. My mom was so upset about the cyst. I hadn't seen my kids in days. Everyone just expected me to be okay. I was not okay. When I saw people on the *kibbutz*, they commented on the fact that I had lost weight. I began a quiet *Shabbat* with my family. Then I woke up on Saturday morning and vomited from the pain.

I did indeed have an ovarian cyst that was about to twist, from the pregnancy that didn't last. I ended up back in the hospital for another three nights. I went to a different hospital this time. I was dehydrated and they admitted me. They gave me pain medication. This was when I got to see the ectopic for the first time. The first one had been on the right. The second one was on the left.

In this hospital, they made more of an effort to talk to me and make sure I was okay. Still, I kept what was happening to myself. I think it would have made a world of difference to me if someone I knew could have been there, even just to sit there with me in silence, or even to just let me cry. I can't do much to change it now. I wish I had been open about it at the time.

The irony of having a cyst connected to a pregnancy that ended was too much to bear. Sometimes I wonder if I needed to go back to the hospital so that I could have a reparative emotional experience with a hospital. Thankfully, I got very good care the second time around.

The nurse I had when I was being discharged went so far as to translate every single word of my discharge papers for me. Her English was horrible, but she stood there and worked on every single word. I tried my best not to cry, my heart so full with her kindness. People don't always understand the impact of being understood.

ALONE, NO MORE

People can say the cruelest things to women going through infertility. I have had people tell me, "Well, at least you have two." You can't imagine how it stings to hear that when you want more babies to mother. I wanted the opportunity to be a mom one more time. I had to wait three months after the ectopic pregnancy to try again. During that time, I met with an infertility specialist in Haifa. The nurse there read my file and saw that I had suffered miscarriages and two ectopic pregnancies. She reached over and gave me a huge hug. I needed that validation so badly.

Thank God, IVF doesn't cost that much here in Israel. In America, I'm not sure we would have been able to afford it. We began treatment. It was a longer process than I had planned. I began telling some friends on the *kibbutz* that I was starting IVF because I needed help making doctor appointments. When I reached out to one friend in particular, she started crying the minute I told her. It turned out that she had also been through an ectopic pregnancy. If only I had told her when it first happened, she could have helped me through it all. She was amazing and made IVF appointments for me. It was so healing to have someone understand.

The more I talk to people about my experiences, the more I realize how common they are and how important it is to share things like this. Before I told anyone, some people would say to me, "Okay, now where is your *aliya* baby?" If they only knew. I recognize now that I need to be able to talk about it. I need to relinquish the shame. There is such a lack of education about ectopic pregnancy, because people won't talk about it. So many women suffer needlessly.

Finally, after undergoing treatment, an embryo took. Now I am sixteen weeks along. It's been harder than I expected but I am so grateful. I should be happy-go-lucky. But I have been preparing myself for tough situations for so long that it is difficult to shake that mindset.

Infertility sometimes feels like a losing game, the pain is so real. But no one's pain is worse than another's. Fear is real in many forms. Now with this pregnancy, I have reached the point where I can share some of my suffering and talk about how things aren't simple for me. I don't have to be alone with my pain anymore.

REFLECTIONS

Questions to Consider

- How important is communication in your life?
- Do you share your personal painful experiences with others? Why or why not?

Words to Remember

> "People don't always understand the impact of being understood."

Group Discussion

Have you ever kept something to yourself that you wish you had shared with others? What inspired you to relinquish the shame so that you could share?

✒

*Take a moment for yourself. What do you need right now?
Close your eyes and be in your own body.
Here is a grounding exercise to come back to yourself:*

Grounding Exercise

Create a safe space in your mind. Use a memory of a happy place as inspiration. What is in your safe space? Is it a lush forest? A sandy beach? Is there fresh air? A cool breeze?

Who is in this safe space with you? Only choose people who make you feel safe and comfortable.

Are there any objects there? Are they things that bring you joy?

Enjoy the peacefulness of this space. Spend as much time there as you like, and as often as you wish. Let the sense of calm fill you with feelings of relaxation and safety.

Finally, come back to your reality when you are ready.

Hadassa's Story

Never Alone and Letting Go

Carmei Gat

MY STORY OF ASSAULT AND HOW I FOUGHT BACK

I was in school in the middle of the week. I wasn't feeling too well that day and the school let me go home early. It was around two o'clock in the afternoon and I decided to take the shortcut to my Jerusalem bus stop.

I was wearing my school uniform, a blue button-down shirt and a calf-length blue pleated skirt with thick tights. I was carrying a heavy bag and I was holding my notebook in my hand.

As I was walking right next to my school, I saw a man sitting. He had a red beard and a black hat. I could tell that there was something going on with him – to me, he looked like he was suffering. It wasn't a typical place where people would come and sit, so I thought it was odd, but I minded my own business and kept walking.

About 100 or 150 meters after I saw him, I felt someone grab my upper arm. I had never felt that before. I had never been touched by a man who was not my relative.

In general, I had never been touched without knowing that it was coming. My school was not touchy-feely; we didn't give each other hugs. My world was so *makpid* on the rules of *negia* that most of the time, women didn't touch each other either.

He grabbed my arm and my first thought was, "What is that feeling?"

297

It was so shocking that it took a second to register. I was schlepping my heavy bag and so I already felt off-kilter. At this point, I was just so disoriented.

I turned around to see who was holding my arm, but his hat was covering his face. Maybe he didn't want me to see his face. He was much taller than me. He started to push me forward toward a more secluded, wooded area.

I realized that he wanted to do something bad to me, but I didn't have the language for it. The only thing I said to myself was, "He is stronger than you, and you are in trouble."

All I kept thinking was, "Try and see his face, so maybe one day you will get justice for what he is about to do to you. Remember his face."

I had the notebook in my hands and all I wanted to do was get that hat off his face.

He was holding his hat over his eyes with one hand and me with the other.

I took my notebook and started hitting him in the face over and over. I felt his grip on me weaken because he couldn't see me. He didn't know what was happening. I hit him repeatedly until I heard him yell out.

He pushed me and we both fell. We were both on the floor backing away from each other.

We made eye contact and I said, *"TELECH!"* – *"GO!"*

I'll never forget his face. He was holding his nose and picked up his hat. Then he ran.

When he saw me for the first time, his expression was pure fear.

I DON'T WANT TO CARRY THIS

I ran in the opposite direction with one thought running through my mind – I need to get to people.

I found a gas station and called my dad. He could hear in my voice that I wasn't okay but I didn't have the words to explain what had happened. I told him to come and get me. My mother had the car, and within moments she was on her way.

I went back to school and didn't know what to do with myself, so I hid in the bathroom. I didn't yet understand what had happened to me and I didn't want to talk to anyone. A teacher found me there and she was very concerned. The first thing she said was, "Don't tell a soul."

The school told me not to call the police. They said they wouldn't believe me and it would just be bad for me. If anyone ever found out that I had been attacked, they would never believe that I fought him off before anything worse happened to me. They told me that the police don't believe religious girls.

The next day, the school installed the security cameras that they were legally obligated to have had all along. They should have had a security guard who could have come to my aid. Footage from a security camera could have been used as evidence against the man who assaulted me. But we had neither.

When my mom came to pick me up, she was trying to do her best to stay calm for me. But I had never seen her so angry and frazzled. It was like her worst nightmare had come true. I told her, "Tell everyone who needs to know about this. But please tell them that I never want to talk about it."

It was starting to dawn on me how much this experience had hurt me. As I walked toward my house, my sisters came out and hugged me. I remember

thinking, "I don't want this to be a part of me. I don't want this. I don't want the sympathy or the worried looks. I don't need this in my life."

I didn't want to deal with this fresh pain.

It felt unfair that I didn't do anything and yet I was the one who had to deal with the repercussions of being attacked in the street. I wanted to be a normal teenager and go to my friends' birthday parties and study for exams. I didn't want to have to carry this with me. I didn't ask for this.

FIGHT, FLIGHT, OR FRIGHT

Within the first week after my experience, my body revolted against the feelings and memories of the trauma. I couldn't eat; I was vomiting. I couldn't sleep or read. I couldn't see clearly.

One of the principals at my school was a therapist and we arranged to have a weekly meeting. I was nervous about calling it therapy, but I wanted to be able to sit with her and talk. I was fifteen, and I didn't understand enough about the power and importance of therapy. I didn't have a hard time talking to her about what happened, but I had a hard time suffering through it. I wanted to be fearless, strong, and confident like my parents were raising me to be. But on the edge of my consciousness, I could feel the fear that the trauma wrought closing in on me.

There are three psychological responses to being attacked: fight, flight, or fright. My response was to fight. If I had responded with fright, I might have frozen and it would have been really easy for him to do what he had intended to do to me. Had I responded by running, it would have been very difficult for him to catch me. But my biological response was to fight him. That just happened to be what my psyche chose to do, and I don't see it as showing strength or bravery. It was not a conscious choice. It was an arbitrary response to the feeling of being attacked.

I have noted for myself that I respond the same way in difficult conversations when I feel like I am being attacked; I fight back. It can manifest itself in many different ways. In my processing of my trauma, I learned this thing about myself.

The first few weeks after being attacked, I was taking final exams. It felt like I had been wearing glasses with a very high prescription and then someone took them away from me. It felt like I couldn't see clearly. Life became one big blur.

Still, I really wanted to go to school. My mom would drive me to and from school instead of me taking my usual bus route. I would go in for my exams,

but I couldn't answer questions on information that I had studied and that I knew. My brain felt fuzzy and I couldn't even read the questions. The school administrators understood what had happened and what I was experiencing and they simply gave me a full pass on all my exams. They understood that they were watching me fall apart.

My rabbi, the principal of the school, would check in to see if I was okay, in a very respectful and appropriate manner. I appreciated that. The message I got was that my teachers and administrators cared about me and believed me, but the other message that they were sending was that the police wouldn't believe me and everyone else would think that I was broken. They encouraged me to talk to them, but to no one else. One teacher went as far as to say that if it got out that I was attacked, I would have a hard time in *shidduchim* because no one would believe that I hadn't been violated.

It was meant to be kept a secret between us. At the time, it made so much sense. I wanted to be seen as a good girl. They were offering me what felt like love and protection.

I felt like my memory was a memory chip that was overloaded. My body was rejecting the memory. I wanted to believe I was fine, so I tried my best to keep going as if nothing happened. I wasn't being brave, though; I was being impatient. I didn't realize how much healing I needed to do.

One night, in my best effort to keep moving on, I went to a friend's house to study. When I was ready to head home, I found that I couldn't walk. I was standing on the corner and my legs wouldn't move. It was starting to get dark and I was aware that there were a lot of men in the street and my legs wouldn't move.

I called my mother and asked her to come and get me. I told her to walk to my friend's house and she would find me on the way. I was so disoriented that I couldn't even describe where I was. She came, took my hand, and I was able to move again. She made me feel safe. It occurred to me that I needed to be with someone else to feel safe. That stayed with me for a long time.

ABILITY TO BE ALONE

I became afraid of men. Every time I would see a man on the street, I would cross to the other side. Once I saw a man holding a gardening tool and I was beside myself with fear, my head filled with catastrophic thoughts of how he could hurt me with that tool. He was just a guy going to work in his garden, but my mind was telling me that I was in danger again.

I didn't want to feel that way about men, but the fear was so strong. In my mind, nothing guaranteed that I would be safe.

I tried to develop some coping strategies to help me with the phobia I had developed from the trauma. I discovered that if I walked with music playing in my headphones, it could tune out some of my fear. When I was ready to begin exploring walking around outside on my own again, I would walk around my block. I would walk up the steps and walk around the block, again and again. I practiced.

Sometimes I would intentionally not charge my MP3 player all the way so that the device would die as I was walking and I would be forced to walk without music, without noise canceling out my fear. I never pushed myself too far, but I felt myself getting stronger. Sometimes when I couldn't handle it and the anxiety got too intense, I would run home.

I would challenge myself to leave at sunset and as I would walk, it would get darker and darker. I was easing myself back into being okay with being alone in the dark, too. I felt confident and it really helped me. I was rehabilitating my ability to be alone.

Later, when I was studying psychology in college, I discovered that I had been intuitively engaging in a form of exposure therapy. At the time, I didn't know that. I was just doing what felt right for healing my mind and my body. It took a month of practicing, and it helped.

After that month, my family took a trip to Thailand together. The experience really helped me break through. Everything looked and felt different – different people, different air, different culture. I felt far removed from the Jerusalem streets where I was traumatized. I felt myself let go of more and more of the event itself.

When we came back, I was much closer to feeling like myself. I was diagnosed with post traumatic stress disorder (PTSD). That diagnosis was very validating, but I had a desperate need to not let the trauma and resulting suffering define me.

FEELING SAFE

I met my husband when we were seventeen years old. It had been two years since I was assaulted and I told him about it quite early into our relationship. I wanted him to know that this experience was a part of me. We were standing at a shawarma shop across from the clearing where it happened and it felt right to tell him.

We went down there together. It was the first time that I had been back there. I felt safe there with him. I always feel very safe with him. All the fears that had been instilled in me that "if he knows, he won't want you" – those feelings melted away at that moment. He accepted all those parts of me too, and I felt a release of that sense of impending rejection.

When I was in college, I needed to take a class on sexual trauma as it was part of our curriculum. I enrolled in the class and didn't realize that it could potentially trigger me. When I came for the first class, I was listening to the lecturer and my body began to shake uncontrollably. I kept saying to myself in my head, "Stop shaking. Stop shaking." But I couldn't stop.

My professor noticed that I wasn't okay and she checked in on me. I had to leave class. I was completely flooded with physical feelings of fear, right back in that moment of assault, and all of the involuntary symptoms that came afterward. I was shaking like a leaf, my mind was buzzing, and I started to cry. I was so embarrassed and taken aback by my reaction. I was so afraid. I didn't want to listen to the topic, I didn't want to read about it, and I didn't want to study it. My teacher was really kind and tried to help mitigate the process for me. She found ways for me to avoid the things that were painful. I wrote a powerful thesis and that is how she graded me for the course. I wrote about PTSD and how gender affects how we are socialized to understand our suffering. It resonated with me personally, and I passed the course.

In general, I have a strong belief in humanity. I think that people are genuinely good. But I had been so naive in my youth. I wish that I had more alertness or awareness that not everyone in the world is good. I'm glad that I know that now, but I wish I hadn't learned it this way. I went from being a fifteen-year-old kid to a fifteen-year-old young woman.

HEALING TOGETHER

In my studying, I made a point to focus on learning *hilchos yichud*, the laws related to men and women being alone together. It was an effort to learn what my religion deems as protections for me. The laws of who is allowed to be alone with whom, and what that should look like, became a part of my safety strategizing. It was a rational guide to my fear.

Religious humans are humans as well. I appreciate the fact that Judaism acknowledges that. People would hope that religious people would never hurt each other, because we hope that religiousness means perfection and goodness. But it doesn't. Religiousness doesn't mean we're protected from inner demons. I was assaulted, and according to my faith that is unacceptable.

Shortly after my assault, a group of friends noticed that I was not myself. They asked me, "What's going on with you?" I put my bag down and told them, "Well, someone grabbed me and I hurt him and I think I'm okay now."

I was expecting them to be shocked and horrified. But that wasn't their reaction at all.

One girl said, "My sister was coming out of the car once and someone tried to do something bad to her and it was really scary. She didn't want to talk about it."

Another girl told us about how her aunt had been attacked. Then yet another girl told a story, and another. As I was standing there, I realized that this is something that happens; people are assaulted all the time. I felt less alone in my trauma. With time, I learned that I would have access to information, to groups, and to communities of women who understood what I had been through. I was going to be able to understand myself better because there were others who had suffered like me. If they could find healing, maybe so could I. It was a moment when hope for myself was born.

I've never blamed myself for the situation. I was at an okay place at a bad time. I learned that I'm not going to apologize for someone else's mistake.

A few years ago, when people started sharing online their stories of assault and abuse, there was a *rebbetzin* whom I love and respect who posted on her Facebook profile about her experience with sexual assault. I was devastated to see that she had experienced it too, but I can't begin to explain how relieved I felt to learn that someone who was holy and good could still be holy and good even through being subjected to sexual abuse or assault. The experience didn't define her or who she could be, and it didn't have to define me either.

I'm telling this story because I know that this experience is so prevalent.

What gave me hope for my healing was knowing that there are other people out there who have been through horrors and back, and yet they can live lives of healing. I know that keeping this story to myself for a long time was a part of my process. And I also know that the fact that I am able to share this story now means that I have finally reached my final chapter of healing.

I think it's important for survivors to share our stories because it will encourage more survivors to speak up. Many times, these cases occur and continue because most cases are not reported. Too often in our community, we silence those who are hurt – and in doing so, we protect those who hurt us. It's easier to act as if these things don't happen where we come from. It is very painful to reckon with the realities of sexual harassment, assault, and abuse. These acts are so unspeakable that we are afraid of what they reflect about us, the evil that lurks within.

But we must talk about it.

Blame belongs with the abusers, not the survivors. We need to shine the light in these darkest of spaces and clear out the mess. The hushed-up nature of these tragedies closes opportunities for healing, on both a personal and communal level. I never should have been told to keep the assault to myself. I should have been encouraged to go to the police. I should have been told that I would be believed, that I was not alone in my suffering, and that it wasn't my fault.

As a victim, I didn't ask for this. I didn't choose this. None of us ever do. What happened to me is not my fault. And yet, the trauma of assault can be stuck in a body like an extra, unwanted limb. One in every three women has endured assault or abuse. Most women have been verbally or physically harassed on the street at one point or another.

I've spent hours in therapy and in conversation, and I've also relapsed on my floor by myself, trembling, afraid, and waiting for the memories that stayed in my body to finally leave. It's been my work to transition from a victim to a survivor. I always knew how this story would end. Of course I could never plan the specifics of it, but I always knew that my story would end with me sharing it. My final stage of healing and growth would be raising my voice and telling others what happened to me, how bad it really was, and hoping that it would have an impact.

Today, I am powerful enough to relinquish this story and own the place where I am. I am deep into a journey of healing. My life is full of blessings. I am strong and ready to share what needs to be heard. My final step is this chapter, and I am eager to be a part of the change that must come.

REFLECTIONS

Questions to Consider
- What does it mean to transition from being a victim to being a survivor?
- What has given you strength in a time when you felt afraid?

Words to Remember

"I think it's important for survivors to share our stories because it will encourage more survivors to speak up. Many times, these cases occur and continue because most cases are not reported. Too often in our community, we silence those who are hurt – and in doing so, we protect those who hurt us. It's easier to act as if these things don't happen where we come from. It is very painful to reckon with the realities of sexual harassment, assault, and abuse. These acts are so unspeakable that we are afraid of what they reflect about us, the evil that lurks within."

Group Discussion

Everyone has a right to feel safe from harm. How can we continue to educate our communities about violence against women? What steps can we take to further raise awareness about this issue?

℘

Take a moment for yourself. What do you need right now?
Close your eyes and be in your own body.
Here is a relaxation exercise to come back to yourself:

Relaxation Exercise

Take a deep breath and fill your lungs with air for three seconds.
Say to yourself silently, "I am relaxed and I am safe."
Release the breath, taking three seconds to do so.
Repeat until you feel centered again.

In Progressive Loss, Love Wins

Modiin

LOVE LANGUAGE

They say that people don't change. I don't know if the essence of someone can change, but I do know that humans are very adaptable.

When I married my very able-bodied, take-charge husband, his love language was acts of service. The way that he expressed his love was doing for others. He was the one who did the grocery shopping and the cooking and fixed everything around the house; he really enjoyed it. His standards were always exacting. He liked things to be a certain way. I am more of a "get it done, it doesn't have to be perfect" kind of person. My husband is more of a perfectionist and since he showed me his love by wanting to do things for me, it worked out better for him to take the lead role in those household chores.

I was the third child and the baby in my family. My brothers would tell you that maybe I had been spoiled and was accustomed to having others provide for me. I always worked and took care of our kids, but if anything needed to be done around the house, Igal did it. He took pride in that kind of work. That balance worked great for our personalities and needs.

We got married in Israel in 2000. We lived in Tel Aviv and about two years later we were expecting our first child. Igal had been an officer in the army, served in *miluim*, went to the gym, ran, played basketball, and even danced in a semi-professional dance troupe for twelve years.

In 2001 on *Taanit Esther*, I was pregnant. Igal and I both noticed that his eyes were going in two different directions. We both thought it was odd, but he didn't get it checked right away. When he went back to the office, his boss said, "That is not normal. You need to go to the doctor and get it checked out right now."

They sent him from the internist to the neurologist and then for an MRI. Pretty quickly, they gave him a diagnosis. They said that he "probably" had multiple sclerosis. We didn't know what that meant. Igal had never heard of it. Plus, it wasn't a definitive diagnosis, and then his eye problem went away. So he was fine. And we forgot all about it.

PROGRESSIVE

While I was pregnant, he had several other episodes. By the time our daughter was born in 2002, he received a concrete diagnosis of MS. Soon after, we up and left Israel. We moved back to the US because I missed my family and since we lived in the middle of Tel Aviv, I was feeling overwhelmed and stressed. I needed a break from the violence of the intifada and I wanted to miss Israel and come back stronger and more connected. We didn't put a plan into place, and so it took a long time to come back. Nine years went by.

While we were living in America, Igal got progressively worse. Over time, his health and motor skills were declining and his pain was worsening. He was still able to work on construction sites as a project manager, but we had begun the process of filing for disability benefits. By the time we got back to Israel in 2012, he had just begun to walk with a cane.

He was able to get a job in the North and he started working. It became clear to us very quickly, though, that he couldn't be on-site anymore. His balance was worse and he wasn't walking as well. Here he was, using a cane and still trying to walk on roofs and through dangerous construction sites. It wasn't okay anymore.

Igal opened up his own architectural and consulting company. But over the last six years since we've been back, he's gone from a cane, to a walker, to a wheelchair, to a scooter, and now, a full electric wheelchair. On *Shabbat* he uses his scooter which is fitted with *Shabbat* settings. He can stand for a few seconds to tuck in his shirt. He needs help getting dressed, showering, and toileting. Our next step is a catheter. And there's the pain, always pain. Mood swings are part of it, too.

It's hard to qualify and quantify how this disease has affected him. Because it is progressively degenerative, small changes appear gradually. It is only when we look back that we fully realize how much we have lost.

MOMENT TO MOMENT

I'm in a Facebook group for family caregivers of people with MS. I have found it very helpful in many ways. It affirms that much of what we are going through is experienced by most families who are challenged by MS. That includes everything from his pain, migraines, and moods, to his anger, sleep problems, being nocturnal, cognitive fog, and losing the concept of time.

Our lives are lived moment to moment. When we are invited to something, now I always say, "We would love to be there, and hopefully we will be, but we never know." It is hard to make plans. Certain things give me some anxiety, like purchasing plane tickets, or concert tickets, or anything permanent that I can't change, or that will cost me money to change, or that will cause other people stress. This affects us a lot. Igal told me a while ago that I should do what I need to do. If he can join me, or help in any way, it'll be a bonus. But I shouldn't expect anything or depend on him at all.

It is a practical approach. What had been happening was that he would tell me that he could and would be able to do something, because he really wanted to do it. But realistically, he couldn't. We need to plan and live for our kids as if Igal won't be able to attend. If he can join us, then that is icing on the cake and we are thrilled. But we can't plan for it. Our lives are pretty up in the air and hard to pin down. It is a real challenge to strike a balance between trying to accommodate his needs so we can do things as a family, and also realistically get things done and be where we need to be.

I needed to let go of a lot of things that used to stress me out and give me anxiety, like timing and being present for certain events. I am not perfect at it. But this is something I have had to learn to do. Somehow, some way, things always turn out the way that they are meant to be. Whether we end up where we are supposed to be or not, the stress and fighting that goes along with planning is never worth it. The result is always okay no matter what it is. It is always the result that is meant to be. I was never that person before.

I have had to become a lot more flexible than I ever was and look at the bigger picture more than ever before. I used to get caught up in the details and get anxious about the small moments. Igal has modeled for me what it means to be calm in the face of imperfection. Whatever it is, it is. There is a lot of acceptance that I have tried to instill in myself.

There is only so much we can do. We are in this situation whether we want to be or not. So why let the things we can't control make us miserable? My motto is: it is what it is.

REALITY

In the beginning, I don't know if I understood the reality of multiple sclerosis. When we had our first baby and Igal would come home from work, I would hand him the baby and want to take a break. He would plop down on the couch and pass out. I would get pretty upset about that. Here I was, up all night and all day with the baby and I couldn't deal with the fact that he wasn't giving me a break. I thought he should be connecting with her, caring for her, and just be giving me a few minutes to take a shower and rest. He couldn't move. Neither one of us really understood what that was about.

There was a lot of tension in the beginning because no one explained to us what was going to happen to him, or how things were going to be. There are many different ways someone can be affected by MS, so they can't give you a handbook to tell you what to expect. We didn't even know that fatigue was a major symptom.

It was less a shock of "Wow, my husband has MS" than it was a feeling of suddenly understanding seventeen years that previously hadn't made sense. I feel guilty looking back on all the symptoms and features that he displayed over that time, when we had no idea that these things were characteristic of MS.

I feel guilty all the time. It is something I work on a lot with my therapist. I've got a form of survivor's guilt. Igal will even say to me at times, "I am jealous of your ability to move so effortlessly." It can be hard for him to see me doing yoga, or running around, or just functioning on a daily basis, cooking, cleaning, shopping, and doing all the things he used to love to do around the house. He describes to me the process that goes into the most basic of tasks. He needs help getting up and he needs to be aware of every angle, every position, and each step. He needs to think about and plan for every single movement.

It's been an experience slowly losing faculties and abilities over time, mourning each loss along the way. The pain, too – lots of pain, both mental and physical. It wasn't like there was an accident, where one moment he was healthy, and the next, he was bound to a wheelchair. I can't actually imagine that.

Because the disease progression is so gradual it is hard to discern what you are losing. One morning we may wake up and say, "Oh, you know, I don't think you can walk as far as you did a few months ago." Or we'll look back and say, "Remember seven years ago when we just got back to Israel and you barely used your cane?" Sometimes Facebook will show me pictures from previous years and we'll be astounded by the things that Igal used to be able to do. Or our youngest will see an old video and say, "*Abba*, is that when you knew how to walk?"

The whole disease is really about perspective, what you realize about the past, now that you have been through other things and now that you have lost certain faculties. The slow process sometimes causes us to be in denial about how things are going. Because it isn't sudden, when he says, "I think I am starting to lose my right hand," it's easy to say, "Are you sure?"

When he tells me that we need a new set of utensils because it's hard for him to eat because ours are too heavy, it's hard to hear. But then I go on Amazon and buy him a new set of utensils, because I know that sooner or later, he's going to need them. He has a hard time accepting that he is going through this, so he won't use them until he has no choice. We both struggle to accept the new losses. But ultimately, we do accept them and we keep going.

MOOD

Igal doesn't currently have a helper at home. We'll hire someone, knowing that there is too much of a burden on me and we really need help. Plus, it's not safe for him to be alone. At first, he'll agree, and then it falls apart. It's hard, because he should not be like this, needing to rely on a helper.

For me, when it comes to the disability, I can help him. I can help him get dressed and use the toilet, turn over in bed, and all the small details of his daily needs. But the hardest in terms of what to expect when I wake up in the morning, what kind of husband I am going to have that day. This disease is so hard on him. That is what I have a really hard time with.

It all affects my own mood. People say to me, "I can't believe you walk around with a smile on your face all day." I feel like maybe I do that because I've lost my mind at this point. I'm not sure that what they see is me being so strong and positive. But every time I go to my therapist, I ask her, "Have I lost my mind yet?" She assures me I have not.

A sense of humor is huge in maintaining our sanity. My husband has been saying lately that he didn't fully appreciate my sense of humor until recently. He really leans on it a lot now, and he appreciates how much it gets us through the mess of MS.

I try to approach the really difficult stuff with lightness and a sense of silliness. There really is nothing else I can do. Sometimes we laugh through the painful moments. Either it's buoyant positivity, or I have truly lost it. But it helps us get through, either way.

WHY NOT ME?

My dad died at a young sixty-four. Before he passed, he said to me, "Bad things happen. It just happens to be happening to us right now."

So that is basically how I live my life at this point. I could be asking, "Why me?" But the real question is, "Why not me?" Why should it happen to the person next door and not to me? What is so special about me that I should only have good things in my life? Some people seem to deal with more and some people with less.

I don't spend a lot of time wallowing in the unfairness of it all. I think my unique ability to live my life moment to moment makes it easier for me to deal with all the struggle. I am not very nostalgic either. I feel like Igal sometimes lives in the past, and it is very difficult for him. He remembers all these wonderful times and opportunities – people he spent time with, climbing Machu Picchu in South America, his time in the army, his dancing years. He remembers everything in detail.

I don't remember much about growing up. I have vague notions about things that we experienced in the past, but most of the details are lost to me. I think that helps me a lot because I don't wallow in old memories.

I see couples in their older years walking hand in hand. Sometimes I get a twinge of sadness that we won't be like that. But then I remember that we can roll down the street together and I still can hold his hand. That feels good, too.

I don't look backward, but I don't look forward either. I am sure that holds me back. I don't look ahead in my career. I don't plan for getting ahead, because I can't. But I don't sit around ruminating over the things that I have personally lost. It doesn't bother me that much. There are so many opportunities that come and go all the time. I tell myself that if there is one that I can't take now, there will be another one around the corner that may work for me and my lifestyle. Maybe one day we'll move to a bigger place and we'll have room for a full-time caregiver who can be with him and give me more flexibility. Maybe it'll happen. Maybe it won't.

READY FOR IT ALL

I'm not always so serene. Sometimes I have outbursts. But I have always had a temper. I am a very emotive person but I am also an open book. I tell everyone everything about me, if they ask. I am not secretive and I am not ashamed. When I share things, it is because I want to put a stop to the shame that many people feel over disease and chronic illness. We have met so many people who have not yet told their families or children about their MS diagnosis because they are ashamed or afraid. We told our children from day one. I can't imagine hiding it from my kids, even in the beginning.

My husband comes from a closed and secretive family culture. They call cancer "the *maḥala.*" He had a very close aunt who passed away recently from stage four lung cancer. We didn't even know that she was ill until the week before she passed. They never spoke to us about it. I have no idea what treatment she got. They were so close; she basically raised my husband. But we did not know that she was ill and so we didn't get to be there for her.

I have met people who have MS whose spouses and children are ashamed of them. They rarely leave the house because the family is too embarrassed. Their school friends don't know. The *shul* doesn't know. So they live with this overwhelming diagnosis in shame. I can't comprehend living like that. There is no shame in this disease. It requires love and nurturing, and family and community support on all sides. My kids are right there in the trenches with me. They help me take care of their *abba.* That is okay. We are all responsible to be there for each other and we can be proud of that.

It is also a wonderful lesson for my kids to see community members stepping in and helping us out. It's been very hard to accept help, but when we need it, I lean on those angels who come out of nowhere and offer a hand. My advice to people who know families going through something similar is don't just ask if they need help. Offer concrete ways in which you can help. Maybe you can pick up prescriptions, go food shopping, drive carpool, or make sure their kids are invited out on vacation days (that's a big one). You can help make sure that the parent who is handling everything is aware when school assignments are due or when they need to sign up for class events. Continue to invite the family for *Shabbat* meals even if you are turned down, and never wait for a reciprocal invitation (another big one). Even just sending a weekly WhatsApp check-in message is enough.

Caregivers also need to learn to take care of themselves. I try to find moments in my life when I can nurture myself. Igal always encourages me to take the time to invest in myself, too. I go to therapy every week. I took a yoga certification course, paid for it, got overwhelmed with the time commitment, and when I couldn't back out of it, ended up benefiting tremendously from going through with it. I had been using St. John's Wort to manage my depression, but I recently upgraded to a selective serotonin reuptake inhibitor (SSRI). I also do aromatherapy. I stay up too late at night because I need the quiet. I need the time to be with my own thoughts, to relax, and to make it possible for myself to have free headspace when I wake up the next day. The next day always comes, and I need to be ready for it all.

REFLECTIONS

Questions to Consider
- What do you imagine are important self-care strategies for a caregiver?
- How do you balance all your responsibilities between work and home?

Words to Remember

> "There is only so much we can do. We are in this situation whether we want to be or not. So why let the things we can't control make us miserable? My motto is: it is what it is."

Group Discussion

Sometimes life throws us curveballs that we could never have anticipated. What has helped you accept hardships and make the best of them? Was it family and friends? Therapy? Investing in yourself?

✒

Take a moment for yourself. What do you need right now?
Close your eyes and be in your own body.
Here is a gratitude exercise to come back to yourself:

Gratitude Exercise

Consider all the people who care for you. Think about all the people who you care for yourself. In your mind, hold all the acts of service that you provide and that are provided for you. Close your eyes and visualize the positive intentions behind each action. Sense the feeling of love and appreciation that flows back and forth between the giver and receiver. Let those feelings of positivity and thoughtfulness make you feel loved and loving in this moment.

Michal's Story

Praying for What Comes Next

Katamon, Jerusalem

WHAT WE ARE SUPPOSED TO DO

In my twenties, I lived in New York on the Upper West side. I was always struggling with my weight. I went back to Toronto for a year, and then stayed for three. I dated on and off. I had one serious relationship. I was working for *Misrad HaAliya* and at a certain point I thought to myself, "If I know where I want to be, why am I still here?"

I was thirty-two and I just wanted a fresh start. I moved around a lot as a kid and whenever I was in Israel, it just felt like home. As much as I loved Toronto and as much as I loved my family, I just knew it was time to start a new chapter. I got on the plane, got a place to live, began *ulpan*, dropped out of *ulpan*, got myself two jobs, and started the next part of my journey.

Subconsciously, I always wanted to be a mom even more than I wanted to be a wife. I know that for many years I didn't get married because I just didn't date. I didn't know myself. I didn't love myself. I went on dates but I was insecure. When I first started dating at nineteen in the *Yeshivish* world, I was told by *shadchanim* that I was "too fat to sell." I left that community but I have seen the lasting impact on my confidence from those experiences. There was just so much pressure.

When you grow up in a *frum* home, you know that by your early twenties you are supposed to get married, have kids, and raise a *"bayis ne'eman beYis-*

rael." But what happens when you don't get to that? Where do you belong? I am the oldest in my family. All my siblings have gotten married at twenty-one and began having children. I am forty-three and aunt to nine amazing, wonderful kids. But I didn't do what we are "supposed to" do.

I wanted to be in a relationship but I don't even think I knew what that meant. I wasn't present enough in my life to even be aware if someone liked me. I think I always thought, "No, he can't really be interested in me. I am too fat to like" (or some other negative thought). Now, I am much more capable of being self-aware, but I am still having a hard time finding what I am looking for in a partner.

WHAT HASN'T CHANGED

I was diagnosed with polycystic ovary syndrome (PCOS) and insulin resistance. Due to those diagnoses, I was constantly struggling with my weight. Around seven years ago, I decided to get gastric sleeve surgery. I don't think I did it the right way. I should have done therapy at the same time, and I didn't. I needed to talk to someone and because I didn't put myself into therapy, it was very easy to put myself back into bad eating habits that are unhealthy for me. It's also way easier to eat chocolate than a piece of chicken.

All these things – weight issues, not really wanting to date, communal pressures, moving, making a new life for myself, and my relationship with God – are all connected. My relationship with God has been a challenge for a long time. I understand that *emuna* needs to be tested, and I am okay with that. It's the communal pressure that upsets me. I don't want to go to *shul* anymore back at home. When I walk into that room, nothing that the community expects to have changed in my life is any different. The milestones that they are waiting for me to reach still haven't happened in more than twenty years. I don't want them to look at me with pity. I am not the same person I was even four months ago, as I am constantly evolving. And yet since the externals haven't changed, they all feel bad for me. Even if they aren't actually feeling bad for me, it feels to me like they are.

It has always felt very easy for me to *daven* for other people but I have a challenging time praying for myself. When I started my IVF journey as a single woman in her late thirties, *Kever Rachel* was the only place where I felt I could pray. I so deeply identify with *Rachel Imenu*, a woman who longed to have children. I remember going there with my grandmother, back when you could just drive up and park right at the front when there were no walls around it in Beit Lechem. Now I have made new memories there as an adult searching for answers in my own life. Every time I walk into the women's space, the women there are crying and pouring their hearts out. There are all types of women there, it feels so diverse, and I love that it is a no-judgment space.

I used to try to *daven* for myself to get married, but there was a part of me that felt like it was never going to happen. Every year on my birthday, my friends and family would tell me, "Don't worry, this year is going to be your year." And then the year came and went, and it wasn't. I just turned forty-three, and so many people were saying to me that they hoped all my dreams would come true. But I don't want to hear that anymore. I just want health, *parnasa*, and calm. My dreams of a family and a spouse haven't come true in any year. Now I need to take another look at my dreams. It's hard to know how to even continue to ask for the things that I want.

EGGS

I began to pray for myself when I decided that as an unmarried thirty-eight-year-old, I should try and be a mom on my own. I had been talking about this since I was thirty-five, but freezing eggs was not as common for single women in their thirties as it is now. It was also far more expensive than it is now. I kept hoping that I would get married and everything would be fine. But I was racing against my biological clock and at a certain point I had to take matters into my own hands. I started learning about my options and going to doctors.

From day one, I had family support. When I started everything, I didn't realize how physically and emotionally draining it would be to go through this without a partner. Finally, I decided to begin therapy and I have found that process very helpful. Another thing that made a difference, and which is unique about doing IVF in Israel, is that the government helps with the costs. Doing fertility treatments while running my own event-planning business and being single has been really difficult. I did my first intrauterine insemination (IUI) and then worked a wedding later that night. The entire IVF journey felt like I was juggling my work and trying to get pregnant. It was overwhelming. Since I couldn't lean on anyone, it all fell on my shoulders. In the beginning, I brought a friend with me to my egg retrievals, but toward the end I just went alone. At that point, I didn't want to share the experience. It was my journey and I needed to do this myself.

As I started the process, I was very open with my friends. But when I found out that I had become the topic of conversation at *Shabbos* meals where I was not present, I just closed up and stopped sharing outside of my inner circle. I felt so betrayed. It was something so personal to me, and I was hurt that people felt that they had a right to violate my privacy and give details that were no one's business. Still, I felt it was important to share with my close friends so that older single women would at least know of the option to freeze their eggs in a timely manner. It had been too late for me.

During the IVF process, I was diagnosed with endometriosis on top of PCOS. They told me that I had plenty of eggs, but that my egg quality wasn't going to work to have a baby. I was devastated.

READY FOR A NEW CHAPTER

After seven cycles, it still wasn't working. When they told me that I was going to have to use donor eggs as well as sperm, I was ready and willing to take a month and start to plan this next step. I visited my family in Toronto, attended a family *simcha* in Chicago, and enjoyed being with everyone before I returned to what I thought would be the next chapter of my life. Arriving back in Jerusalem, I suddenly fell apart and hit rock bottom. I was overwhelmed, so depressed, and unable to fully function. I realized that I was in deep mourning for the child that I would never have, a child that was biologically mine with my DNA. I was in therapy the whole time, and it took two years to realize that I had never truly mourned and allowed myself to feel the loss and the impact of those seven cycles that were unsuccessful, as well as putting on more weight and doing everything all on my own. It took a great deal of time for me to become comfortable with myself.

My therapist suggested to me that I should go to the *mikve*. My mother was a *mikve* attendant while I was growing up, and I had always thought that going to the *mikve* was such a special experience. The whole concept of engaging in purity after pain is something that really resonated with me. One of my best friends is a *kalla* teacher and she offered to go with me.

The preparations were so meaningful to me. I had felt that for a long time, this ritual – which I was raised to expect would be part of my life – was withheld from me. To finally engage with it made me feel like I was preparing for a new chapter in my life. I was opening myself up to the future. I was there to pray to Hashem for a baby, but even just the beauty of the experience was something that I had been craving to do my entire life. When I did it, it was such a powerful moment. Taking off my earrings and my other jewelry somehow mirrored taking them off when I went in to be put under for my egg retrievals. It all felt so connected, and here I was looking to budge some sort of emotional or spiritual block. I was trying to get through to a new chapter. It was restorative and transformative.

ONE LAST TIME

When I was ready to begin the process again, I knew I needed to consult a *rav*. I wanted to make sure that however I brought my child into the world, there would be no question that it had been done according to *halacha*. I needed a halachic understanding of the ramifications of doing A, B, and C. The information I received was that I needed to get the eggs and sperm from a specific place, to ensure that they were donated by people who were not Jewish. Then, after the hypothetical baby was born, there would be a truncated conversion process even though I, as a Jewish mother, carried the baby.

I found a doctor who specialized in egg donation here in Israel. I went to see him with another of my best friends, who is a gynecologist. We asked all our medical and halachic questions and I decided to go through with it again. Everything was 100 percent vetted.

I saved 45,000 shekels for the procedure and I bought tickets to Cyprus, where the procedure was done. The doctor got two high-quality embryos. This past December, I went and did the first implantation. Two weeks later, I found out that it didn't work. My doctor has a very high success rate, and he was very upset that it didn't work. He told me that we should try it all again. Since we had the second embryo, I flew back to Cyprus and did it again. I had full belief that this time it would work. Eleven days later, following an early-morning blood test, I checked the online system for the results after a full day of meetings. It failed one last time.

I kept trying to wrack my brain. Maybe I did something that made the procedure fail. I kept going over that moment when I tripped. Or maybe I reached too high when I screwed in that lightbulb? Maybe I drank too much coffee? Why didn't it work? This was time number nine. When you are single, and you don't have a partner to comfort you at home, it can seem insurmountable. How much more could I put myself through?

WHAT SHOULD I PRAY FOR NEXT?

At this point, God has given me *parnasa* and a beautiful life here in Israel, and I am truly grateful for it.

That doesn't mean that things feel simple to me. I decided that I can no longer go through IVF as a single person. People tell me stories about the women who did IVF for ten years, and then one day, miraculously, got pregnant. But I don't have the support of a spouse to do that. Doing it all by myself has been so challenging, but it was my journey. I did what I had to do.

My father said, "Don't worry Michal, you'll just get married now and it'll be OK." I had to explain to him, "No Abba, that's not how this works. If this last one didn't take, that's it. I might not ever get to be a mother. I can't do IVF again as a single person." In addition to the financial issue, which is significant, there is also the mental and emotional exhaustion that takes a toll on me.

During the whole IVF process, I used to go to *Kever Rachel* once a month, and for many months after I stopped doing fertility treatments, I wasn't able

to get in my car and drive the five minutes down the road. I was torn about going because I felt like I had nothing to say. I didn't even know what to ask for. Perhaps if I went there, all my pain would come pouring out.

But now, I feel differently. I have mourned and mended. I have moved on. I have returned to Mama Rachel and I felt her there in all her glory; when I was able to pray at the *kever*, it felt like she was hugging me and telling me it was going to be OK. I *davened* not just for me, but for my friends and family, and for all our good health. I prayed for all our dreams to be realized.

For me, hope is not lost, it just took me time to see behind the clouds. Recently, I created a vision board, a representation of my goals for the future. I wrote down all the negative feelings that have been draining me and put them in a small bag and mentally sent them away.

Once they were gone, I was able to see the vision of my future clearly. A vision of a successful business, of a family, a partner, a home.

I still may not know how or when I will become a mother and what form that will take. But I know there are still options open to me. I am ready and open for all the blessings waiting for me.

REFLECTIONS

Questions to Consider
- Have you ever struggled with feeling like your prayers aren't being heard?
- What are your feelings about your own time being single?

Words to Remember
> "My relationship with God has been a challenge for a long time. I understand that *emuna* needs to be tested, and I am okay with that. It's the communal pressure that upsets me."

Group Discussion
What inspired you to keep going when you felt like you didn't know what to ask for next?

&

Take a moment for yourself. What do you need right now?
Close your eyes and be in your own body.
Here is a breathing exercise to come back to yourself:

Breathing Exercise
Sit comfortably with your back straight. Place one hand on your chest and the other on your stomach. Breathe in deeply through your nose and fill your abdomen with air until it appears full. Only fill it to a comfortable limit. Release the air out through your mouth. Repeat until you feel centered and relaxed.

Chana's Story

Finding Space to Breathe

Hispin, Golan

INSIDES AND OUTSIDES

When I was six years old, I told my parents that I couldn't hear. They took me to a doctor and tested my hearing and there was absolutely nothing wrong. That was one of the first times I remember expressing that something didn't feel right.

I learned how to read very early. In kindergarten, when everyone was learning their ABCs, I was already reading. I tried to skip to first grade but it didn't work out. Before I skipped, I had been among the youngest in the class, so some of my new classmates were almost two years older than me. The kids felt the difference and made fun of me for being so young. I went back to first grade. However, after a few more years, I skipped sixth grade. The difference between girls in fifth grade and those in seventh is vast, but this time I stuck with it. I entered high school at an unusually young age.

I am the oldest in my family and I took the responsibility seriously. My father, a lawyer, and my mother, a psychologist, had to work evenings. As a sensitive kid who was (overly) attuned to my parents' moods and struggles, I always wanted to make it easier for them. I tried to take care of my younger sisters and have things cleaned up before my mother got back from work. During this time, I suppressed my negative feelings; I am not sure how aware I was of them. I distinctly remember, though, that there were times I wanted the school bus to keep going and not drop me off at home. Something within me still didn't feel right.

By the time I got to high school, there were many days that I didn't want to get out of bed. I felt so sad all the time, but I kept it bottled up on the inside. On the outside, I was doing well. I had a perfect report card and I was the head of the school band. But the truth was that I was shutting down. I went to a very religious high school. Ultimately, I made some close friends there, but the school was not a good match for me. We were not encouraged to ask questions.

When I got depressed, I mostly withdrew. I didn't cause any trouble, and I kept inside any doubts I may have felt. In eleventh grade, I was the only girl out of some ninety-odd girls in my class to take the PSAT in preparation for college. I was called into the principal's office and told, "We didn't think that you were that type of girl." But I had plans. I wanted to go to medical school and become a doctor.

I started playing piano at a young age and I learned how to play the drums from my fellow band members in high school. I have many painful memories of myself just sitting at the piano and drums, frozen, not feeling that I could bring forth the music. But I would rally myself, and the music would come.

My insides did not match my smiling outside. I probably should have started medication in high school to treat my depression. But I didn't.

CONFUSED

As a clinical psychologist, my mother tried very hard to help me. However, giving therapy to your own child is nothing like counseling others. Toward the end of high school, I met with a therapist from a nearby community. She was too unfamiliar with the culture in which I was growing up and we were not able to communicate well.

When I was sixteen, I went to seminary in Israel. I had never really been away from home before. I became severely depressed and I stopped getting out of bed altogether. I felt very locked up and was not able to reach out and connect to others in my new environment.

My parents came to visit in January. I thought they were coming to see me but really, they were coming to take me home. Somehow, I managed to convince them that I was okay and that they should let me stay. By *Pesaḥ* I was doing better and I started appreciating the freedom to meet new people and explore new things.

I had decided in high school that I wanted to be a doctor, maybe a neurologist or psychiatrist. Before leaving for seminary, I had received a full scholarship to a four-year city college program in New York City and after returning home from Israel, I started school there. I was on the premed track, but I decided to major in music, not the typical choices for a religious girl. The scholarship that I received came with free board. I accepted the dorm room, thinking that it might be useful at some point if I had any late classes that were required for premed. I started using the dorm room once a week, but it quickly turned into two or three times a week. Before I knew it, I had moved into a room in a coed dorm and I was staying there the entire week. My parents didn't know what to do, and I didn't know what to do with myself, either. I felt a strong need to move out of my home and deal with my depression, which was creeping up on me again. All of a sudden, I had a different place to be. I was also questioning my religiosity and needed the space to figure it out. It would have been easy for me to start drinking or doing drugs in the dorm, as they were being offered all over campus. Thank God, I never did. I think that if I started up, it would have been really hard for me to stop.

I was in the middle of two worlds at school – the premed, highly competitive crowd and the music major, where many just sat in the hallway and strummed their guitars. And I was definitely in two different worlds between the dorm and my parents' home. I toyed with not being religious. I hardly ever called home during the week, but I went home every *Shabbat*. The weekends at home were difficult. Soon enough, the depression reared its ugly head again.

I started therapy with a psychologist in Manhattan. Her therapy was largely analytic. She told me that in order to start dealing with the depression, I needed to stop confining myself and become less stifled. I needed to do what I wanted to do, without worrying about my family and the community's expectations. Sometimes I was so depressed that we would just stare at each other for forty-five minutes in silence. It was a confusing time.

Ironically, although I didn't even know where I stood religiously, I started a kiruv program at my school. I made friends through this group, as well as through other venues. I also became friends with a couple of other people who were also struggling with mental health issues. One of my closest friends had a severe case of anorexia and and at one point, she was so sick that I needed to take her to the emergency room.

I went out on a few *shiddukh* dates, but they didn't go anywhere. I had no idea who I was, let alone what kind of man I wanted to marry. I was in my last year of college and I just scrapped the whole idea. It was definitely not the time for me to be dating.

Struggling with depression, I had trouble concentrating in class and during exams. In my last semester of organic chemistry, I handed in mostly blank tests. I became afraid of my dream to go to medical school. I was scared of how I would be able to get through medical school if I couldn't even get through the premed courses. This was the first time that my mental illness stopped me from pursuing my goals.

EASY

Thinking that it was a good compromise, and that the courseload might be more managable for me and yet still a challenge, I decided to become a physician's assistant. I got accepted to an excellent PA program and decided to go to Israel for the summer before I started. I arrived in Israel on a Thursday and found myself without plans for *Shabbat*. There was a family I had wanted to go to when I was in Israel for the year, the Machlis family. They had hundreds of people each meal on *Shabbat* and accepted anyone who needed a meal without questions.

I went that Friday night and found a seat between a drunk person on one side and a young Mormon man on the other. The Mormon was quite curious about the goings-on and he was asking me non-stop questions about the significance of everything he was seeing. I went to help in the kitchen to escape and found myself talking to a boy from Texas named Eitan, who was a student of the Machlis family and was frequently at their home. I stayed in the kitchen with him and the Machlis daughters until early in the morning.

The next morning, Rebbetzin Machlis, *a"h*, went up to him and said, "I saw you talking to a girl last night. *Nu?*" Eitan told her that with my very *frum* New York background, he didn't think it would be a good fit. She wouldn't hear any excuses and called me the next day. It wasn't a hard sell. I had wanted to go out with him.

I called my parents and let them know that I wanted to go out with someone I had just met. They panicked. "He's from Texas? Is he Jewish?" This wasn't the *shiddukh* dating that my community and friends were experiencing. My parents, not knowing what to do, told me that I could go out with him once. We went out once with their blessing and then didn't tell them about the next date at all.

With Eitan, it was so easy. I found myself slipping into talking about our future kids. His religious observance really ressonated with what I was looking for. He grew up in a family that had slowly become more observant over time. I suddenly didn't have so many religious questions. I had been looking for a model of healthy observance for me, and I had found it. I was very attracted to that. I didn't go to too many classes that summer. We would walk to the *Kotel* and talk until four o'clock in the morning. It was just so easy being with him. He told me that he wanted to move to Israel after finishing school. I was game.

I told Eitan early on about my mental health struggles. He was extremely supportive. We were young and optimistic and falling in love. We both had no idea how much my depression would impact our marriage. I think it is one of those things that you can't know until you have gone through it.

WE NEED HELP

I started PA school and Eitan was in *kollel*. There were some months during our first couple years of marriage, especially in the winter season, that my depression really took over. During those months, I was on the couch a lot and avoided social situations as much as I could. My husband attended *shul* and other functions alone. I took the antidepressants that I was given to manage my depression and even during the rough times, I went to school and got good grades.

As a teenager, my husband had gone to Poland to visit the concentration camps, and he was heartbroken by the devastation there. He decided on that visit that he wanted to have twelve or thirteen kids. He wanted to do his part to rebuild our nation after the *Shoah*. To me, it sounded amazing and very touching.

Before we got married, we went to seek advice from a *rav* who my husband held in high regard. With an understanding not common among the clergy twenty years ago, he explained to us that in my case, I should only try to have children during time periods when I was doing well emotionally, and when my psychiatrist agreed that I was up for it. At that point, we had no idea that having children would not come easy to us.

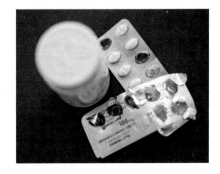

I got pregnant with our daughter after a year and a half. As was the current recommendation among the medical community during that time, I stopped taking my antidepressants. As the pregnancy progressed, I became more and more depressed. After I gave birth, I stopped sleeping. I was nursing at night, and I would not be able to sleep between feedings. This was our first baby and we didn't know what was normal. Eitan would wake up in the morning and I would be reorganizing closets and doing things on our to-do lists that we had never gotten around to doing. Then I started to speak faster than usual.

I wasn't myself. I wasn't making good decisions. I was taking the baby out for walks in the middle of the night in our unsafe neighborhood in the city. I had gotten a job at a local high school as a tutor, and one of the teachers noticed that I wasn't quite right. I was acting out of line and it was obvious to others that I wasn't acting in a typical way. When I think about that time period, I feel so embarrassed.

I had a new baby at home and things were deteriorating. I was getting paranoid, I was not able to think clearly, and I didn't sound healthy. I had become manic. However, I was in touch with reality enough to realize that we needed help. I told Eitan that things were not okay, that we needed to go away and get some help. He must have been so scared. I told him that we should go to Texas to be with his parents.

When we were dating, I told him that he was free to share my mental health issues with his parents. But he didn't. He didn't share it with anyone, not even his closest friends. He was dealing with it all on his own. But now it was time to reach out. Eitan called up his parents, and seemingly out of the blue said, "Chana is sick. We need help."

TERRIFYING

My in-laws didn't know what to expect. We got off the plane with a new baby and they had a psychiatrist, a good family friend, waiting for us at the house.

He had come prepared with tranquilizers in case I needed it. He gave me sleeping pills to help me sleep. They worked, but my husband told me that I had nightmares and woke him up screaming a few times that week.

Medical consensus at the time was to not nurse while on mood stabilizers, so I had to stop nursing my baby. I now had painful engorgement in addition to everything else. My in-laws took care of us and I came down from the mania. We stayed in Houston for a few weeks.

After being in *kollel* for a few years, my husband decided to go back to school for a physical therapy degree. He got accepted to a program in Houston and we moved at the end of the year. I got an amazing job as a PA in radiation oncology at one of the best cancer centers in the US. I was still experiencing bouts of depression, but was overall doing much better. It was helpful for me to be with the cancer patients I was treating, because when I feel depressed, I find it difficult to talk. Being with them helped me get out of myself and be present for other people. They needed me and I was able to focus my attention on them.

We started talking about having another child. We promised ourselves that we would be aware of the signs of mania and would stop it right away if it happened. I would start medication immediately if there was any suspicion. We were prepared.

But getting pregnant wasn't as easy this time. I found out that I wasn't ovulating at all. I was diagnosed with polycystic ovary syndrome (PCOS) and needed to start fertility treatments in order to get pregnant. Pregnancy was becoming more complicated. We began fertility treatments, and *barukh Hashem*, with just Clomid, I was able to get pregnant. I stayed on my antidepressants this time, as the medical world had made strides in acknowledging the importance and safety of many antidepressants during pregnancy. My mood during this pregnancy was much better than it had been during the first one.

I gave birth to my second daughter in March of 2006. We had promised ourselves that if I started to experience mania again, we would treat it before it got too bad. If I stopped sleeping, we would tell the psychiatrist right away. But denial is a strong adversary. I convinced myself and my husband that my lack of sleep was solely due to caring for a newborn. But the other signs of mania were beginning to show.

When I was two months postpartum, my older daughter started complaining of stomach pain. Her pediatrician felt a mass in her abdomen and an ultrasound identified a tumor. The doctors explained that until they did surgery, we wouldn't know if it was benign or not. They estimated about a 50 percent chance that she would need to go on to have chemotherapy or radiation. I can't imagine how terrifying it was for my husband. His wife was experiencing mania, his daughter had a tumor, and he had a newborn baby at home. Our daughter had surgery within a few days and thank God, the tumor was benign. But I was getting worse and worse.

A few weeks later, I was put back on mood stabilizers. I came back down to myself, but it was not a swift process. I went back into therapy. We went to marital therapy as well, but I wasn't ready to deal with it all. I wasn't ready to talk about how my illness affected our marriage negatively.

Slowly, I started getting better. Our two girls were wonderful babies. My husband graduated from school and started working.

He had told me when we met that he wanted to make *aliya* in the future, and after five years in Houston, we decided that now was the time. Our oldest was going into first grade and it would only get harder to move as the kids got older. It was time to make the move.

MAYBE ONE DAY

We made *aliya* to Ramat Beit Shemesh in 2008. Everything was going well. After a few hard months of job seeking, Eitan found a job. My daughters were in school. I was working from home as a medical consultant for a software company that sold programs to physicians.

I began fertility treatment again, but this time the Clomid didn't work. I started treatment with various injections and got pregnant. On the ultrasound, they saw two sacs. The thought of twins was too overwhelming for me to talk about. But within a few weeks, ultrasounds identified only one baby. Since my last pregnancy, the medical world had grown even more accepting of psychiatric medication during pregnancy. This time, I stayed on both of my antidepressants. Together with our psychiatrist, we decided that I would start taking a mood stabilizer immediately after birth, without giving myself any time to develop mania. The pediatricians I consulted with thought it was best if I didn't nurse while taking this medication and I tried to prepare myself emotionally to not be able to nurse again.

My third child was born via emergency C-section after a long labor. Knowing that I wouldn't be able to nurse, I asked for medication to dry up my milk. The neonatologist on call informed me that the most current research showed that it was indeed safe to nurse while taking the dosage of the mood stabilizer that I was preparing to take. I was so happy to be able to nurse my baby. The medication worked and I didn't develop mania. We were terrified that I would. Every time I had a bad night of sleep, we were so frightened. It brought back so many bad memories.

I continued working from home. During the times that I was feeling down, working from home was both a blessing and a challenge, for the same reasons. I didn't have to get dressed and I didn't have to interact with other people. It was easy to hide.

I miss working in my field. I miss working with patients. I dream about going to medical school here in Israel. Maybe one day.

BREATHING

About six years ago, after realizing that we would likely never be able to afford to buy something substantial in Beit Shemesh, we started looking elsewhere in the country. As the most affordable places in the country are the Negev in the South and the Golan in the North, we started looking in the Golan, as I am not a fan of the desert heat. After visiting the *yishuv* of Hispin multiple times, we decided to move and build our home in the Golan. Not long after we got here, I surprisingly got pregnant without any fertility treatment. I gave birth to my youngest shortly after we moved into our new home.

Moving up here took guts. We left a vibrant community of people similar to us back in Beit Shemesh. I find the culture gap between us and the native Israelis here can be challenging, but there are many other things that make up for it. Our religious experience here on the *yishuv* has been so positive. There is a warmth in the Golan between different types of Jews, both observant and non-observant. The *yishuv* lifestyle, along with the surrounding springs and agriculture, is wonderful for us. I feel like I can breathe here. There is more room for everything – religious expression, personal development, and a beautiful landscape. There is even room for mental illness.

I have been on the same two antidepressants plus a mood stabilizer for almost ten years. I don't know if I will ever stop taking them. I am so grateful that these medications exist and that I found them. I still go through one or two hard days every week. I try to talk myself through it and not get scared. I'll fall asleep at the computer or hide under the covers. I'll cry a little more. But then I come back to myself.

Last year we found out that for a medical reason, I needed to have my ovaries removed. When that happened, I woke up from surgery immediately in menopause. We were very nervous because the huge hormonal shift might have been very destabilizing to my mental health. Thank God, though it brought me down, it did not derail me.

I am very sad that I can't have another baby. But I truly believe that this was another message from God, guiding us as to what is best for our family. It is nothing short of miraculous that with my infertility and mental illness, I have four beautiful children.

Being here in the Golan is like taking a long breath of fresh air. I feel like I can do what I want and be myself. After ten years of working remotely, I am signing up for an EMT course to start doing what I love in Israel. I am looking to the future and am so thankful to God, my family, my friends, and the good mental health care that has helped me get here.

REFLECTIONS

Questions to Consider
- What do you do to care for yourself when you are feeling down?
- Have you found your own space to breathe?

Words to Remember

"I feel like I can breathe here. There is more room
for everything – religious expression, personal
development, and a beautiful landscape. There
is even room for mental illness."

Group Discussion
Think about a moment when you needed to ask for help. Was it hard
for you to accept help? What changed for you that allowed you to
open yourself to others?

✍

Take a moment for yourself. What do you need right now?
Close your eyes and be in your own body.
Here is an affirmation exercise to come back to yourself:

Affirmation Exercise
I value myself for the things I love and the things I struggle with.
I feel joyful about every step in the right direction.
I make time to nourish myself, body, mind, and soul.
I love myself and I believe in myself.
Every day, there is hope to grow stronger.

Alana's Story

Seeking Spirituality

Har Nof, Jerusalem

IMPRINTS

When I was child, I remember having romantic and beautiful feelings about Israel. I was deeply in love with Israel; I yearned for it. Anytime a family member or friend went on a trip to Israel it felt like a really big deal. Why? I don't know for sure, but I do know that it came from my family – pure Zionism.

My first trip to Israel was a divine experience. I exercised free will to go, but I also know that my going was divine providence. Over and over, I've seen that everything in my life is meant to happen in a certain way. Hashem willed me to go in a specific direction, provided the settings to enable me to go in that direction, and I freely chose to follow that path. No fiat, no instruction, no directive, but a direction for sure.

At the end of my junior year of college I wanted to go to South Africa to attend a highly competitive study-abroad program. I wasn't accepted and I was heartbroken. I went to speak with a woman who worked in the international affairs office at my school, and she suggested I go on a trip to Israel that was being arranged. It was very late in the process of being placed in an international trip or program, and I impulsively said, "Sure!" It was 2007, less than a year after the Second Lebanon War. Israeli tourism was not very attractive to many students at my school, but I decided I was going. I had no background in Hebrew and had no premeditated thought to visit Israel, but the suggestion felt like an opportunity. The program took place at Ben-Gurion University in the Negev. We lived on campus, and I was totally secular at that point in my life. I found the experience very difficult. The technical and cultural differences were vast. Everything was nuanced and variable; nothing was simple. My roommates were Arab-Israeli and their spoken language was Arabic, while obviously throughout Israel I mostly heard Hebrew other than in my classes, which were in English. Days in the Negev burned hotter than a furnace and I was always depleted.

My volunteer project was teaching English to Ethiopian children at an absorption center in the South. They were all new immigrants. Some of them had been in Israel two weeks and others had been there just under a year. English was to be their third language. Many of the children were orphaned. All of them had a story – sad stories, sorrowful stories, spiritual stories. I wanted to adopt them all.

I enjoyed teaching the children, but I mostly cherished the gift of connecting with these warrior souls who had barely escaped with their lives to come be in the same country which I had entered in a comparative calm. I cried every day, but one day in particular, my tears would not stop. We received a call that still rocks me to my core. We were told not to come in because the father of one of my students had mortally stabbed his wife. This meant that my student had lost his mother. Most of my friends on campus were disin-

terested. It also barely made the news. But I struggled to cope. I was naive and unable to process the energy of Israel. During this period, I internalized the pain and struggles and it felt like there was also beauty in my pain. There was no crisis counseling and support, no coping as a community or public gatherings. It was a rocky experience.

Overall, my time in Israel was a like a literary European love story. It was very long and dramatic. Just when I thought it was almost over another plot twist would be revealed. I had the privilege to see a lot of the country and had many lovely moments. But there was something missing.

When I left Israel and came back to the States, it felt like I was in mourning. I was in bed for nearly two days. Eventually I went on with life. I put that semester in a lockbox, knowing I'd come back to it but still unaware of the imprint that my time in Israel had etched within me.

A NEW JOURNEY

Time passed. I changed. My personal journey continued and things really shifted for me. I matured, grew up, became religious, and I went to graduate school. The cycle of life continued.

At some point, over the last year and a half, I started feeling this pull to return to Israel. It was a really foreign feeling. I had never felt it before. I had friends constantly going back and forth to Israel and I had done lots of traveling, but it never crossed my mind to go back there. When it hit me, it was slow at first, but over time, I knew it was something I had to do.

I had no idea how it was going to happen. At the time I was working at a law firm during the day and I had just started filming a documentary that I was co-producing and directing. I was in New York, I was dating, and I had a social life. There was no reason to leave. I was in the middle of this chapter of my life.

But the feeling was strong, in a deep internal way. It wasn't scary; it wasn't painful or loud; it was simply steady and true. I started telling people very close to me that I was going to Israel. I had no idea how it was going to happen. I wanted to go for a year and I started researching seminaries because it was clear to me that it was going to be a spiritual journey. I needed to strengthen my religious foundation and I was looking for spiritual growth. Seminary seemed like a good place to do that. I was in my early thirties, not the typical age for someone going to seminary. I thought I might be the oldest person there by a decade. Honestly, though, it didn't matter because I didn't care.

I was choosing between a long list of schools and I received guidance from many people to help me narrow down my choices. It seemed as though it was becoming increasingly more common for *baalei teshuva* of all ages to make their way to Israel and study in full-time learning programs. Around November of last year, a *kiruv* rabbi connected me with a woman who is a *baalas teshuva*. She works in *kiruv* and guides many women, eventually sending many of them to seminary. We spoke at length. Over the course of several hours of conversation, my list went from ten schools to one school. It was very clear to me that I had found where I needed to be.

EMUNA

I immediately began researching funding options to finance my trip to Israel and a year in seminary. I realized late in the process that the funding options initially presented to me were not going to work. Overnight, I went from thinking that I had funding fully secured to having no funding at all. At that point, it was the summer, and I was planning on coming for the *Elul* semester. I didn't tell anyone that I didn't have the funding. I was still planning on going. But I didn't know how I was going to make it happen. It was beyond anything logical. It really seemed like everything was falling apart. But I knew I had to be in Israel and I knew that somehow Hashem would put the pieces together for me.

Many organizations that offer scholarships said no to me. Because, because, because – because I wasn't learning with their rabbis, because they were a *kiruv* organization and I was already religious, or because I was too old. They were looking for specific types of people, like women who were in their twenties and grew up with no Jewish background, or they had the background but had left that in the background. In any event, I didn't thread their needle. My story of being in my early thirties and religious for quite a few years but with no formal Jewish education just wasn't the story they funded. I felt like I was falling through the cracks. I kept praying, moving forward, going through all the motions, and reasserting to myself that I was going.

One night I went out with a friend. I told her that I didn't think it was going to work out. It just seemed like there were too many hoops and I wasn't successfully jumping through them. I was wondering if it was the responsible thing to do, after all. Maybe I should be spending my energy in New York City trying to date and find my soulmate. Maybe I need to finish my documentary. Why was I going on this spiritual adventure? My friend said to me, "You need to think about what you really want." I knew that what I deeply wanted and needed was to go to Israel. I knew that I wanted to learn. I knew that I wanted to grow, and that I needed to grow.

The day after I spoke with my friend, I was in touch with a rabbi who was helping guide my process. Within twenty-four hours he called me; he had gotten the funding all in place. I called a travel agent, and within the week I had a one-way ticket. I was going to fly to Israel and be ready to start learning after the *chagim*. I would be arriving *Erev Yom Kippur*.

CLARITY

Funding secured, I began finalizing my arrangements and working through all the logistics. Despite family and close friends having difficulty accepting my thought process and decision to depart, I think everyone knew it was for my best. I felt supported. When I bought the one-way ticket, I didn't know when I was coming back. I didn't know what Israel had in store for me. Everyone was asking me, "Are you making *aliya*?" or "Are you staying for a week? A month? A year?" I honestly had no idea. I still have no idea.

When I got here, I felt totally embraced by the faculty and staff at my seminary. They made it clear that if I felt like I needed to stay longer, they would help me find the resources to continue to make it work. Everyone here has stayed true to that, especially the leadership. I am more than a student to them. I am a person, a person who wants to be here, and they make up an institution that wants me to thrive and feel a sense of belonging. The holistic and nurturing approach of my seminary has made it a true source of energy and sustainability for me.

The learning has been amazing. I think that I have gotten a lot of clarity in a lot of areas in my life. The more clarity I get, it opens more windows into ambiguities that I didn't know existed before. Making this jump was a huge leap of faith. And perhaps that is the most significant skill and value that I have gained through this process thus far: when I take a leap of faith and I choose to be sure about something really important and meaningful and which I feel to be a deep truth, there will be a net to catch me. This has been shown to me not only practically but also analytically and textually. Learn-

345

ing about and from the Matriarchs and Patriarchs, seeing their struggles and what they went through, and studying their faith-based life decisions has brought me to understand more deeply my own decision and continues to inspire me to leap further and higher on a daily basis.

I know I'm not done here. My work has just gotten started. I know I have a lot more to learn and grow. And I also know that I have no idea how long that will take.

SEEKER

Reflecting on my first months in Israel and the choices I made in order to come here, I've begun to realize how rare it is to go down the path I did. My reflections have really been sharpened by external feedback. As I meet people in Israel and speak with those I left behind in America, I've noticed that people reflexively express excitement for me. Some will riff on the idea of being true to yourself and others identify with living in, and with, what you need in the moment. I think that there can sometimes be this paradox: I came here as someone and I know I want to be myself when I leave. But I also want to be the most highly elevated – or at a minimum, a more elevated – version of myself when I leave. Even so, I don't want to be some-

one else, or erase any of the artistic sides to myself. I need more understanding of the religious rituals that I do so I can have more appreciation for their inner drivers. Only then can I hope to illuminate my spirit with the spiritual without being rote and ritualistic.

I feel like at some point I went backward on the age scale. I was very serious in my twenties and now in my thirties, I feel something has settled in for me. Socially, it can be challenging here, as almost all my fellow students are far younger than me. I am in a different head and heart space than most of the women in my program here in Israel. There is a certain level of growth based on age, maturity, and physical realities that I have gone through already. I was secular and in my twenties while I was passing through uncertainty and self-discovery. But now, at this stage, I know who I am. It is a beautiful thing and

I think everyone goes through these phases or windows of life progression. Now I am in a stage of growth and change that comes from knowing myself. There is this dynamic of evolution that comes from being more settled. It's less about moving with the crowd and engaging with mob mentality; now is the time when I want to do the best for myself and I know that following that growth pattern is how I'm going to develop.

When I was younger, I found there was a lot of people-pleasing. At this age, I don't feel the need to live for others. More importantly, I do feel like living for me. It is interesting to engage in this spiritual journey while being focused on my true inclinations and spiritual direction, as opposed to juggling and balancing inner contradictions of spiritual growth with people-pleasing. My growth is mine. Growth that comes from a place of pleasing others doesn't last. It wouldn't even make me happy, because I wouldn't be growing the "me" whom I'm tasked with making. No matter where you come from and where you end up, even if those points are exactly the same, life isn't really lived if there isn't a momentous moment where you actually choose your destination and end point for yourself.

I identify as a seeker. My life is a quest for more, a search for something deeper. I was happy in the life that I had back home. But through my experiences here, there will be things that I will want to let go because I will have outgrown them. Maybe, more importantly, I'll be empowered to let go of those things. I know that after doing that, the things that I keep with me will be so much stronger. There will be more nuances in the details. It will all rest on more solid ground.

There are things I left behind and mourned when I first became religious, such as the opportunity to be in a Broadway play. My whole path in life had been leading there; that is what my whole cohort from school is doing now.

But I knew that this type of religiosity was what my soul needed. So even though there is loss and sadness over a path that was excluded from my possibilities, I do have hope that the system will change and that there will be more opportunities for *frum* women to perform in the future. I know that it was hurtful to me and very confusing to many around me, especially all those who believed in me, that I could no longer work toward the goal of performing.

I have been an artist my entire life. My identity has revolved around singing, dancing, acting, writing – that was it. The darkest times of my life have been the times when I didn't engage those creative talents. Now I am saying that I am committing to a lifestyle which does not seem to be in sync with my art. It is a struggle. Part of the way that I reconcile the two is by creating anything that I can possibly create. I force myself to work in the spaces that are available to me now. This was the catalyst for me to produce some of my creative projects. I always hope that I will be cast in something that will work with my religious sensibilities.

In life, we need to pause, put things on hold, and explore what calls out to us. I can't have any regrets about being attentive to all my needs. I think that in the long run, I will have a far more fulfilled and satisfied life.

HEART EXPANDED

At the end of my time in seminary, I boarded a plane out of Israel. My departure shocked my syste, just like the heart-snapping jolt I felt upon arrival. My entire stay felt wholly unearthly. Often, the journey I took in Israel felt like an out of body experience. I felt like I knew my soul in a different way. I felt embodied in a new way. I felt guided, but not by any mechanism that I controlled. As the natural end of my stay fast approached I grasped at anything I could to stay in Israel, but all logical roads pointed to America. I experienced enormous difficulties with my immigration visa, my subtenant in NYC needed to move out, and I also had a sick close relative back home. I accepted what felt like Hashem's direction, knowing that this fate and these facts were from Him too.

Coming back to America was difficult. I was changed, and I had new and different priorities. Immediately after returning I still felt the holiness of Israel. My prayers still felt like a conversation I wanted to have rather than a speech I had to give. I felt Hashem everywhere. *Hashgacha pratis* became my status quo and there truly were moments when I was unable to distinguish between an expected pattern and a miracle. My vessel felt full and even at times overflowing. I still wished I was living in Israel, but I also knew I had to come back with what I needed. I went to Israel with a thirst to learn and I came back with the ingredients to do; to act, to be – for me and for others.

When I landed in the US, the external pressure to get married was strong. It started my first *Shabbos* back. There had been periods of my life when I took dating seriously, other times I wasn't even in the mix, and on occasion it felt like a big bad joke. This time I decided I was going to put in my fullest effort and leave the outcome to Hashem. I knew what kind of man I wanted to marry and the kind of Jewish household I wanted to have.

A year after leaving Israel I met my husband. We became formally engaged six weeks after meeting and married a month later. Our wedding was during the height of the Covid-19 pandemic. There were ten people at our wedding. Neither of us had any relatives present. Still, one of the holiest and happiest days of my life. All of our friends and family were able to watch on live stream.

I joined a small social justice theater company that accepts all aspects of who I am. From day one they knew that I wouldn't be able to perform on *Shabbos* and it was a non-issue. Today that is essential in every partnership in which I participate. Full acceptance of my whole self is my prerequisite for all of my collaborative commitments. I also now work with women seeking to improve their lives on a one-on-one basis. I facilitate guided meditations and hold space for women who want to grow into their most fully realized selves. I'm still seeking spirituality – I hope I always will – and what better way to stay focused on my own spiritual growth than helping others to do the same.

Now I live in Brooklyn with my husband, Yisroel. I have three amazing bonus daughters from my husband's previous marriage. Becoming a mother on my wedding day was one of the greatest gifts of my life. Every day my girls teach me, with mercy and kindness, how to be a better person. They have the ability to see my potential for greatness as well as my weaknesses all in the same moment – and they still love me. With the help of Hashem, I look forward to continuing to grow my family. My heart has expanded. My vulnerability has been radicalized. I might physically be in America but my heart, soul, and mental state are very much connected to *Eretz Yisrael*.

REFLECTIONS

Questions to Consider
- Have you ever wrestled with the conflict between your religious life and your career aspirations?
- At your current stage in life, what would you like to invest your time in learning?

Words to Remember
> "It is interesting to engage in this spiritual journey
> while being focused on my true inclinations and
> spiritual direction, as opposed to juggling and
> balancing inner contradictions of spiritual growth
> with people-pleasing. My growth is mine."

Group Discussion
People are constantly evolving and growing.
What growth are you experiencing in your life right now?

Take a moment for yourself. What do you need right now?
Close your eyes and be in your own body.
Here is an inspiration exercise to explore further:

Inspiration Exercise
Close your eyes and think about the following:
- When did you first begin to identify your own spirituality?
- What are the sacrifices you make in your life?
  Do you feel they have been worthwhile?
- Do you have dreams that you want to accomplish? What steps can you take to get closer to your goals?

Worth Every Moment

IS THIS NORMAL?

During my first pregnancy, we were so young. We were married for five weeks when we found out. I had been twenty years old for a total of three weeks. I was sick right away. We were naive and we didn't understand that this was different, that what I was experiencing was above and beyond typical pregnancy symptoms. I was hospitalized at one point for dehydration, but even then I didn't understand that it wasn't typical for a woman who is thirty weeks pregnant to not be able to at least keep down fluids. My mother was the only person who told me that what I was experiencing wasn't normal. Not that I didn't believe her, but she worries about me, so I thought it was just my mom worrying about me. I didn't think it was something unusual or weird.

When I became pregnant for the second time, it was much harder for me because I already had a baby at home. I could barely be a functional human being. That is when I started to understand that this experience was not typical of other women's pregnancies. I have so many traumatic memories from that pregnancy, such as having contractions because I couldn't keep anything down and I was dehydrated.

Though this second pregnancy wasn't the beginning of having difficult pregnancies, it felt like the beginning of real life. I was mothering, I was working, and I was finishing school. I took the CPA exam during that pregnancy. I took one section of the CPA exam each trimester. One of these tests was right before *Shavuos*, and my husband bought me a piece of cheesecake. It was the most decadent cheesecake with strawberries – heaven. We didn't have a lot of money at that time. We never splurged on things like that. But he bought it for me to celebrate. I got in the nineties on my test; I knew that I deserved to celebrate. But I sat trying to eat this piece of cake, struggling to choke it down. That is not normal.

My doctor told me that whatever I could get into my body, I should, regardless of whether it was considered healthy. I just needed caloric intake. I was told, "If you can eat it, eat it." I found that many people in my life had zero understanding of how sick I was. They didn't understand what it meant that I could barely eat and that I was miserable all the time. It made me feel like there was an enormous divide between my experience and a typical pregnancy. That left me feeling so alone.

BREADWINNER

In every pregnancy, my first sixteen to twenty weeks were hell. From about week twenty to week thirty, I had some sort of relief. From week thirty until I gave birth was horrible again. In the beginning, I would vomit anywhere from three to ten times a day.

I have always been the main breadwinner. At that time, like most of our peers, we had chosen a *kollel* lifestyle and we had no money. There was no one who could help us financially and I had no one else to rely on. So I would go to work. My nausea would be so bad that sometimes I was paralyzed. If I moved or opened my mouth, that meant that I would be sick. It especially became an issue when I drove to work and when I had meetings with my colleagues at the beginning of my work day.

Shabbos was always the hardest day of the week. *Shabbos* food is often not conducive to a person who is so sick. As we got older and we became more mature – to the point where we understood that we needed to make adjustments to our lifestyle – we stopped serving traditional *Shabbos* food while I was pregnant. It wasn't that we didn't think it was important, but rather we understood that it wasn't going to work while I was ill.

I always told my boss about my pregnancies right away, after the first appointment when there was a heartbeat. That also meant that when I lost a baby, my boss knew right away too. I have always told them early because I felt I needed to tell them. I was weaker and I needed to explain why. It wasn't because I was lazy or slacking off. I give my job 110 percent, and I needed them to understand why I wasn't pushing as hard as always.

When I was in a more corporate environment, they really didn't get it. But once I had a boss in that environment who was an amazingly strong woman who was totally supportive of me. She was the boss I had when I lost a baby at four months pregnant.

When I moved to a smaller company but had climbed higher up the corporate ladder, it was better. I had my own office, so when I got sick, it was less of a scene. At one point, my boss's wife was pregnant too. When I told him I was pregnant and how ill I get during pregnancy he said, "Don't worry, I get it." But he didn't get it. He expected me to function like a regular pregnant woman. He made me jump through hoops and take calls late at night when I was barely functioning. It made me so angry. He didn't understand why I was so angry. At my evaluation that year he told me, "I don't think you handled that appropriately." He was my boss, so there wasn't much I could say. It just wasn't right.

There were days when getting up to go to the printer to get a document felt impossible. We forget what food does for our bodies. It gives us the energy to move. It makes all your bodily functions work. When you don't have that, and when you don't have it on a long-term basis, you can become really ill. Something like standing up to pick up a piece of paper can become more than you can handle.

PARENTING WHILE PREGNANT

On the days that I made it through work, I would come home and I couldn't move. On the weekends, I couldn't move.

One of the things that was the hardest about all of this was all the judgment that I got about how much my husband would do in the house. People didn't understand how sick I was. My husband understood and supported me completely. He would never get angry at me. Sometimes he would get stressed by the burdens of the household and worrying about me, but he was always understanding.

Other people would say things. Once his *chavrusa* said to him, "Your wife takes advantage of you." My husband was sitting there thinking, "My wife is throwing up ten times a day, while she goes to work to support me while I am learning in *kollel*, and she takes advantage of me because I am serving dinner?" People really spoke that way to us, and it was hard. They didn't understand what we were going through.

Another pivotal moment happened while I was in my sixth, and likely last, pregnancy (fifth baby). I was really ill and the pregnancy was very complicated. My husband has an autoimmune disease and is one of those people who looks fine on the outside but might not be fine on the inside. He had CMV, which is a form of mono. CMV can also be very dangerous for pregnant women. He was very, very sick.

I don't walk around telling people that I am pregnant in the beginning unless they need to know, especially because I had a late pregnancy loss. My sisters have always been able to figure it out because I drop off the face of the planet; I don't have the energy to talk to them. Of course, I would tell my parents right away. But generally, I keep it to myself. But during this time that my husband was sick, someone confided in me that she was expecting. I was relieved to tell her that I was expecting, too. My husband had not been able to pick up the slack in the same way that he had in the previous five pregnancies, and this time we had four kids.

There I was sitting on this park bench, with my friend who also was in her first trimester. After I confided in her about what was happening at home, she ended up cooking *Shabbos* for us for three months. My husband was too ill to stand in the kitchen, but he was able to drop off groceries and bring the cooked food home. I couldn't eat the food myself, but we had four children who needed to eat. It was another moment where I felt this huge divide. This woman was also pregnant, but she was able to care for us while we were barely keeping it together.

Around this time, I went to parent-teacher conferences and the teacher told me that my eldest was acting odd. She would cry at the drop of a hat, while in class. I was ten weeks pregnant at the time and I looked at the teacher and said, "I am pregnant and my husband is ill. I am not parenting my child. She is the oldest and a lot is falling on her."

As painful as it was to admit it, I knew then that I needed to be done having children. I already have children who I need to raise. I can't raise them when I am pregnant.

At twenty weeks, I was able to open the fridge and not fall ill. I can't explain the joy of opening the refrigerator and putting something in the oven for my kids to eat. I had so much gratitude for being able to do the smallest thing, like preparing a meal for my children.

HUNGRY AGAIN

In my first few pregnancies, I didn't understand that I had hyperemesis gravidarum (HG). I am a perfectionist, and it was hard for me to admit that something was too hard for me. Everyone else could do things a certain way, and I couldn't – that felt hard to accept. When we started the journey of having kids, we were so young. We were a lot less self-aware and a lot less mature. We were a young *charedi* couple doing what young *charedi* couples do, which is have babies. There was so much pressure for us to keep up.

That being said, I love my children so much. I don't regret any moment I spent struggling, because now they are my world. At some point when they are new, I hold them and think about every moment that I was sick, and how every ounce of suffering I experienced was worth it, just to hold them for that moment. I still feel that way.

For the first six months after my babies were born, I would just feel relieved about the fact that the pregnancy had been successful and I was alone in my body again. After my loss at four months, I was completely heartbroken. When I got home from the dilation and curettage (D&C), the procedure that clears the uterine lining after a miscarriage, my husband made me a plate of chicken and I could eat it. For one minute, I was so happy that I could eat lunch that the acute pain of the loss didn't hurt as badly.

For my third birth, I had a superfast delivery. My mom always says that since I have hard pregnancies, God gives me easy labors. I gave birth in triage, still wearing my clothes. I had a *charedi* nurse who cursed at the top of her lungs when she realized that I was giving birth right then and there. Once they took care of the baby, they brought me to a recovery area.

Since it was early morning, my husband went to *daven*. A volunteer approached me in my bed and asked me if I wanted something to eat for breakfast. She brought me a tray of cottage cheese, eggs, and Israeli salad. Nothing so fantastic or interesting, but I sat there eating that cottage cheese and I cried. The minute the baby was out of my body, I could eat again. I was completely and utterly thrilled to bring my baby girl into the world. But for one moment, I was just celebrating the fact that I could eat again.

Hyperemesis gravidarum made me suffer. But the babies were healthy and I was back to myself when they were born. We wanted to have a large family. Inborn in our value system is to have a large family. In our community, children are seen as blessings. I thought of the challenges of these pregnancies as a sacrifice that I wanted to make. It was a matter of time and pain in the moment so that we could live a lifetime raising and enjoying our children. Though it was hard, I wanted these kids so much.

LAST

I think I was in la-la land during my first pregnancy. As much as I was extremely sick and it was a very difficult pregnancy, we were newly married and didn't have any other kids yet. We were still in *shana rishona*, and we were head over heels for each other (which we still are). We were unaware of some harsher realities of life.

Around seven months into the pregnancy, we realized that maybe something wasn't right with me (besides for my undiagnosed hyperemesis gravidarum). My body was pretty swollen. We went to the doctor. I had read about preeclampsia in one of these baby books, and I told the doctor that I thought that I had preeclampsia. The doctor looked at my chart and thought my blood pressure looked fine, but I told her to look further back and see that typically, my blood pressure is on the lower end. She became alarmed. After that, they monitored me very closely. They induced me as soon as they thought that it was medically unsafe for me to be pregnant anymore. It was a difficult labor, but the baby came out and we were all okay.

Everyone told us that this was a fluke. The doctors said that preeclampsia can happen in first pregnancies but typically will not return with subsequent pregnancies. The younger you are or the older you are, the higher the risks. My first pregnancy was basically a teenage pregnancy, considering how young I was. They assured me it would not happen again. I was monitored for every pregnancy afterward, but mostly it was fine.

My last pregnancy was by far the hardest. With both my husband and I being so sick, we struggled to make it through. We were kicked out of our apartment and we had to move to the only place that was available. We did not love this new apartment and it was on the seventh floor of the building.

Just as things usually start getting better, around twenty weeks, we went to the doctor and found out that the baby had a skull deformity. We spent the rest of the pregnancy having no idea what would happen to our baby. They called it a structural abnormality and said that typically, babies with this condition have some sort of chromosomal abnormality. The rest of the time I was treated like I was giving birth to a child with a chromosomal abnormality.

We decided not to do an amnio because they wouldn't do it until thirty-two weeks. At that point, we felt that we would not risk any harm to the baby by doing more testing when the baby would, God willing, be present in person soon enough. They would have sent the results to Europe and we would not have any answers till I was thirty-six weeks along, anyway. We went through the rest of the time with a high-risk OB, being highly monitored all the way.

I was still vomiting and sick and all the while, I didn't know if I would have a healthy baby in the end. I kept having to go back for very invasive internal ultrasounds. I was in a room surrounded by doctors who thought that my baby might have fluid in his brain. It was very important to keep coming back for more ultrasounds so they could determine what kind of delivery he would need.

SWOLLEN

I had gotten a bit too swollen. Whereas in my first experience with pre-eclampsia, the symptoms came upon me in a slow, calm fashion, this time it sprang on us out of nowhere. At thirty-seven weeks, I saw my high-risk OB on Wednesday. On Thursday I went to work and I was having visual disturbances. I didn't understand what was happening. It was November in Israel and it was very sunny. I thought maybe the sun had bothered my eyes. In the office, I was seeing stars and lights in my eyes. But it passed.

When I got home that night my whole body was shaking. I thought I was having anxiety. I was thirty-seven weeks and worried about my baby. Makes sense, right? I was feeling sick as a dog, and on *Shabbos*, I had to walk up seven flights to get to our apartment. My husband said afterward that he knew something was really wrong when I was panting and not able to stand when I got to our place. I do those stairs all the time, no problem, even through pregnancy. Something was just wrong.

It took us time to put all the pieces together. It was only on Saturday night that I turned to my husband and asked, "Do my fingers look swollen to you?" I had these shakes that were coming on and off. He responded, "Not only do your fingers look swollen, but your face looks swollen too."

Maybe we should have called an ambulance right then, but it was eleven o'clock at night. We made a decision – I don't know if it was the right or wrong one – that in the morning, we would drop the kids off at school and head straight to the Center for Women's Health. When we got there, the nurse was very calm. She put me on the monitor and checked my blood pressure and went off to talk to the doctor on call. I feel really lucky that we live in a society in which our insurance companies have women's clinics, because I got immediate care. One of the OBs looked at my file in the system, and then looked at my blood pressure and said, "This woman needs to go to the hospital immediately."

They induced me right away and it went really well. Our son was born within six hours of getting to the hospital. He was perfectly healthy. Though my nausea abated, my blood pressure didn't go down and so they kept me in the hospital for a week so I could be monitored by a hematologist. I found out afterward from her that the shaking I experienced wasn't from anxiety. It was my body reacting to the preeclampsia. This whole experience taught me that I really need to listen to my body when it sends me a message.

We had kind of known that this pregnancy was going to be my last. We knew we were going to have to discuss not having more children. Now the preeclampsia made that decision for us. My husband has said over and over again, "I would rather have five children and my wife. I don't want six orphans." For us, that seals the issue.

The HG was so difficult for us both. And yet, because I love my children so much, I might have considered making the stupid decision (for me) to put myself in that compromised position again. The preeclampsia made it so I can't make this decision anymore. I feel my body saying, "Enough already. Ayelet, you are done."

THE NEXT ONE

Being *charedi* and having a husband who is a rabbi puts us in a specific position. If you look at the people around us – our siblings, friends, peers, and the rabbis he works with in yeshiva – it's clear that almost none of them are stopping at five children. Everyone is having more.

I was telling someone that all my sisters and sisters-in-law are pregnant right now, with babies that will be number four, five, six, seven, or eight. I find that people look at me waiting, expecting, and wondering. In my world, people don't say, "Five kids and you are done." In my world, they always say, "*Be'ezras Hashem*, the next one…" People don't even consider that there might not be another one or that for me, they are just pouring salt on an open wound.

I was talking with a relative about all the family babies being born, and they said to me, "Oh, are you getting baby fever?" waiting to find out if I was pregnant as well. There is just such tremendous pressure. People in my world think that having five children means you have a small family. They look down on you for it.

I think we do a huge disservice to women by making us feel like we aren't enough. I've always heard, "She is such a *tzadekes* because she has ten kids in a tiny apartment." Why can't you be a *tzadekes* and have fewer than ten kids? I always wanted to be that *tzadekes* with ten kids. I won't be. The perfectionist inside me struggles with that. I am not used to not following the program. I got married at nineteen. I supported my husband through *kollel*. I did everything according to the values and expectations of my community. I did everything "right." Now I feel like I am doing something wrong. Obviously it is not wrong. But Hashem took the ability to choose away from me. That leaves me heartbroken because I am not whole with the decision. This decision didn't come from me feeling at peace with my circumstances, it came from the circumstances themselves. I am not whole yet.

PUSHING MY LIMITS

We talk about infertility. We talk about loss. I know loss. But we define infertility as the inability to get pregnant. I am a woman who gets pregnant

immediately. That is how God made my body. But He also made my body respond to pregnancy with struggle and pain. It is not the same struggle as someone who waits for a child. But my family size is also being determined by my body, and not by my heart.

One of the things we have been trying to do lately is have fun. That is not something we could do for the first ten years of our marriage. From nineteen to twenty-nine, I was either pregnant and sick or nursing. Now, we go away on small vacations. We play. We go to fun restaurants and eat fun food. We take our kids out. We got a seven-seater car so we can go anywhere we want. It has been an extremely special experience for me, in the sense that I am myself again. I feel like a person. Fun is something that is still really hard for me. It was never on my list of priorities. But now, fun has become part of my healing process.

I have decided that I want to run the Tel Aviv Marathon next year with my husband. He has been running it for the last two years. So far I am on four weeks of running, three times a week. I am trying really hard and I'm doing it for a reason that you might not normally hear a *rebbetzin* say. I am doing it to reject the limits placed on me by the negative side effects of my pregnancies. I am doing it to discover the new limits of what my body can do. There is so much more I can do with my body than just have babies. I keep dreaming about how I'm going to feel when I finish that race, knowing that for so many years I was so limited. I could barely get off the couch. Eating felt impossible. I couldn't or wouldn't prioritize going out and living my

life. What is going on inside and what people see on the outside are just so different. People saw me as a successful young *charedi* woman, having babies, climbing the corporate ladder, and going about my life. But inside, I was the woman who couldn't choke down a slice of cheesecake.

I am investing in myself now and allowing myself to be a human being. I am seeking health and joy. I am enjoying every second of raising the children I struggled to carry. I am thrilled to be a wife and an employee. I got promoted this week and I am flying. I can't wait to continue to explore this new lease on life. I am eager to push my limits till they bring me health and continued happiness. I am grateful for all my blessings and thank God for His many gifts.

REFLECTIONS

Questions to Consider
- Has anything influenced your family size, such as illness, finances, or career?
- What is your relationship with your body? What sweetness or struggles has it brought into your life?

Words to Remember

> "People saw me as a successful young *charedi* woman, having babies, climbing the corporate ladder, and going about my life. But inside, I was the woman who couldn't choke down a slice of cheesecake."

Group Discussion

Communal pressure can be painful. It can make us feel like we are not keeping up with our peers or that we are doing something wrong. When has communal pressure affected your life?

Take a moment for yourself. What do you need right now?
Close your eyes and be in your own body.
Here is an affirmation exercise to come back to yourself:

Affirmation Exercise

My body is my home and I can take care of it.
I can enjoy the feeling of strength.
My body can do many things.
I deserve to feel good, inside and out.

Zehavit's Story

Complicated Love

Tel Aviv

PAINFUL BEGINNINGS

I never really considered myself to be a second-generation Holocaust survivor. I never thought about it in that way. Some people live all their lives with that title. I have issues, but I never connected those issues with the *Shoah*. All my life, I knew I had a hard childhood. I knew that my parents didn't do so much to contribute positively to my mental health. I just thought, "This is just how it is" – until recently.

My father came to Israel from Poland before the Holocaust, in 1933. He came with his parents and their six small children. He and his siblings had a rough upbringing. Their mother died when they were young and their father remarried and threw all the children into an orphanage. Maybe all of this was less traumatic for my father because he was already fifteen when his mother died.

My father later fought in the Palmaḥ, the elite fighting force of the Hagana. His friends died in wars and he suffered many losses. He married his first love, and then she died of cancer. Later, he met my mother and after their marriage, I was born. Whatever relationship my parents had, it was undoubtedly not easy. Their painful pasts played out in our household.

My father never liked to talk about the terrible things he witnessed. When I was young, he talked about his bravery and how he saved lives. He also said many times that God loves him, because of all the moments that he was spared. My mother always talked about her life. However, the first time I heard it described completely was when she wrote her book later in her life. Before that moment, I gathered fragments of her memories and wove them together in a haphazard way. It was only while editing the book for her that I got a full picture of what she had experienced.

My mother was born in Slovakia. When she was about ten years old, in the last two years of World War II, she was forced to wear the yellow star in school. People spat on her in the street. On my mother's side, my grandfather was a medical doctor and the manager of the local Jewish hospital in the Slovakian town of Nitra. My grandmother was a pediatrician. Twice, the Nazis came to arrest my grandfather to force him to work for them. The first time, his assistant chose to go in his place, because my grandfather had a family. The second time, he pretended to not hear them calling for him and escaped out the back door of the hospital.

When it became more dangerous, my grandfather tried to convince his siblings to sell their gold and jewelry so they could have money, because it would be getting worse and they would need the money to pay for hiding. No one listened to him because he was the youngest in the family. He came up with an idea that it would be easier to bring his wife and kids to a local small village, because there it would be easier to hide. He convinced the town doctor to declare that he needed help, and he arranged to give that doctor his salary so that they could have a cover. There were only non-Jews in the village.

He had an agreement with his brother in Nitra. If one of them heard that the Nazis were coming to take the Jews, he would send the other a message in Hebrew, *"Ham me'od,"* which means "very hot." They were preparing to hide. They got a contact person who they paid to secure a house for them if the Nazis came searching. The night when the message came through was so stressful for my mother, then a young child. She said that the villagers were so curious about what would happen to this family of Jews living with them, that they just kept coming all night to her father's medical clinic, which was part of their home. They were pretending that they had pains, just so they could watch. Eventually, my grandfather closed the clinic because it became really late in the evening and they really needed to start going.

My mother and her younger brother were already brought to the place where they were going to hide. The family split up to make their presence less noticeable. My grandparents left the clinic and walked in the opposite direction of where they were supposed to go, carrying two heavy suitcases. The villagers followed them to see what they would do, knowing that the Nazis were after them. When the villagers finally gave up following them, my grandparents went to the house where they were supposed to hide.

Because it took so much longer than it should have for them to arrive, the people who were supposed to be hiding the family were very anxious. "What if they dropped off the children here and left? Maybe we should kick them out?" My mother, a young child, was panicking but she responded quickly. "Oh, my parents are looking for something they couldn't find. They will be here soon." They waited a little longer and eventually her parents made it there.

The Christians who were hiding them took a huge risk. There were rumors that our family was hiding there. They received a letter threatening them. At some point, some of our other relatives came to hide with them, too, but they made too much noise. My grandparents had so many impossible decisions to make. Should they try to save other family members even if they put their immediate family in danger? Shortly after, the villagers told my grandparents they had to get out.

HIDING

They bounced around from house to house, over five or six houses, over a span of six months. Depending on the place, they were hiding in various uncomfortable spots: an attic, or a room with a German soldier living right behind the door. They needed to be very quiet so no one could hear them. They had food because they paid for their board. Surprisingly, in one place, the woman who was hiding them asked what they wanted on the menu.

My grandparents were so clever. They devised creative ways to communicate with each other. They used their smarts together to stay alive, which meant continuing to convince the villagers to hide them. It was hardest for my mother on one occasion when there was no room to hide them all together and they needed to split up. They sent her to a hole in a field when there was nowhere else to go. She counted the hours too quickly while she waited for them to retrieve her. She panicked, thinking that she was left behind and forgotten.

Once they were hiding in a barn of a village family when people unexpectedly came by and discovered them. My grandfather offered his watch to them as a bribe to stay silent about the fact that they were there. Eventually, they learned that these were the parents of the man who was hiding them. His parents had no idea that their son was hiding Jews and didn't do anything to harm them. They did not take the watch, either. The image of her father looking so poor and helpless never left my mother's mind.

One stressful night, they were thrown out of their hiding place. They had communicated via telegram with a new family who would hide them, and they hoped that they would pick them up from the field before someone worse picked them up. When they got to the house, the mother of the family showed them a jacket that had been made for her by my great-grandfather. She told my family what a good person he was and how she felt obligated to help his family.

My mother's family started running out of money. They had a Christian relative whom one of their cousins had married, and she was willing to help them. They asked her to go around to my grandfather's patients to collect money to help them hide. She did, and a lot of money was given. But the man who was making the connections for them was a gambler. He

thought that he could double the money for them, but instead, he lost most of it. The Christian woman went back out to collect more, but this time the patients did not give her that much, as they suspected she was stealing their charity. The man who was making the connections was a good man and felt very guilty, so he stashed the family at his brother's house for free. His brother was a widower and his fifteen-year-old daughter took care of the house and the younger children. She became responsible for also taking care of the Jewish family in the attic. She was not that much older than my mother was at the time.

We kept up the connection between our family and that last family who saved them. Over the last few years, I have been to visit this family several times. They always welcome me very nicely and I like meeting with them very much. I was lucky to have the chance to meet the woman who cared for our family. I saw the attic myself, too. It was still there last year. It was a small space with no windows. The floorboards were not that stable, so I couldn't walk all the way into the corners where they hid.

At the end of the war, my grandparents went back to Nitra. They needed to find a new flat, as theirs was already taken by their neighbors, and their belongings pillaged. My grandfather went around to all the neighbors demanding his belongings and furniture back. Most of it was returned.

As a teenager, my mom got involved in local Benei Akiva (religious youth movement) groups, and it was decided that she and her younger brother would travel to Israel in 1949 with Benei Akiva, and that their family would meet them there. She missed her parents and was afraid, again, that they would not come to rejoin her. She traveled with her brother by train and by boat. Though she was happy to be in Israel, she encountered other Jews there who were resentful that she came after the War of Independence and had not been there to fight. They had no idea what she had been through.

My grandparents packed two large suitcases to go to Israel. When they went into hiding, my grandmother had also packed two large suitcases – that time in the dead of winter. You would have thought she would have filled them with sweaters, jackets, and blankets. But half the suitcases were filled with *sifrei kodesh* and *maḥzorim*.

This time, they packed their most precious belongings, including pieces of Hungarian crystal. They brought only two bags because they got a message the next morning that doctors would not be able to leave the country. That night, they pretended to go to Vienna for the weekend. In reality, that had begun their escape to Israel.

BLOCKED OUT

Living in a Benei Akiva camp in Israel, my mother was seventeen years old when she married her music teacher. She told me that she was afraid that no one would marry her. She had no money. At the time, people who came to Israel from the *Shoah* were looked down upon. They were married for seven years and never had children. He was always obsessing about money. Even forty years after their divorce, he made her send her wedding ring back to him.

My mother later met my father when she was set up by a matchmaking service. My father is a charming man, and many women fell in love with him. He is ninety-one now, and he still has women falling in love with him. I imagine it wasn't that hard at forty-five. He was not religious and my mother was. He liked to go to synagogue because he liked to be a *ḥazan*. But after a few years they kicked him out of the synagogue because he drove on *Shabbat*. After that, he left home for *Shabbat*.

He was looking for a clean home and good food. He didn't find that at home and so they were not happy. My father had a longtime mistress for many years, since I was a baby, or maybe even earlier. My mother confirmed her suspicions by hiring a private investigator and taping their conversations. I still have the tapes. My parents fought a lot.

I don't remember most of my childhood. It was probably my way to block it out. My mother has told me stories about the things that have happened to me, how more than once I was left alone. This seems impossible considering how much she stressed over my whereabouts even as an adult.

My parents had very different values and moral codes. It wasn't a surprise that my mother and father's marriage did not last. I was eight years old when they divorced.

EXTREME

My mother exhibited some extreme behaviors. I could sit with her and we would talk and laugh. Then I would say one word or sentence and she would panic. I would regret everything that I said and all the things that I confided in her. I could never anticipate what would set her off. She would get anxious, and it was like we were living in a life-or-death scenario.

I would go on class trips as a kid and my mom would have to sign a permission slip. It would be just your run-of-the-mill "if something happens to your kid, you can't blame us" form, and it was always so hard for her to sign them. I was always the last child on the bus. She would sign it while I was waiting to sit down on the bus. She would walk around the bus and test the tires. She did not want to sign those slips. She did not want to let me go.

I understand this. It is a horrible thing to have to sign something that talks about something bad potentially happening to your child, especially for her, a person who had seen so many fearful things. I understand this now. But as a child, I found it so embarrassing and difficult.

WARNINGS

My mom cooked food without salt and without spices because she thought that it was healthier. When I got older and I would go to my friends' houses where the food was so much tastier, I would be so frustrated that her food was so bland. Now that I am older, I recognize that some of the things she made were healthy, even if they didn't taste great. But at the time, I felt deprived and tried to eat out of the house as often as I could. I would tell her that I wanted her to cook different foods, but she wouldn't change the menu. She was cooking healthy foods so that we both would be healthy and live. However, it didn't help make the plain boiled chicken taste better.

She used to tell me that spicy food was terrible for you and would cause peptic ulcers. That idea really got in my head. When I first went to India, I had my mother's voice in my mind telling me that I should avoid spicy food, that it wouldn't be good for me. Later I started learning Indian medicine, which teaches that in every meal you need to have all of the tastes, including spiciness, and that spices are actually very good for you. Knowing that helped ease my concern about eating spicy food.

A lot of my mom's fears stay in my mind, though. At her essence, she was so panicked about my well-being. Even things that were natural or a part of growing up were terrifying for her. She would climb a ladder into her old age, but she made it seem like it was dangerous for me to do. I am still afraid of climbing a ladder or a step stool in the house. I was afraid to ride a bicycle until I became an adult and moved to Tel Aviv. I was afraid to swim, and I still don't know how.

When it came to me, everything felt scary and dangerous for her. The terrible things that she experienced early in life made the world feel unsafe. She wanted to protect me no matter what it took. Often, it took a toll on us both.

PREPARED

There were always things that my mother would keep that she didn't need. When I moved my mother out of her apartment, I found things that no one could ever need, even from before I was born. There were things still there from my grandparents' house that should not have been saved. She never could throw anything out. As I got older, I needed to throw out my own things, because there was no room for my stuff in her house with all the things that she had hoarded.

She never wanted to waste anything. One time I had a boyfriend who came over and went to use the toilet, and there was a note taped with a sticker from the egg carton. He said to me, "I could not believe this was the house of a woman in hi-tech," meaning me. My mom took reusing to an extreme. She wouldn't throw away any item, thinking that it could somehow be useful in the future. Perhaps being in hiding during the *Shoah* taught her the value of every item she owned. She knew what it was like to be left with nothing and to be unable to depend on anything. But I guess living as a single woman, and later as a single mom, without much income could have been an influence as well.

She always had in her mind to be prepared for the inevitability of war coming again. Once I found a case of water bottles in her apartment that was from the Persian Gulf War, which had happened many years earlier. Along with the old newspapers and other random items that she kept, she also kept water and food stowed away in her place. If we couldn't get out of the house for a week because we were in the middle of a war, we would all be in trouble. But not my mom. She was ready for anything.

It was hard for me to grow up in a house that was always a *balagan*, with things and mess everywhere. But when I grew up, I stopped caring about it and she also didn't care about her living environment. She was always afraid of being robbed as an older person. But she was right – older people are more likely to be robbed. I know that she intentionally made her things messy, so that no one would think to rob her. She created a shield and a wall to keep herself safe from danger.

INDEPENDENT

I always felt the need to prove that I could take care of myself. I felt that my mother never thought that I could be okay on my own, that I could be responsible to take my own risks, even as an adult. She always treated me like someone whom she needed to control. She was always so worried about me. But the irony is that when the serious decisions came up, I was the one who needed to make them, for her well-being and my own.

I love to travel and I do it very often now, but in the beginning, it was not commonly done in my generation. Now for young Israelis, it is very common to travel the world after serving in the army, but when I was that age, most of my friends started to study immediately after the army and never traveled the world on long journeys. My mother used to compare me to my friends and say, "This person isn't traveling. Why do you have to do it?"

When I travel, I feel freer. I don't plan so much; I don't think so much. I just go with the flow. It is the opposite of what I usually do when I am home. When I leave, I am more open. I let things happen. I meet new people. I go with my feelings and go to good places.

Every time I go, I have my own fears. Additionally, every time I planned a trip, my mom used to lecture me about the dangers of traveling. She would bring a tall stack of articles about all the catastrophic events that had happened in the country or region I was planning to visit. She did this to make me more careful and sometimes even tried to prevent me from leaving, which never worked but always stressed me out. Later on, I would just call her from the airport. By that point, there was no time for all her warnings.

When she would call me, she would always talk to me in codes as if someone was listening. She would call and tell me things that were public knowledge, news items and information that was plastered all over the internet. But she was afraid that someone would hear that information and use it against

us, either personally or as a country, as if the terrorists were listening to our calls and planning their next target. Growing up in the time of the Nazis and Communists deeply affected her. I would say, "Do you think that anyone is actually listening to us on the phone?" But I believe she did. In some ways, she was reacting to another time. The trauma lived within her.

A relative one time commented to me that she thought that my mother was jealous of me because I was going to locations that she would never visit. Maybe instead of the disapproval that I felt from her for so long, it was admiration for the fact that I wasn't plagued by fears like she was, that I was free from those memories. Her experiences affect my attitude toward travel in positive ways, too. Even during those times when my mother and her family lived in a country in which most people wanted to kill them, they found good people who helped them. Maybe it is because of this that I believe I too will find good people along the way.

So many times in her own life, my mom made choices not to do things that she wanted because of her own parents' disapproval. She made choices out of respect for her father, as opposed to what she really wanted to do. It must have been really difficult for her that I didn't live my life to please her, like she did for her parents. And yet, one time my therapist made me understand that I wasn't fully independent from her like I thought. I wasn't always making choices based on what I wanted. I was making choices specifically to not please my  mother. I was living in a reaction to her. My therapist told me to imagine a good child and a bad child. The good child will do what he is told, and the bad child will do the opposite of what he is told. Then there is the independent child, who does what he or she likes. She told me that as much as I thought I was independent, I was actually making choices based on what would upset my mother. At a certain point, I enjoyed getting a rise out of her, because she put so much of a burden on me. Sometimes I would call and say, "Hey mom, guess what I did…," even if I knew it would make her upset.

This realization also showed me that I was always much closer with my mother than I thought. I cared about what she thought. It meant something to me that she would react. I didn't just tell her things to antagonize her. I told her things that were important to me. I shared parts of my life with her. She knew everyone in my life. She really knew me. Even if I regretted telling her some details of my life, I still always wanted to share again.

GOODBYES

I thought that my mother's life would be so much longer. But now that I think about it, after she had to move out of her apartment and into assisted living, the thought that she would have another two years popped into my head. I don't know why, but that is what I told myself. I told myself that if she had two more years, I would spend more time with her. It was two years, and I didn't spend more time with her. I don't know why I didn't listen to that voice in my head. There were other gut instincts that I ignored as well. In my heart, there were things that I knew were wrong. Those choices gave me problems, too.

Sometimes I would go visit my mom and she was so friendly and relaxed. It was fun to be with her. I would think to myself, "Hmm…maybe she should live closer to me so I could see her more." Then the next day she would call me up and make me upset about something.

She fell one afternoon and didn't want to disturb me before my classes, so she didn't call me. The week before, I had been upset that she disturbed me just before my class with some problems regarding her computer, and she didn't see the difference in disturbing me for a computer problem or because of a medical issue. I had a bad feeling when after class I tried to call her and she didn't pick up. But then I forgot about it, and when I remembered that she hadn't answered, it was later at night and I didn't want to disturb her. I didn't know that she had fallen and couldn't stand up on her own.

I heard from the hospital. I was in the middle of class when I got the call. They told me that since it was Friday, if I didn't get there by one o'clock, they couldn't operate on her that day. They told me that she didn't want to go into an operation without seeing me. I rushed over there as quickly as I could and I felt good that I was able to get there in time. We were glad to see each other. We called the people in her life so that they could wish her good luck. I was there through the surgery. I gave the nurse all her updated medical information. She was happy that I came, and I felt I was handling the situation well.

The next morning, I had a meeting scheduled in advance with my ex-boyfriend to meet and talk about getting closure between us. I didn't want to cancel, but I hoped to start and finish this meeting as early in the day as I could. It took much longer than I thought. By the time I got to the hospital, I was so emotionally exhausted. My mother was distraught and panicked because she had been alone for so many hours. I was so embarrassed that I hadn't been there. After the surgery, she had been clear-headed. Now she was not herself. Later I realized she was in a lot of pain. I couldn't believe how quickly bedsores are created.

The last time I saw her, she asked me to hold her hand. I said no. I was so emotionally wrecked from the morning. I did not want to be comforting anyone. I was still reeling. A family member took me aside and told me to rest. He could see that I was close to a breaking point and that I needed to go home. I had a whole plan. In the morning I would wake up early, buy her a special mattress, arrange for a private nurse, and be there all day. I couldn't find the right phone numbers to arrange it that night. They gave her medicine to sleep and I went home. I couldn't sleep that night. The whole night I had in my mind to go back to the hospital, but I forced myself to sleep so I could be there for her the next day.

When I was looking for parking in the morning, they called me. They told me not to come to her room, but to come to a different department. I understood it was bad. Her swift decline had started a few hours earlier but no one called me. They didn't even try. If I had known, I would have jumped out of bed and come to be with her. She had passed while I was looking for parking. They didn't call me in time.

I was relieved that she didn't suffer more than she already had. But I still hurt over the way that she passed. I wish I could have been there. The doctor pointed out something challenging for me to realize. He said, "At any point in your relationship with your mom, it would have been the same. That was your relationship. You always would have felt the same." It ended as it always was: complicated. I just thought I would have her for so much longer. You never think that the end is coming. I thought that I would have been by her side for her whole recovery process.

When I saw her body after she passed, I sat with her for an hour. I took her hand. I told her all the good things that maybe I never told her but I wanted her to know. I thanked her for the cooked food that she provided me, for the roof over my head, the life lessons she taught me, and the time and effort she invested in me. I thanked her for teaching me sewing, cooking, and crafting, how to find solutions for things, how to figure out how to fix things – to make them better and save them. I thanked her for teaching me honesty and morality, and for showing me how to be kind to people and animals. She taught me so much – everything I know. She loved me. I loved her too.

REFLECTIONS

Questions to Consider
- Has your family been touched by the *Shoah*?
  Are there lasting effects on your family culture?
- What role have your parents played in your life?

Words to Remember
> "When it came to me, everything felt scary
> and dangerous for her. The trauma that she
> experienced early in life made the world feel
> unsafe. She wanted to protect me no matter what
> it took. Often, it took a toll on us both."

Group Discussion
Is there a way to share the stories of the *Shoah* without sharing intergenerational trauma?

֎

Take a moment for yourself. What do you need right now?
Close your eyes and be in your own body.
Here is a gratitude exercise to come back to yourself:

Gratitude Exercise
Close your eyes and imagine:
  You are at home.
  Your bed is warm.
  You are nourished by food.
  And you are safe.

Tamary's Story

Promises Made, Promises Kept

Naharia

PROMISES

It all began when my youngest brother was born. It was fourteen years ago and I was twenty years old. As soon as I saw him, I knew there was some- thing different happening, even though he was just hours old. My mother had refused any genetic testing, but this pregnancy had still been considered high risk because she was in her early forties. Looking back at any ultrasounds or testing, there was no evidence that something was different. There were no markers that he was not typical. Even after delivery, they still weren't clear about what was going on with him. But to me, it seemed clear. No one said anything, so I didn't say anything.

A few hours later my father called me and said, "They are bringing him to the NICU because he is having problems eating and breathing at the same time." I was twenty and my friends were having babies, plus I was the oldest of eight. I had a lot of experience with babies.

Later that night my father called again and said, "The doctors suspect that the baby may have Down syndrome." The only thing I thought was, "As long as he is healthy, then we are going to be just fine." It was a bit harder for my

381

mother. She didn't talk about it a lot, at least with me. But when she held him, I saw that she was so in love and kissing him.

He was an eight-pound baby in the NICU next to all these preemies. They told me that they weren't ready to tell my younger siblings until the blood tests confirmed it. I called my brother who was in Israel for the year to come back home. We needed the family to be all together and support each other. Still, though, in my mind, this was my baby brother and as long as he was healthy, that's all that mattered.

Toward the end of his NICU stay, my mother said to me, "What's going to happen in twenty years from now, when I am older? Who is going to take care of him? I don't know what his functioning is going to be like. Who will be with him?"

I answered, "He has seven siblings who love him. It is not a question in my mind that someone will take care of him. There are no other options. He will have family and whatever he needs. I will make sure that there is always someone to take care of him."

She told me that it was a very overwhelming, big responsibility and that I shouldn't just say that. When he came home right before *Pesaḥ*, we spent *ḥag* with my whole extended family. Everyone came in for his *brit mila*. During that time, nestled in the back of my mind was the knowledge that there would always be a possibility that one day he would be in my care.

Shortly after that, I got married and moved to Israel. But I never forgot what I promised my mother in the NICU.

DEGENERATION

Netanel's birth had a big effect on my family. Going forward, many of my siblings worked in camps for kids with special needs and went on to get degrees in the field. I feel like I missed out on that part of our family culture. I missed out on volunteering with individuals with special needs, and the specific education that comes with it. When I was a young adult, it wasn't a passion of mine. But so many of my siblings changed their careers and desires based on their experiences living with a sibling with special needs.

Netanel and I grew up with the same parents but in completely different households, and many years apart. I had already practically moved out of the house by the time he was born. My life path was pretty set. I felt left out a little bit when it came to him. I consoled myself by saying that I would make myself available to help out with whatever I could, either at that time or in the future.

I would see him once a year when we would come to visit my family in America, and every so often, he would come with my parents to visit me here in Israel. But it all changed five years ago when my mother got sick. She wasn't diagnosed right away. She was falling a lot and at first, they thought it was vertigo. They did every test; they thought it was a brain tumor and it wasn't. She started slurring her words. They didn't know what was going on for at least a year. Finally, she was diagnosed with ataxia, a degeneration of the cerebellum. They couldn't find an underlying cause. Ataxia affects balance and speech. It's not usually genetic, and it causes slow degeneration. After more testing, they discovered that she has multiple system atrophy. That means that every system in the body atrophies until it stops working altogether. The prognosis is awful and it progresses somewhat quickly.

At first, she was doing everything that she used to do, though she struggled with walking and fell often. It became harder to understand her speech and it slowly got worse. She came to visit us here in Israel after I had a baby and we could see her muscles were weakening. At that point, she was still driving and maintaining her independence. But then she needed a walker and she stopped driving. One of the most difficult things to experience is watching her independence slowly be stolen from her.

It got to a point where Netanel would come home from school and she was no longer able to care for him, even though that was what she wanted to do. Up until this point, she had done everything for him so lovingly. She spent her days devoted to him, taking him to every therapy he could possibly get, and fighting for any funding or extras that might be available to him.

Netanel was in a local public school in Baltimore. There were no appropriate Jewish schools for him, nothing that offered the education he needed. The truth is that even the public school wasn't a good fit for his needs. He would come home and sit in front of the TV. My mother is an incredible mother who raised seven children before him. She was so involved, always taking us places and doing projects with us. But she wasn't able to do any of that with him.

Netanel would eat whatever he wanted and take advantage of the situation. He is really smart and he knew how to make it work to get what he wanted. He knew no one would follow him or run after him if he ran away. My dad would come home from work in the evening and take care of him, feed him, and put him to bed. But from two in the afternoon till seven at night, he was alone in the house with my mom. He has ADHD and is impulsive, which made the situation more difficult. He would run to any neighbor he wanted. He would cross streets he wasn't supposed to cross alone. He knows what is right and wrong, but often, he doesn't think the rules apply to him. Netanel would run away on *Shabbat* when my father was in *shul* and he was home alone with my mother. She would call Hatzalah (Jewish emergency medical services) or the police because she didn't know what else to do.

I told my sister, "If the police are called enough times, they are going to call Child Protective Services." Someone was going to get involved and I was scared of what was going to happen if that occurred. I was afraid they were going to take my brother away. Being so far away, it was difficult for me to hear about everything that was happening. The childhood I had with my amazing mother was so different than Netanel's childhood.

BEST FOR THEM

It was so difficult for my mom to accept help. She was the one who was always helping everyone else, making meals, giving people rides, and taking people to doctor appointments. It is hard to accept outside help when you are the one who is used to helping others. It's hard to be on the receiving end, even when you know and understand that people are helping out of love.

Netanel had afternoon programming here and there, but it wasn't much. They tried a Jewish day school for the afternoon hours, but it wasn't equipped to handle his needs. My fantastic siblings and their special spouses also helped and continue to help out whenever and however they can.

My sister made *aliya* three years ago. I have been here for thirteen years. The day she landed was one of the best days of my life. I was so happy to be reunited with her. While all of this was getting worse at home in Baltimore, I spoke to my sister. I wondered out loud, "Do you think we could bring him here?" Netanel wasn't doing anything in school. I was devastated that he wasn't going to have access to the kind of education he needed to reach his potential. He didn't have enough discipline or boundaries, though that was certainly not due to a lack of effort by those around him. I felt awful and I was torn up inside. My parents gave him the best that they could. My mother, always so devoted, was doing everything in her hands to raise him. But they were deeply stuck trying to facilitate my mom's care, working to support the family, and trying to deal with the terrifying reality they were facing. It was too much.

I wanted to start looking into programs here. I knew there were amazing programs for kids with Down syndrome in Israel. When these individuals grow up, they are treated as contributing members of society. I wanted that for Netanel. I looked into it a little bit and it seemed complicated.

Meanwhile, my mother was getting worse and I felt the need to do something. I mentioned the idea of bringing Netanel to Israel and my husband said, "Whatever you think is best for him, we will go along with it." When I mentioned it to my sister, I didn't say that it would be her responsibility at all. That is a huge thing to put on someone else. I told her what I was thinking and she said, "You're crazy. It's a huge amount of work."

I knew where she was coming from. I have six kids. My oldest is twelve. But I told her, "I'm not thinking about this because I want to make things harder for myself. I just don't see any other option. What is going to be for him?" I had these visions of Child Protective Services coming and taking him away and putting him in foster care in Baltimore.

My sister and I kept talking about it. One day she called me up and said, "If you are really serious about this, then I am behind you one hundred percent. We will do this together." We figured out the details and decided that it was time to pitch the idea to our parents.

Last *Pesaḥ*, my parents came with Netanel to Israel and made him a beautiful bar mitzva in the Old City. Over *ḥag*, I mentioned the idea to my father. I can't imagine how overwhelmed he must have been, taking care of both my mother and Netanel's needs. He has a full-time job; he has all the financial stress. He was worn so thin. The emotional stress was wearing him down. He was very receptive to the idea. He thought it would be great for Netanel and that it would make their lives more manageable. He would be freed to focus on my mom's increasing needs. Netanel would be in a place where he could thrive.

My sister and I approached my mother and we tried to be extremely sensitive. I brought up the promise I had made to her when Netanel was born. "Remember when I told you that I would care for Netanel when you were no longer able? I still stand by that promise. No one expected it to happen when you were in your mid-50s. But things are happening. We are ready to help you and help him get what he needs. With your agreement and consent, we would like to bring him to Israel."

It was so emotional. Her initial reaction was, "How could I send my baby away?" After she absorbed the facts and thought about it, though, she knew that it was best for him. I also knew it was what would be best for her, because the stress of knowing that Netanel wasn't getting what he needed was not making her illness any easier. We talked about how my father had been thirteen when he left home to go to a high school outside his town, and how sometimes individuals with special needs go to group homes when they can no longer live at home. All sorts of people leave home as teenagers for many reasons. This didn't have to have a negative connotation. It could be seen as a part of what Netanel needed to thrive. This could be the next stage of his life.

People had suggested that we send him to a group home in New York. First off, he isn't a New York resident and the waiting list for residents is already super long. Secondly, we don't have any siblings in New York, so who would visit and be there for him there? Wouldn't it be better for him to live with family if he could?

We decided as a family that he would come to Israel. We found a family lawyer to help us with the bureaucracy. We got help from Nefesh B'Nefesh to figure out the process of *aliya* and transferring custody to me. He couldn't make *aliya* because he was a minor, and he couldn't make *aliya* without someone taking custody of him here in Israel. I needed to get those papers signed first, and then he could make *aliya*. Once he officially made *aliya*, he could get health care and then he could be registered for school. These were our goals. The lawyer laid out a simple plan. Little did we know how complicated it would get.

CONSISTENCY AND BOUNDARIES

In August I flew with my two daughters to get Netanel and bring him back to Israel. We came in for a week. We did a lot of fun stuff. We began to say goodbye to his friends and family. He was so excited to make *aliya* and become Israeli.

The day we flew, he was so nervous. I took him to the supermarket to buy some snacks for the flight and he threw up in the store. He called my father right away telling him that he was sick and he couldn't go to Israel.

Netanel mainly lives in the moment. Depending which moment it was, he would take in everything differently. The day he was leaving, a ton of our relatives came to say goodbye to him and he wouldn't talk to anyone. He was so anxious. It was hard for me to know exactly what he was feeling, because it is hard for him to explain his feelings. He was getting presents and attention, but he refused to look at anyone.

We went to the airport and everything was fine until it was time to say goodbye. It was too emotional for me to watch. I felt the enormity of the situation. He and I had barely even lived together in the same house. This was such a big step for both of us. The flight was fine. We survived. Our family here in Israel was so excited that we arrived. When my husband and I discussed everything with our kids, they were just excited that their uncle was coming to live with them. They did not say a single negative thing about the huge changes that were coming to our household, even though we discussed it with them at length. But they also didn't grasp what was really happening. My older kids were considerate of everyone's feelings – their grandparents, Netanel, and all the grown-ups making decisions.

I hadn't been scared off by the huge responsibility. My mother stopped working when Netanel was born and dedicated her life to caring for him. He has had therapies since he was six weeks old. He learned how to swallow properly. He speaks clearly. She gave him all the foundational support he needed. I had a feeling that he would respond well again to more therapies and boundaries. I knew we could all make this work if we worked together.

Netanel went to my sister's house when we landed so I could sleep a bit. We were trying to come up with a schedule of where he should be at which

times until we got our paperwork and school started. We thought that after *Sukkot* – or maximum, Ḥanukka – he would be in school.

My sister signed him up for loads of *ḥugim*: basketball, personal training, Hebrew support. He could already read Hebrew slowly, but it was very intimidating for him. Anytime someone spoke to him in Hebrew, he would shout, "I'm scared! I'm scared!" It was hard for him to come and not know the language. We did our best to provide him with language support as well as activities in English.

We began to encourage him to eat healthier and be more active. He was in a new environment so he was a bit timid. He didn't know what we expected of him. We laid down rules from day one. He would be splitting his time, living with my sister from Monday to Thursday and then with me from Thursday to Monday morning.

My sister has a master's in special education and she worked tremendously hard to get him on the right track as soon as he got here. She had charts for him and was incredibly consistent. She has three little kids but wasn't working outside the home at that time. Halfway through the year, I got a job outside of the home. We all knew our roles and whatever she decided and worked on with him, I followed through with it when he was at my house. She worked so hard on his behavior both in the house and out of the house. He learned how to go to the supermarket and he loved helping out in the store. Both of our husbands were also very consistent with him. But it was exhausting.

Immediately, though, we saw Netanel begin to thrive and feel happy with our routine. We live on a *yishuv* and he has a lot of freedom. He walks to *shul*, and he can go to the *makolet* when he wants. He can go to the park if he feels like it. He has so much independence and he tells me, "I'm a teenager. I'm allowed to go out when I want." But he also knows that there are adults in charge and he takes comfort in the boundaries that we've set for him.

A JEWISH BOY

My mom calls every day. Netanel loves folding laundry, so they video chat while he folds and tells her about his day. She is super involved in every decision we make. Both our parents are a part of everything. Even when we went to go look at schools, we had them on video so they could see everything, too. They are updated on his behavior, goals, and accomplishments. They miss him very much, but they are relieved to see him thriving again.

But it was not all simple. The paperwork didn't get sent to court until November. They have three months to respond and they took all of that allotted time. We had a series of meetings to begin the process of getting custody. My sister will soon be moving to my *yishuv* and then we will petition for her to have custody, too.

I went to all the meetings. I was under the impression that I would have a meeting with the social worker assigned to our case, and that she would sign off that we were a good living situation for Netanel. But she explained to me that it was not like that at all. It was a series of meetings, then a home visit, then they had to discuss it amongst themselves in the *Revaḥa*, and then they would have to write up a whole report. She told me that it took time, but I was anxious for it to begin so he could go to school. Netanel came with me to almost every meeting. I had no coverage for him on the days that he was with me, so he came along for the ride. The days that I was able to go to meetings were the days I was off from work, and he was with me and not at my sister's house.

My parents came in February, so our lawyer requested a court hearing so they could give their part of the story to the judge, hoping we could speed up the process. It was hard for my mother to travel and we didn't know when she would be able to come back. The problem was that the report hadn't yet been filed. The judge and the lawyer told us, "He is America's problem. Why are you bringing him here?"

I was horrified. I said, "Netanel is a Jewish boy. He has a right to make *aliya* just like any other Jewish person in the world. As you can see, our family is all advocating for the same thing. There is no fighting here. We are all lovingly willing to help change his life. And you are saying that he is not Israel's problem?" I understand that allowing Netanel to make *aliya* is expensive for Israel because of the money that the government would have to put into his education and care. But there is nowhere in the right of return that says that you have to be over a certain age, or that you have to be neurotypical, to make *aliya*. A Jewish person is allowed to come to Israel. Period.

The technical issue was that he was a minor, though we were all happy and willing to transfer custody so that wouldn't be a problem. But the judge said he was only going to go with what the *Revaḥa* decided. They wouldn't even give us temporary custody so he could start the school process. It was not normal for a fourteen-year-old boy to sit at home all day and do nothing. The judge wouldn't let me speak. He only wanted to hear from my parents and the lawyer. I was just sitting there biting my tongue. I had so much to say to him. We were denied.

He told us that Netanel had to go home with our parents. He put a stop on my parents' tickets so that they couldn't leave the country unless he was with them. My mother was so overwhelmed. After everything we had done to get him to Israel to give him a better life, Israel was throwing him out.

FLIPPED UPSIDE DOWN

I was so angry. I was shocked by the outcome. I could not believe that none of these people with authority could see beyond their jobs, that they couldn't open their minds or their hearts to this young man. They saw my mother in her wheelchair, struggling to speak. I couldn't understand how they had no compassion for our family.

The courthouse is right around the corner from Nefesh B'Nefesh. After we were denied the temporary custody, we all marched over to the NBN offices and begged for some assistance. They so graciously convened an impromptu meeting, grabbing all the staff members who could help. We tossed around ideas and discussed different options of how to move forward. The wonderful and dedicated staff there did so much for us, not only at that meeting, but also throughout the process. They were a great sounding board and made use of their helpful connections in the government offices. They pushed for Netanel's *aliya* to go through and they were there to answer any question that came up along the way.

We met with the deputy mayor of our *yishuv* about our situation. He reached out to some of his government contacts for us. He asked me what I needed. I said that I first needed Netanel to be able to make *aliya*. The custody could come later, but in order to get health coverage and attend school, he needed his *aliya* benefits. The deputy mayor knew someone high up in a politician's office. But when he asked for his help on our behalf, this contact said that he was not willing to go against the court. They wanted to wait for a final court decision first.

Our lawyer requested an emergency hearing the next day. We went back to court. My mother was crying and said, "Everyone is forgetting that this is my child we are talking about. He is not just a number on the piece of paper about a court case."

They sent a new lawyer for the *Revaḥa*, who happened to originally be American. Thank God for that, because it made it easier for my parents to communicate with her. She made it clear to us that she had empathy for our case. Because it was an emergency case, we got a new judge, whoever was on call that day. The new judge was a lovely and sweet older gentleman. He said, "I wish I could give you custody right now, but I can't. What I can do is take the stop off your parents' tickets and place it on you, because someone needs to be responsible for this young man."

He asked me, "Are you prepared to take responsibility for Netanel?"

I told him, "That is what I have been doing all along. I voluntarily brought him here and with my sister, I have been caring for him since he has arrived."

The lawyer spoke up toward the end. "The judge didn't rule on the temporary custody yesterday. Could you give us a ruling so this child can go to school?" He said, "Of course I can!"

It was amazing to me how someone's life could change depending on which judge is assigned to his case. In two seconds, I had temporary custody. I was amazed at the timing of this decision too; it was the day before *Purim*. One day earlier, we had been so angry at the judge for ruling against us. Today, the whole decision was flipped upside down, just like in the *Megilla*.

I was so thankful. I couldn't thank the judge enough. I don't know if it was appropriate for the setting, but I said, "You can't understand what a life-changing decision this is for Netanel. You are amazing. This is huge. You have saved this boy!" He tried to understand, but I don't know whether he ultimately understood the gravity of the situation. We were all so relieved.

Finally, we were able to begin the process of getting Netanel into school. We still had a long way to go.

PRECEDENCE

We met with the school. My parents came to see it. It is an excellent school that is so impressive. They were so sensitive to us and were ready to take him. They helped us with whatever paperwork we needed.

It took until after *Pesaḥ* for him to be able to start school. I called every bureaucratic office a million times to try and make it happen. I was begging. Every step was a battle, but he started school. My parents came in for *Pesaḥ* and were able to escort him on his first day. It was so special and beautiful. I was so happy for my mother to be able to be there for that moment. It felt almost worth it to wait till they were there, just for them to be able to share in that moment. She was able to see him go into school and be welcomed with open arms. He literally dove into his new teacher's arms and was embraced in the biggest hug. At the end of the day, my parents were able to pick him up and see how happy he was.

Our community coordinator made thousands of calls for us. Our deputy mayor was helping us non-stop. They helped us get him a van to and from school, which he should have been eligible for automatically.

Netanel hadn't had health coverage all year. There were appointments that he needed to make that were long overdue. This was my main argument against everyone who was fighting against me making a life here for him. My brother needed health care and so they needed to let him make *aliya* ASAP. He was the first case of his kind – an American child, whose parents were not Israeli citizens and who lived in America, was making *aliya* by himself, with his sibling getting custody. There was no precedent for us.

Misrad HaPnim told us in November that as soon as I got custody of him, he would be able to make *aliya*. When my parents were here, they signed a document giving their permission, and it went into his file. But when I told their office that I got custody, they said to me, "But he's only fourteen. How do you know that he wants to make *aliya*? Did you ask him?"

It was ridiculous. They were trying to claim both sides. You can't say I need custody because he is a minor and also that we need to ask his permission. You don't ask a child to decide what is best for them. Hundreds of families make *aliya* every year, without asking their children's permission to go. You

can discuss *aliya* with your children, but ultimately you don't let them make the decision for you. As the parent, you make the decision. Out of curiosity about what he would say, I asked Netanel if he wanted to make *aliya*. He said, "I moved to Israel and made *aliya* last summer. Why are you asking me that?"

It took time. We kept working on it. Our deputy mayor pulled more strings to get to the high-level politician he had contacted during Netanel's court case. By *Shavuot*, I was able to connect with him. He asked me to send him all the paperwork I had. I sent it to him one morning last week, and that afternoon I got a call that Netanel's application had been approved.

We went to *Misrad HaPnim* to make it official. It went how it usually does. We waited forty minutes. We just waited. The head of the branch who we were supposed to be meeting was very busy. My brother got bored and made himself comfortable by putting his feet up on her desk. But we walked out of there with a *mispar zehut*, an identification number. He is Israeli. It says "*oleh*" as his status. Finally, after all these months, we accomplished our goal.

I went to the *kupat ḥolim*, the socialized medicine group my family joined, to add Netanel to our plan. There was no precedent as to how to add him. Just two days ago now, I brought my other children to the pediatrician, and the doctor asked me about my brother. When would I be sending the doctor his files? I told him the secretary was still trying to figure out how to add him. The doctor said, "I'll tell you what I've learned. It's easier to ask for forgiveness than permission." He stuck him in the computer as if a new baby was born in the family. He said, "*Mazal tov*, it's a boy!" And now he has health coverage.

FUTURE POTENTIAL

Yesterday I had the end-of-the-year meeting at Netanel's school (even though he was only there for three months). I met with the entire staff: teachers, speech therapist, physical therapist, occupational therapist, music therapist, principal, assistants. They prepared a short video clip of his time at the school so that we could see how happy he has been. They all spoke about how well he is doing, and how he even encourages all the other kids to keep doing their best. I was crying the whole meeting. There are no words to describe what has changed between where he was last year and where he is now. Every day he comes home from school with new words. He is making a ton of progress with his Hebrew.

Last week, on *Shavuot*, I watched all the kids in our neighborhood playing ball in the street. There were twenty-five kids of all different ages. Netanel was playing among them as an equal. He was following all the rules, catching and throwing. When he got out, he left gracefully. When he went back in, he did it with joy. I watched him through my tears. I hadn't had time to prepare anything spiritually for myself for the holiday, but watching him play was the uplifting spiritual moment I needed. In America, he had rarely played with anyone his own age. It blew me away to see him now, and to see other kids speak to him and include him as if he is one of them.

My parents are amazed at the school's approach, and at how well Netanel is getting along with my kids and with my sister's kids. They are amazed at his progress. We have hope that he is going to reach his potential. We know he is going to do well in life. My goal is for him to go to school here till he is twenty-one. If he wants, he could go to the army. It's definitely an option for him here. Our end goal is to see him get a job and live in an assisted group home for young men like him. We want

him to contribute to society, be part of a community, and if he wants, get married. Ultimately, we want him to have fulfillment and be happy.

This entire process, from the moment I had the idea to bring him here, to this moment now when he is thriving here, has been really humbling. It is amazing how much a person can accomplish if they keep striving for a goal. The work that my sister and brother-in-law have done with Netanel's behavior, getting him back on track, has been awe inspiring to watch. Another part of it has been my own persistence in following through with the bureaucracy to get him what he needed. It was so humbling to go through the process of one step forward, ten steps back, refusing to give up (even though there were times that I almost wanted to), and succeeding in the end. I know that whatever we will need to do in the future, we can do it, because my sister and I have the full support of our husbands, siblings, kids, and of course, our parents. I am so grateful to them all for loving Netanel like I do. I also believe that I have what it takes to make things happen for him.

Ultimately, though, it is my mother and father who have sacrificed and persevered the most, always doing what is best for him even if it is painful or a struggle for them. My mother's dedication to Netanel, and all her children, provides me the motivation I need every day to keep caring for him. I will be eternally grateful for the example of giving and sacrifice that she has imprinted on us all. Most of all, she has taught us to love unconditionally and how to care for each other. No matter what happens going forward, what could be more important than that?

℘

A message from the author

In August 2020, Tamary's brave and dedicated mother lost her battle with MSA (Multiple System Atrophy). It had been almost a year since she was able to see her children in Israel, due to the global Covid-19 pandemic. She died knowing that her Netanel was in good hands, thriving in his new life in Israel in the homes of her beloved daughters.

After her mother's passing, Tamary shared these words with me:

> I know she was at peace with her decision to send him to live in Israel. I hope my sister and I (and our husbands) can raise him up to her standards. I am so grateful that we were able to settle him here before my mother passed away and she was able to see how we continued to give him what he needs.
>> I know that she was so proud of how we fought to bring him here. I pray that I continue to make her proud always.

Join me in praying for an *aliya* of the *neshama* of Chava bat Yitzchak Mordechai *z"l*.

REFLECTIONS

Questions to Consider
- What was a time when you needed to advocate for yourself or someone else?
- Are you a caregiver? How does that role manifest in your life?

Words to Remember

"But there is nowhere in the right of return that says that you have to be over a certain age, or that you have to be neurotypical, to make *aliya*. A Jewish person is allowed to come to Israel. Period."

Group Discussion

What is the role that persistence has played in your life? What have you accomplished through never giving up?

⊘

Take a moment for yourself. What do you need right now?
Close your eyes and be in your own body.
Here is a gratitude exercise to come back to yourself:

Gratitude Exercise

Being grateful often helps put our lives into perspective. I am grateful...
for the parental figures who cared for me;
that I was able to go to school and learn;
for my ability to communicate;
that I can contribute to society.

Chaya's Story

Discovering My Roots

Rehavia, Jerusalem

WHERE I TRULY BELONG

Many people ask me why I immigrated to Israel. They say that I come from a beautiful country and I had everything I needed. What would entice me to leave? I usually respond with a big smile, "In short, there is no place like Israel."

I was born and raised in Puebla, a city next to Mexico City. My father is a Christian and my mother is not. My parents got divorced when I was a small child. Most of my childhood, I had mainly been close with my father's family.

When I was fifteen, I started spending more time with my mother's family. They were different than all the other families in the area. They didn't work on Saturdays. They didn't go to church. My mother always taught me about how there was only one God. She taught me to have faith and encouraged me and my siblings to read the *Tanakh*. She learned *Tanakh* while she was being raised by her uncles, as her mother passed away when she was four years old.

My great-grandmother's last name was Valencia. She came to Mexico from Valencia, Spain. We believe that she was a Jewish woman, though we have no records to prove it. We have no birth records for any of her children, either. We have no paperwork or documentation. All we have are the stories that we heard growing up and the undeniable fact that my mother's family seemingly always kept the Jewish faith. My great-grandmother never explained why or where this belief system came from. She never called it Judaism, but we believe that she was born Jewish.

The family observed certain customs such as wearing modest clothes. The women in the family wore only skirts, which was unusual in a secular environment. They celebrated *Shabbat* on Saturday, in contrast to most other people where we lived, who kept the Sabbath on Sunday. There were separate pots for milk and meat and we were strictly forbidden to consume pork and seafood.

We all went to school with Christian children. My mother made it clear that though we should respect them and their faith, we were different.

When I was a child and my friends or my father's family had events in their churches, my mom was always hesitant to let me go. She would say, "It's better that you don't go." I never understood why. I would go because I wanted to be there for my friends and my community. I did know that I was never there to observe the Christian faith.

In Puebla there was no Jewish community. I knew I felt different but I had never seen a Jewish community so I had no way of knowing where I truly belonged.

LIVE A GOOD LIFE

As the years went by, my extended family became more religious. By the time I started spending more time with my mother's family, my great-uncles were keeping *Shabbat* fully and learning Torah. They started teaching me about the Jewish faith.

Because there was no way to prove that they were officially Jewish, my uncles decided to convert so they could have all the paperwork they needed in order to make *aliya* to Israel. There was a rabbi in Mexico City who made their conversions official. He is no longer there and therefore, there are no longer conversions that occur in Mexico.

At the time, a rabbi came to our family home in Puebla and began to teach us all about Judaism. I have two siblings and I am the oldest in my family. At that time, he was preparing the conversions of my uncles and their families, so he knew that perhaps I would be interested in conversion as well. When I was eighteen, the rabbi made me an offer. He said that I could go to Israel and attend *midrasha*. He wanted me to see if I liked it there. He wanted me to see if I would choose to be Jewish.

At the time, though I knew my extended family was going through the process and planning *aliya*, I was not sure of it myself. I was coming to terms with who I really was and where I truly came from. The question was, did I want to commit to that identity? I could have just chosen to be a Noahide. I could have believed in one God, kept the *sheva mitzvot benei Noaḥ*, and lived a good life.

I was afraid. I was fearful of leaving everything I knew behind. I was learning new things and I was processing what they meant. I was trying to understand what it would mean to keep all the *mitzvot*. It felt like an extreme change. You can believe in a faith, but the style of life was very different. I had never spent time in a Jewish community. It all felt so foreign.

THE OFFER

My uncles finished their conversion process and were able to make *aliya* to Israel. Shortly after, I followed them when I took my rabbi up on his offer. I was coming to Israel to learn and to see if I would like it enough to consider conversion and *aliya*.

I went to a fantastic school and I lived with one of my uncles who had completed his *aliya* years earlier. There was a special program for Spanish speakers, so the learning was in my native language. I made a lot of new friends. I came with a solid background because we were already keeping *Shabbat* at home, but there was still much to learn. The intensive program that I joined allowed me to learn so much so fast. Having different rabbis teach me different perspectives and the many hours of class each day helped me absorb the material. I was soaking it all up and I was so excited. I told my mother, "You need to come." I thought she would love this life and I knew it would be great for my siblings.

I loved Israel. The people were so kind. The land is magical. You can't explain it with words. I felt I belonged here. I felt I had a job that I could only accomplish here. It was hard because I left everything behind me. I felt I was starting at zero. I didn't know how or why, but I knew it was worth it.

I was investing in something that someday would reveal how it would manifest for me. I was ready to take the next step and make my commitment to Judaism official. I was ready to live this lifestyle and officially accept my birthright.

There was a conversion process that was connected to the seminary that I was attending, but instead, I chose to convert with my uncle's rabbi. He was here in Jerusalem and I had been in contact with him since I arrived in Israel. He had his own *midrasha* for Spanish speakers that was more *ḥaredi*. I learned so much with him and loved the lifestyle.

He helped me to convert and I did it in Benei Berak. I went to the *mikve* nine months after I arrived in Israel. I felt like I had been gestating during my time here and finally, when I came out from the waters, I was reborn. That timing made me feel in awe of the way that Hashem runs the world. Nothing is an accident.

CONVERSION

I did a full conversion. I sat with seven rabbis from Benei Berak. My rabbi was with me and helped translate for me. I was so scared. I didn't speak Hebrew. They asked me questions about *ḥagim, kashrut, Shabbat*, the Thirteen Principles of Faith, and more. I knew all the answers and I passed their examination.

The *mikve* was very nice. It was a special experience. Though it has been eleven years, I remember that I cried. I had a mix of emotions afterward, but in the end I accomplished my mission. From that moment on, I could begin to live. From that moment, I could be who I really am.

But I needed to convert again. This first conversion was not recognized by the State. In Israel, only the Chief Rabbinate is allowed to convert people and set their status as recognized by the State. I was already considered Jewish, but in order to make *aliya* I needed to do it again through the Chief Rabbinate. I knew about this requirement in advance, but it was important for my family that I do it first through the *Beit Din* of Benei Berak.

A few weeks after my first conversion, I went to the *mikve* all over again because that conversion was the one that would be recognized by the State. My process was finally finished. I was so excited to start my new life.

A LIFE TOGETHER

Shortly after, I went back to Mexico to prepare for *aliya*. I had to get my paperwork done, pack up my things, and send my life across the world.

At that time, my mother was also preparing to move to Israel. She wasn't making *aliya* officially but she was on her way. She hadn't converted yet with my siblings. There is an *ulpan* of conversion at Shavei Israel, and they have classes in Spanish, Portuguese, and Italian. That is where they were going.

I was overjoyed when they came. I had been so happy to be here in Israel. It was wonderful to have my uncles, aunts, and cousins here. But you cannot compare the joy of being reunited with your mother and your siblings. I wanted them to come here to study, live here, and share this amazing experience with me.

My personal conversion process was kind of miraculous. Normally it takes much longer to go through. It's a very difficult bureaucratic process. For families, it is even harder. Because my sister was under eighteen, my mom needed special papers to bring her to Israel for the visa that would allow her to stay. My father gave permission for her to go since she was still a minor.

I had always been in touch with my dad by phone. He was against all of us moving to Israel because he would miss us. Originally, the plan was for all of us to be here for only one year. But at the end of the day, he understood that this is where we wanted to be and where we belonged. He accepted that we needed to stay. We all studied Hebrew and started to build a life together.

BODED

My mom needed to go back to Mexico with my little sister to settle things and sell her house. She decided they would go for a year to work everything out and then come back. In the meantime, my brother joined the army. He was a *ḥayal boded* and a combat soldier. I was so proud of him. He and I were living together. I was his home base when he got off from the army. Shortly after he joined, war began in Gaza. It was *Tzuk Eitan*. I would sit alone in our apartment feeling so worried about him. I would cry wondering where he was and whether he was exposed to danger. I would pray to Hashem to protect my brother and make sure that he came home to me safely.

A *ḥayal boded* receives a benefit that he gets a month off from the army to visit his family in his home country. Suddenly, in the middle of the war, his *ptor* came through. He was free to go home for a few weeks. We were so surprised, but I was so relieved. We were planning to go back to visit in the summer anyway, but then the war started. I did not purchase tickets because I didn't think it would be possible for him to leave. I found out that he got permission to leave because he surprised me by buying tickets and telling me we could go. We went for a few weeks. By the time we came back, the war was over.

He finished his army service and I went back to school. I went to college in Jerusalem and studied Hebrew. I did a year of *mekhina* for *olim*, to prepare me for school in Hebrew. I studied marketing and finished my BA, specializing in tourism management. I began to work in hotels. For five years, I did every job there was: reception, human resources, accounting, reservations. Everything. I loved that work.

One day, I got a call from someone at Shavei Israel asking me if I wanted to work for them. I had always wanted to work with *aliya* and *olim*. I was happy where I was, I had been promoted where I was, but my passion was to help *olim* and to share my experience. I had three interviews and there were seven candidates. They chose me.

Now I work with Shavei Israel's conversion *ulpan*. I work with people who are coming here not only from Spanish- and Portuguese-speaking countries, but also people who want to make *aliya* from all over the world. I manage their cases and their paperwork. Since I've done it myself and I know exactly what it is like, I know how to help and guide them.

This past year, I had more of my family members come to Israel from Mexico. It was I who managed the process for them through Shavei Israel. It was so hard. The bureaucratic process is so difficult. You don't always have the answers when you want them; you have to wait till the committee decides. They had to wait six months to find out whether they could convert.

I helped them translate their documents and get their recommendations. I collected a copy of the *teudot zehut* of all our family members here to help recommend them to the committee. Sometimes the committee says no. They don't find the candidate to be a match for the process. I understand why everyone can't be accepted, though it is hard. I have seen cases where people ask to convert because they want to come here for other reasons. They don't end up keeping the religion, or they want to come to Israel to start a business. Not everyone is doing it for the intended reason of wanting to be a Jew.

But this time, the committee said yes, and I believe that our family's support and advocacy assisted their acceptance. Thank God, they finished. They will be making *aliya* soon. Now I have family living in Be'er Sheva, Ashdod, Ashkelon, and Jerusalem. We have more than thirty family members here. There are uncles, aunts, cousins – whole families getting married, having babies, and growing here. It's incredible to be a part of this new chapter in my family's history.

LOOKING TO THE FUTURE

I find that people generally like people from Mexico because they love our culture, our warmth, and our willingness to help our neighbors. I have found nothing but welcome here in Israel. Every place I go, I meet people and make connections. There is a huge Spanish-speaking community here in Jerusalem. For a long time, I didn't even feel the need to learn Hebrew because there are so many people who speak my mother tongue.

I live in Rehavia with two Israeli female flatmates. My mom lives in Armon HaNatziv, where there is a huge Latino community with people from Argentina, Venezuela, Brazil, Mexico, Colombia, Peru, and Puerto Rico. It is an amazing, supportive community. The *ḥesed* here is like nothing we've seen in the world. We spend *Shabbat* and holidays with our family all over Israel.

I go on dates and I would like to get married someday. I think that is the next thing for me. Until now I didn't feel pressure to get married, but now that I have turned thirty, I feel it is time. I am dating more seriously. I've dated all kinds of people – Israelis, Latinos, Anglos, French.

I put my conversion on the table from the beginning. I am very proud of my journey and I love to talk about it. There have been people who aren't comfortable with this, because it would be an issue for their family. Usually, when I am dating someone, if it ends it is not because of me being a convert.

At this point, I feel very integrated here. My Hebrew is strong now. I feel ready for the next chapter in my life.

REFLECTIONS

Questions to Consider
- How much do you know about your family's genealogy? What places do you come from?
- How do we balance the beauty of *aliya* with the stress of the process?

Words to Remember

> "I went to the *mikve* nine months after I arrived in Israel. I felt like I had been gestating during my time here and finally, when I came out from the waters, I was reborn. That timing made me feel in awe of the way that Hashem runs the world. Nothing is an accident."

Group Discussion

Some families enjoy closeness, while others function better when they have space apart from each other. What dynamics have you seen play out in your own family life?

✒️

Take a moment for yourself. What do you need right now?
Close your eyes and be in your own body.
Here is a gratitude exercise to come back to yourself:

Gratitude Exercise

Think about your family and community. Find the spaces where you belong. Bring up strong memories connected to beloved people, places, and events. Hold them in your mind and smile. Feel the warmth of those things in your heart. Let them fill you until you feel joy.

Losing Control and Finding Myself

Hashmonaim

LOST AND ALONE

When I was fifteen, my friends and I were trying to figure out who we were. It became clear to me that we were growing in different directions. I felt very lost and alone.

I moved to Hashmonaim from America when I was nine. Growing up in a religious *yishuv* raised many religious questions for me. While many of my peers were becoming more committed to their Jewish life, I was trying to figure out if I would follow them and whether I truly believed in this lifestyle.

I was also unhappy in school. I was struggling with integrating into Israeli society as an immigrant, even after all those years. I was going to a new school in Jerusalem, with only one friend. I had started dating my first boyfriend. I was in a big transitional moment where things were changing quickly. As I began to ask myself all these questions, I began fighting with my parents, even though I had always been very close to them. I felt very alone.

In the middle of tenth grade, my parents realized that I was not doing well and they took me to a therapist to get help. My father told me that he felt like they were walking on eggshells around me. I would explode at the smallest issue. I was irritable and angry all the time. I was not myself.

409

I had always struggled with opening up and I was not upfront with my therapist. I started self-harming and I did not inform anyone. I got into a fight with someone one day and I was so angry and upset. I don't know what made me decide to do it, but I had a pocket knife in my room. I cut myself for the first time. I think the sense of being in control was the first thing I felt. It was really appealing to me. This time I was the one causing the hurt, and that made me feel in control.

After two months of treatment, my therapist felt that I was withdrawn, so she sent me to a psychiatrist. They started me on antidepressants. I continued on that treatment path for another two months. I was still self-harming, and doing it a lot. I had a friend who knew what I was going through and she happened to see all my cuts one day. She told my parents what she saw on my arm. My parents told my therapist and they all decided I needed more intensive treatment.

NO CONTROL

I was not going to school and I was not doing well emotionally. I began to binge eat. At night I would just eat until I felt that I couldn't eat anymore. Shortly after I began doing that, I began purging as well. I would eat an excessive amount of food and then quickly purge afterward. I didn't do it every time I ate and therefore it was easy to hide.

My parents were trying to figure out what to do for me. They did a lot of research and discovered DBT, dialectical behavior therapy. They knew that I would really benefit from that kind of treatment, but they found that at the time, it was not commonly practiced here in Israel. They reached out to different centers abroad and found a center in New York that agreed to take me. My mom and I were going to go to America for six months, which was the time allotted for each course of treatment.

My parents felt that even though it would be really hard on the entire family, it was what they needed to do for me. At the time, I was very angry. I wasn't given a choice. I felt out of control and I felt that my parents didn't know what was best for me. Just when I was trying to feel in control of my life by cutting and by binging and purging (which my parents did not know about), this significant decision was being made for me. It made me feel even more out of control. I was sixteen and I thought I knew what was best. No one was asking me, and I thought I was the only one who knew what was right for me.

We went to New York and stayed with my grandfather on Long Island. I began my course of treatment. It consisted of going to therapy once a week on my own, once a week with my mom, and once a week in a group session with other kids and parents to learn coping skills. I got a job as a waitress part-time because I needed to have something to do every day. I was not in school and had decided to get my GED, but that wasn't enough to keep me busy. I did not want to sit around all day.

Even though all these pieces of my life began settling in, I still felt this void. Very quickly, my mom learned about the purging. The perspective that my therapist took was that it was another manifestation of my need for control. She decided that if she ignored the purging, it wouldn't become a big deal. Giving attention to it would make it a bigger issue.

I had a chart that I had to fill out before every session that monitored my mood and my behavior. While I was being honest about what I was doing, the therapist wasn't sure if I was. She sent me to a doctor to monitor my health. I started seeing this doctor once every few weeks. At the same time my psychiatrist was changing my medications.

I had this feeling that if I couldn't fix all my issues and all the ways that I felt broken and empty, at least I could fix my body, which I decided I no longer liked. That is when I realized that I could restrict.

SPIRALING

I stopped eating breakfast. I ate fewer carbs. I started purging more after my meals. All of a sudden, I felt like I had control again. I think in the beginning, it was a cry for help. I thought that maybe if I did something more extreme, they would pay attention to it. I was scared of what I felt I was capable of doing. I wanted to be taken seriously. I felt that no one was taking my eating issues seriously and if they weren't going to take me seriously, I would make them.

My treatment team wasn't taking it seriously. I think that my mom didn't know what to do and she was depending on my team's guidance because they were the experts. My medical doctor was the only person I felt was actually listening to me. I was very open with him because I felt like he was an advocate for me. My weight was in the average range and so he thought it would be best to send me to a nutritionist to help me regulate my eating.

This status quo lasted for a while. Then my doctor told me that he was getting worried. He said there was an eating disorder clinic and that maybe I should be admitted to it. I told this to the DBT clinic and the clinic director told me that because I was in the middle of treatment I needed to finish and that it would help me. I wasn't happy with that answer. I felt alone and unheard. At that point I realized that I was spiraling and I wasn't in control anymore. I was frightened. I think my mom knew that I wanted help for my eating issues, but I was not upfront with her about how bad the situation was and how I felt so out of control. At that time, I harbored a lot of anger toward her for forcing me to come to America. Our communication was not great and I didn't share what I needed to share with her.

After the meeting with the head of the DBT clinic, my mom and I went home. I felt so alone. When I get upset, I clean. I felt the need to do something and so I busied myself cleaning my grandfather's kitchen. He was a pharmacist, and as I was putting away mugs in the kitchen, I found a bottle of pills. I felt very hopeless and I took the bottle of pills and went up to my room. I sat there and counted all the pills in the bottle. I grabbed a bunch of them in my hands and swallowed them. I felt an immediate sense of relief. I was relieved at the thought that I wouldn't feel anything anymore if I was dead.

All of a sudden, it occurred to me what my mother would feel if she came into my room and found my body. I was overwhelmed with the feeling that I could not do that to her. I could not hurt my mother that way. I ran into her room and woke her up. I told her what I had done.

She rushed me to the hospital. They admitted me and pumped my stomach. I had done some damage to my liver, so they had to hook me up to an IV and keep me for several days. They sent in a team of psychiatrists to come in and talk to me. After talking to me and talking to my mom, they decided that I was a danger to myself and I couldn't go home.

RESTRICTING

My mother was so frightened. She told them that she could take care of me and that she wanted to take me home and care for me there. She had a whole plan. My uncle, who was a doctor, was going to help her. The psychiatrists told her that if she tried to take me, they would get a legal warrant and keep me in the hospital.

They admitted me to a short-term psychiatric unit. I was there for three weeks. During the time I was there, I completely shut down. I stopped eating. There were visiting hours every night, and my mom would bring me food. I would starve myself all day and then she would visit me and I would eat with her. When visiting hours were over, it was shower time. I would make sure that I would be the first one to get to shower. Though we were being watched all the time, the one time I was alone and unwatched was in the shower. Every time I got in the shower, I purged what I ate for dinner.

I was dropping weight rapidly. I was going for days without keeping food down. One day after treatment, we were meant to go to our rooms. I stood up and all I could see was black. I lost my vision and stumbled over to the nurses' station. I said, "I don't feel good" and promptly fainted.

Realizing that they needed to be more on top of me about eating, the staff tried all different ways to force me to eat. They left me all alone in my room as a punishment for not eating and since no one was watching me, I exercised all day. I was not complying with what they wanted me to do and they were out of their depth. The plan was that once they felt that I was psychologically clear, they would release me to the eating disorder program.

At this point, it was still about control. I had zero control over my life. I was stuck in the hospital against my will; they wouldn't let me go home. I was in a country where I didn't want to be. There was nothing that I could do about it. I just needed to feel in control of something. I knew restricting

413

my eating made me feel like I was in control. There was power in not eating. I needed to feel those feelings. I needed to feel like I was good at something, capable of something. That is how I felt when I was restricting.

The fact that I attempted to end my life made me feel so sad. I felt like I didn't even know who I was as a person anymore. I didn't know how to get back to who I wanted to be. I felt sad about the pain I caused my family. I felt sad about the pain that I was causing myself. I felt it would be easier if I wasn't living. But I did not regret the fact that I hadn't died. I was just lost. I felt very empty. I wasn't feeling my emotions. I was shut off.

ON MY SIDE

My mom and I had a conversation in the hospital and I told her that I needed to get out of this place. She told me that she was trying so hard to help me, and get me better and out of there. She was fighting for me and doing everything she could. We were both sitting there crying. At that moment I realized that my mom was on my side and that she had always been my advocate. I decided that if she was fighting for me, I had to do the same.

My mother made a deal with the hospital that she could come and eat every meal with me. For every meal from that point on, I sat with either my mother or my uncle and I slowly began to eat. I was relinquishing control, but I let it go to people who I felt were on my side.

After a few days of eating, they released me as a day patient to the eating disorder program. I was there from nine to five every day, but I was allowed to sleep at home. I didn't feel like I could trust myself yet, but I was eating all my meals at the program so I was still being supervised. I no longer had any suicidal ideation, but I was still very depressed.

Overall, the program was very good for me. I was there for three months. I became weight restored and then the work became about helping me release control of my eating disorder. Near the end of the program, my entire family came in from Israel. We did three

weeks of family therapy together. It had been almost a year of us not living together. The six months had turned into a year. There was so much to work through together. There were sessions with me and my parents, sessions for me and my siblings, and sessions for just me and my sister. There was a lot to unpack. One of the most amazing things to learn was how supportive my family still was, even after everything that had happened. By the end, things had become clearer for them. I did a lot of explaining in therapy. Even though I had been in contact with them while I was in America, it was not the same. We spent a lot of time reconnecting.

One of the amazing things that my parents did during that time was that they made sure that when we were not in therapy, we were doing fun things together. I felt so much less alone with them around. At the end of those three weeks, I felt like I had my family back. I felt like I was getting there, and that I was finding myself again.

RELAPSE

We came back to Israel right before *Purim*. It would have been my senior year. All my friends were talking about the army and *sheirut leumi* and I was just trying to find myself and my equilibrium. I was still in the process of finding a treatment team on this side of the world.

Within a month of being back, I relapsed. I felt very out of control again. My friends all knew what they were doing with their lives. My family had settled back into their lives. And I was still lost. I didn't know what my life was. I turned back to the one thing I could control, the one thing that was a comfort for me.

Within three weeks I hit the lowest weight that I had ever reached. My family was very worried. It was the first time that I was actually scared for my health. There was one morning when I woke up and I was dry heaving and my body was convulsing. I asked myself, "Oh my God. Is this when I die?" But it still wasn't enough to set me straight.

My parents found a dietician for me here in Israel. I believe this saved my life. I saw her twice a week. They also found me a new therapist. I was on a very strict food plan. The first six months I didn't follow the protocol at all. I would fight with my parents over eating a pickle. I was scared to drink a cup of water because I was afraid that I would gain weight. If I gained weight, I would be losing control. I wouldn't even hold high-calorie foods in my hands because I was afraid that the fat content would seep in through my skin and make me gain weight. This was the worst my eating disorder had ever been.

I had no concept of what I looked like. I had gotten it into my head that I needed to be perfect, and that my body didn't fit that ideal. I thought that if I hit all the goals I set in my head, I would be happy. But each time I hit my goal weight, I still didn't feel happy. Then I would set it lower. I thought I would feel happy because of the satisfaction I felt when I restricted. I felt powerful. I felt better than everyone else. I didn't need food. I was stronger than everyone else. I never wanted that feeling to go away. If I kept losing weight, maybe I could feel that way all the time. Maybe I would finally feel less empty.

I was at this point where my entire life was falling apart. There was a part of me that wanted to get better, but I didn't know how. Until you realize that you are not okay, it is not going to matter what other people say. Until I hit rock bottom, I didn't realize how bad it had gotten.

I could see that my parents were falling apart. They were watching me deteriorate in front of them and they could do nothing about it. I couldn't walk the two staircases up to my room without having to stop because I was out of breath. I started to realize all these things, and I began to try and get better. My dietician gave me back my control. She knew what I needed. Everyone was taking me seriously. Everyone gave me back the control. Once it was mine, I felt that I could take ownership over my healing process. I could start to get better.

RELINQUISHING

I slowly started eating again. My medication was changed and though it was not supposed to affect weight, I gained weight from it. This put me much closer to a healthy weight. It made the transition to a healthy weight smoother from a physical perspective, but emotionally it was challenging as I gained a lot quickly. I was not prepared for that.

I think that was the start of my recovery process. From there I did another year of therapy and meeting with my dietitian. Even once I hit a healthy weight, I was still struggling, this time with guilt. Every time I ate a meal, I felt guilty for being at a healthy weight and needing food. But my whole team was working together and my treatment was centralized, which really helped.

Since then, I haven't had any serious relapses. I have had minor relapses and I think I will always wrestle with having an eating disorder. I still struggle with some things. There are still some foods that I cannot bring myself to eat. There are days that I find myself back in that old mindset. And other days, it's quieter. It's still about that feeling of control. It gets bad at times when I am feeling a loss of control.

When I started dating my husband, he was in school studying social work. That was extremely helpful because it made it easy to tell him my story. I told him everything. He was so supportive. He told me that I was amazing and that I had come so far. He said that he was proud of me. When I told him that I wanted to talk about it publicly, he told me that I would be a role model for others. I knew that he was the right one for me.

When I was planning my wedding, the old mindset was stronger. I felt that lack of control. I felt that stress tightening my grip, and I wanted more control. Figuring out the root of my eating disorder helps me prepare myself for a possible relapse and helps me know how to deal with it.

Around a year ago, I was on the verge of a relapse. Though I kept eating, mentally I was struggling. But my husband was there for me, supporting me through it all. Sometimes in a relationship you need to give up control. I am able to do that because it feels safe for me to share the control with him. I know he is on my side and that it's safe to relinquish control to him. He just loves me for me. He makes me feel very blessed.

THE BIGGEST BLESSINGS

I think that I was forced to grow up very young because of this struggle. Though it was hard, I really understand everything I have been through – the root, the cause, and the solution. It will help me moving forward because I don't really have open-ended questions anymore. I learned a lot from everything I've experienced. I want to use it to move forward in my life. When I look ahead, I can see how I use my faith and security in my experiences to propel me into the future. It all happened to me for a reason.

My family is so close now. It is one of the biggest blessings in my life. People will come for *Shabbat* and be blown away by how close we all are. The people in my family are my biggest supporters. My sister is my best friend.

My brother can always put a smile on my face. I have only gratitude toward my parents for all their interventions on my behalf. I have no idea where I would have been if they hadn't done what they needed to do and brought me to America to get help. I am so blessed that they supported me through everything. I have the best relationships with them now. We are all so proud of each other. They are all my most loyal advocates. I always know that I can go to them for help when I am struggling.

So much of my pain stemmed from loneliness. But I have learned that I have an amazing support system and no matter what happens, they will always be there for me. I feel so lucky to have them all in my life.

REFLECTIONS

Questions to Consider
- What role does trust play in your life?
- Has there ever been a time when you set yourself free?

Words to Remember

> "I had this feeling that if I couldn't fix all my issues and all the ways that I felt broken and empty, at least I could fix my body, which I decided I no longer liked. That is when I realized that I could restrict."

Group Discussion

For many people, the issue of relinquishing control in our lives can be very challenging. How big of an issue is control in your life? What makes you feel more in control? What makes you feel out of control?

ॐ

Take a moment for yourself. What do you need right now?
Close your eyes and be in your own body.
Here is a mindfulness exercise to come back to yourself:

Mindfulness Exercise

Notice any thoughts or anxieties that may have come up while reading this chapter. Note them without judgment, and with understanding. Then remind yourself of moments that brought light into your life. Slowly let go of the stressful thoughts and divert toward the ones that bring you peace.

Adena's Story

Keeping the Fire Alive

Efrat

MY MOTHER, THE ZIONIST

Her entire life, it was my mother's dream to make *aliya*. This dream was planted throughout her childhood, growing up in a Zionistic home in Brooklyn full of artwork representing Israel, with bookshelves full of Zionistic books. They were always talking about Israel and conversations including buying Israel bonds. She was raised with a love for Israel. In those days, people didn't travel easily to Israel the same way people do today. But her love grew and grew. Today my siblings and I look back and we laugh about how when we were kids, we would cringe with embarrassment when our mom made little baggies of dried fruit for us to take to school on *Tu BiShevat*, or little blue and white cookies on *Yom HaAtzma'ut*. No other kids' moms did that, but ours did.

My mother did a lot of needlepointing. She would choose scenes of Israel and spend her time focusing on spiritual vistas and landscapes. Hebrew was very important to her and she made sure to sprinkle Hebrew words into our conversations and send us to schools where we would learn the language. These were all these little things that seemed small at the time, but now looking back, it makes me realize how those small things grew into big things. As we got older her bond with the Holy Land got stronger. She read more books, followed the news, learned more history, and went to hear speakers.

It took many years, when I was married with kids and my brothers were grown – that she was finally able and ready to moved to Israel. She had a few friends who had made *aliya*, but she had really only been to Israel a handful of times before she decided that it was the path that she wanted to take. In the 1990s, her brother had already made *aliya* and she was married to her second husband (my parents divorced when I was a young teen). Once they made that decision to go, they traveled back and forth frequently. My youngest sister was born by then, and they made lots of connections geared toward building a life in Israel for the three of them.

My mother knew that there were levels of difficulty for kids who are *olim*, depending on what age they are when they move to Israel. At this point, she would be moving only with her husband and my sister, Atara, because my brothers and I were grown and out of the house. She figured it would be best a year or two before high school. Their goal was to make *aliya* after her bat mitzva so she would have seventh and eighth grade to acclimate.

We lived a mile away from each other on Long Island. My kids slept there all the time; we were very close and we would see each other all the time. I was already pregnant with my fourth child when they made plans to move. Even with all the talk of making *aliya*, I was in denial about my mother leaving. I didn't believe that it would happen soon. It felt more like, "Sure, one day."

But then it became real. They were making concrete plans. They found a place to rent and they had a plan. All of a sudden, I was not okay with the decision. "What do you mean you are going to leave?"

My mother assured me, "Don't worry, we are going to find you a place that you are going to love in Israel and you will come soon and join us. We will pave the way for you." I said okay. It was all theoretical and I didn't think any of it would happen. My three little girls were devastated that their

Aunt Atara, whom they idolized and who was like a big sister to them, was leaving. They were heartbroken that their *savta* was leaving too. I was left feeling, "Where are you going? What are you doing? How could you leave us?"

The year was 2000, and the intifada had already begun. Everyone advised her to wait, push it off. They told her that now was not the time. She would respond, "No, this is exactly the right time. We need to go and give *ḥizuk*. This is the best time to go." She didn't put off her plans.

They left at the end of August. My mother was full of hope and joy that she finally got to take the next step and fulfill her dream.

DOING HER PART

They moved to a house near my uncle in Efrat so that my mother could be near her brother and Atara could be near her cousins. My mother immersed herself in helping my sister acclimate. She was so happy. She would call me and go on and on about every detail of her new life. She raved about the smells of the flowers and how it was *Shemitta* year, so they got to keep extra *halakhot*. She immediately did *ulpan* to learn more Hebrew and about Israeli culture. She joined the women's *beit midrash* in Efrat and began a course of study and made many friends. She was thriving.

The plan was that she would come back to me in the States when my baby was born in December. The baby was born early and my mom was able to fly in and make it in time. She came with my sister and they were with us for ten days. We had missed them so much. It was great to see them again. A few months later, we went to visit them for *Pesaḥ*. We had a beautiful trip. They printed T-shirts that said "*Pesaḥ* with *Saba* and *Savta*" and we did day trips, we stayed up North, and went all over the country. My mother was so excited to show us her new life, her home, and her new friends. When we came to her house, we saw that she had put sticky notes all over the furniture with the Hebrew words for all the items, so she could learn them. We have so many pictures and so many memories. The next plan was that we would be together for the summer. They were going to come in to the US and we were going upstate together for a few weeks. I was really looking forward to it.

My younger brother went to Israel to be with my mom for *Shavuot*. I was home with my husband, my four kids, and my other brother who was single, at our home on Long Island. They has planned to spend *Isru ḥag* – the day after the holiday in Israel, a rare day off – at the *Kotel*. In America, that day is the second day of the holiday. They were going to have an enjoyable day together in the Old City. My mother loved the Old City, Hevron, *Kever Rahel* – she would spend so much time visiting these places. She just felt so lucky to be able to be there.

It was the heat of the intifada and traveling the roads where they lived was difficult. A lot of people did not travel. Many people wouldn't travel in private cars, only on bulletproof buses. But my mother cautiously continued to go by car because she felt strongly that it was important to continue to live her life, and not let terrorism win. She wasn't super brave or an extremist, but she had her value system and her beliefs, and she stuck to them.

Kever Rahel was often the target of violent attacks, and many people avoided going there. The buses were often completely or nearly empty. My mom and her friends from Efrat would ride the empty bus as often as they could, back and forth, to make sure that they would keep the bus line running. If they closed the line, no one would be able to get to *Kever Rahel*. If no one could get there, we would lose it. They would have *shiurim* on the empty buses or at the *Kever*. She would also go to Hevron and go to the little Jewish shop there and buy anything – a pen, a magnet, a book. She did this to let the shopkeepers know that even though there was no tourism at the time, there were people who were with them and supporting their endeavors. She did the same thing in the Jewish Quarter in the Old City.

My mother would carry around American candies and chocolate bars and give them to all the soldiers at the checkpoints. She would say, "These are young boys, giving them some chocolate while they are on duty is the least we can do to show them that we support them." She always kept them in her bag to give chocolates out wherever she went.

This is how she spent her time in Israel, supporting the economy, going to *shiurim*, doling out whatever emotional support she could offer. She did her little part that made her feel like she was making a difference.

I spoke to my mom *Erev Shavuot*. It was almost *ḥag* by her. She had finished her cooking already and she told me all the details of all her classic *Shavuot* food that she made. It was one of our favorite holidays in our family because my mom really loved dairy. She made blintzes and souffles and fish and she told me about her adventures trying to find all the ingredients she needed in the Israeli supermarket.

I rushed off the phone. "That's great, Mom. I love you and miss you. I gotta run because I haven't even done my shopping for *ḥag* yet. Have a good *Yom Tov*."

I had no idea that those would be the last words I would ever say to her.

OPEN FIRE

The day after *ḥag* in Israel, my mother, stepfather, brother, and two *trempistim* who they picked up on the way out of Efrat, were all on their way to the *Kotel*. My brother was on his way back to the States and wanted to visit one more time before he left.

Shortly after leaving Efrat for Jerusalem, they were on Highway 60, right after the entrance for Neve Daniel. A car came from behind and as it passed them on the left, the people in the car opened fire, shooting through the back window, the side window, and the front windshield.

My brother was sitting behind the driver, and was badly injured from bullet wounds in his arm and shoulder. A nineteen-year-old *bat sherut* named Esther, was sitting next to him and was killed from her bullet wounds, falling into his lap as she died. My mother's husband, the driver, was badly injured from shrapnel and glass in his eyes, nose, and face, rendering him unable to continue to drive. My mother was the front-seat passenger, and was shot from behind, through the back window.

There was a road of full traffic that morning, because it was a rare day off in Israel and because many were on the way to the funeral of another terror victim who was killed just a day earlier in the Gush. Many people saw the shooting, many stopped to try and help. Ambulances were on site immediately, and the injured were treated at the scene. My brother was taken by ambulance to the hospital, and my mother was taken in a separate ambulance in an attempt to try and save her life. She didn't make it to the hospital, and was declared dead before they reached Jerusalem. They turned around, and returned her body to Gush Etzion.

ARE YOU SURE?

It was early afternoon in America. We were in *shul* on *Shavuot* morning. I had a house full of company. It was a beautiful day.

My uncle from Efrat came to my brother in the hospital. He told him that our mother had been killed. He knew that he had to reach me and our other brother and tell us what was going on. They called my father, knowing that he would answer the phone. My father had to process this information, be reassured that my brother would be OK, and then come to find me and family. He drove over and told us. It was surreal. I fainted when they first told me.

Within a few minutes, my house was full. People found out really quickly. The press came to the house. Rabbis of the local *shuls* came over. People from Hatzalah (Jewish emergency medical services) heard the news on their radios and came over to see if we were okay. People were running around telling each other. When the press found out that my mother had been from Lawrence, they went to her *shul* there and asked her rabbi for a comment. That is how he found out. My mother had been so close to him.

The next thing we knew, we were giving interviews and talking about my mother in the past tense and they were asking for pictures of her. We found pictures from our trip on *Pesaḥ*. People were on the phone making plans – when we would leave, when we would come back, who would fly, and who would be with the kids. It was a crazy amount of details and decisions that needed to be made so quickly in this state of shock. I was just doing what people told me to do. I was nursing my baby and people kept telling me, "Drink, drink, drink." I didn't understand why people were telling me to drink.

I remember one of my friends saying to me, "We have to pack. What shirt do you want to rip?" and I said, "What do you mean?" Thank God, people were telling me what to do. I remember phone calls with my uncle in Efrat. He was making all the arrangements and doing everything. I asked him, "Are you sure? Did you see her with your own eyes?" He promised me that he had. I asked, "Should we come?" I was asking weird questions because I could not process that my mother was gone.

I remember telling my kids, "*Savta* died." And they were like, "Okay, can we go back out and play in the yard?" I let them. Everything was just happening around us. It made no sense.

Somehow the day passed; people were coming in and out. People kept forcing me to drink. *Yom Tov* ended and a car came to get us to bring us to the airport. It was myself, my husband, my baby who I was nursing, and my brother. My father and my cousin took us to the airport. I don't even remember leaving instructions about my kids. My two best friends were going to take care of them, with my housekeeper who was helping me raise them. I just left.

My uncle had made all the arrangements. He told me, "Just bring your passport. When you get to the airport, they will be waiting for you." I didn't understand what that meant. When we got to the airport, my aunt and uncle were waiting for us, too. I was so confused and I asked them, "How did you know?" They, of course, had gotten calls just like we had. More family members showed up as time passed.

There were El Al representatives waiting for us. They knew that we were "the family." We gave them our passports and they took us straight to the plane. The flight was surreal. I kept saying to my husband, "My hands are tingling. My arms are burning. Something is wrong with them." I didn't know this was an effect of trauma. I was having a hard time holding my baby. Still to this day, when something triggers my PTSD, I get that feeling in my arms.

I think the loss of my mother sunk in during the flight. I couldn't sleep. I wasn't sedated and I was crying non-stop. Even while I was talking, I was sobbing through my words. I kept saying, "I feel like this is not real. I feel like there is something wrong. I feel like this has been a mistake."

Before I left the house, I told my uncle on the phone, "I need to see her. Make sure that I can see her." He told me, "Don't worry. Let's decide when you get here." I told him, "No, you need to promise me that I can see her." He promised me. On the plane, my aunt kept telling me that I shouldn't see her, that it shouldn't be the last image I have of her in my memories. But I needed to see her. I needed to understand that it was real. I needed to know that it was her. I needed closure.

The stewardesses and crew of the flight knew who we were and why we were there. I think that much of the plane's passengers had heard as well. When we landed, they made an announcement, "Please, everyone stay seated. There is a family that needs to get off the plane very quickly. Clear the aisles." They didn't say why.

No one moved. It was silent. No one stood. As I walked through the aisle people touched my arms, or held my hands for a moment. They knew. When we got into Ben-Gurion, there were more people waiting for us, whoever they were. They took our passports and walked us through. My uncle was waiting for us. It only got more painful.

IN THE DARK

My grandmother, my mother's mother, was living at home with my uncle in Efrat. He had to protect her from hearing the news in the wrong way. They knew that once the press and public found out, it would be inevitable. They

427

sent neighbors to barricade the house. They wouldn't let her turn on the TV. He needed to tell her himself.

At the airport, they put us into a big black van. I asked a lot of questions. I told them I needed to see her, and they took me straight to the *Ḥevra Kaddisha*. It was a room in a caravan, somewhere in the Gush. I remember my uncle said to me, "Your grandmother said that if you go to see your mom, she wants to go with you." I didn't think it was right for her to go with me. But she insisted. I remember that my hands were stiff and had that tingling, burning feeling. They walked me in to see her. My grandmother stood by the doorway. She didn't want me to be alone. I went in. My mother's body was wrapped up, but they left her head and her face open. I was able to see her face. She looked beautiful. Her hair was soft. I kissed her and she was cold and hard. But she was her.

The woman from the *Ḥevra Kaddisha* came to me and said, "Are you okay? Your mother is okay." It was the first time that anyone talked about my mother since the whole ordeal began. But now I had seen her and I saw that she was okay.

The funeral waited for us. Efrat had two funerals that day. The first was for the young woman who was killed in the car with them. She was buried right away. Then everyone gathered, waiting for us to begin my mother's funeral.

The *shul* where the eulogies were being held is only steps away from my uncle's house. When we got out of the van, they told me, "Okay, you need to go to the funeral now." I told them, "No. I need to nurse the baby." Everyone was waiting. But I didn't care. I went into the house and went to the bathroom and nursed my baby. I changed my shirt and gave instructions to the babysitter someone had sent.

When I walked outside to go to the funeral, I realized why they thought I was crazy. The streets were closed. The police, army, press, and tens of thousands of people swarmed all over the streets of Efrat, waiting for me, to start the funeral.

I have visions still of the massive banners that the Benei Akiva kids had put up lining the streets, supporting us and loving us. There were signs welcoming us to Israel. We didn't live in Israel. We didn't know this part of what it means to live in Israel. We didn't know how people bind together to love and support strangers, our brothers and sisters. We didn't know.

We wondered, "Who are all these people? How do they know us? Why do they love us?" They told us, "Everyone here is here for you. We are here to support you."

When I came into the *shul*, I saw my brother who had been shot. It was the first time I had seen him since the attack. He was signed out of the hospital by a doctor who took responsibility for his care so that he could be at our mother's funeral. His bandaged arm was in a sling, he was attached to an IV, and he had patches on the bullet holes in his arm and shoulder. He looked white. But he had a blazer hanging over his shoulders. We just hugged. There were very few words.

My grandmother was there. My thirteen-year-old sister was there. The rabbi spoke and the mayor spoke. One of my mother's friends from the *beit midrash* spoke. My sister wrote something for the funeral but she couldn't read it. I read it for her, but I could barely get it out. I don't even have a clue what it said.

My sister was my first baby. I am eighteen years older than her. I raised her. When I had a house of my own, she practically lived with me. I am her sister, but I am also a mother figure to her. There we were at our mother's funeral and I kept saying to her, "Don't worry. I am going to take care of you. You are not alone. You are mine."

When the eulogies were over, we had to walk along the cobblestoned, winding, hilltop streets to get to the hearse. We were walking through a sea of people. I don't remember much. People told me afterward that I was screaming. I remember I had to go to the bathroom again because they kept telling me to drink. There were paramedics around us. When I went to the bathroom, a paramedic told me, "I'm just going to stand here in the bathroom with you." I couldn't understand why. I was so out of it. They must have been really worried about me. My husband told me to let him stand in the doorway and I just let everyone tell me what to do. The paramedic stood in the doorway.

As we got to the top of the block, I saw a sea of people. Tens of thousands of people, in the dark of night. Before we got into the van, I saw my mother's best friend from childhood. I saw her and I lost it. "Judy! You must be so sad – she was your best friend!" That is what came out of my mouth. We just hugged each other and sobbed.

The van drove our family from Efrat to the cemetery at Kfar Etzion a few miles away. The highway was lined for miles with people holding Israeli flags and candles. We couldn't understand what they were doing there. We were told, "It is for you. It is for your mother. It is for us." We couldn't fathom it.

The cemetery was pitch black. The cars used their headlights to light the cemetery. The hills of the cemetery were blanketed with people, in the dark. We couldn't get through. My brother was transported in an ambulance. There was so much to comprehend at one time. This kind of experience is not within our lexicon of understanding, coming from the States. It was just pure shock. None of it made any sense.

We buried her late at night in the darkness. I just remember the loud wailing and the crying. I don't remember anything else.

SITTING

That night I slept in my mother's house. I slept in bed with my sister. My husband brought me the baby every few hours when she needed to nurse.

I woke up very early. My sister was sleeping in my arms. I looked out the window and saw the most gorgeous view of the sun rising over the Judean hills. It took me a second to remember what had happened and why I was there. I remember thinking, "It is too beautiful out. I can't be this sad when it is so beautiful."

We sat *shiva* at my uncle's house down the block for the whole week. The first morning I got there very early and there were all these chairs set up in a circle in the living room. I sat down and my uncle sat down across the room from me. I looked at him and said, "Is this real?" Then *shiva* started. There were tens of thousands of people who came for *shiva* – people we knew, people who my mom knew, and people who no one knew. There were Israeli politicians, army generals, American politicians, and the press. It became a political event. Though my mother's husband was in so much pain, he and my uncle were able to convey our tragic loss to the media. It was a blur to me.

It was hard for me to nurse the baby. I felt like I had to stop. I thought the milk I was producing was soured from stress, and it would be bad for my baby to be nourished by it. I nursed all my babies for a long time, over a year, and here she was at seven months old and I had to stop. In the middle of *shiva*, it was over. I was in pain and she cried, but I just couldn't do it anymore.

My brother was in the hospital for the first few days of *shiva*. The community of Efrat would not let him be alone. There was someone with him around the clock. But he didn't know anyone and he wanted to be with us. A doctor who is a close family friend signed him out under his care, so that he could sit *shiva* with us. At least we were able to be together.

My mother's husband had patches over his eyes because they were full of glass from the windshield that shattered from the bullets, directly into his face. His whole ENT system was messed up. He couldn't hear or see. It seemed to me that he was screaming and crying the whole time.

My grandmother was very calm and very dignified. She didn't scream or cry in front of people. She talked about her daughter and she liked to hear stories. She was very proud of my mom. She was very happy that my mom had been happy and didn't regret that she made *aliya*. She didn't regret that she got in the car that day. She was so very strong.

There were a lot of beautiful moments amongst the craziness. Many people came to pay respects to a stranger, because she was a terror victim. The phone was ringing off the hook. It was surreal. But my family was together. There was something about this place. We felt my mother's presence here. We felt a pull, a connection to the community, to Efrat. I thought about going home and sitting *shiva*. But I didn't want to leave. I didn't want to go home. When people say at the end of a *shiva* visit, "*HaMakom Yenaḥem*" – it's true. There really is something powerfully transformative about being in a certain place and the comfort that it can bring you. We certainly experienced that in Efrat.

AL KIDDUSH HASHEM

When *shiva* ended we had so many logistics to figure out. My husband had to go home to be with our other three children and so he took the baby with him. My brother was still too injured to travel back to the States, so my two brothers and I stayed for another two weeks. We packed up my sister to get her ready for her summer trip to the US. I packed up my mother's things and went through her house. We divided up jewelry and needlepoints. We donated her wigs and clothing to a *gemaḥ*. We did as much as we could while we were all together. I flew back home with my brothers, and a few weeks later my sister came to us for the summer.

After the summer she came back to Efrat and I was doing a lot of parenting her from afar. I came back and forth to Israel a lot. I came for big events and small events, and we flew her to visit us a lot, too.

During *shiva* one night, we were lying next to each other and I said to her, "You know, I think the best thing is that you come back and live with me. I will take care of you." She was practically raised in my house as it was. "You will come live with me, and then we will make *aliya* together. We will come back soon." She said to me, "If I come back with you, you will never

431

come. Mommy wants us here and she wanted you to come here. So if I stay here, it will make you come."

She was right. We came.

It took time. We had a business and a home. My mother was killed in 2001 and we made *aliya* in 2004. I didn't think that Israel needed me. But I felt that I wanted to honor my mom. I needed to keep her passion alive. We had such an emotional, strong connection to the people here, the people we knew and the people we didn't.

There is a famous story we tell in my family, about how one night during *shiva* it was twelve o'clock at night and finally everyone had left. We hadn't stopped all day and we hadn't eaten. As we were unwinding, there was a knock at the door. Someone came in, carrying a stroller, wearing a *mitpaḥat*, and wearing her small baby in a carrier. No one recognized her. Finally someone asked her, "Who are you?" She said, "I don't know anyone here. I just came to be *menaḥem avel* your family." We asked her why she had come so late. Where was she from? She told us she was from Hevron. She left her house at nine o'clock and it took two and a half hours of traveling by *trempim* with her baby to come bring us comfort, to come visit people she didn't even know.

We just started crying. What is this place? Things don't happen like this where we are from. We felt such strong love and connection. We wanted this for ourselves. We wanted to raise our kids here. With every visit, the feelings got stronger.

I was not afraid. The intifada continued for a year or two after my mother was murdered. I remember one winter shortly afterward, we were here in the Gush. In the winter, the roads are dark and foggy and you can barely see them. No one was going out. Efrat had a *gemaḥ* for people to borrow bulletproof vests, in case you were driving on the roads. We were here as tourists, with our rental car, and we borrowed vests for ourselves and our kids and drove to Jerusalem. My mother was not afraid, and I was not going to be afraid either. We kept coming. We did what we had to do. We were just inspired, connected, and drawn to this place.

I think that God has a plan. I don't like it when people say that God picks the special ones to be martyrs for His name. But I have to understand that yes, my mother died *al kiddush Hashem* and I am not going to take that away from her. There is something very holy about her. But to me, she was just my mother – sometimes messy, not a great cook, always loving. It is hard to connect the woman I knew with the sainthood of a terror victim. She became a symbol. There are girls named Sara out there who are not related to us, named for my mother. She inspired people to make *aliya*. We, her children, came on *aliya*, and that is beautiful. But for her to be so inspiring to the rest of the world is incredible. I have an entire extended family that made *aliya* because of her. We have a whole tribe here living in Israel to honor her memory. She would love that. She would love to know that my daughter Sara was born here in her beloved homeland. They took a Sara, and we brought back a Sara.

My daughter calls this the "butterfly effect." I know that if my mother was alive right now, we wouldn't be living here in Efrat. We would be commuting, living in the States and visiting Israel frequently. My kids are so Israeli now, so it is hard to imagine.

I have five girls and one boy and I keep my mother a permeating presence in our lives. When I sing a song, I'll ask my kids, "Do you want to hear a song that *Savta* used to sing?" Her favorite color was purple and everything I buy now is by default, the color purple. Everyone who knew her knew how much she loved the color purple. My kids don't remember my mother, but they know she loved purple. They know she gave chocolate to the soldiers. They know she loved *Kever Rahel*.

We chose to move to Efrat because we felt my mother here. There is something about it. She loved it here and I love it here too. I feel her in the Old City, in Hevron, and when I see soldiers at a checkpoint. When I got remarried after my divorce, I chose to get married in Gush Etzion, because I knew she would be here.

It has been eighteen years, and it is still a journey. I am still healing, learning, and evolving. I am only now almost at a point where I feel I can give

advice to someone. Time doesn't always heal as fast as we would like. It is such a long journey and I don't think it ever ends. Healing means learning to live with it. There are moments that out of the blue on some random day, I just get the urge to call my mom. Recently I was crying in the supermarket because I had a question about which vinegar to buy, and my first instinct was to call my mother. And I couldn't.

I feel it is my duty and my job to keep all the things that were important to her alive and fresh in all our minds. As the eldest, I feel responsible for passing on everything she wanted us to learn. Only recently did I discover that my experience of losing my mother is different from the experience of each of my siblings. That hit me like a ton of bricks. We all have different pains. We all have different memories. Healing looks different for all of us.

We need to keep her alive. We can't let the fire go out.

REFLECTIONS

Questions to Consider
- Has there ever been a time where you stood up to fear?
- Recall a time when you were grieving. What gave you comfort?

Words to Remember

> "I didn't think that Israel needed me. But I felt that I wanted to honor my mom. I needed to keep her passion alive. We had such an emotional, strong connection to the people here, the people we knew and the people we didn't."

Group Discussion
In what way does Israel need you?
What does Israel bring to your life?

✍

Take a moment for yourself. What do you need right now?
Close your eyes and be in your own body.
Here is a gratitude exercise to come back to yourself:

Gratitude Exercise
Think of someone you have lost. Recall this person in your most favorite moments – cooking together, holidays, everyday life, and special occasions. How does this person still exist in your life? Is it through memory, or perhaps food? Is it through items that were given to you, or names carried on in the next generation?

Glossary

Jews from all over the world pronounce words differently.
This glossary reflects two different denominations of spelling
utilized by the women in this book. Entries are listed as they appear in the text.

Abba: father

Aliya: moving to Israel; ascending

Al kiddush Hashem: to sanctify the name of God

Am Yisrael: Nation of Israel

Amuta: non-profit organization in Israel

Arayot HaYarden: "The Lions of Jordan" – a coed infantry unit in Israel Defense Forces, stationed at Israel's eastern border and in the area of the Jordan River.

Avodat Hashem: service of God

Baalat teshuva, baalas teshuva/ḥozer biteshuva, chozeres biteshuva: secular Jew who becomes observant

Balagan: state of confusion and disorder

Balanit: *mikve* attendant

Barukh Hashem/baruch Hashem: Thank God

Bayis ne'eman beYisrael: "A faithful home among the Jewish people"

Be'ezras Hashem: God willing

Benei Menashe: sect of Jews from India who began to return to the religion of their ancestors, starting in the 1970s and continuing to the present

Beis midrash: study hall

Beit din: rabbinic court

Beit knesset: synagogue

Bekarov: soon

Benot Sheirut Bodedot: young women who voluntarily serve in Israel's national service while their families live in the Diaspora

Berakha, bracha/berakhot, brachos (plural): blessing

Bet: second letter in the Hebrew alphabet, equivalent to "B"

Bitachon: belief, trust

Bochurim: male yeshiva students

Brit mila/bris mila: circumcision ceremony performed on Jewish males on the eighth day from birth

Brita/simḥat bat: celebration over the birth of a girl

Bubby: grandmother (Yiddish)

Caracal: 33rd Battalion in the Israel Defense Forces; a coed infantry battalion in the Arava region of Israel

Chasidus: movement in Judaism started by Rabbi Yisrael Baal Shem Tov

Chulent: *Shabbat* stew

Dam Yehudi lo hefker: "The blood of a Jew is not free"

Daven: pray

Dayan: judge

Derech: path, referring to the path of Jewish observance

Dod: uncle

Eishet ḥayil: woman of valor

Elul: month in the Jewish calendar, usually coinciding with parts of August and September

Emuna: faith

Eretz Yisrael: the Land of Israel

Erev: day before a holiday

Frum: religious (Yiddish)

Frumkeit: religiosity (Yiddish)

Gabbai: person who assists in the running of a synagogue and its ritual services

Galut: exile

Gan: preschool in Israel

Ganenet: preschool teacher in Israel

Gar'in: seed group

Gemaḥ: repository of useful items that people may borrow and then return at a low cost or at no cost

Gemara: rabbinic commentary on the *Mishna* that forms the second part of the Talmud

Geula: redemption

Gibbor: man of strength

Givati: brigade in the Israel Defense Forces

Giyoret: convert to Judaism (f)

Giyur safek: second conversion to preclude any doubt about the validity of the original conversion

Ḥag/chag, ḥagim/chagim (plural): Jewish holiday

Haggada: text recited at the *Seder* telling the biblical story of the Exodus from Egyptian slavery

Hakol beseder: "Everything is fine"

Halakha, halakhot (plural): Jewish law

HaMalakh/HaMalach HaGoel: one of the blessings that the biblical Jacob gave his children, traditionally sung today as a lullaby

HaMakom Yenaḥem: phrase of comfort said to mourners at the end of a *shiva* visit

Ḥanukka: festival commemorating the rededication of the Second Temple following the Maccabean Revolt

Ḥaredi/charedi: Orthodox Jewish sect characterized by strict adherence to the traditional form of Jewish law and a rejection of modern secular culture

Harei at mekudeshet li: Jewish marriage vow

Hashgacha pratis: divine intervention

Hashkafa, hashkafic: Jewish worldview or guiding philosophy

HaTikva: Israeli national anthem

Ḥatzitza: something separating the body from the purifying waters of the *mikve*

Hatzlacha: success

Havdala: Jewish religious ceremony that symbolizes the end of *Shabbat* on Saturday night. It features lighting a candle with several wicks, reciting a blessing over a cup of wine, and smelling pleasant spices.

Ḥavrusa: Torah study partner

Ḥayal boded: "lone soldier," a soldier who voluntarily comes from outside of Israel to serve in the Israel Defense Forces while his or her family lives in the Diaspora

Ḥayim: life

Ḥazan: cantor

Ḥesed/chesed: charity, generosity

Ḥevra: group of friends

Ḥevra Kaddisha: organization of Jewish men and women who ensure that the bodies of deceased Jews are prepared for burial according to Jewish tradition and protected until burial

Hilchos yichud: the laws related to men and women being alone together

Hishtadlut/hishtadlus: personal effort

Hitnatkut: the Disengagement – the unilateral dismantling and withdrawal of Israeli communities

439

and the Israeli army from within Gaza in 2005

Ḥizuk: strength

Ḥoger: Israel Defense Forces identification card

Ḥugim: after-school activities

Ḥumash: volume containing the five books of Moses

Ḥuppa: Jewish marriage canopy

Ima: mother

Iriya: local government in Israel

Kabbala: Jewish mystical tradition

Kablan: building contractor

Kalla: bride

Kapo: Nazi concentration camp prisoner forced to supervise other prisoners (German)

Kashrut: ritually fit to eat or use according to Jewish law

Katzin: commander in the Israel Defense Forces

Ketuba: religious marriage contract

Kever: burial grave

Kever Rahel/Kever Rachel: the burial place of *Rahel Imenu*, Rachel the Matriarch.

Kibbutz: collective community in Israel that was traditionally based on agriculture

Kibbutz galuyot: ingathering of the exiles to the Land of Israel

Kiddush: blessing over wine on Friday nights to sanctify the *Shabbat*

Kipat Barzel: Israel's Iron Dome defense system that intercepts rockets, artillery, and mortars

Kiruv: practice of bringing unaffiliated Jews closer to Jewish practice

Kita gimmel: third grade

Klita: absorption

Kol HaNe'arim: part of the prayer service on *Simhat Torah* when the children are called up to the Torah for a blessing under a large canopy of *tallitot*

Kollel: full-time advanced study of the Talmud and rabbinic literature

Kotel: the Western Wall

Kupat holim: medical clinic or medical insurance

Lamed: letter in the Hebrew alphabet, equivalent to "L"

Limudei Kodesh: Jewish religious studies

Maabara: immigrant absorption camp

Mahala: "The Illness"

Mahzor/mahzorim (plural): festival prayer book

Makolet: Israeli corner store

Makpid: particular or conscientious, especially related to Jewish law

Mashiah: promised deliverer of the Jewish nation as prophesied in the Hebrew Bible, the Messiah

Mazal: luck

Mazal tov: congratulatory expression (lit. "Good luck")

Megilla: scroll of the story of Esther and Mordekhai and their saving of the Jews, read on *Purim*

Mekhina/mechina: college preparation for immigrants to Israel

Melaveh malka: meal after the end of *Shabbat*, considered to escort out the *Shabbat* Queen

Menaḥem avel: paying a condolence call to comfort a mourner

Merkaz klita: absorption center

Meshuga: crazy (Yiddish)

Midrasha: religious school for women

Mikve: ritual bath used for spiritual purification for conversion, family purity, or before praying

Milchig: dairy (Yiddish)

Miluim: army reserves

Mincha: afternoon prayer service

Min hashamayim: sent from the heavens

Minyan: prayer quorum of ten men

Mirpeset: porch

Miskeina: "Poor thing" (f)

Mispar zehut: Israeli identification number

Misrad HaAliya: Ministry of Immigration

Misrad HaBitaḥon: Israeli Ministry of Defense

Misrad HaChinuch: Ministry of Education

Misrad HaPnim: Ministry of Interior

Mitpaḥat: headscarf

Mitzva, mitzvot/mitzvos (plural): commandment or good deed in accordance with Torah values

Moshav: cooperative community, settlement, or village

Motza'ei Shabbat: Saturday night after *Shabbat* is over

Naḥat: pride and enjoyment

Nakh: acronym for *Neviim* and *Ketuvim* (Prophets and Writings), the second and third sections of the Hebrew Bible

Negia: Concepts in Jewish law that forbid or restrict physical contact with a member of the opposite sex

Neshama: soul

Nidda: laws of family purity

Nu: So? (Yiddish)

Olah (f)/*oleh* (m)/*olim* (plural): immigrant to Israel

Olam HaBa: World to Come

Onen: status of a mourner before the burial of an immediate relative

Parasha: passage of the Torah assigned for weekly reading during synagogue worship

Parnasa: sustenance

Pesaḥ/Pesach: Passover, the Jewish festival commemorating the liberation of the Israelites from Egyptian slavery

Peyos: side curls

Ptor: army release papers

Purim: festival celebrating the rescue of the Jews from extermination at the hands of the Persian minister Haman

Rabbanut: Israeli government body of rabbis who make legal and halakhic decisions

Rabbonim: rabbis

Rakezet: guidance counselor (f)

Rashi: Rabbi Shlomo Yitzhaki, Torah commentator from medieval France

Rav: rabbi

Rebbetzin: wife of a rabbi

Reḥov: street

Revaḥa: social services in Israel

Rosh Chodesh: first of the month on the Jewish calendar

Rosh HaShana: Jewish New Year

Rosh yeshiva: head of school

Saba: grandfather

Sabra: native Israeli

Savta: grandmother

Seder: Jewish ritual service and ceremonial dinner on the first night (in Israel) or first two nights (Diaspora) of Passover, in which the story of the Exodus from Egypt is retold

Shabbat/Shabbos/Shabbatot (plural): Saturday, the seventh day of the week, a day of rest and spiritual enrichment

Shabbaton, shabbatonim (plural): weekend seminar during *Shabbat* with enriching Jewish content

Shacharis: morning prayer service

Shadkhan/shadchan: matchmaker

Shalom Aleikhem: traditional song sung on Friday nights before the *Shabbat* meal (lit. "Peace be unto you")

Shalom bayit/bayis: peace in the home, usually a reference to marital harmony

Shana rishona: first year

Shavuot/Shavuos: festival commemorating the giving of the Torah

Sheirut leumi: national service in Israel; religious women often choose this as an alternative to army service

Shema Yisrael: central prayer in Jewish worship

Shemitta: sabbatical year when the land of Israel rests and various Jewish agricultural laws come into effect

Sheva mitzvot benei Noaḥ: seven Noahide laws

Shiddukh/shidduch/shid-

duchim (plural): introduction arranged by a matchmaker

Shiur, shiurim (plural): Torah lecture or class

Shiva: seven days of mourning following the burial of a first-degree relative

Shivat HaMinim: Seven Species of the Land of Israel: wheat, barley, grape, fig, pomegranate, olive (oil), and date (honey)

Shleimut: wholeness, completion

Shloshim: seven days of mourning following the burial of a first-degree relative

Shoah: Holocaust

Shoḥet: slaughterer who works in accordance with the laws of Jewish slaughter

Shomeret (f): person who watches over the body of the deceased before burial

Shtetl: small town with a large Jewish population (Yiddish)

Shuk Mahane Yehuda: large outdoor market in Jerusalem

Shul: synagogue

Simchas Torah: Jewish holiday that celebrates and marks the conclusion of the annual cycle of synagogue Torah readings, as well as the beginning of a new cycle

Simḥa/simcha, smaḥot/smachos (plural): joy or happy occasion

Sokhnut: the Jewish Agency for Israel

Sponja: Israeli-style mopping

Sukkot/Sukkos: Festival of Tabernacles

Taanit Esther: Fast of Esther, occurs the day before *Purim*

Tafkid: function

Taktziv: budget allocation

Tallit/tallis, tallitot/talleisim (plural): prayer shawl

Tante: aunt (Yiddish)

Tefillin: phylacteries, a pair of black leather boxes containing parchment inscribed with biblical verses, worn by men on the head and upper arm during weekday morning prayer services

Tehillim: psalms, recited during times of duress, thanksgiving, or prayer

Terumot and *maasrot*: food from the Land of Israel that is separated according to Jewish agricultural laws

Teudot zehut: identification cards

Tikkun: fixing/rectification

Tisha B'Av: Ninth of Av, fast day commemorating the destruction of the two Temples

Tiyul, tiyulim (plural): day trip/hike

Tovim: good (plural)

Tremp, trempistim: hitchhike, hitchhikers

Tu BiShevat: New Year for the trees

Tzaddik: righteous man

Tzadekes: righteous woman

Tzebrochene: broken (Yiddish)

Tzniut: modesty

Tzuk Eitan: Operation Protective Edge, Gaza war in the summer of 2014

Ulpan: intensive Hebrew course for new immigrants to Israel

Ulpana: girls' high school

Yerushalayim: Jerusalem

Yeshivish: non-hasidic *charedi* Jews

Yishuv: Israeli village or settlement

Yom HaAtzma'ut: Israel Independence Day

Yom HaShoah: Holocaust Remembrance Day

Yom HaZikaron: National Remembrance Day observed in Israel in honor of all Israeli military personnel and victims of terror who have lost their lives for the sake of the State of Israel

Yom Kippur: Day of Atonement, the biblical holiday of fasting and repentance

Yom Tov: holiday

Zayde: grandfather (Yiddish)

Index

For those who are interested in reading about a particular topic, or for those who are looking to avoid certain topics, here are the chapters that either discuss or mention the themes below:

About the Author

Photo: Tzipora Lifchitz

Shira Lankin Sheps is a writer, photographer, and clinically trained therapist. She is the creator and publisher of *The Layers Project* magazine, an online magazine that presents in-depth insights into the challenges and triumphs of the lives of Jewish women, and is passionate about creating spaces for stories that need to be told and changing the dialogue around stigmatized topics.

Shira Lankin Sheps earned her BA in English Literature at Stern College of Yeshiva University and an MSW from the Silberman School of Social Work at Hunter College. She made *aliya* in 2018 and lives in Jerusalem with her husband and children.

Check out *The Layers Project Magazine:*
www.thelayersprojectmagazine.com
Follow along on social media:
Facebook.com/TheLayersProject
Instagram.com/thelayersproject
Facebook.com/shira.l.sheps
Instagram.com/shiralankinsheps